STALINISM AT WAR

STALINISM AT WAR

The Soviet Union in World War II

Mark Edele

BLOOMSBURY ACADEMIC
LONDON • NEW YORK • OXFORD • NEW DELHI • SYDNEY

BLOOMSBURY ACADEMIC
Bloomsbury Publishing Plc
50 Bedford Square, London, WC1B 3DP, UK
1385 Broadway, New York, NY 10018, USA
29 Earlsfort Terrace, Dublin 2, Ireland

BLOOMSBURY, BLOOMSBURY ACADEMIC and the Diana logo are trademarks
of Bloomsbury Publishing Plc

First published in Great Britain 2021
Reprinted 2021

Cover design by Ben Anslow
Cover Image: 1944, Members of a Soviet tank battalion being greeted by
people in the war torn city of Lodz, Poland. A soviet T-34 tank stands behind them.
(Photo by Victor Temin/Slava Katamidze Collection/Getty Images)

A catalogue record for this book is available from the British Library.

Library of Congress Cataloging-in-Publication Data
Names: Edele, Mark, author.
Title: Stalinism at war: the Soviet Union in World War II / Mark Edele.
Other titles: Soviet Union in World War II
Description: London; New York: Bloomsbury Academic, 2021. | Includes bibliographical
references and index. |
Identifiers: LCCN 2021007708 (print) | LCCN 2021007709 (ebook) | ISBN
9781350153516 (hardback) | ISBN 9781350153523 (epub) | ISBN 9781350153530 (ebook)
Subjects: LCSH: World War, 1939-1945–Soviet Union. | Soviet Union–Politics and
government–1936-1953. | Soviet Union–History–1939-1945. | World War, 1939-1945–
Social aspects–Soviet Union. | World War, 1939-1945–Campaigns–Eastern Front. | World
War, 1939-1945–Campaigns–Asia.
Classification: LCC D764 .E244 2021 (print) | LCC D764 (ebook) | DDC 940.53/47–dc23
LC record available at https://lccn.loc.gov/2021007708
LC ebook record available at https://lccn.loc.gov/2021007709

ISBN: HB: 978-1-3501-5351-6
ePDF: 978-1-3500-6531-4
eBook: 978-1-3501-5352-3

Typeset by Deanta Global Publishing Services, Chennai, India
Printed and bound in Great Britain

To find out more about our authors and books visit www .bloomsbury .com and
sign up for our newsletters.

To my companions in the Covid-19 spaceship:

Debra, Anna and Chino

CONTENTS

List of illustrations viii
Acknowledgements x

Introduction: Stalinism at war, 1937–49 1

1 Preparing for war 13

2 The war begins in the east, 1937–9 29

3 War in the west, 1939–40 47

4 Armageddon, 1941–2 73

5 Recovery, 1941–2 93

6 Triumph, 1943–5 115

7 War of ideologies 135

8 The war after the war, 1944–9 151

9 Impact and aftermath 175

Appendix: Maps 193
Notes 202
Index 254

ILLUSTRATIONS

1 Georgy Zhukov at Khalkhin Gol, 1939 42
2 Japanese doctor treats injured Soviet POW during the battle of Khalkhin Gol 45
3 German and Soviet officers shake hands on the Soviet–German demarcation line 51
4 Soviet soldiers distributing newspapers in eastern Poland, September 1939 54
5 Red Army enters Vilnius, 15 June 1940 60
6 Machine gunners of Far Eastern Army, 1941 67
7 Germans attack the Soviet Union, 22 June 1941 74
8 German vs. Soviet forces, 1941 81
9 Red Army soldiers at frontline near Leningrad, 1941 84
10 Zoia Kosmodemianskaia's body, 1942 85
11 Ration cards in Leningrad, 1941-2 96
12 Dead German soldiers outside Stalingrad, 1943 109
13 Victim of starvation in Leningrad 112
14 German personnel losses in the Second World War (thousands) 116
15 Roosevelt, Stalin and Churchill in Teheran, 1943 117
16 Red Army tanks in the streets of Leipzig, March 1945 118
17 Soviet production as a multiple of German production, 1941–4 123
18 'The Last Jew of Vinnitsa', 1941 140
19 Soviet propaganda posters at the frontline, Leningrad region, 1941 143
20 'In the Headquarters of the Soviet Partisan Movement' 147
21 Raising the Red Flag over the destroyed Reichstag in Berlin, 2 May 1945 169
22 Ukrainian resettlers from Poland to the Soviet Union, 1946 172
23 A deported Ingush family mourns their dead daughter in Kazakhstan, 1944 172

Maps

1   The Soviet Union in 1937 193
2   The eastern front, 1938–9 194
3   The western front, 1939–41 195
4   The frontline, 1941–2 196
5   Evacuations 197
6   Soviet successes in the west, 1943–4 198
7   Lend Lease Routes 199
8   Soviet Empire in the West 200
9   The eastern front 201

Tables

1   German and Soviet war production, 1941–4 (thousands) 124
2   Crime statistics for Soviet Union, 1939–49 (reported cases) 164

ACKNOWLEDGEMENTS

This book was started over a decade ago in Western Australia. After years of research travel, it was completed in 2020, in Melbourne, during the apocalyptic year of unprecedented bushfires and a global pandemic. The Covid-19 crisis nearly derailed the project. First, my roles as a university bureaucrat and as a university teacher expanded during this emergency. Once I could devote at least part of my attention to the project again, travel was impossible and I had lost access to the physical library collections, both a large part of my professional library in my university office and the university library. Lockdown was emotionally draining to everybody subjected to it. Home-schooling drove us all mad and cabin fever became increasingly severe as we were confined nearly constantly indoors.

I drew inspiration, however, from the example of Soviet scholars in the Second World War. During the siege of Leningrad, they continued academic writing, some starving to death over their manuscripts. Compared to their suffering and their heroism, Melbournians' collective 'house arrest' to slow the further spread of the deadly virus seemed positively luxurious. In the end, the crisis slimmed down my notes, a fact my colleagues whose work has been omitted shall never forgive me. Most readers, however, will probably appreciate the shorter endnotes.

Our little collective – my wife Debra McDougall, our daughter Anna Edele and Chino, our fierce Labrador – supported each other through the weeks of stage 4 restrictions. I therefore dedicate this book to the three of them. I'm not sure I would have gotten halfway sane through the final weeks of working on this manuscript without their support.

The bulk of the research and most of the writing of this book were funded by a generous four-year Australian Research Council Future Fellowship in 2015–19 (FT140101100). But this book also builds on two decades of reading, thinking and writing about this war, starting with my first published article in 1999. Since then, a succession of smaller grants allowed preliminary studies which in many ways culminate in this book: an Australian Research Council Discovery Project (DP130101215; 2013–15); a University of Western Australia Research

Development Award, 2010; and a University of Western Australia School of Humanities Staff Travel Grant, 2011.

Over the years, I have benefited from the research assistance of a group of incredibly talented scholars, including Iva Glisic, Oleg Beyda and Rustam Alexander. Natalie Belsky generously shared research notes which made orientation in the interview transcripts in the New York Public Library much easier than it would have been otherwise. Sandra Wilson has answered my questions about Japan over the years and Neil Diamant was an essential interlocutor on Chinese history. Alan Barenberg advised on the Northern Pechora Railway. A conference on the Soviet Union in the Second World War, held in Paris in 2011, influenced me deeply. Particularly, conversations with Urufu-san (aka, David Wolff), Mie Nakachi, Tsuyoshi Hasegawa, David Holloway, Alexander Statiev, Terry Martin, Lennart Samuelson and Amir Weiner remained with me for the following decade.[1] In Kyiv, Iurii Shapoval was an essential supporter and companion. In Melbourne, my earlier collaboration with Filip Slaveski shaped my views on the origins of the post-war crime wave. Oleg Beyda, David Goodman and Brandon Schechter read the penultimate draft of the manuscript. Their commentary, critiques and observations helped immensely in the final revisions.

An earlier draft of parts of Chapter 1 was first presented as 'Was the Soviet Union Prepared to Fight the Second World War?' at the Murdoch University World Wars Research Group Colloquium 'Preparing for War, 1914–1945', 17–18 June 2013. One paragraph was published as part of my review of Alexander Statiev's book on mountain warfare in *European History Quarterly*, 49 No. 3 (2019): 536–7, and parts of the section on Stalingrad in Chapter 5 first saw the light of day as a book review of David Glantz's three-volume history of the battle, published in *New Zealand Slavonic Journal* 45 (2011): 181–3. Earlier and more extensively footnoted versions of sections of several chapters were first published as part of '"What Are We Fighting For?" Loyalty in the Soviet War Effort, 1941–1945', *International Labor and Working-Class History* 84, no. Fall (2013): 248–68; 'Toward a Sociocultural History of the Soviet Second World War', *Kritika: Explorations in Russian and Eurasian History* 15, no. 4 (2014): 829–35; 'The Soviet Culture of Victory', *Journal of Contemporary History* 54, No. 4 (2019): 780–98; 'Who Won the Second World War and Why Should You Care? Reassessing Stalin's War 75 Years after Victory', Journal of Strategic Studies 43, No. 6-7 (2020): 1039–62, published online 2019. I am grateful for the permission to reuse these materials here.

A note on terminology. The Soviet Union abounded in acronyms, putting even Australian universities to shame in this respect. I have tried to avoid them as much as possible. The Soviet security organs, or secret police, form a special problem for the writer intent on not littering his text with sequences of letters in caps. Formed as the Cheka in 1917, it became the GPU under the Commissariat of the Interior (NKVD) in 1922 only to be renamed OGPU in 1923, and GUGB under the NKVD in 1934. In 1941, the security services were separated into NKVD and NKGB, reunited in the same year only to be split again in 1943 and renamed 'ministries' (MVD, MGB) in 1946. During the war with Germany, the Red Army had its own policemen, united eventually in the fearfully named organization 'Death to Spies' (SMERSh). In order to not confuse the reader, I have avoided these changing acronyms wherever possible and used the terms 'security forces', 'security services', 'security troops' of 'police' instead. The latter term can also refer to the regular 'militia' and at times I use the informal term 'chekist', which both friend and foe continued to use to describe a member of the secret police.

Purists might also be annoyed by my use of more popular transliteration of names ('Lavrenty Beria' rather the more scientific 'Lavrentii Beriia') or my propensity to use the current spelling of Ukrainian cities (Kyiv) rather than their until recently more common Russian spelling (Kiev). In footnotes, I give short titles of archival document in English translation rather than in transliterated Russian or Ukrainian, but I do use standard transliteration of scholarly publications, in order to make it possible for other scholars to locate them, should they wish to do so.

INTRODUCTION

STALINISM AT WAR, 1937–49

Victory

Our Soviet people did not spare its strength or its labor in the name of victory. We lived through hard years. But now every one of us can say: we won. From now on we can consider our fatherland delivered from German invasion from the west and Japanese invasion from the East. The long-awaited peace for the peoples of the entire world has arrived. . . . May our Homeland live long and may it prosper!

It was the 2 September 1945 when Josef Stalin gave this address to his people. 'Comrades!', he proclaimed, 'the end of the Second World War has come'.[1]

The dictator had reason to be proud. His Soviet Union had won the greatest and most terrible war in human history. On the night of 8–9 May 1945, Germany had surrendered. Hitler had killed himself earlier, on 30 April, just as the Red Army was storming Berlin in an incredibly costly battle lasting until 2 May. A week later, on 9 May, the most destructive land-war in history was over.[2] Four months on, Japan followed the German example. Its war economy had collapsed, its navy and air force were already barely functional, disabled by US supremacy in the air and on the seas, and the country had been under sustained air attack since June 1944. On 6 August, the US Air Force dropped a new and terrifying weapon on Hiroshima. On 9 August, Soviet forces started racing through Manchuria. On the same day the Americans dropped their second atomic bomb, this time on Nagasaki. Given this concerted onslaught from every direction, Japan's government gave in. On 15 August, the Emperor announced Japan's surrender; on 2 September, the Foreign Minister signed the formal document: the Second World War was finally over.[3]

The Soviet Union was an essential part of the war-winning alliance. While in the Pacific or in Africa, most of the fighting was done by the British Empire and the United States, in Europe the war was essentially won by the Red Army.

Soviet forces faced the largest number of German troops and killed more of them than anybody else. Stalin's soldiers also destroyed or captured the largest share of German military equipment.[4]

For this victory over National Socialism, the Soviets paid a heavy price: 27 million war-related deaths, or about 12 per cent of the pre-war population. According to a government commission collecting data on the devastation, 1,710 towns and cities had been destroyed, more than 70,000 villages burned and bombed. The destruction affected more than 6 million buildings, some 32,000 industrial enterprises and 98,000 collective farms. Millions were homeless; millions more were disabled and sick, traumatized by years of relentless misery and horror. To make things worse, soon after Stalin's triumphant address a terrible famine ripped through the war-weakened population, killing between 1 and 1.5 million people in 1946–7. Fighting continued in the newly acquired borderlands of Western Ukraine, Western Belarus and the three Baltic republics of Estonia, Latvia and Lithuania. In these regions, which the Soviets had taken over in the opening stages of the war in Europe, Soviet troops faced off against nationalist guerrillas resisting the Sovietization of their country. Pacification here had to wait until a round of brutal deportations in 1949 upturned the soil in which the insurgency was rooted.[5]

Asian beginnings

The Soviet Second World War, then, was considerably longer in some parts of Stalin's empire than is usually appreciated. Soviet and later Russian war memory focused on the war with Germany, the 'Great Patriotic War' as it continues to be called in Russia. This war began on 22 June 1941, with the German attack, and ended on 8–9 May 1945, with German surrender. What happened before and after was, at best, a prequel and a post-script to the real war.[6]

Nothing could be further from the experience of Ten San Din and his family. In the autumn of 1937, the 19-year-old student from Vladivostok was deported to Soviet Central Asia. He had not done anything to deserve this fate, but was swept up in the first Soviet deportation of an entire ethnic group: Soviet Koreans, who were moved away from the border regions of the Soviet Far East and dumped in the steppes and towns of Kazakhstan. By 29 October 1937, the operation was nearly complete. A total of 171,781 Koreans had already been packed into cattle cars, as Stalin's chief policeman reported. Only 700 remained, to be despatched by 1 November.[7]

This deportation was a reaction to the outbreak of war in China in July 1937, which Stalin hoped to exploit to his best advantage. Japan had long held ambitions on Soviet lands and Stalin knew it. But as long as the eastern imperialists were busy elsewhere, Stalin calculated, they might not attack the Soviets. Hence, in August 1937 the Soviet government signed the Mutual Nonaggression Treaty with China. The hope was to help the Chinese nationalist government bog down

Japan and hence keep it from attacking the Soviet eastern flank. But should Tokyo nevertheless decide to do so, the Soviets would be ready. Hence the deportation of the Koreans, whom Stalin saw as potential fifth columnists – enemies within the gates who might help the Japanese invaders. The two decisions were linked: they were both taken on the same day, on 21 August 1937.[8]

Ten San Din's Second World War was entirely Asian. Deported because of the outbreak of war in China his attempts to join the army were knocked back repeatedly. He was eventually drafted in 1945 and fought in a swift operation in Korea, as part of the Soviet attack on the Japanese Empire in the summer of 1945. Petr Fedorovich Katasonov provides another corrective to Euro-centric narratives of the Soviet war effort. Born in 1914 he served in the Soviet–Japanese border war of 1938–9, fighting in the battle of Khalkhin Gol in 1939 as a machine gunner. After the war was over, he was demobilized and worked in a collective farm in the Buriat-Mongolian Autonomous Republic, located in the south of the Soviet Union. After the German attack on 22 June 1941, he was again mobilized into the army, but not sent to fight against the invaders. Instead, he served at the Manchurian border. 'In 1941–1942', he remembered, 'there were constant provocations at the border. We helped the border forces to catch all kinds of spies and saboteurs.' Once the war in the Pacific heated up, his frontline quieted down, until, on 9 August 1945, 'we went on the offensive against Manchuria'. He fought against the crumbling Japanese forces in northern China, guarded prisoners of war and was demobilized shortly after Japan's capitulation. His war, like Ten San Din's, was an entirely Asian affair.[9]

Such war experiences run counter some of the most basic assumptions we have about the Second World War in general and the Soviet Second World War in particular. European historians do not usually begin this war in Asia and in 1937, but in Poland on 1 September 1939; Russians tend to start their own 'Great Patriotic War' only in June 1941 with the German invasion; and from an American perspective, the Second World War did not begin until December of that year, with the entry of the United States into the war after the attack on Pearl Harbor. While some Japanese historians push the start of what they call the '15 Year War' even further back to the invasion of Manchuria in 1931, English-language historians have often ignored the Asian theatre, maybe because few white men fought there, maybe because the bloodletting in the Pacific preoccupied the American public more than the strange war in a far-away land or maybe because the enormity of the European war, the German–Soviet front and, not least, the Jewish Holocaust pushed everything else into the shadows. [10]

Eurasian war

This book instead follows recent efforts to cast the borders of the Second World War wide enough to account for the Asian experience as much as the European or American one. As we know from Stalin's address as well as the recollections of the two veterans, the Soviet war was not just a European affair. It was a Eurasian war fought both on the Soviet Union's eastern front in Asia and its western front in Europe. And it was a war embedded into a wider, global war, which was, in turn, an amalgam of several armed confrontations.[11]

Five distinct wars made up the Second World War: an Asian land war, which started in 1937 with the outbreak of the Sino-Japanese conflict; a European war, starting with Hitler's attack on Poland in 1939; a north African war fought from 1940 to 1943; the German–Soviet war from the summer of 1941; and a Pacific war, beginning with the bombing of Pearl Harbor in December of the same year. Late 1941 marks the moment when these separate conflicts were linked together in a global conflagration.[12]

Soviet participation in this Second World War began in 1937 with involvement in the Asian war, a defensive war in the east. Stalin provided aid to China, secured his eastern front through ethnic cleansing and a troop build-up. Soon, his Red Army fought an oft-forgotten but crucial border war with Japan in 1938–9 (battles of Lake Khasan and Khalkhin Gol). Next came an offensive war in Europe, where the Soviets joined forced with the Germans in dismantling Poland in September 1939 before striking out alone in the Winter War with Finland in 1939–40 and annexations of Estonia, Latvia, Lithuania, the Northern Bukovina and Bessarabia in 1940. In the third phase, the Soviets were again on the defensive, this time in a catastrophic war with Germany starting in the summer of 1941. The fourth phase then saw Soviet victory against Germany in a war of attrition from early 1943, and, after victory in Europe, an offensive war against Japan in the summer of 1945. The final phase was one of pacification and consolidation. It began with the liberation of territories from 1943 and ended in the heartland with the abolition of food rationing in 1947 and the conclusion of mass demobilization in 1948. In the western borderlands, meanwhile, another aspect of the Soviet war came to the foreground: the conventional Soviet war against Germany and Japan was entangled in Civil Wars against groups of the population, some armed and fighting back, many others simple civilians targeted as enemies of Soviet power because of their sociological or national profile. The war as Civil War continued until 1949, when large-scale deportations in the west and the victory of Chinese communists in the east marked the end of the Soviet Second World War.

Scope and sources

This history of the Soviet Union in the Second World War brings together the history of international politics and military operations with studies in the economy, culture and society of the wartime years.[13] Its perspective shifts continuously between individual stories and the larger histories they were a part of. This book thus combines an anthology of war experience with the historian's bird's eye view on larger social, economic, cultural and governmental structures. The state's view is reconstructed from once secret archival data from Russia, Ukraine, Latvia, Lithuania, Estonia, Germany, Australia and the United States.[14] But archives are depositories of government-produced documents and do not always capture the human side of this war. Hence, this book also uses extensively diaries, memoirs and oral history interviews with survivors. Some of them were conducted close to the events in question and have been published in important source collections; others were written or documented outside the Soviet Union by émigrés, such as the Harvard Project on the Soviet Social System or the oral history collection of the Dorot Jewish Library in the New York Public Library. Others were recorded after the end of the Soviet Union, such as the large collection of interviews with Red Army veterans now available in a growing online database.[15]

Lamentably, Stalin did not keep a diary or leave memoirs. For this central actor, we are reliant on the views of those who knew him, as well as the traces he left in the archives. A distinguished biographical literature can inform our reading of these sources.[16] Understanding Stalin is central, as the Soviet Union in the 1930s and 1940s was one of the most repressive dictatorships of the twentieth century. Stalin held the country, his Communist Party, the state apparatus and his closest associates in an iron grip. Quite naturally, therefore, he plays a central role in our narrative. Nevertheless, this volume is neither yet another biography of the dictator nor a study of Stalin's war alone. Instead, the leader is surrounded by other actors, big and small: civilians and soldiers, communists and their opponents, men and women, generals and privates, workers and peasants, bureaucrats and scholars, loyalists and resisters, Russians and members of a large number of national minorities. This kaleidoscopic view of the war precludes deep explorations of Stalin's diplomacy or detailed recounting of military operations. These have been covered by other scholars in sufficient detail to be relegated to short sketches here.[17]

Professional historians, meanwhile, might hope for more coverage of scholarly controversies and historiographical debate. They can find these in my more specialized essays and monographs which emerged on the way to the current volume. *Stalinism at War*, by contrast to these earlier studies, was written for a non-specialist readership. Therefore, historiographical discussion, scholarly polemics and bibliographic footnotes are kept to a minimum.

Domestic impact of the war in each phase

Bringing together the broad sweep of Soviet history with individual experiences raises the question of how important the different stages of the long Second World War were in the lives of ordinary citizens. Seen from a domestic perspective, the different periods of the Soviet Second World War varied in their impact. Unless you were Korean or an active Soviet serviceman in China, Mongolia or the Far East, the defensive war in Asia of 1937–9 would have only peripherally touched you, largely as a reader of newspapers. A total of 97,000 troops were involved in the fighting and losses were fairly minimal, maybe 11,000 dead.[18] Stalin's Great Terror impacted on many more lives during this period: in 1937–8 alone, 1.6 million people were arrested, 682,000 of them shot.[19]

In the second phase of 1939–41, the war would be much more widely felt. The number of troops involved went from tens of thousands to 1.3 million, not counting those involved in the Baltic and Bessarabian acquisitions. Some 128,000 Soviets were killed in the fighting in Poland and Finland. At the very least half a million servicemen saw the outside world in Poland and the Baltics, a disorienting experience.[20] The Hitler–Stalin Pact of August 1939 caused widespread ideological confusion and deportations from the western borderlands extended the Korean experience to 383,000 more victims. The increasing shift of resources into armaments production together with the food deliveries to Germany as part of the Hitler–Stalin pact further depressed civilian consumption, increased shortages, lines, inflation and labour turnover. Economic output per head stagnated between 1937 and 1940, civilian consumption fell significantly and instead rearmament gobbled up more and more resources. The authorities reacted with the introduction of rationing in certain areas of the country and with a nation-wide imposition of labour laws which put industrial workers on a wartime footing in 1940.[21]

But it was the third and fourth phases – the life and death struggle with Germany of 1941–5 – which truly universalized the experience of war. Consumption dropped catastrophically, for civilians sometimes to starvation levels. Altogether 34.5 million men and women served in the armed forces during this period, and 7.8 million died as a result. Everybody who did not fight was mobilized to work and the death toll among civilians was more than three times higher than among soldiers.[22]

In the final phase, the experience of war was again localized, this time to the western borderlands. Here, insurgencies of Estonian, Latvian, Lithuanian, Polish and Ukrainian nationalists were put down with force. The open military confrontation was over in 1945, with the anti-Soviet partisans subdued by the superior firepower of the Soviets. The resistance then shifted to terrorist tactics, which continued to make life deadly for supporters of Soviet power. As late as 1946, communist officials in the Latvian countryside would routinely carry automatic weapons for self-defence.[23] Losses were nowhere near the scale of the wars with Germany or even Japan, however. Overall in the western borderlands, some 70,000 counter-insurgency troops were involved in the fighting. They lost no more than 6,000 men.[24] However, the anti-Soviet partisans killed multiple times this number outside of direct military confrontation, mostly 'soft targets' – civilians, seen as collaborators with the Soviets.[25] In 1948, in operations against the Lithuanian underground, to cite an example we explore in more detail in Chapter 7, Soviet security forces killed nearly ten of their opponents for every casualty they suffered themselves. But if we add the victims of anti-Soviet attacks on civilians, the kill ratio is nearly even: 1.6 partisans for every one 'Soviet' death.[26]

Elsewhere, the main story of these years was no longer of war but of reconstruction. Demobilization, the return of displaced persons, re-evacuation and rebuilding of the economy were the order of the day, as was a concerted fight against war-related violence and crime. Once people survived the post-war famine of 1946–7, life began to return to normalcy, albeit a Stalinist one. Repression returned, but by and large in a less lethal form: people lost their jobs because they were accused of 'rootless cosmopolitanism', or they were locked up under the draconian theft laws of 1947. Exceptions were the Leningrad (1949–50) and Mingrelian Affairs (1951–2), which resembled miniature great terrors in the trumped-up charges but led to the execution of a relatively small number of people.[27] Repatriates who returned also sometimes faced arrest, either during the original verification process or later in life. However, archival research has shown that this phenomenon was much smaller than older literature had speculated.[28] Once the counter-insurgency in the western borderlands came to an end with the 1949 deportations, these new regions of the empire also joined Stalinist normalcy: everyday life under extraordinary conditions even in peacetime.[29]

A changing vision of the Soviet Second World War

This book's re-casting of the Soviet Second World War as a long Eurasian war stretching from 1937 to 1949 thus does not negate the centrality of the experience of the 'Great Patriotic War'. Instead, it places it into a wider geographic and historical context. What does this reconfiguration imply for our understanding of the Soviet Second World War?

For one, the role of the Soviet eastern front becomes much more crucial. China played a central role in keeping the Soviet Union's back free until at least 1942, when the United States Navy took on the brunt of the Japanese military's attention. Even then, however, China continued to pull its weight. While the Americans engaged the Japanese fleet and air force, it was the Chinese who bogged down the ground troops that could have presented a threat to the Soviets. Allied aid (Lend-Lease) through Japanese waters to Vladivostok and hence the Trans-Siberian Railway was essential to the Soviet war effort and only possible because Stalin had managed to secure peace with Japan in 1941. There were other routes for the delivery of supplies – via Arctic waters or through Iran. But as we shall see in Chapter 6, these were much more problematic than shipping through the Pacific, which soon became the principal connection of the Soviet Union to its Allies.

Despite its neutrality in the Pacific war, the Soviet leadership never lost interest in the Far Eastern front and troops there never dropped below 1.1 million. The region became transformed into a huge troop training ground where raw recruits were made battle ready before being sent to the front. And once the war against Germany was won, Soviet citizens like Ten San Din or Petr Fedorovich Katasonov also did their bit to force Japan to surrender.[30]

Second, displacement becomes a central theme in this history. Be it soldiers, people mobilized to work, deportees, arrestees sent to the Gulag, refugees, evacuees and re-evacuees, plenipotentiaries and trouble shooters: nearly everybody was on the move in the wartime Soviet Union. Stalin, however, remained stationary, with Viacheslav Molotov at his side presiding over the entire flux. In 2013, historian Peter Gatrell called on his colleagues to integrate the history of refugees into mainstream accounts. This book goes further by arguing that any history of the Soviet Union at war needs to take seriously the various forms of displacements which defined the experience of war for a large sector of the population. [31]

Third, the Soviet Second World War was multinational. While both contemporary observers and later historians often wrote of 'Russia's war', about half of the Soviet population, a significant share of the fighting forces, and more than half of the civilian victims were made up of non-Russians.[32] Hence, this was not just 'Ivan's war' but also Ten San Din's, Susanne's or Nachman's – and, of course, Stalin's, a Georgian who spoke heavily accented Russian.[33] In this book we will encounter a rich variety of Soviets: Koreans, Germans, Jews, Poles, Ukrainians, Lithuanians and, of course, Russians. Our attention to the borderlands in the east and the west brings displaced Koreans, Balts or Poles into focus. We pay particular attention to the suffering and the heroism of Soviet Jews, who only recently have been written back into the history of the Soviet Second World War. They included a significant number of 'new Soviet Jews' who entered the Soviet story during the aggressive phase of 1939–41.[34]

Fourth, the totalitarian aspect of the Soviet Second World War, which many historians have stressed for the western borderlands, both was an all-union experience and followed its own unique dynamic. The Soviet Second World War began with the deportation of Koreans in 1937 and ended with the deportation of 'kulaks' and their families from the west in 1949. The Great Terror of 1937–8 was the backdrop to the international crisis in the east in 1937–9 and was motivated as preparation for war. With the German attack came more violence against the own side, what one historian has called the 'Great Terror of 1941'. Once Soviet forces liberated territories from German occupation, Stalin's police and, with it Stalinist terror, returned. However, it had changed its nature since the early 1940s: repression became more widespread but also much less lethal. In Estonia, to cite one particularly well-documented example, the arrest wave of 1944–5 targeted a broader group of people than its 1940–1 predecessor had, but a much larger percentage now survived. The death penalty was used less frequently now and was abolished in the Soviet Union as a whole in 1947; conditions in detention had improved. The 1949 deportations followed the same pattern: they victimized twice the number of their 1941 predecessor, but the death rate now was down to 15 per cent, compared to 60 per cent in 1941. Somewhat surprisingly, then, the immense suffering and the unrelenting brutality of the Soviet Second World War did not brutalize Stalin's regime. It had the opposite effect: in the post-war years, historians have observed the replacement of terror with regular if heavy-handed policing.[35]

Structure of the book

This book develops these themes in nine roughly chronological chapters, each addressing a different question about the Soviet Second World War. Chapter 1 asks if the Soviet Union was prepared for war when it broke out. The answer is ambiguous: Stalin's policies of the 1930s both helped and hindered war preparation; the Stalinist way of waging war was both effective and inefficient; terror, conceived as part of war preparation, had adverse effects on readiness.

Chapter 2 tells the story of the oft-forgotten phase of the Second World War when Stalin managed to avoid a major threat that concerned him deeply: a war on two fronts. It asks what role the Soviet Union played in the war in Asia in 1937–9. While Stalin's policies during this phase were destructive domestically, they were crucial internationally. Soviet aid helped China resist Japan, and Soviet victory in the border war of 1938–9 pushed Tokyo towards a 'southern strategy' which both kept the Soviet eastern front quiet until 1945 and brought Japan into conflict with the United States. Thus, Soviet actions during this period were pivotal for the entire further history of the Second World War.[36]

In Chapter 3, covering 1939–41, the major action moves from the east to the west. It answers the question about the role of the Soviets in the opening stages of the war in Europe. These were the years of the alliance with Germany, when the Soviets acted aggressively in Eastern Europe and not only annexed foreign lands but subjected them to totalitarian terror of immense proportions. The ambivalence many feel today about this period is rooted in the experience of these years, which were deeply unsettling for many Soviet citizens. In the borderlands itself, these years were marked by foreign conquest and violence. But in the old Soviet Union, too, they were perturbing. How could one make sense of a situation where a supposedly anti-fascist, anti-imperialist, socialist state made common cause with the Nazis and took over neighbouring lands by force of arms? Opportunism had dictated Stalin's tactics: he wanted to play for time, increase the reach of his state and hope for the best. As we shall see, this strategy failed and the expansion to the west left the Soviets more vulnerable than they had been before 1939. Moreover, such cynical Realpolitik was a hard sell and the Soviet leadership groped for a formula which would explain its actions not only internationally but also domestically. Eventually, it was found: Soviet expansion was not imperialism but national liberation; it freed fellow Slavs (Ukrainians, Belarusians) from Polish oppression. While this logic could not explain the annexation of the Baltic countries or the aggression against Finland, it pointed to things to come: the ethno-national principle would become central to the way post-war borders would be drawn.

Chapter 4 is concerned with the first period of the German–Soviet war, that is, 1941–2. It asks what caused the catastrophe and how it was survived. As Stalin recognized in moments of weakness, the initial chaos was his fault: he had weakened the army in the Great Terror; he had supported and supplied the Germans since 1939; he had refused to believe that an attack was imminent. War preparation was fundamentally botched and the widespread anti-Soviet feelings in the population – caused by the terror against the own population since the start of collectivization in 1929 and the terrorist takeover of the western borderlands from 1939 – did nothing to prepare the country for defence. And Stalin's immediate response was more terror, which further destabilized the situation. Nevertheless, the dictator did not give up and neither did a hard core of supporters all over the Soviet lands. Within the general breakdown and the widespread chaos, determined resistance continued. The tactic of relentless counter-attack by sections of the Red Army frightened German soldiers at the time. As more and more historians agree, it also broke the German war effort already during the first half year of the war: by the end of 1941, Hitler had already lost the war in the east. He just did not know it yet.[37]

How the remarkable recovery was possible is explored in Chapter 5. It shows that the Soviet regime underwent a dual process of centralization (of decision making) and de-centralization (of implementation). While individuals and their families navigated the mobilizational system's cracks and fissures, the Soviet government recovered from the shock of the first weeks, consolidated its wartime structure and began to mobilize the country. The dictator was central to this effort, both as the actual linchpin of the entire system and as a symbol for a strong and determined government. But Stalin did not act alone. The dictatorship became much more flexible than it had been before the German attack, which allowed massive mobilization of resources for defence. The contradictions of Stalinist war preparations, however, also played themselves out.

On the positive side, Stalin's successful attempt to avoid a two-front war now paid off: the east remained calm and could be used both to relocate industry and to train troops for the fight in the west. The leadership had gained valuable experience in crisis management in the domestic upheaval its war preparations had caused ever since 1929. Their skills as trouble shooters helped Stalin's 'team' during the chaos of war. Force-paced industrialization with a focus on heavy industry also paid off now: the Soviets could outproduce their enemy with massive numbers of standardized equipment. And the dictatorship was strong enough to mobilize the vast majority of the population to either fight or work for victory. On the negative side, however, the poor productivity of Stalinist agriculture was further exacerbated by the effects of the war, and hunger was a constant companion of Soviet citizens during wartime.[38]

The following two chapters then deal with the follow-up question: why did the Soviet Union win the war? Chapter 6 covers the years 1943–5, a period of triumph against Nazi Germany and, eventually, Japan. It makes the case for the centrality of the Soviet war effort for victory in Europe and explores the role of Allied aid and Allied support to Soviet success. It also discusses the lesser role the Soviets played in the victory of war in Asia and again reminds readers of the role China played in keeping Stalin's back free. It analyses the origins of the wartime food crisis and the role of coerced labour in the war effort.

Chapter 7 switches from economic to cultural history. It shows how and why an increasing proportion of Soviet citizens supported Stalin's war effort against Germany. Repression alone did not win this war. Even during the darkest days of 1941, when Stalin felt compelled to ratchet up repression in order to save his regime, he could still rely on a core of committed supporters on all levels of the political and social hierarchy. Everywhere – from the trenches to the Kremlin, from the factory floor to the Central Committee apparatus – there were ideologically committed men and women who believed in the Soviet cause and often also in the leadership of comrade Stalin. They were decisive in organizing the resistance to the Nazi onslaught. As time went on, the group of supporters grew. Revenge, patriotism and anger at what the Germans had done combined with a growing enchantment with the successes of the Soviet state and the Red Army in their fight against the Wehrmacht. As time went on, the core of supporters thus grew to encompass larger and larger sectors of the population. More and more Soviet citizens began to feel that their interests coincided with those of the regime. The exception were the western borderlands where the struggle took on the quality of multiple Civil Wars within the conventional war.[39]

Chapter 8 then turns to these borderlands and explores the counter-insurgency in the newly acquired territories during the years 1944–9 before turning to the more general pacification of a society marred by war-induced violence and swept by a terrible crime wave. It shows how the Soviet state struggled to re-establish its monopoly of violence, but how it eventually succeeded in this quest.[40]

The final chapter then shifts to putting the Second World War into the larger context of Soviet and post-Soviet history. It asks what impact the war had on Soviet society and how it is remembered in the successor states after the breakdown of 1991. It thus links this history to the present, which continues to be shaped by it.[41]

1 PREPARING FOR WAR

Doom and gloom

'Do you want our socialist fatherland to be beaten and lose its independence?'
Stalin was at his most rhetorical when he spoke to an assembly of his industrial
managers in 1931.[1] The dictator posed this question at a time his strategy to
prepare the Soviet Union for war had produced chaos, even catastrophe. There
were successes, to be sure. In the wake of the dual decisions to industrialize at a
forced pace and order the peasants into collective farms – Stalin's first 'revolution
from above' – both employment in industry and gross industrial production
more than doubled between 1928 and 1932. But this Industrial Revolution came
at the price of plummeting living standards and at the cost of worker resistance,
which had to be suppressed. Calorie consumption declined by between 20 and
30 per cent and Soviet workers would not eat as well as they had in 1928 until
well after Stalin's death. Housing was cramped and unpleasant. The most fortunate
lived in communal apartments, with one family per room and shared kitchen and
bathroom facilities, if there were any. Others lived in barracks, in tents, in hastily
constructed dugouts or in sheds nailed together from whatever material could be
found. Workers grumbled about their hard lives: was this really socialism?[2]

But if life in the cities was dreary, catastrophe loomed in the countryside. Stalin
could not know it, yet, but a famine of major proportions was afoot, killing millions
in 1932–3, especially in Ukraine, the Northern Caucasus and Kazakhstan. This
famine was a direct result of Stalin's agricultural policies, especially the relentless
grain requisitioning to pay for industrialization and the confiscation of cattle to
feed the cities. The government soon learned what was going on, but the dictator
refused to act decisively, either because he did not believe that things were really
as bad as reported to him or because he was willing to sacrifice Ukrainian peasants
and Kazakh nomads for the good of his socialism.[3]

It was in this context of social, economic and political crisis that Stalin
argued for his type of crash developmentalism. Russia, he claimed, had always

been beaten by foreign powers, because the country was backward culturally, technologically and militarily. The Soviet Union, he implied, was the successor of the Russian Empire and beholden to the same geopolitical laws: either overcome backwardness or perish. That the red empire was also the only socialist country, an island in the sea of capitalism and, according to those believing in the doctrines of Marxism–Leninism, humanity's only hope for a better future made the choice only starker: a war would come, Stalin insisted. Marx, Engels and Lenin had taught that capitalism necessarily led to war. As he had lectured a foreign reporter in 1929, just a month after the stock market crash which inaugurated the Great Depression in the capitalist world: it was not clear 'when, where, and on what pretext' a war would start. But that it would come was not in question. 'It is inevitable', the dictator explained the contours of his worldview, 'that the efforts of the stronger powers to overcome the economic crisis will force them to crush their weaker rivals'. In the long run, this dynamic could have but one outcome: eventually, 'the giant powers must fight for markets among themselves'. The interwar order, instituted with the peace treaty of Versailles in 1919, was doomed to break down, the dictator explained and Europe was an armed camp.[4] The Soviet Union better be ready. A peasant country with backward agriculture would again lose, as Russia had in the First World War. The task was to transform it into an industrialized war machine able to win modern wars.

Stalin's predictions of a coming war were correct. But was the strategy he had developed in response successful? Was the Soviet Union prepared for war when it broke out, first in Asia in 1937, then in Europe in 1939? The answer is ambiguous.

The dictator and his country

In 1931 Stalin could not know what the outcome of his efforts would be. But he did know where he was heading. He also knew where he came from. His Soviet Union had emerged from the First World War and its violent aftermath in Eastern Europe. Beaten in war and rocked by political and social unrest, the tsarist empire had broken apart into a patchwork of new states, most barely able to restore even the most basic functions of governance: to monopolize the means of violence. Lenin's Bolsheviks, Stalin among them, turned out to be adept at this task. They had taken control over the Russian heartland around Moscow, where they built the core of their new state. It proved itself best suited to reassemble the defeated and fractured empire – a paradoxical outcome, given their anti-imperialist ideology. In 1920 and 1921, the Red Army would reconquer much of the tsarist lands. Only Poland, Finland and the three Baltic republics (Latvia, Lithuania and Estonia) remained independent for the time being.[5]

The state they built in the process did cover much of the same real estate as its tsarist predecessor, but it was a fundamentally different polity: not only a dictatorship but a dictatorship of a new kind. Because the Bolsheviks had few technical cadres of their own – bureaucrats, doctors, engineers, statisticians, army officers etc. – they needed to co-opt a good part of the old elite. These people, of course, could not be trusted and hence some kind of surveillance mechanisms needed to be established. Part of the answer was the secret police, but this situation also called for political leadership of the 'bourgeois specialists', as Lenin called them. The answer was found in what would become a central feature of Leninist states: the duality of party and state administrations. In order to keep a good eye on the state, staffed with what were considered hostile specialists, a parallel hierarchy was created of Communist Party positions, which would oversee the work of the technocrats.

While Lenin's men had managed to reassemble the empire, it was a starving country they now controlled. The working class, in whose name these Marxist revolutionaries governed, had all but disappeared in the conflagration of war, revolution and Civil Wars. What was left of tsarist industry – once growing at a rate faster than any other – produced a pittance. Gross industrial production, which stood at 8,431 million roubles in 1913 and had grown to 9,220 million roubles as a result of the wartime armaments boom by 1916, had collapsed to only 1,718 million roubles by 1920. The regime, popular in 1917–18 for ending the war and giving land to the peasants, was confronted with political unrest: by 1920–1 workers were on strike, peasants rebelled and revolutionary sailors asked for the end of the Bolshevik dictatorship. Lenin reacted with a two-pronged policy: the uprisings were suppressed with unrestrained brutality; economic concessions decreased discontent.[6]

The result was the New Economic Policy (or NEP, 1921–7), a compromise solution. It combined dictatorial government with a planned state economy and a growing private sector ruled by market forces. This settlement was doomed for a complex mix of reasons. It was haunted by economic contradictions and was politically unpopular among rank-and-file members of the ruling Communist Party. Many communists were upset that they seemed to have shed their proletarian blood during the Civil War only for petty bourgeois tradespeople and tight-fisted peasants to reap the benefits. NEP also depended on foreign credits and access to world markets (for grain, especially), which proved problematic with the deterioration of the world economy culminating in the stock market crash of 1929. In order to work in the medium term, NEP also required fairly level-headed economic management at a time when Lenin's deputies were embroiled in a nasty succession struggle after the leader's premature death in 1924. Finally, the NEP allowed only for relatively modest economic growth at a time when Soviet relative backwardness vis-à-vis the capitalist world threatened doom. While the NEP had allowed recovery of most indicators to pre-war levels by the late 1920s, this was a return to an economic performance under which the Russian empire had lost the First World War over a decade earlier. And this normalization was concentrated in consumer goods, not in the heavy industries which could form the basis of a modern war economy. 'We are fifty or a hundred years behind the advanced countries', summarized Stalin this view in 1931. 'We must make good this distance in ten years. Either we do it, or we shall go under.'[7]

The NEP thus found its gravedigger in Stalin. Once he buried it, he would become one of the most ferocious dictators of the twentieth century but also the man who presided over the Soviet Second World War with an iron fist. Stalin had been one of the few plebeians in a pre-revolutionary Bolshevik Party dominated by intellectuals. He had stayed in the country and worked in the underground while Lenin had nursed his migraines in Switzerland. He had shown himself a practical politician before the revolution and proved his mettle after the Bolshevik takeover as a terroristic dictator over Tsaritsyn, the city later renamed Stalingrad in his honour. As commissar (minister) for Nationalities, he presided over the management of the national question in the multi-ethnic Soviet empire. In 1922, Lenin installed him as general secretary of the Bolshevik Party, the single most powerful position in the Soviet dictatorship save Lenin's own. After his teacher's death, Stalin proved more skilful in the succession struggle than his more sophisticated competitors. Once in power by 1928, he inherited a Soviet economic system in deep crisis and a country which could expect war with Japan in the East, Poland or Germany in the West and Finland in the north. It was not likely to win such a war unless it acquired a modern industry.

Stalin's strategy

Stalin developed a three-pronged strategy to deal with this problem. The state would sponsor crash-industrialization, buy state-of-the-art equipment from the capitalists abroad and employ foreign specialists to install this technology and train the domestic workforce. In order to pay for this massive investment in heavy industry, the peasantry had to be brought to heel. Forced into collective farms, the agricultural population lost control over its labour and the fruits of its work. It was subjected to arbitrary grain collections. Third, a new elite of proletarian origin was trained to take over from the fickle intellectuals beholden to the old regime.

Together these three revolutions made up Stalin's first revolution from above – the industrial revolution of the First Five-Year Plan, the agricultural revolution of collectivization and the cultural revolution of challenging the old elite by training its replacement. It built the basics of the warfare state that would win the Second World War: a subdued population, a growing police apparatus, a centralized economy, a propaganda machine trying to direct the entire population to the regime's ends and a group of beneficiaries – young, upwardly mobile cadres who owed their advancement to comrade Stalin and his socialism. Together with younger and thoroughly indoctrinated communists of the next generation, they would form the 'core' of the Soviet Union's fighters in the Second World War. These cadres had a stake in Stalin's system and had made the goals of his socialism their own. Rather than brainwashed automatons, they were creative actors, engaged in a continuous process of self-indoctrination. Seeing themselves as part of a global struggle for a better world, they were disciplined, hard-working and committed to a cause – attributes which would serve them well in the coming war.[8]

Crucially, however, Stalin's revolution preserved the central feature of the duality of state and party apparatuses, which had originally been developed to control a state not staffed by cadres loyal to the regime. In an example of the preservation of structures which have outlived their original justification, the party–state duality remained a fundamental feature of the Soviet polity. As we shall see in later chapters, until 1941, Stalin was not technically heading the state hierarchy at all: he was the general secretary of the Communist Party, nothing more. Eventually, this would change. From the summer of 1941, Stalin would stand at the head of both hierarchies as the top official in charge of everything.

By the time Stalin gave the speech about Russia having been beaten, beaten and beaten again because of her backwardness, however, his revolution from above was incomplete. Yes, new cadres had been trained but the levers of power in the Bolshevik Party, the wider state apparatus and the economic management were still largely in the hands of pre-revolutionary specialist or old Bolsheviks loyal to the party of Lenin but not necessarily content with Stalin as leader. In Stalin's eyes, this situation was risky: in times of war, elites of dubious loyalty might well make revolution, as they had in 1917. But then, the revolution had been against tsarism, capitalism and imperialist war. Next time it would be against the only bastion of socialism, the one and only radical alternative to the capitalism responsible, in Stalin's Marxist mind, not only for exploitation but also for war. This risk could not be taken. Extreme measures were called for.[9]

The Great Terror

On 1 December 1934, Stalin found a pretext for launching his second revolution from above. On this day, a slightly deranged gunman shot the Leningrad Party boss dead. Stalin immediately took charge of the investigation into his comrade's murder and used it to 'uncover' all kinds of 'enemies' within the party ranks. Some of the victims of the emerging Great Purge were truly in opposition to Stalin. Many more were loyal Stalinists who had confessions beaten out of them. Each arrest triggered several others, as the accused were forced to point fingers at alleged co-conspirators. The purge began in the Party and the state apparatus but soon broadened to include the military, decapitating the Red Army. Three out of five Marshals did not survive the decade. More army-level commanders were shot between 1936 and 1941 than had been in these positions at the start of the period:

the terror chewed up replacements, too. Many more experienced cadres saw their careers destroyed even if their lives were spared. Lower down the hierarchy the impact was less spectacular and reinstatements lowered the overall share of victims to about 8 per cent of the officer corps in 1937 and 4 per cent in 1938. But the purge truly only became the Great Terror after it spread to the population at large in a series of 'mass operations' in 1937 and 1938. Overall, in these two years, nearly 1.6 million people were arrested, and a staggering 681,692 of them shot. More died in detention, as a result of torture, malnutrition, overwork, disease or accidents, increasing the death toll of these two bloody years to maybe 1.5 million.[10]

To Stalin, this bloodletting was an essential part of war preparation. Wreckers were everywhere, he told the Central Committee in 1937. They were ready to 'do their spoiling work . . . in the period immediately preceding war or during war itself'.[11] The closer his police looked at personal networks within the party, the more conspiracies they thought they saw. The more he learned about the views of the population, relentlessly eavesdropped upon by party members and police agents, the more isolated he felt. A public debate about a new constitution, the promise for more open elections and a census of the population all revealed widespread hostility to his form of socialism. In the context of the looming threat of Japan from the east and a militarizing Nazi Germany from the west, it was clearly not enough to just purge state, party and army from hidden enemies. Formerly well-off peasants ('kulaks'), whose property had been confiscated and who had been sent into exile as part of collectivization at the start of the decade, people who had fought with anti-Bolshevik armies in the Civil War, officers and civil servants of the old regime, members of competing socialist or non-socialist parties, clergymen, common criminals, 'anti-Soviet elements', Poles, Germans, Finns, Latvians, Chinese, Koreans and other diaspora nationalities all fell victim.[12]

Did Stalinism prepare the Soviet Union for war?

When Stalin stopped the bloodletting in November 1938, he had achieved his goal: there was no opposition left in his empire and in his party. Even his closest colleagues in the Politburo were now so terrified that nobody dared to contradict the dictator. It was now, between 1938 and the German invasion in the summer of 1941, that Stalin was as close to a totalitarian ruler as he would ever be. And it was now that he launched into the foreign policy adventures explored in Chapter 3: making common cause with Hitler, he completed the re-gathering of the old Romanov lands which had successfully resisted the Red Army in 1918–21. Having consolidated his power at home, Stalin was ready to export his revolution. The foreign policy decisions of 1939–41, which struck so many contemporaries as puzzling at best and scandalous at worst, were not those of a collective leadership any more. They were born of Stalin's own idiosyncrasies, not checked by an independent apparatus or a strong leadership team. Stalin could now embark on foreign policy adventures because his rule seemed safe domestically and his country ready for war.

But was it? Had Stalin's two revolutions from above really created a totalitarian warfare state prepared for modern war? To assess this question requires clarifying what it means to state that a country is 'ready for war'. Military historians distinguish the ability to fight and to continue to do so ('military effectiveness') from doing so in the least costly manner, that is 'efficiently'. Economic and cultural history further broaden our view to include economic and cultural factors. Such a broad framework allows assessing the extent to which the Soviets were ready for war when it erupted in China in 1937, in Europe in 1939 and in the Soviet heartland itself in 1941.

Military preparedness

In one sense, of course, we know the answer: after all, the Soviets won. They won against the Japanese at Lake Khasan (29 July–11 August 1938) and at Khalkhin Gol (11 May–16 September 1939); they won against the Polish army in (17 September–6 October 1939); they won against the Finns (30 November 1939–13 March 1940); they won against the Iranians (25–28 August 1941); they won against the Germans (22 June 1941–9 May 1945) and against the Japanese (9 August–2 September 1945). So, the Soviets were clearly 'militarily effective'.

But they were not efficient. Lake Khasan was a slaughter of Soviet infantry won by sheer numbers. Khalkhin Gol, another limited campaign, was a mixture of highly modern warfare with typically Soviet methods of threats and executions to motivate the troops, as we shall see in Chapter 2. The Polish campaign, discussed in Chapter 3, was won at the cost of 1,475 dead Soviets and 2,383 wounded against an enemy overwhelmed and beaten already by the Nazi war machine invading from the west while also engaged in a Civil War with home-grown insurgents. The war against Finland killed a staggering 126,875 Red Army soldiers, while another 264,908 others were wounded, frostbitten or fell ill during the campaign. The catastrophe of the first year of the German–Soviet war is described in detail in Chapter 3; the Iranian army, again confronted with a two-front campaign (against the Soviets from the north and the British from the south), collapsed nearly instantly, the Soviets suffering only fifteen fatalities, the majority of them drownings, and eighteen wounded; during the war against Germany, the Soviets consistently lost more men than the enemy, the ratio dropping from a catastrophic 10:1 in 1941 to 3:1 in 1943; and the Manchurian campaign in Japan in the summer of 1945 was fought against relatively weak forces of an already collapsing empire, but still at the cost of 6,729 dead in China and 528 in North Korea.[13]

In military terms, then, the Soviets were effective without being particularly efficient. This characterization also holds for the overall performance of the Soviet Union in the Second World War. In strictly military terms, two aspects are particularly important: the technological, doctrinal and institutional preparedness of the Red Army for a relatively modern war; and the level of military training in the population at large.

The latter is easily overstated, as official discourse loudly celebrated relatively modest gains. Once the Germans attacked and civilians had to be drafted in large numbers, the military struggled with high levels of unpreparedness. 'The overwhelming majority of soldiers do not have modern military training. They do not know how to use their rifles', wrote a professor serving among peasants in a newly formed rifle company in October 1941. 'I have also never shot before, I do not know my weapon and I hoped that we will be given the opportunity to prepare a little, if only quickly.' Soldiers were assigned to machine guns they had never seen, let alone used before, as a veteran remembered later. 'Here, comrades', they were instructed 'we have the newest machine gun . . . four people are required to work it. . . . To shoot, you have to press it, press it, pull it, insert it and shoot. Understood?!' While the thus instructed all cried 'understood' in response 'nobody understood absolutely nothing. And with such knowledge of the machine gun we marched towards the frontline and were immediately shot at.' Even officers, both in the Finnish war and later in the Great Patriotic War, could not always read a map or use a compass, and among the troops as a whole, even basic literacy was often lacking. Officers, particularly lower-level troop leaders, continued to be scarce throughout the conflict.[14]

These shortcomings were compounded by severe and continued shortage of materiel, in particular motorized transport, but also automatic weapons, not to speak of communications equipment. The impressive production statistics we explore in Chapter 5 need to be seen in the context of both extremely high losses and the massive expansion of the Red Army. As a result, normal rifles remained the standard weapon of infantry, and horses and boots their basic mode of transportation. When Soviet forces began their attack against Japan on 9 August 1945, to quote a very late example, they had more horses than cars at their disposal and more troops than personal firearms (rifles and machine pistols).[15]

This only partial modernization of the army was in striking contrast not only to the thoroughly mechanized British and US armies, but also to the Soviet doctrine of deep operations. This Soviet equivalent of the German blitzkrieg called for complex interactions between highly mobile arms. How could this vision be made reality given the shortage of skills, weapons and motorized transport? The leadership solved this puzzle by creating a two-tier system. On the one hand were elite troops, maybe 20 per cent of the total, who were well educated, well trained, lead and provisioned. These also had a very high level of unit cohesion, Communist Party and Komsomol membership, and ideological commitment. They tended to be younger than regular infantry. These crack troops made up the mobile spearheads of the deep operations, which had been trialled at Khalkhin Gol in 1939 and became the standard mode of operation of the Red Army by 1942/3. The rest of the army followed behind, marching. The foot sloggers were supported by horse-drawn transport, an essential element of Red Army mobility from Lake Khasan in 1938 all the way to the Manchurian campaign of 1945. Regular infantry fighting was less complex than the elite equivalent, and relied on massive artillery preparation (conducted by another elite branch of the army), followed by frontal assault by foot soldiers taking heavy casualties.[16]

Military preparation, then, was patchy. It was also somewhat discontinuous, as the experience of the Spanish Civil War (1936–9) led to wrong conclusions about tank warfare, the Great Purges eliminated many of the most enterprising and sophisticated officers, and the Finnish campaign led to a misguided focus on siege warfare. Hence, the Red Army while quite ill prepared for war at the start of the 1930s, had made great strides by 1937, which were partially undone by 1940. A partial re-orientation and a massive re-organization from 1940 had not been concluded when the Germans attacked.[17]

The story of mountain warfare can stand for Soviet war preparation in general: it showed a pattern of progress in war preparation in the first half of the 1930s followed by a destruction of many of these achievements in the second half of the decade. There were real advances until 1937, with a large number of mountaineers trained and some thought given to how to deploy them in case of war. Soviet climbers were more than a match to their European counterparts. 'By 1937, the Soviet Union had more men who had climbed peaks over 7,000 metres than any other country', as their historian has pointed out. But then came the Terror. The soldiers who had pressed for the creation of specialized mountain troops perished, the system of alpinist camps for civilians was dismantled and some of the most accomplished mountaineers were shot as alleged fascists and terrorists. When the battle for the Caucasus erupted in 1942, the Soviet troops involved did not know how to tie a knot, how to ski, how to avoid avalanches or how to use crampons. They were regular infantry without climbing equipment or even appropriate footwear. And they were confronted by some of the best trained and equipped mountain troops in the world. The results were predictable.[18]

A parallel story evolved with regards to irregular warfare. The Soviets had prepared guerrillas (or 'partisans', as they called them) in preparation for foreign occupation. In the early 1930s, special partisan schools were established by the army, their graduates taking part in regular army manoeuvres, and the security forces also trained special squads. Weapons caches were prepared in regions susceptible to enemy occupation: Ukraine, Belarus or Leningrad region. By the mid-1930s, however, this 'impressive, if limited, partisan program' came under fire. The new military doctrine called for any attack to be repulsed at the border and then turned into an offensive destroying the enemy swiftly on his own territory. Thus no foreign occupation would occur; hence no preparation for guerrilla war was necessary; hence the proponents for preparing for such an eventuality were either defeatists or, more likely, enemies (what did they hide all these weapons for?). The programme was dismantled and soon many of the most prominent champions of partisan warfare as well as an entire corps of instructors were arrested and shot in the Great Terror. When the time for partisan war came in the summer and fall of 1941, nobody was prepared.[19]

Economic preparedness

As Stalin understood, however, in industrialized mass warfare – the kind of war fought between 1914 and 1945 – military efficiency was of secondary importance. What counted was numbers: how many men, machines and guns a country could field and at what rate it could replace losses. Military effectiveness, then, relied on the economic system.

What makes a society economically ready for total war? The economy needs to be able to produce and distribute enough food to feed the army and the industrial workforce and hence ensure the most minimal base for sustaining the war effort. Second, the industrial system has to be able to produce the weapons necessary to win the war. Both the Soviets managed to do, but at an incredible price, which contrasts poorly with the performance of democratic warfare states like Britain or the United States during the same period.[20]

The 1930s were a period of massive expansion of military spending, both in terms of weapons and ammunition production and in terms of infrastructure investment. The rate of growth was staggering. In 1930 defence production made up 2.6 per cent of all industry; by 1940 this share had grown to 22.5 per cent.[21] In the context of overall enlargement of industry, investment in armaments was massive, as economic historians have pointed out: 'Between 1932 and 1937 the defense budget increased by 340%.' If in 1929/30 defence outlays constituted 1,046 million roubles, or close to 8 per cent of the state budget, by 1932, expenditure had jumped to 4,034 million roubles, close to 11 per cent of the budget. In the following years, both absolute and relative numbers remained in this ball park until 1936, when expenditure rose to 14,858 million roubles, constituting 16 per cent of the budget. The next significant shift came in 1939, when 39,200 million roubles were spent, over a quarter of the budget; followed by a third, or 56,752 million roubles in the following year. By 1940 military spending consumed close to one-third of state expenditure: more money 'than the entire state budget of 1934'.[22]

The capacity to produce armaments had thus increased by leaps and bounds. When Stalin took the reins of the Soviet state in the late 1920s, his country owned

45 defence factories and research facilities. By the end of 1936, this number had grown to 183, to reach 218 by 1939.[23] The average annual production of aircraft had risen from 869 in 1930–1 to 3,758 in 1935–7. The equivalent numbers for tanks were 740 and 3,139; for artillery pieces, 1,911 and 5,020; and for rifles, 174,000 and 397,000. In 1936, the Red Air force had more planes at its disposal that Germany and Japan combined. By 1937 the Soviet armed forces had reached 1.4 million men and Stalin's Soviet Union had become the 'world's leading military power'.[24] This increased military capacity explains Stalin's remarkable about-face with respect to Japan. In the first half of the 1930s he had done what he could to avoid conflict; in 1938 and 1939, by contrast, he made a stance and fought at Lake Khasan and Khalkhin Gol, as he could now afford to (see Chapter 2).

These impressive numbers hide extreme inefficiencies, however. Soviet industrial production created an incredible amount of waste: the compulsion to fulfil plan norms lead to hoarding of materials on the one hand and 'storming' at the end of the plan period, on the other. Both led to shortages: much was stockpiled at factories in anticipation of the mad rush at the end of a plan period, in stocks invisible to central planners. These materials were unavailable to other factories and could only be acquired through time-consuming informal negotiations, employing so-called 'pushers' (*tolkachi*). The mad rush to the finish line, in turn, produced a lot of shoddy products, which had to be discarded, further adding to the pervasive shortages. During the war, Stalin's lieutenants and a whole army of lower-level trouble shooters would spend much of their time trying to cut through this nexus of shortage – which of course only made the entire process even more chaotic and unplanned: if a bottleneck in one part of the economy would be overcome with ad-hoc measures by an emissary of Moscow, this solution would only create shortages elsewhere.[25]

Moreover, the entire strategy of the pre-war years was premised on stockpiling huge amounts of weaponry, which inevitably led to obsolescence. 'In a sense', wrote one historian in a path breaking study of the militarization of the Soviet Union in the interwar years, 'the Soviet Union rearmed for World War II six or seven years too early. By producing so much ordnance during the early and mid-1930s, the Soviet Union began the Great Fatherland War burdened with tens of thousands of obsolete tanks and planes.' Instead, Stalin should have 'de-emphasized current production, turning instead toward building capacity and improving design and technology'.[26] At the same time, this costly way of providing for the war had an important positive side effect, as another economic historian has stressed: it 'embedded' the 'experience of mass production . . . in factories and work teams before the war broke out'. It was because of the extremely inefficient and costly path Stalin had taken to make the Soviet Union ready for war that 'Soviet industry was able to produce larger numbers of tanks and aeroplanes in fewer models and longer runs than its German adversary'.[27] The Stalinist industrial system thus combined effectiveness with inefficiency.

The second aspect of economic preparation pertains to food production. Here the record is even more mixed. The intended result of collectivization had been to establish a grain reserve for half a year of fighting until 'the peasant' came to his senses and began defending his country, as Stalin had explained to the Central Committee in July 1928.[28] This goal was not reached. By 1940, per capita grain production had not yet recovered to pre–First World War levels; and on the eve of the German attack in the summer of 1941, the regime had only one month worth of supplies in grain, cereals and flour in storage. As one historian has observed: 'Quite simply, collectivized agriculture did not provide the state with vast reserves of grain.' By 1941, 'the Soviet Union found itself in an extremely precarious position with regard to food supply.'[29] The country survived anyway, because the regime concentrated on feeding the urban workforce and the army, as we shall see in Chapter 4.

We again encounter effectiveness coupled with inefficiency: starving civilians to feed the army is not a very efficient way to run a war; it might nevertheless be effective, as the following hard- headed analysis makes clear:

When war broke out, the policies of collectivization and rearmament paid off. . . . In food supply the important step was to have turned the peasants into residual claimants of food . . . . As a result there was no urban famine, except in Leningrad . . . . Widespread hunger could not be prevented elsewhere, but supplies to the army, the defence industry and the urban population were protected. This outcome was the opposite of the experience of the First World War – and it was the intended result of collectivization.[30]

This analysis might strike readers as inhumane. But it was exactly the way Stalin and his leadership team thought: the end always justified the means; peasants were expendable. And the war against Germany was not just a struggle for life and death in the mind of the Stalinists. It was in reality as well.

Cultural preparedness

In total war, economic, military and administrative practices interlocked. The economy, the military and the administration, meanwhile, were not abstract entities or self-running machines, but made up of people connected through more or less stable relationships. And these people and their relationships were informed by norms, ideas, symbols and beliefs. Part of the preparedness of a society for total war, then, was cultural. Cultural preparedness included loyalty towards the extant regime and knowledge of how to act in wartime circumstances.

At the time Stalin gave the speech cited at the start of this chapter, his regime had massive problems with loyalty. Collectivization and de-kulakization, an onslaught on the peasant way of life by the godless city people, had left the majority of the population thoroughly alienated.[31] Peasants, by and large, hated the regime, wanted Stalin dead and the collective farms disbanded.[32] This basic hostility of the rural majority would remain a fact of life throughout Stalin's years in power, but in the early 1930s he faced other troubles as well. The working class, in which name the regime ruled, was rebellious, too. In the Ivanovo Industrial Region alone, 16,000 workers were on strike in 1931.[33] Most troublingly, within the Communist Party itself, there was rising opposition to his leadership and the policies of crash industrialization and forced collectivization, expressed most famously in the March 1932 'Riutin Platform', a text which compared the great leader to a pile of excrement.[34]

Stalin's reaction to this widespread hostility had four prongs: First, he eased the economic burden by shifting some resources from heavy industry to consumer goods, inaugurating the 'three good years' of 1934–6, where civilian consumption was allowed to recover somewhat and life became, in Stalin's famous 1935 phrase, 'more joyous'. Second, he did what he could to avoid war, appeasing Japan by selling the Manchurian railway to the Japanese puppet of Manchukuo in 1935. Third, he stepped up repression, beginning with cleansing the cities of undesirables in 1933 and a purge of the Communist Party from actual or assumed critics beginning in the same year, all of which culminated in the Great Terror of 1937–8. Finally, he shifted the tactics of propaganda. It became increasingly clear that agitation for 'socialism' was not enough to ensure loyalty among the majority of the population – at least not as long as a regime of war-like austerity forced to project the attainment of the material benefits of this socialism into the indefinite future. During the years 1932–6, Stalin's propagandists began to develop a more popular line, which combined focus on heroes in the military, in production and the party, with a promotion of love for the socialist motherland. According to recent research into popular opinion, this shift was moderately successful. More and more Soviets, in particularly among the younger generation, began to believe that sacrifices were reasonable in order to defend the nation from the enemies surrounding it on all sides. The economic relaxation of the 'three good years' only added to this mellowing of popular hostility.[35]

While in 1931 the loyalty of Soviet subjects was in serious doubt, by July 1937 things might have looked somewhat brighter, were it not for the Great Terror. The coincidence of the start of the war in Asia with the move to mass killings (by quota) of allegedly 'anti-Soviet elements' (order No. 00447 of 30 July 1937) did for loyalty what the blood purge of the army had done for military preparedness: intended to increase it, it had the opposite effect. Not only were many ordinary Soviets touched by this purge in one way or another but an entire pantheon of heroes fell victim, destabilizing the workable ideological line of hero-worship and Soviet patriotism.

By September 1939, then, the Soviet Union was worse prepared for this war, than it had been in 1937. And by 1941 the loyalties were divided enough for a substantive minority to welcome the Germans as liberators, while the majority waited to see what would happen. Only a minority rallied to the red flag. Even the renewed mobilizational effort during the Great Patriotic War was a failure as far as ensuring loyalty was concerned. 'What saved Stalin's day', the most in-depth study of Soviet wartime propaganda has concluded, 'was less his propaganda than the reality: Hitler's regime offered no livable alternative to Stalin's.'[36]

Practical knowledge

Cultural preparation for war also included knowing what to do and how to live in wartime. This practical knowledge was widespread. Stalin and his entourage were not untypical for the society they tried to mobilize insofar as prior war experience was concerned. If we assume that children retain memories from the age of four, all those born in or before 1910 would have at least some memory of the entire First World War, those born in or before 1912 of the Revolution and the ensuing Civil Wars, and those born in or before 1916 of this conflagration of violence. Substantial shares of the population, then, had direct war experience: in 1939, for example, 22 per cent of the inhabitants of the Russian Republic were older than twenty-nine, that is the groups with memories of life during the crisis years after 1914. Moreover, life in the 1930s was in many ways reminiscent of wartime, defined by rationing, scarcity, censorship, propaganda, police control and far-reaching restrictions on freedoms of movement. [37]

Civilians thus knew what to do in war: hoard foodstuffs, be prepared to flee or be evacuated (deported), circumvent the various restrictions if necessary, find alternative sources of information, look after their own family and friends, as only they will ensure survival, and so on. The functionaries of the state, too, had a lot of experience with crisis management. It was this experience – gained by some in the Civil War, by others in the domestic crises of the 1930s – that prepared these men well to deal with wartime chaos.

Wartime administration was an extreme form of the normal way the Stalinist command economy worked in peacetime. In this system, lower-level functionaries worked with more autonomy than is sometimes supposed. They were what one historian has described as 'subcontractors under force' – relatively independent economic actors threatened with severe, sometimes lethal consequences if they did not perform.[38] Historians often stress the extreme centralization of Soviet wartime state, but this focus on the formal structures is somewhat deceptive. As we shall see in Chapter 5, in practice the war was run by constant trouble shooting by strong men sent out by Stalin to take care of things. These plenipotentiaries had considerable decision-making powers, as long as they could get the job done.

Ready or not

Did Stalin, then, succeed in what he had proposed in 1931: make good the economic gap with the capitalist countries and build a warfare state ready to withstand the onslaught of modern, industrialized, mass warfare? By 1945, it seemed so to many, not least the dictator himself: in the 1930s, the Soviets had built a mighty war industry more or less from scratch; they had accumulated enormous supplies of weapons and machines; they had trained civilians for the coming war and had manned the largest land army in the world. Between 1937 and 1945 they won every military contest they entered, notwithstanding the poor performance against Finland or the catastrophe of the second half of 1941.

Stalin's first revolution from above of 1928–32 had built an enormous warfare state gearing everything and everybody to war preparation. Forced collectivization and rapid industrialization focusing on heavy industry had not created abundance, social cohesion, wide-spread loyalty or a smoothly running planned economy. It had, however, given the state control over the main levers of economic life, the ability to confiscate most of the agricultural production to distribute on its own terms and the capacity to mass produce standardized military hardware in prodigious quantities. A massive police apparatus could suppress any opposition and an equally large propaganda state could keep the population on message. This warfare state was not particularly efficient. But it was effective: it could and did mobilize for war and it could get the job done, albeit at incredible cost.[39]

At the same time, part of this Stalinist war preparation was counter-productive. The subjugation of the peasantry through collectivization and the expropriation of the most successful farmers in 1929–32 as well as the ensuing famine of 1932–3 had created a large class of seriously disgruntled second-class citizens not very likely to put their lives on the line for the regime. Even industrial workers, in whose name Stalin ruled, were far from content with their lot. Even more disastrous was Stalin's second revolution from above: the Great Terror of 1937–8 was meant to eliminate any and all potential opposition which could challenge the regime in the coming war. Instead, it created chaos in production as managers and engineers disappeared into labour camps and execution chambers, seriously undermined the officer corps' ability to lead the Red Army, and sowed confusion even in the ideological sphere, where an entire pantheon of heroes had to be replaced. As a result, the Soviet Union was better prepared for war at the start of 1937 than in 1939.[40]

Moreover, the enemies Stalin's country faced were relatively minor ones, comparatively speaking. The 1938–9 war against Japan was fought by a sub-section of the army group securing Manchuria (the Kwantung Army), not by the full force of Japan's ground forces, which were busy fighting China. Poland was already on its knees when the Soviets invaded on 17 September 1939. That tiny Finland posed an obstacle at all is remarkable. Even Germany was a relatively poor country at the eve of the Second World War, despite its great engineers, disciplined workforce and well trained and tactically skilled military. While the average German was richer than the average Soviet, the same was not true for the size of the overall economies: here, the Soviet Union has a slight edge over its enemy. What would have happened had the Soviets really had to fight against the 'capitalist encirclement' they claimed they faced? It was Stalin's good fortune that his own ideas about 'the imperialists' and 'the capitalists' were wrong and the centre of world capitalism – the United States of America, with a GDP well over twice the Soviet Union's – did not attack the 'first socialist country'. And once this confrontation actually eventuated after 1945, he had the prestige of victory and soon the atomic bomb on his side. This war would be fought as a cold one: by threats and mutual intimidation.[41]

We are left, then, with a paradox: the Soviet war machine was effective but not efficient. Stalinist preparation for this war was successful but wasteful and chaotic. When war did break out in earnest, the Soviets were not ready. But they were ready to be unprepared: the entire experience of the 1930s had nurtured a culture of improvisation which accustomed officials and rank-and-file citizens to the trouble shooting necessary at times of war. They would need every bit of this preparation in the conflagration of the Second World War.

2 THE WAR BEGINS IN THE EAST, 1937–9

Orienteering accident

When war came in 1937, it was the result of an orienteering accident. On the night of 7 July, a Japanese soldier lost his way south of Beijing. His commander believed him captured by the Chinese, setting in motion a chain of events with far-reaching consequences: the start of the Second World War in Asia.

Japanese troops had been stationed in China since the Boxer Protocol of 1901. They had pried Manchuria loose from the mainland in 1931 to form the puppet state of Manchukuo in 1932. Various confrontations continued throughout the 1930s. In the night of 7–8 July 1937, negotiations between the two sides ensued, broke down and were confused by independent action of other Japanese units. Fighting for the Marco Polo bridge erupted. The structure changed hands twice before a fragile truce was reached. It would not last long: the 'Incident at the Marco Polo bridge', as it came to be known, would start full-scale war between Japan and China, and with it the Second World War in Asia. The war would last until the Japanese surrender in 1945 only to seamlessly transform back into the Chinese Civil War it had interrupted. The Communists won the latter in 1949.[1]

China had little real chance of withstanding the Japanese military. By the end of 1937, the major industrialized regions were under enemy control. The cities of Beijing, Nanjing and Hangzhou had been taken. The government of Chiang Kai-Shek was reduced to weaponizing the size of the country. He retreated to Chongqing and sat out the war there, repeatedly harassed by bomber attacks. His stubborn refusal to surrender had important effects on the further development of the global conflict, as historians increasingly recognize. It 'guaranteed that Japan would have to fight a two-front war throughout World War II, one against Western Allies and another on the Asian landmass in China, where substantial Japanese forces remained tied down'. As we shall see in this chapter, the Soviet Union would be both a crucial supporter and a major beneficiary of China's war effort.[2]

Supporting China

Stalin soon decided that taking China's side was in the strategic interest of his state. The Soviets had long assisted the Kuomintang (KMT), nationalist revolutionaries led by Chiang Kai-Shek. The first weapons and advisors had been sent in 1924, and despite at times rocky relations between Moscow and the KMT, the Soviets remained 'the decisive foreign influence in China'.[3]

Stalin was a veteran revolutionary and a committed Marxist–Leninist. One might therefore imagine that his support for China was driven by ideology: the hope to expand socialism into Asia. Instead, hard-headed geopolitical calculations animated Soviet policy. Stalin and his team were confronted with potentially aggressive powers in the east (Japan) and in the west (first Poland, later Germany). These enemies had all participated in the 'Russian' Civil War after the First World War. German forces had occupied Ukraine and later fought in the Baltics as part of 'White' (anti-Bolshevik) troops. Japan had intervened in the Far East in 1918–22. Poland had defeated revolutionary Russia in one of its most spectacular early wars (1919–21), a humiliation which continued to rankle. None of these neighbours accepted the existence of a socialist state and all of them were considered aggressive imperialists by Moscow.[4]

A two-front war is problematic under the best of circumstances, but in the Soviet case the sheer distance between the two potential theatres was a particular obstacle. In 1905, the Tsar had been unable to resist revolution in the heartland, because he could not bring back troops fighting Japan in the Far East. The rail link between the European and Asian part of the empire had improved since then, with more of the Trans-Siberian double-tracked. But it continued to be a long trip: over 9,000 kilometres from Moscow to Vladivostok.[5]

This realistic assessment was not in opposition to Stalin's ideology or even to his self-interest in holding on to power and survive the coming war. Rather, the personal, the ideological and the real-political neatly interlocked in the leader's view of the world. After all, the Soviet Union was the only Marxist–Leninist state on earth. Stalin conflated its survival with the survival of the communist movement more generally. And as the leader who had risked all and dragged that peasant country into industrial modernity, he also associated his own interest with the interest of the state.[6]

A two-front war seemed a real possibility in the 1930s. Historians often focus on Soviet relations with Germany, the country that turned out to be the main opponent in 1941–5. But throughout the 1930s, Stalin took the threat of war in the east as seriously as the danger from the west. The Soviet Union shared a 4,083-kilometre border with Manchuria, a 24-kilometre frontier with Korea, and a 132-kilometre line with Japan. In 1931, after he received intelligence about aggressive Japanese intentions, Stalin was worried enough to shift resources into military industries, a militarization of the economy furthered even more once the Japanese marched into Manchuria in September. Stalin saw this invasion as a 'serious' matter. 'It''s not excluded and even probable', the dictator hypothesized, 'that Japan will stretch out its hand to our Far East, and, possibly, to Mongolia', the Soviet satellite in Asia. In 1936 he noted that it was hard to predict if the eastern or the western 'hotbed of war' was more threatening. 'So far, he added, the Far Eastern hotbed is more active, but it is possible that the center of this danger will move to Europe.' (When asked for the 'main reason' for this persistent war danger from all sides, the Marxist dictator deadpanned: 'capitalism'.)[7]

Such worries continued throughout the decade. In 1936, Japan and Germany, signed the Anti-Comintern Pact, which raised the spectre of a military alliance of the two states against the Soviet Union. At the end of March 1937, a high-ranking commander of the Far Eastern Army discussed the 'problem of war on two fronts', referring to Stalin's analysis of the geopolitical situation: there were 'two hotbeds of war', one in the east, fanned by Japan, one in the west, stoked by Germany. The Soviet Union had to be ready to repulse a joint attack. In this eventuality, the question would be: How to limit the war in the east to throw as many troops as possible against Germany? And the Japanese threat was not just a figment of a paranoid imagination. The eastern front was far from quiet: In 1935, there were 136 border incidents along the long border between the Japanese and Soviet empires. In 1936, that number increased to 203.[8]

While frantically preparing his country for war through industrialization, the building of a warfare state, and the liquidation of presumed enemies, Stalin tried to avoid war, cost what it may. Not believing his country ready for war and unsure if he could avoid a confrontation on two fronts, he opted for appeasing the Japanese imperialists. Rather than standing his ground, he buckled and sold the Manchurian railway – long a bone of contention between Russia and Japan – to the Japanese puppet regime in Manchukuo.

But appeasement was flanked by the attempt to encourage the aggressors to engage elsewhere. The start of war in China seemed to offer an opportunity for this strategy. If the Japanese imperialists could be bogged down in China, they would have neither time nor resources to fight the Soviets. Hence, Moscow renewed its commitment to the KMT by signing the August 1937 Mutual Nonaggression Treaty, which stipulated that both sides would 'refrain from any aggression against each other' and would not aid any other aggressor. Subsequently the Soviets would deliver thousands of automatic weapons and tens of thousands of rifles, hundreds of planes and ground vehicles, including tractors and tanks. They also made available the loans to pay for this equipment.[9]

This aid was despatched at very short notice. Already in October 1937 the Soviets sent a column of trucks from Alma-Ata (today: Almaty) in Kazakhstan to

Lanzhou in Northwest China – a hard, 3,000-kilometre track. As one participant remembered:

> The route passed through mountains, deserts and semi-deserts with creeping sand dunes. Sandstorms were frequent. You could drive for hundreds of kilometres and not meet a single water hole. Thus, besides the military cargo, we needed to carry more than one water tank for people to drink and to cool the truck engines. It often happened that a sudden squally wind ripped the best attachments of the R-5 aircraft out of the ground, lifted the machine into the air like a paper plane, and threw it back a good one hundred meters. The Gobi desert constantly reminded us of its harsh character. On the road, even in good weather, clothes, ears, noses, hair – everything was covered in fine sand, which was impossible to get rid of. It constantly crunched between our teeth.

Every 200–250 kilometres, bases were built to support the transportation crews and allow repair of the trucks. They also served as base stations for two-way radio communication along the track, powered by diesel generators. [10]

People came, too. First were volunteer pilots and their planes, ready not only to train their Chinese counterparts, but also to challenge Japanese air superiority themselves. 'We were warned', recounted one of them later, 'that we would have to fight under assumed names'. The pilots either picked their mother's maiden name or their favourite classic author, calling themselves Pushkin or Gogol. Thus equipped they travelled to Alma-Ata by train, claiming to be norm-busting industrial workers to anybody who asked. In Kazakhstan, they took possession of Soviet fighter planes with Chinese markings which they flew to China at the end of 1937. 'We fought in civilian clothes', remembered the veteran, 'without identity documents – we only had a security certificate issued by the Chinese authorities'.[11]

The Soviet pilots participated in the defence of Nanjing in 1937, as well as other forgotten battles of the Second World War. One was the air war over Wuhan in 1938, where 150 Soviet fighter pilots fought with the aid of 500 Soviet planes. 'Almost every day in August', writes one historian 'crowds came out into the streets to watch Russian and Chinese pilots . . . duel in dogfights with the Japanese Zeros . . . Dozens of Russian pilots were shot down; their sacrifice was memorialized elaborately at the time and is still remembered today.' Soviet aircrews continued their service after Wuhan was lost. Between June of 1939 and May 1940, 405 pilots flew bombing missions and engaged in air combat with Japanese fighters. They shot down 'up to forty' enemy planes and destroyed many more on the ground. The Soviets lost thirteen aircrew during these raids. Another seven were wounded.[12]

Overall, of the 5,000 Soviet pilots, advisors, medics and technicians sent to China, 227 were dead or missing in action by the end of the intervention. Other sources speak of 'more than 200' Soviet aviators alone, who 'gave their lives to the cause of the Chinese people's freedom'. That might well have been what they fought for. Their task, however, had been to tie down the Japanese to preserve Stalin's freedom of action in the unfolding World War. As the dictator put it in toast 'to our fighters in China': it was better 'to fight the Japanese fascists in China than in the USSR'. This mission they accomplished successfully, as it turned out. By 1938, the majority of Japanese ground troops were deployed in China: twenty-seven out of thirty-seven divisions.[13]

Stalinist war preparations in the east

As events unfolded, however, that outcome was far from clear. Whether or not Soviet help to China would be enough to distract Japan from attacking the Soviet Union was anybody's guess. Hence, Stalin shored up his defences on the eastern front. By 1937 the Far Eastern districts of the Soviet Union commanded 17 per cent of all artillery pieces and 22 per cent of all tanks the Soviet armed forces had at their disposal. Military manpower increased from 242,311 men in early 1935 to 354,093 in July 1936 to reach 450,000 men at the start of 1939. They were supported by 5,785 artillery pieces and over 3,000 tanks.[14]

Stalin prepared for the war with Japan also in a way typical for his paranoid style of politics: he cleansed the border regions of Soviet Koreans, who had migrated across the border since the second half of the nineteenth century, partially in search for agricultural land, partially fleeing Japanese imperialism. Many had resisted the Japanese intervention in the Far East after the revolution, and by the 1920s, most of the former settlers and their offspring had become Soviet citizens. At the start of 1937, there were 168,259 Koreans in the Soviet Union, nearly all of the (165,165) of them in the Far Eastern Region. Stalin now suspected them of potential spying for the Japanese. Their removal would stop 'the penetration of Japanese espionage activity in the Far Eastern Region', as the top secret resolutions ordering this deportation stated.[15]

These suspicions predated the outbreak of war in China. Already in 1922 a plan to remove Koreans from the border regions had been contemplated because they were suspected of collaborating with Japan. In the context of the witch hunt of the Great Terror, such fantasies became convictions. On 23 April 1937 *Pravda* reported that the 'Japanese imperialists' were active in the Far East, systematically preparing for an 'expansionist war' against the Soviets. They collected information on the Soviet fleet and the train lines, planted spies among the population and organized sleeper cells of 'saboteurs and terrorists' in defence enterprises, among railway personnel, and within the Communist Party and the Youth League. They would be activated at the time of attack. These hidden enemies were well trained and expertly masked and could not be easily distinguished from the rest of the population. They also wormed their way into the confidence of ordinary citizens, recruiting them to work for the enemy (or so the writer thought).[16]

Another *Pravda* article, written by a secret police man and passing across Stalin's desk just two days before war broke out in China, was equally alarmist. It warned that Japanese spies often infiltrated 'pretending to be Koreans or Chinese' and then recruited various 'kulak', 'declassed' and other 'elements' among Soviet Koreans. 'In the Soviet Far East', the author warned darkly, 'exists a large number of Korean laborers, living in a compact mass. Japanese agents artificially create group and faction fights between Korean social organizations. They try to destroy them from the inside and recruit new members for their work.' The article was published two days after the war had broken out in China. The hostilities at the Marco Polo bridge were reported on the same page.[17]

By now, what might have been conceived as the start of a purge of the Korean community in line with what was going on elsewhere in the mad year of 1937, instead became an even more pressing task. On 21 August Stalin ordered the NKVD to 'remove the entire Korean population of the border zone'. Just to be safe, a month later a follow-up resolution broadened the deportation to all Koreans in the entire Far Eastern Region.[18]

How urgent Stalin thought this matter was illustrated by a telegram he sent on 11 September to the men in charge of the Far East: first secretary of the Far Eastern Region Iosif Vareikis, the commander of the Special Far Eastern Army, Vasily Konstantinovich Bliukher and the new head of the Far Eastern branch of the Commissariat of the Interior, Genrikh Samoilovich Liushkov. 'It is clear', the dictator mentored his subordinates, 'that the eviction of Koreans is a matter of urgency. It is possible that we are somewhat late already. But if this is the case, the eviction must be carried out all the faster .... I propose that each of you take strict and urgent measures in your area of jurisdiction in order to ensure exact and timely execution of the eviction plan. People who sabotage this matter', Stalin warned, 'whoever they may be, must be arrested and punished as an example to others'.[19]

That Koreans, whose homeland was occupied by Japan since 1910, would make common cause with those same imperialists they or their parents had fled was, of course, absurd. But Stalin's suspicious mind often worked in mysterious ways. Who could tell the difference between a Korean and a Japanese? Were they not loyal to forces outside the Soviet state? He was right insofar as Korean patriots were beholden not just to his Soviet Union. Ten San Din, whose wartime experience began this book, remembered how his father, arrested by Stalin's police and shot in 1938, had told him repeatedly: 'My son, I might not see this day, but you should seek to fulfil the main goal of my life: liberate the country from the Japanese.' The country in question, of course, was Korea, not the Soviet Union. But Stalin's state could help. The 'hatred towards the occupiers' motivated the son to volunteer for the Red Army and eventually to participate in the Manchurian campaign of 1945: Stalin's military goals happened to coincide with Ten San Din's wish to free the land of his forefathers from the Japanese imperialists. Such complicated loyalties were suspicious to comrade

Stalin, however: they were too unpredictable for a man used to thinking in red and white.[20]

Stalin's unease with non-Russians and in particular with diaspora minorities – those who could look towards a foreign state as a potential home – went back to his time as Commissar for Nationalities during the post-revolutionary and Civil War years (1917–23). And they kept surfacing once Stalin was in power. Throughout the 1930s, his terror policies again and again targeted non-Russians, suspected of 'bourgeois nationalism', secessionist tendencies or spying for foreign powers. But it was only in the context of the outbreak of war in Asia that 'the concept of the enemy nation . . . fully emerged', as the leading historian of the nationality problem in the Soviet Union writes. The forced removal of the Koreans in 1937 marked an important moment in this evolution of Soviet nationality policy. It was the first deportation of an entire national group without regard to age, sex, social class, party membership or loyalty to the Soviet cause. Koreans were removed not for anything they had done, but for what some of them might do. Other 'enemy nations' would soon follow.[21]

The operation to remove the Koreans from the border was planned with military precision and the NKVD officers and railway personnel involved were later congratulated by the government for 'exemplary and precise fulfilment of a government task related to transport'. By 29 October 1937, 171,781 Koreans had been shipped off in 124 echelons made up of cattle cars. Seventy-six of the trains had arrived; the rest were still en route. Of the 36,442 families, 16,272 were sent to Uzbekistan (75,525 persons) and 20,170 to Kazakhstan (95,256 persons).[22]

Overall, the trip took a month or more. Trains were the first point of call only for those who lived in cities or near train lines. Other deportees first needed to be transported to a rail head. This transfer could be accomplished by barge, by truck or by foot. Once at the train station, waiting ensued, frequently without any food provided. 'The whole waiting mass of Koreans', reported one witness who experienced the deportation as a 5-year-old, 'was guarded by a solid ring of soldiers with rifles. The frightened people did not even think about hiding from the resettlement.' After loading into the box car, more waiting followed. 'It is impossible to describe without trepidation the conditions we faced while waiting to be loaded into the wagons, the moment of departure of each echelon from the station', the memoirist continued. 'Before departure, the soldiers closed the doors, but the hands of the crying, grief-stricken people did not allow to close them tightly. Screaming, crying and groaning continued to emanate from the trains.'[23]

The echelons moved in fits and starts, often standing on side-tracks to make way for other trains or to wait for locomotives. The rail lines were overcharged and transportation was often fairly improvised. One British diplomat witnessed how 'a few miles from Barnaul where the Biisk branch line joins the Turksib . . . a number of cattle trucks' full of Koreans were 'hitched on our train.'[24] The box cars were cramped, each laden with around thirty people, who 'slept, ate, fell ill, died, and relieved themselves' in these confined spaces.[25] Life soon fell into a depressing and anxiety-laden routine.

> In the freight car, people were placed on three-level bunks. Between the rows of bunks stood a cast-iron stove, in which they kept a fire going day and night. Children were, as a rule, placed on the third shelf. The carriage was packed with people like herring in a barrel.[26]

The sanitary conditions 'got worse every day. There was no water to wash our hands, to say nothing of a complete wash. People began to suffer from lice. . . . Just the memory of the dirt we lived in makes me feel disgusted.'[27] Food was another problem. Those with money could buy food at train stations along the way, if local peasants came to the cars to sell food. Venturing out themselves was forbidden, the guards threatening to shoot offenders. Selected men were sent under guard to get hot water and food at some of the stations.[28]

Many of the deported Koreans were sent well beyond any rail heads, frequently after further delays waiting for transport, such as barges, if there was a river, or sleds, if there was none. By now, it was fall or even winter. 'We travelled on sleds for an entire day and a night', remembered one survivor. 'Hungry and frozen to the core, we wanted only one thing – that all of this would come to an end.'[29]

But arrival did not spell the end of woes of the 'resettlers', as they were called euphemistically. When the deportation had been announced, the Koreans had been told there would be work and accommodation for them. Now, they found themselves simply dumped in villages and towns, with no work, no money and at best improvised housing. 'People started to dig mud huts and make do, everyone as good as he could', reported one witness. 'People were accommodated in some kind of club', remembered another. 'We spent the winter days of the first year of the resettlement in inhumane conditions.' Months later, many were still waiting to find work. Their children were going hungry. No wonder they wanted to return home, but to do so would have meant breaking the law. Technically, the Korean deportees had all the rights of Soviet citizens, except one: they were not allowed to leave the region of their re-settlement. Attempts to receive internal passports failed.[30]

In theory, the deportees were allowed to take movable property and livestock with them, but there was seldom enough space in the box cars to accommodate such massive baggage. On 5 September 1937, the Politburo reacted to this problem by limiting the property to be taken along to household goods and agricultural materials, while livestock was to be taken over by the state and the owners later compensated. In practice, however, even greater restrictions applied. 'They allowed us to take only the most necessary things', remembered one survivor, 'food for five or six days'. Another memoirist reported an allowance of 30 kilograms of baggage per person. Deportees were also supposed to be compensated for whatever property was left behind. That, too, remained an empty promise. After the arrival in Kazakhstan, remembers another witness, 'we lived during the first winter together with ten other families and their sheep' under one roof. 'The promised housing did not materialize. Compensation for the housing we gave up and the property we left behind was not provided. Our livestock was not returned to us.'[31]

Thus, the deportations amounted to yet another state-sanctioned confiscation and forced impoverishment of the targeted population. The material impact would be remembered for decades:

> We had to leave everything behind: the new house, two horses and a milk cow, the entire rice harvest, salted kimchi . . . a full chest of linen, and all the dishes: copper pots, deep and shallow bowls, dishes, spoons and chopsticks, all made of copper polished to a shine. . . . All the dishes remained behind, lying all over the floor.[32]

But loss of property was the least of it. The deportations were accompanied by the arrest of 2,500 Koreans. They were part of a larger pattern. Koreans were arrested all over the Soviet Union, from Moscow and Leningrad to Omsk and Barnaul. These were the years of the Great Terror's mass operations, after all: 'In 1937–38 nearly the entire Korean intelligentsia [in the Soviet Union] was shot', as one witness noted with only slight hyperbole.[33]

And, of course, there were fatalities, both during transport (554 according to official figures) and after arrival in Central Asia. 'Many died on the way', remembered one who survived. 'Particularly children died a lot. . . . Our neighbor in the box car, Ivan Kim, lost two children: his son, who was about six, and a little three-year-old girl.' The daughter burned herself terribly on the red-hot metal oven heating the car, and the mother, trying to come to her aid, tipped over the kettle of boiling soup which seared her son. The parents tried to hide the deaths, hoping they would arrive soon and bury their children where they could visit the graves. Even this small consolation was denied them, though, as the corpses started to smell after three days. Security guards removed them from the train. 'Such instances happened every day in the echelon', reported the witness. 'One could hear people cry all the time.'[34]

The dying continued after arrival.

> People who lived in mud-huts started to die because they lacked the most elementary conditions supporting life. In our family the children died: the nine-year-old daughter of my oldest brother, my third brother's five-year-old daughter and six year old son, the three-year old daughter of my fourth brother

as well as his new-born baby. Nearly everybody suffered from diarrhea, from coughs, the children from measles. . . . My mother died in December.

The first winter in exile was terrible. 'People began to swell from hunger. They died of cold.' The worst was over only once spring arrived.[35] As in other deportations before, during, or after the war, the initial death rates during transport and arrival declined rapidly once the survivors had arranged themselves with life in their new surroundings. 'A great battle for life began', noted one survivor. 'Our building brigades worked day and night to build dugouts, each accommodating two families.' Rice fields were planted and the harvest in late 1939 was good. 'Thus began the heroic labour of the resettlers', he proudly remembered these hard years of his childhood.[36]

Indeed, Koreans did not show the kinds of catastrophic decline in numbers Kazakhs or Ukrainians suffered as a result of the famine of 1932–3. According to the available census data their population instead grew faster than the Russian equivalent. This was a result of their own resilience, however, not the care the Soviet authorities extended to these 'human resources'. That Ten San Din could fight the Japanese in 1945 was the accomplishment of his family and their friends who had won in the struggle for survival against all the odds created by Stalin's toxic suspicion against his people.[37]

Terror

Minority nationalities of Asian appearance were not the only hidden enemies Stalin felt compelled to neutralize in order to safeguard his eastern front. Could there not also be traitors in the ranks of the eastern army itself? As he told Liushkov, the hatchet-man he sent to both deport the Koreans and to incriminate and arrest supposed opponents within the Far Eastern army: 'War with Japan is inevitable; the Far East is undoubtedly a theatre of war. It is necessary to clean up the army and its rear in the most determined manner from enemy spies and pro-Japanese elements.' He gave the Far Eastern NKVD chief his marching orders: 'terrorize the district and the frontier so as to prevent any Japanese work.'[38]

Stalin's security forces had long suspected that the Far Eastern Army was riddled with traitors and foreign agents. In late 1936 and early 1937 new material buttressed this conviction as surveillance of the Far Eastern Army was ratcheted up. Increasingly, even 'seemingly harmless acts by servicemen were considered political crimes'. Arrests for 'counterrevolutionary agitation' as well as for spying now grew in number. By August 1937, fifteen brigade, division and other high-level commanders had been arrested and shot. Headquarters of corps, divisions and brigades also lost leading personnel to the blood purge. Arrests continued throughout the following year. Overall, at least 432 Far Eastern commanders were arrested, the vast majority of them were shot, died in prison or committed suicide. [39]

The terror did not spare the top men in the party, army and police, who had just done their bit in the deportation of the Koreans. In October 1937, the party boss Vareikis was arrested. He was convicted in July 1938 and shot as one of the Far Eastern leaders of an imaginary military conspiracy against Stalin. Army boss Bliukher had participated faithfully in the military purge in the Far East, handing over his fellow commanders to Stalin's torturers. He followed in October 1938, after he had won the Battle of Lake Khasan at great cost. Stalin's policemen accused him of sabotage and other crimes and tried to beat a confession out of him. 'His entire face was black and blue', reported the prison physician. There was 'hemorrhaging in his eye. It was overflowing with blood.' Bliukher died soon after. [40]

Of the three men responsible for the Korean deportations, only Liushkov escaped Stalin's paranoid fear of supposed traitors and spies of the Japanese enemy. The 38-year-old chief of the secret police in the Far East was no fool. He had watched the purge he implemented among the Far Eastern security forces, the party, and army move closer and closer to himself. In the spring of 1938 he was summoned to Moscow. Such recalls were often the first step to arrest, as had been the case with Vareikis. Any experienced operative would know the procedure. Liushkov thus suddenly found his inner anti-Stalinist and decided to run. Having done the dictator's dirty work, he now wanted to 'carry on the good fight against Stalin from the outside'. Wearing a spring coat and a hunting cap over his uniform, he crossed the border to Manchuria in the early morning hours of 13 June 1938 to become the most spectacular defector to Japan in Soviet history.[41]

Soviet–Japanese border war

The defection of such a high-ranking official was a shock to a leadership nervous about a military conflict on two fronts. It triggered the final war Bliukher would fight before his arrest: the Battle of Lake Khasan, or what the Japanese would call the Changkufeng Incident (29 July to 11 August 1938). A bit less than three months earlier, Boris Mikhailovich Shaposhnikov, chief of the General Staff of the Red Army, had penned a report on the strategic situation facing the Soviet Union.

> Japan is weakened because of its use of part of its human and material resources in the war with China. It has to keep a good part of its divisions in the territories it has occupied there. At the same time, Japan has an already mobilized army, which has already been completely transferred to the [Asian] mainland. That is, it is not inhibited in the critical period by sea transport.
>
> Even if Japan would suffer serious losses in the war with China, in the event of armed conflict in Europe between the fascist block [i.e., Germany and Italy]

and the USSR it would be compelled by this block to initiate war against the USSR. . . .

Thus, the Soviet Union needs to be ready to fight on two fronts: in the West against Germany and Poland and partially against Italy; . . . and in the east against Japan.[42]

In this situation, a defection of a high-ranking officer was alarming. Clearly, the border needed to be sealed more tightly, which is what the Soviet side tried to do as a result. Troops occupied the Changkufeng hill, a commanding outpost in the poorly mapped and strongly disputed border region between Korea, Manchuria and the USSR.[43]

Japan claimed this hill as its own territory and sent troops to expel the invaders. A Soviet counteroffensive followed, sparing no men in frontal, uphill attacks on entrenched positions. The fighting was hard, the location remote. In this region lived 'not a single person', as the commander who had initially taken the hill reported after the battle to the political and military leadership of the country. A few border outposts were the only human beings far and wide, Georgy Mikhailovich Shtern noted. Moving troops and supplies was a problem. 'As a matter of fact, there are no roads in this sector, only a path on which a cart or a car of the frontier guards drives every three days.' Further into the Soviet interior, roads existed, but were intersected by dry channels which after rain would turn into raging rivers. There were no bridges over these, hence bad weather completely disrupted transport. 'We had great problems with moving our forces', reported Shtern, 'all our marching plans fell apart'. Given the territory – no woods, 'not even a small shrub' – troop movements could not be hidden from the enemy during daytime. Hence the Soviets marched at night, which further slowed them down. Tank units moved at a snail's pace of between 1.5 and 2 kilometres an hour. On the other side of the frontline, the situation was much better. The Japanese had many roads, river-transport and a railroad went 'straight to the battlefield'.[44]

Eventually, Bliukher himself took over command of the battle. He overcame the logistical and tactical problems by brute force, sending in three times more men and four times more artillery than the Japanese defenders could muster. Wave after wave ran on against Japanese fire. Artillery, tanks and infantry cooperated poorly, as Commissar for Defense, Kliment Voroshilov, pointed out after the battle: 'It seems to me that we not only failed in the so-called coordination of arms, but it brought us no end of trouble.' Nearly a thousand dead Red Army men and over 3,000 wounded later, the hill was back in Soviet hands. For every Japanese soldier killed, nearly two Soviets had to lose their life in battle. This generous use of Soviet lives for a questionable objective and the lack of tactical skill in the use of military assets were previews of things to come later in the Second World War.[45]

Nevertheless, Stalin had sent a signal to Tokyo: feeble responses to Japanese provocations were history. Lake Khasan was a major departure from the Soviet policy of appeasement towards Japan, in place since the beginning of the decade. The objective situation was, of course, still pretty dire, with the country reeling from the destruction of the Great Terror which had struck well before the chaos had been overcome which the First Five-Year Plan, the terror of collectivization and the great famine had caused earlier in the decade. But Stalin appeared much more in control in a country where nobody spoke truth to power anymore and where production statistics created the illusion of strength.

Moreover, Stalin knew that Japan remained engaged in China, which bolstered his position at the eastern front – the decisive point nudging him towards taking a militarily more assertive stance in the Far East. Only a year earlier, and just before the escalation at the Marco Polo bridge, the Soviets had backed down in a similar border clash: the Amur River incident near Blagoveshchensk on 30 June 1937. It began with Japanese forces sinking a Soviet gunboat patrolling the river between Manchuria and the Soviet Union, and damaging two others. Survivors swimming to safety were machine-gunned. At stake was whether an island in the middle of the river was Soviet or Manchurian territory. After the attack on the gunboats, the Soviets backed down, evacuating the island and leaving it to the Japanese. This skirmish inspired a famous Soviet war song about three tank drivers,[46] but the reality was far from heroic: a humiliating back-down to avoid confrontation with the Japanese army. A year later, with the enemy busy in China, the Soviets instead stood their ground.

The test case of this new-found confidence would be the battle of Khalkhin Gol, or 'Nomonhan incident', in its Japanese rendering. Technically speaking, it was not a Soviet–Japanese 'border incident' as it took place on the unclear demarcation line between Mongolia and Manchukuo – Soviet and Japanese satellites, respectively. Mongolia was the first Soviet puppet regime. Established in 1924, it served as a model for similar arrangements in Eastern Europe after the Second World War. Manchukuo, founded in 1932, was Japan's way to rule Manchuria by proxy. Where exactly the border between the two states ran was a matter of dispute. One bone of contention was if the line ran along the river Khalkha (Khalkhin Gol in Mongolian) or at the village of Nomonhan, some 16 kilometres east. After skirmishes in May and Japanese air strikes in June, a full-scale battle began in July.

On the Soviet side, in command was now the 42-year-old Georgy Zhukov, a rising star in the army. Zhukov, like Stalin of extremely humble origins, had fought in the First World War and then the Civil War and remained in the Red Army to make a career. It accelerated in the 1930s because the massive expansion of the army and the purge of superiors eased his way. In his autobiography he presented himself as a near-victim of the purges and his daughter reported that he kept a bag packed in preparation for arrest. However, as his biographer points out, his arrival in Mongolia was as a victimizer, not a victim: 'he was sent to the Far East to conduct a purge'.[47]

Zhukov arrived in Mongolia on 24 May, between the initial skirmishes of 11–12 May and the first larger-scale engagement on 28 May. He sent a series of scathing reports on the shortcomings of command, tactics, and training in the region. As a result, he was appointed to command the 57th Corps on 12 June. He imposed order, organized intelligence gathering and improved training. When fighting resumed in July, he threatened subordinate commanders with military tribunal if they failed to lead their troops:

> For manifest inactivity in organizing the fording [of the river] and for failure to establish control of his troops in preparation for battle I reprimand regimental commander, comrade Stepanov, and military commissar, comrade Musin, as well as chief of staff, comrade Nerot. I hereby warn them, if the regiment will not be put in order, if commanders and staff remain inactive, I will raise the question of trial by military tribunal with the People's Commissar of Defense.[48]

These were no empty threats. 'On 12 July the commander of a machine gun company, Potapov, was demonstratively arrested and shot in front of his soldiers', reported a political officer a few days later. Battalion commander German, who had 'personally provoked his soldiers to retreat', was likewise executed. Examples were also made of rank and file soldiers. Red Army men Nikitin and Maltsev, who had shot themselves in the left hand to escape battle, were sentenced to death by shooting with confiscation of all property. 'Death to contemptible cowards and traitors!', exclaimed Zhukov's order to the troops

ILLUSTRATION 1 Georgy Zhukov at Khalkhin Gol, 1939. After winning the battle of Khalkhin Gol for Stalin, Zhukov would go on to become one of the most celebrated Soviet military leaders of the Second World War. © Heritage Images / Getty Images.

announcing these executions. Such words and actions would recur throughout the Soviet Second World War.[49]

The battle of Khalkhin Gol was more than a border incident. It was a series of skirmishes and battles raging over a large front for months, beginning on 11 May and concluding only on 16 September, more than two weeks after the war in Europe had broken out after the Germans attacked Poland on 1 September. At the very least, the multiple battles of Khalkhin Gol constituted 'a small undeclared war', as one historian put it. One could well go further and see them as a culmination of the Soviet–Japanese border war of 1938–9, which itself was part and parcel of the global Second World War. At Khalkhin Gol, 100,000 men and 1,000 combat vehicles joined battle in several engagements stretching four months. The 30,000 to 50,000 killed and wounded on both sides also indicate the level of the fighting. And Soviet victory, as we shall see, had immense consequences for the further unfolding of the Second World War.[50]

If it is remembered at all, the battle of Khalkhin Gol usually serves to celebrate Zhukov's brilliant use of massed armour and motorized infantry, supported by air-power and coordinated with artillery fire – a model of 'deep battle'. It was an indication what the Red Army could do now, if its modern, mechanized forces were given into the hands of the right commanders. Just the logistics were daunting, with a supply line from the closest railway track of 650 kilometres. A fleet of 4,900 trucks and other automobiles, including combat vehicles such as artillery tractors, shuttled back and forth delivering 18,000 tons of artillery shells, 6,500 tons of aviation ammunition, 22,500 tons of lubricants and fuel, 4,000 tons of food and 4,000 tons of 'other goods'. The drivers were 'heroes as from a fairy tale', marvelled Zhukov in his memoirs. They did 'the practically impossible: in conditions of sweltering heat and dry winds they repeatedly completed the round trip of 1,300 to 1,400 kilometers, which took five days each time!'[51]

As an example of mechanized, multi-arm, coordinated warfare, then, the battle contrasted sharply with Lake Khasan. In retrospect, it can be seen as a sign of things to come, when from 1944 the Red Army steamroller flattened the Wehrmacht in offensive battles implementing the theory of 'deep battle'. This view has recently been nuanced by military historians who have pointed out that the reality was less ideal than Zhukov's later recollections. Even under his leadership, the Red Army was effective despite a lack of efficiency. Tank forces were committed without infantry support, the coordination of arms was often poor and had to be compensated through the use of 'overwhelming force'.[52] Moreover, Zhukov's modern Red Army – both in 1939 and later in 1941–5 – was embedded in a nineteenth century army relying on horses, trains and forced marches for its mobility. Indeed, war at Khalkhin Gol was peculiarly motorized, as the distances involved made auto transport absolutely essential for supply and the terrain favoured manoeuvre warfare with mechanized forces.

Nevertheless, there were plenty of horses in Mongolia, too. 'In January 1939', remembered one veteran, 'I arrived in the 6th Cavalry Brigade in Mongolia. . . . I took over a platoon. There were 30 people and 60 horses.' Why so many beasts? Because the artillery was horse drawn, too, with every piece in need of four animals. 'So in the platoon there were more horses than people', he concluded. The opening skirmishes were indeed fought by cavalry forces, and by 8 August, the sixth and seventh Mongolian Cavalry Divisions had lost more horses (553 dead and 558 wounded) than men (133 dead, 407 wounded and 8 missing in action).[53]

The results of Soviet victory in the east

Neither the Soviets nor the Japanese called the fighting along their border a 'war'. To Stalin, Lake Khasan and Khalkhin Gol were 'small episodes . . . trifles rather than war'.[54] Historians would inadvertently follow his lead, treating the 'border incidents' as inconsequential. They happened in some god-forsaken place, in areas most Europeans, Americans or Australians would not be able to find on a map. And very little territory changed hands as a result of these engagements. The borderline remained relatively stable, despite the lives lost along it. At best, these skirmishes were a minor war in its own right, but not part of the Second World War. More recently, this downgrading of the Soviet–Japanese border war has been challenged by historians who understand the history of Asia as an integral part of the global war. There are good arguments for this view.

For one, the battles of Lake Khasan and Khalkhin Gol were part of a larger pattern. Soviet–Japanese border clashes occurred in the winter and spring of 1936, in June 1937, in July and August of 1938, in February 1939, and then again in May through August of the same year. If we observe a series of military 'incidents' between the same players along the same border, we might as well call it a 'war'. Second, these 'incidents', still minor engagements in 1936 and 1937, were serious battles in 1938 and 1939. It was one thing for Stalin to belittle them from his vantage point in the Kremlin. It was quite another to experience these trivialities. 'For us, the pilots of the 22nd air fighter regiment', noted one veteran, 'the Great Patriotic War began in the spring of 1939'. To other participants in the fighting, too, it was 'completely obvious that what happened at Khalkhin Gol . . . was not a conflict but a real, albeit undeclared, war'. The nearly 10,000 Soviet dead and missing at Khalkhin Gol, let alone the 25,000 'irrecoverable losses' on the other side of the trenches were those of a 'real' war. In 1939, the Germans lost only 16,000 men in Poland, and nobody suggests that this was an 'incident' or a 'border clash' but not a war. The Sino-Japanese war, too, is accepted by historians as the real thing, although in 1939 the Japanese leadership was more preoccupied with the Nomonhan 'incident' than the 'war' with China.[55]

ILLUSTRATION 2 11 July 1939: Japanese doctor treats injured Soviet POW during the battle of Khalkhin Gol (Nomonhan), Mongolia. The oft-forgotten Soviet–Japanese border war of 1938–9 was an integral part of the Second World War. © The Asahi Shimbun / Getty Images.

The Soviet leadership, too, was on tenterhooks. Until 1937, the Soviet economic effort had followed what planners called the 'American model': they built 'dual purpose industries' which could produce for civilian needs during peace and would be re-tooled for defence production in times of war. In the years 1938 and 1939, by contrast, they shifted to a more thorough militarization of industry, as all-out war now seemed on the horizon. Khalkhin Gol marked one high point of this war scare: On 1 August 1939, Commissar of Defense Voroshilov ordered all forces in the Far East to prepare for battle immediately. They should be prepared to go on the offensive, if attacked. The eastern front seemed ready to erupt any moment.[56]

Third, the fighting between Japanese and Soviet forces in 1938 and 1939 was deeply entangled with the Sino-Japanese war. We have already seen how the start of fighting in China encouraged a more assertive Soviet stance at the border with Japan, leading to the all-out battles of 1938 and 1939. Soviet involvement in China's fight for survival also contributed to the unfolding border war with Japan. The Soviet war effort at Nomonhan was aided by the military advisors active in China: the intelligence they had gathered about the Japanese military in China helped defeat the enemy in Mongolia. Conversely, the battle also contributed to the Chinese fight against Japan by drawing away troops and equipment from the battle of Wuhan.[57]

Fourth, and most importantly, the results of the Soviet–Japanese border war of 1938–9 were far reaching: 'a great lesson' for 'the samurais', as one veteran put it. 'Even when the Germans stood outside Moscow' during the low-point in the Soviet Second World War in late 1941, 'Japan did not decide to come to the aid of its ally Hitler: the memories of the rout at Khalkhin Gol were still too vivid.' The determined Red Army resistance in Manchuria and Mongolia convinced Tokyo that the Soviet Union was a foe to be reckoned with. 'Estimates of what would be required to defeat the Russians were revised upwards', writes the author of a pathbreaking diplomatic history. Japanese planners now envisioned that 70 per cent of Japan's land forces were just enough to attack the Soviet Union. 'In these circumstances', concluded one historian, 'there was no way Japan could contemplate war on two fronts'. Hence a decision had to be made and the outcome of Khalkhin Gol strengthened the faction arguing for a 'southern' or 'Pacific' strategy and weakened those who saw the Soviets as the main enemy. Eventually, this turn south would lead to war with the United States after the attack on Pearl Harbor on 7 December 1941, among the most important turning points of the Second World War. It brought the largest economy of the world into the war-winning alliance. From 1942, the US Navy would take over much of the role China had played for the Soviets from 1937: it saved Stalin from having to fight a two-front war. Hence, the 1939 battle at the Mongolian–Manchurian has been rightly called 'the most important World War II battle that most people have never heard of'.[58]

While it was a war of consequence, the Soviet–Japanese border war was not aggressive but defensive. The Soviet leadership made sure that the fighting would remain localized. The Red Army did not exploit its victories by trying to conquer new territories. Instead, the fighting was about defending the border line and keeping what the Soviets already claimed as theirs. This defensiveness contrasts strongly with what would follow in the west after the battle of Khalkhin Gol had been won.

True to this defensive stance, eventually the Soviets signed a non-aggression treaty with Japan in April 1941, just months before the USSR would be attacked by Japan's German partner. It would hold until Stalin broke it in the summer of 1945, after having finished off Hitler. Until then, the Soviets remained officially a neutral power in the Pacific, which helped them in two ways. First, it kept their back free and allowed them to concentrate their forces on the war in the west. While never denuding the eastern front of troops, neutrality against Japan allowed the Soviet Union to throw much more into the western front's meat grinder than otherwise possible. At critical junctures, most notably the Battle of Moscow in the winter of 1941–2, this ability to transfer troops to the west was decisive. Finally, as we shall see in Chapter 5, neutrality in the Pacific also kept a major path for Allied assistance open throughout the war with Germany: the shipping lanes through Japanese waters.

Thus, we must conclude not only that the war with Japan of 1937–8 was a real war but also that it was a major Soviet victory. Together with convincing the Western Allies that Eastern Europe should be his backyard after 1945, it was victory in the east, and the resulting neutrality pact with Japan, that was Stalin's greatest military-diplomatic success of the Second World War.

3 WAR IN THE WEST, 1939–40

Pact with the devil

'The last minutes before I leave. Good bye, dear diary. I have been called up and am on my way to the induction point.' Stepan Podlubny, a frequently despondent diarist whose chronicle of the 1930s has gained some notoriety among historians of Stalinism, got ready to die in the war that had started in Europe. Yet his entry of 11 September 1939 was not his last. His call-up turned out to be a mistake and he continued, for the time being, with private life. Like many Soviet citizens, he had been aware of the war in the east, which was present in Soviet media throughout 1938 and 1939. 'There were the events on Lake Khasan, the battles at Khalkhin Gol', a later volunteer, Maria Iakovlevna Starchukova, born 1924, remembered. 'We constantly felt the threat from militarist Japan. There was always news that the border guards were catching enemy saboteurs hiding in the taiga. That's how we were prepared for labor and defense.' The Soviet Union, wrote Podlubny on 17 September, had fought a 'small war against the Japanese and the Manchurians', following earlier skirmishes. 'Somehow one got used to hearing about the conflict in the east.'[1]

The west was different. Here, everything had been quiet until now, thought Podlubny. Then, on 22 August, Soviet citizens had learned about impending negotiations with Germany; two days later the pact was published in Soviet newspapers and celebrated as a major step to secure peace; immediately after its ratification by the Supreme Soviet on 28 August, the Germans attacked Poland on 1 September. That day, the entire front page and a third of page three of *Pravda* were taken over by Commissar for Foreign Affairs, Viacheslav Molotov, defending the pact. The start of war was reported on page two the following day. Then, on 17 September, Molotov informed the Soviet population in a radio address that the Soviet high command had ordered the Red Army to march into Poland.[2]

Podlubny was astonished. 'Now we get ready', he lamented, 'to conquer a piece of what Germany has nearly already conquered completely. We have left the democratic states in the lurch and formed an alliance with the fascists.' But all would be well, he convinced himself. The march into Poland would begin a turn against the Germans who would be chased out of Poland by the Red Army.

Podlubny was not alone in his confusion about the Hitler–Stalin pact, a radical reversal of Soviet policy towards Germany. Since Hitler had taken power in 1933, Germany had replaced Poland as the main threat in the west. Soviet citizens had learned about the barbarism of 'the fascists' and the danger they posed to world peace. Moscow had become a major destination for German communists fleeing persecution in their homeland. Many of them subsequently fell victim to the Great Terror but now some of the survivors were handed over to the Nazis.

Reports on the mood of the population in 1939, besides the obligatory support for the new line, included many expressions of 'confusion, shock, and numerous questions of the type, "Why before did they shout that fascists are enemies, and now they make a treaty with them?"' 'They accused England and France of betraying Czechoslovakia in Munich', one such rank-and-file commentator pointed out, 'but they don't talk about the fact that in Moscow we have now betrayed Poland to Germany.' The USSR was 'implementing a great power policy no different to what pre-revolutionary Russia did', remarked another. The goal was, he speculated, to recover the borders of the old empire. Making common cause with Hitler was immoral, noted a third, exclaiming: 'What happened to our ethics?'[3]

The unease about the Treaty of Non-aggression between Germany and the USSR of 23 August 1939 continues to this day. More commonly known as 'Hitler–Stalin' or 'Molotov–Ribbentrop' Pact it included a secret protocol which divided Eastern Europe into 'spheres of influence'. 'In the event of a territorial and political rearrangement in the areas belonging to the Baltic States (Finland, Estonia, Latvia, Lithuania)', the secret protocol stated, 'the northern boundary of Lithuania shall represent the boundary of the spheres of influence of Germany and the USSR.' Such 'rearrangement' was also forecast for Poland. Here, the respective 'spheres of influence' would be 'bounded approximately by the line of the rivers Narew, Vistula and San'. Whether or not a Polish state would continue to exist was left open. The two parties would 'resolve this question by means of a friendly agreement'.[4] In the context of Hitler's persistent quest to undo the post-First World War settlement in Europe, this could only be read as endorsing war. Hitler no longer had to worry that the Soviets would come to the aid of Poland. The question contemporaries asked and historians continue to ponder to this day is why did Stalin align himself with Hitler, given that war in Europe was the logical result?[5]

Some historians argue that Stalin had no choice. The Soviet position throughout the 1930s had been to try create a framework of collective security against Hitler. But France and Britain consistently spoiled these attempts, the argument goes. Worse, still, under the Prime Ministers Ramsay MacDonald, Stanley Baldwin and especially Neville Chamberlain, Great Britain actively abetted Nazi Germany with a policy of 'appeasement'. The high point of this disastrous approach to a dictator actively seeking war was the Munich Agreement of 1938 – the betrayal of Czechoslovakia. Great Britain and France agreed that Germany could take over the Sudetenland. Hitler, of course, was not content with this surrender by the democracies and gobbled up the rest of Bohemia and Moravia as well. Other parts of Czechoslovakia became a Nazi puppet regime or were annexed by Hungary and Poland.

If Munich in 1938 was a desperate, morally repulsive and indeed politically inept attempt to avoid war, Moscow in 1939 was an opportunistic move to hasten war and expand their own sphere of influence into Eastern Europe. After the disaster of Munich, France and Britain had finally taken a stance and declared any invasion of Poland grounds for war. With Hitler set on attacking Poland, the Soviet Union had to decide what was more advantageous – stand with the Western Allies against the Nazis or gain some advantage from the situation. When Germany proposed a deal, Stalin took it. 'In regard to Poland', Stalin's eventual successor Nikita Khrushchev remembered the leader's explanations to his inner circle, 'Stalin said that Hitler would attack it, occupy it, and make it his protectorate.' The First Secretary of Ukraine further explained the leadership's reasoning:

> A war was about to begin, with the West encouraging Hitler to go at it with us, one on one. With the signing of this treaty, as it turned out Hitler would be the one to start the war, which was advantageous for us from the military, political, and moral point of view. By his actions he would challenge Britain and France to declare war on him, because he would be attacking their ally Poland. As for ourselves, we would remain neutral. . . . we simply had no other alternative.[6]

Of course, there were alternatives: a neutrality pact with Germany which included safeguards against aggressive war; actual neutrality eschewing formal alliances with either side; or an alliance with Britain against the Nazis. The latter was still a real possibility. While negotiations with the Soviets were slow and incompetent, since May 1939 the British government was ready to accept an agreement with Stalin and actively worked towards that goal. Stalin had a choice. He just took the better offer.[7]

Accepting it put Stalin 'in a very good mood' on the evening of 23 August. He thought he had 'outwitted Hitler', but also the British and the French, whose diplomatic missions were still in Moscow, trying to close their own deal with the Soviets. 'They're going to leave empty-handed', Stalin gloated.[8]

The dictator had never trusted the western powers. To the suspicious conspiracy-theorist the glacial speed and frequent ineptitude of British negotiations looked like sinister tactics by capitalists who wanted to use Hitler to destroy the first socialist state. To the Marxist Stalin, the difference between Nazis and conservatives was at best one of degree: both were capitalists; both were imperialists; both were anti-communists. An alliance with either was always tactical. What mattered was what served Soviet interests.

Stalin knew that war was coming. His troops were already fighting against Japan in the east and he did not know yet how this war would end. He wanted to avoid a two-front confrontation at all costs, because he rightly saw it as an extreme danger to his state. The pact with Germany was likely to speed up the march towards war between Germany and Poland, which in turn was likely to lead to war between the Reich and Britain as well as France. This development could keep Stalin's western front quiet, while he tried to make sure the east was safe and continue to prepare the country for war. If the Soviets could remain outside the European war, they could shore up their defences and get ready for war while the capitalists would bloody each other. 'We see nothing wrong', said Stalin to his closest comrades in a 7 September 1939 meeting in the Kremlin, in the capitalist countries 'having a good hard fight and weakening each other'. It would be excellent, the dictator continued, 'if at the hands of Germany the position of the richest capitalist countries (especially England) were shaken'. Hitler, in effect, did the world revolution's bidding, Stalin explained: 'without understanding it or desiring it', he was 'shaking and undermining the capitalist system'.[9]

If things went really well, war would lead to revolution, as it had in the First World War in Russia, Germany and elsewhere in Eastern Europe. If things went poorly, the Soviet Union would have more time to get ready to fight against whichever capitalist won. In any event, it would fight an enemy already weakened by previous battles. Whatever scenario would play itself out, the Soviet position would be more advantageous than now, when it was surrounded by hostile capitalist powers presumably intent at destroying the first proletarian state.

Joining the war against Poland

At first, things went according to plan. Germany attacked Poland on 1 September and on 3 September the French and British Empires declared war on Germany. But then things started to go wrong. The allies did not actually do anything to help Poland: neither Britain nor France attacked Germany and the Wehrmacht made terribly fast progress. On 5 September, the Soviets refused a Polish request to deliver military aid or let third parties deliver it through Soviet territory. 'The Soviet Union', Molotov lied 'does not want to be drawn into this war'.[10] On the same day he also answered German requests to act on the August agreement and attack Poland from the east. Fighting at Khalkhin Gol was still ongoing and Stalin steadfastly refused to be drawn into a two-front war. Hence Molotov politely declined: 'It seems to us that haste can spoil our cause and facilitate the consolidation of our opponents.'[11]

Only once a cease fire in the war with Japan had come into effect on 16 September, did the dictator set his Red Army in motion in the west on the 17 September 1939, breaking the Polish–Soviet Pact of Non-Aggression of 23 July 1932. The Soviets denied that they had done so, because there was, they said, no more Polish state with which to have a binding agreement. They proclaimed neutrality in the European war. Sophistries aside, however, the fact of the matter was that on 17 September 1939 Stalin had joined the Second World War in Europe. And for the time being, he was on Hitler's side. His Commissar of Foreign Affairs said as much in a published speech before the Supreme Soviet of the USSR on 31 October: 'It turned out that all that was needed was a quick strike on Poland, first by the German Army, then by the Red Army, and nothing was left of this ugly brainchild of the Versailles Treaty.'[12]

Why did Britain not declare war on the Soviets? The published Agreement of Mutual Assistance with Poland would have made such a move possible, even if a secret addendum specified that the 'European power' which might be the source of the aggression referred to Germany alone. But given the secret nature of this clause it could have been set aside. So why leave the Soviets alone after they chose Hitler's side and spoil British war plans, which relied on exploiting naval power in order to prevent Hitler from supplying his armies? With Soviet supplies, the blockade was essentially broken.

The first part of the answer is that the actors at the time – in sharp contrast to us today – did not know about the secret protocol dividing up Eastern Europe. This

ILLUSTRATION 3 German and Soviet officers shake hands on the Soviet–German demarcation line; Poland 1939. © Sueddeutsche Zeitung Photo / Alamy Stock Photo.

ignorance made Soviet obfuscations believable: the claim to neutrality, the pretence of intervening to save civilians and the posturing that their blockade breaking was just legal trade between a neutral country and a belligerent. Churchill, then still First Lord of the Admiralty but soon to become British prime minister, certainly gave Stalin the benefit of the doubt. Rather than condemning Soviet aggression in Poland, he respected 'the assertion of the power of Russia'. His much quoted radio address of 1 October continued:

> Russia has pursued a cold policy of self-interest. We could have wished that the Russian armies should be standing on their present line as the friends and allies of Poland instead of as invaders. But that the Russian armies should stand on this line was clearly necessary for the safety of Russia against the Nazi menace. At any rate, the line is there, and an Eastern Front has been created which Nazi Germany does not dare assail.

What would happen next was impossible to foresee, he added in a famous phrase: 'Russia' was 'a riddle wrapped in a mystery inside an enigma; but perhaps there is a key. That key is Russian national interest.' That self-interest demanded to limit the German advance into Eastern Europe and this interest coincided with Britain's.[13]

A declaration of war also seemed ill-advised to many in the British foreign policy establishment, because Britain was not just a European power, but a global empire. War with the Soviets might open up a new front in the Soviet Union's south, threatening British oil interests in Iran and Iraq, an air base in the latter country and eventually even India, separated from the Soviet Union only by Afghanistan, created as a buffer state between the two empires during the 'great game' for Central Asia in the nineteenth century. Geopolitics thus reinforced wishful thinking born of ignorance: some hoped that the Soviets would resist the Germans, others that Germany would see the light and unite with Britain in a campaign against the Bolsheviks, and in any case it seemed better if Germany was not the only major player left in Eastern Europe. Thus, Stalin's aggression remained unpunished.[14]

The campaign went without too many glitches. 'When the Red Army went on the offensive the Polish army was already demoralized to such an extent, that it nearly did not resist at all', wrote Deputy Commissar of Defense Grigory Ivanovich Kulik in a top secret report a few days later. The Soviets had taken 'very many' prisoners, for whom they were not prepared. Thus many ran away and returned home to their families. The Soviet advance was slowed not by the Polish army but by heavy rains, swollen rivers and chaos on the roads. The drivers were inexperienced, infantry not used to travelling on trucks and commanders unprepared for the demands of traffic control. As the soldiers advanced, they left behind a power vacuum for a day or two, until political workers arrived to take power. Brewing ethnic tension escalated, erupting in fights between Ukrainians and Poles.[15]

Although the Polish supreme command had ordered the troops not to resist the Soviet invaders, there were moments of heavy fighting. In Grodno, on 21 and 22 September, Polish forces barricaded themselves in houses and hurdled gasoline bottles at enemy tanks. The Soviets lost 16 tanks and three armoured vehicles. Forty-seven Red Army soldiers were killed in the fighting for the city and 156 were wounded. Overall the campaign involved some 466,000 troops, of whom 1,475 died or went missing and 2,383 were sick or wounded. They gained Stalin 200,000 square kilometres of territory and 13.5 million new subjects.[16]

Onlookers were stunned by the appearance of the Red Army, an incongruous combination of modernity and poverty. 'A few dozen steps behind the tanks rode the cavalry', remembered one witness. 'Instead of saddles they covered horses with blankets.' The animals were underfed and exhausted. They 'would fall under the riders. . . . They were so thin that it was fearsome to look at them.' But it was not just the horses who had suffered from malnutrition in Stalin's warfare state. 'When Soviet forces entered the town', wrote another memoirist, 'one immediately noticed their physical appearance and their poverty. Those of us who were used to the healthy, grown up looks of the Polish soldiers were amazed at the short stature of these arrivals.' The hardships of the Soviet decades since the Revolution had physically stunted these men. And the equipment of the rank-and-file was often wanting. 'Terrible', is what one onlooker called it: 'torn uniforms, dirty coats, hands and faces, they washed their boots in puddles, they picked up papers off the streets and rolled cigarettes. They were pitiful.'[17]

Interactions between occupiers and occupied ranged from the hostile to the ridiculous. Internal Soviet reports speak of random executions, rape and plunder. Soviet soldiers were amazed at the wealth they found in this fairly poor corner of Europe. They went on a shopping spree but sometimes also took what they wanted by force. Wrist-watches were a particularly popular item among the rank-and-file, as they would be later in Germany, Manchuria or Korea. Poles, in turn, amused themselves by ridiculing the occupiers' ignorance. 'Do you have oranges?' they would ask a peasant lad in Red Army uniform. 'We produce them in factories', came the answer. 'Do you have Amsterdam, or Greta Garbo?' the prankster would up the ante. 'We have plenty', was the confident reply. The obvious poverty of the occupiers also led itself to taunts, sometimes countered by the Soviets with a pithy summary of the difference between capitalist economics and Stalin's warfare state: Poland had perfume and silk stockings; the Soviet Union had invested in 'tanks, guns, and airplanes'.[18]

On the other end of the spectrum, the Red Army was welcomed as a liberator from Polish oppression. 'Even our advance units who fight their way [into eastern Poland] are showered with flowers', reported the boss of the Main Political Administration of the Red Army, Lev Mekhlis, on 21 September. Many of the locals, he added 'cry from happiness'. Ukrainians, Belarusian and Jews – groups who had felt discriminated against under Polish rule – were most likely to react in that way. In the case of the latter, relations soon soured as the Jewish bourgeoisie as

ILLUSTRATION 4 Soviet soldiers distributing newspapers in eastern Poland, September 1939. The invasion of what would become Western Belarus and Western Ukraine was embedded in a propaganda war attempting to win over in particular the Belarusian and Ukrainian population of the borderlands. © Popperfoto / Getty Images.

well as politically active, non-communist community members were targeted for expropriation and sometimes deportation. Michael Goldberg chronicled his own disillusionment in an unpublished memoir. He grew up in Pinsk in a left-wing, Zionist–Marxist family. 'At that time we believed, with all our hearts, that only to the East was the real paradise.'[19]

Before the war, Goldberg had been 'active in the illegal Marxist movement'. Now his friends from underground days became 'top leaders in the regime' and brought him in as well. 'When the tailor cooperative was organized, I became the manager', he recounted. 'Suddenly, I found myself in the role of the boss over my father and others like him.' In late 1939 he was sent to a party conference in Minsk. 'There I had my first glimpse of the real conditions of life in the Soviet Union.' First doubts started to nag the true believer. It did not help local enthusiasts that Soviet soldiers sometimes warned them that bad times were coming. They expressed their disappointment 'that they had brought communism to Poland instead of being liberated from it at home by the Poles'.[20]

Drawing borders

Like later historians, many new and old Soviet citizens thus struggled to make sense of this phase of the Soviet Second World War. Ideological confusion proliferated.

Both internally and externally, the Soviets had portrayed their country as peace-loving, anti-imperialist and anti-fascist. Since the Hitler–Stalin pact, however, they behaved like war-mongering imperialists, invading a neighbour and making common cause with the Nazis. Soviet citizens drew dangerous conclusions: with the signing of the non-aggression pact, the Soviet Union had become responsible for the German attack on Poland, thought one rank-and-file analyst of world events. 'I believe there is also a secret agreement between the USSR and Germany', he added. 'Obviously, this agreement provides for the division of Poland', he concluded, correctly. 'Fascism and communism are the same concept', exclaimed another Soviet citizen. 'Confirmation of this is the agreed partition of Poland.' The Soviet government was aware of such sentiments: both the Communist Party and the secret police regularly compiled dossiers on the mood of the population, and in the summer and fall of 1939 these were full of expressions of incomprehension and alarm.[21]

The original justification for the Soviet invasion of Poland had been that in the wake of German attack the Polish government had collapsed and 'de facto' no longer existed (a claim disputed by Polish authorities then and Polish historians ever since). The Soviets then marched in to defend Ukrainians and Belarusians from attack by their Polish neighbours, to 'take under its protection the life and property of the population of Western Ukraine and Western Belarus', as Molotov put it. The war, he continued, was the fault of the Polish leadership and the Soviet troops would bring peace. This argument 'was to make the intervention of the Soviet Union plausible to the masses', as Molotov explained to the German Ambassador on 10 September, 'and at the same time avoid giving the Soviet Union the appearance of an aggressor'.[22]

This carefully thought out public relations line was popular. Many Soviet citizens thought all Ukrainians should live in Ukraine and all Belarusians in Belarus. On 1 November, V. I. Motorkin, a Moscow resident giving his full address, wrote to the Soviet legislature, describing his initial confusion and subsequent epiphany. How could a pact with a country like Germany come about, and so quickly? How could one explain the fact that Germany, 'a bourgeois state', retreated from territory it held and handed it over to the Soviets without a fight? 'But it is no longer necessary to be astonished' about 'the wise policy of our government', he added with relief. He had finally grasped the higher meaning of Soviet policy: it was about 'the liberation of the peoples of Western Belarus and Western Ukraine from the yoke of the capitalists and landowners of the former Poland'. This national-communist explication clarified everything.[23]

The problem was that the boundaries drawn in the secret protocol did not accord with this theory: such national thinking had at best played a minor role in the original negotiations, which, on the Soviet side were driven by opportunism informed by an overall strategy to avoid a two-front war with Germany and Japan, while also weakening the capitalist powers. The point of the pact had been to isolate Japan in the east and in the west 'pit one side against the other'. As a result of the treaty, the capitalists would fight each other 'as fiercely as possible', as Stalin explained to his inner circle. The Soviet Union would then pick up the pieces: 'What would be the harm', Stalin asked rhetorically, 'if as a result of the rout of Poland we were to extend the socialist system onto new territories and populations?'[24]

Now, however, it had turned out that a nationalist interpretation worked extremely well to sell red imperialism as a humanitarian intervention. The Polish campaign was not war, but an operation to save fellow Ukrainians and Belarusians. To make this explanation internally coherent, the borders drawn in the secret protocol had to change – and Soviet negotiators made sure that they did. A frontier treaty of 28 September 1939 assigned overwhelmingly Polish-settled regions to the German sphere but compensated the Soviets by conceding interests in Lithuania. Earlier plans to create a separate Polish republic to join the Soviet Union were thus dropped.[25]

Stalin, the old revolutionary, remained ambivalent about this further shift towards nationalism. Even after the realignment of borders in September 1939, significant numbers of Poles lived on Soviet occupied territory. They were often treated badly by the new authorities, who bought the anti-Polish line. Polish was treated as a taboo language, Polish refugees were ignored by the authorities, and Poles were refused jobs, as Stalin complained in a July 1940 telegram to a local party boss. This state of affairs was unacceptable. 'The Central Committee of the Bolshevik Party', wrote Stalin sternly, 'asks you to take personal responsibility to liquidate these and similar problems and take steps to establish fraternal relations between Ukrainian and Polish laborers'.[26]

The Baltics in 1939

That Stalin had not suddenly become a Russian nationalist was demonstrated soon. If the Soviet Union had really have transformed into a national homeland for eastern Slavs, as the propaganda about the Polish acquisitions implied, why re-conquer the Baltics? There were significant minorities of Russian living here, but nothing on the scale as Ukrainians or Belarusians in the former borderlands of Poland. But Stalin's thinking was muddled, mixing revolutionary, imperial, nationalist and strategic concerns. Latvia, Lithuania and Estonia had been part of the Russian Empire before the First World War; crucially, they were also strategically important to the Soviet Union's defence.

Stalin used somewhat more subtle methods than in Poland. Having demonstrated that the Red Army was willing and able to invade neighbours, Latvia, Lithuania, Estonia and Finland were pressured to concede sovereign rights to the Soviet Union on their own accord: Stalin wanted military bases. The argument for them was made more convincing by the real threat of military invasion of superior forces: the three Baltic dwarfs had no chance of resisting the Red Giant. Treaties were signed with Estonia on 29 September 1939, allowing 25,000 Red Army soldiers into the country. Latvia was next, on 5 October (30,000 soldiers), and Lithuania five days later (20,000). These were more than just advance bases for defence, however, as a close collaborator of Stalin's noted in his diary on 25 October: 'in our pacts of mutual assistance (Estonia, Latvia, Lithuania) we have found the right form to allow us to bring a number of countries into the Soviet Union's sphere of influence.'[27]

War with Finland

While the bullying of the three Baltic states had produced the desired outcome, in Finland things did not go according to plan. Like the Baltic republics and Poland, Finland had been tsarist territory at the eve of the First World War. It had broken away during the revolution and retained its independence after the wars of succession of 1918–21. A short but brutal Civil War had ended with victory of the anti-Bolshevik 'Whites' and a bloodbath among communists. Bringing Finland back into the Soviet empire could thus be seen both as completing the regathering of the Romanov lands under the red flag and as revenge for the earlier defeat of the Finnish communists. More important, however, were again strategic considerations. Finnish territory was too close to Leningrad, the cradle of the revolution, the unofficial second capital and a major industrial centre – 'one of the largest producers of weapons and ammunition in the world' at the time, as historians have pointed out.[28]

Stalin made that point when defending his decision to go to war in front of the country's top military brass after the humiliating conflict was over. Could it have been avoided? No, answered Stalin. 'The war was necessary, because the peaceful negotiations with Finland did not lead to results and we had to secure Leningrad, because its security is the security of our fatherland. This is the case not only because Leningrad represents some 30-35 percent of our country's defense industry . . . but also because Leningrad is the second capital of our country.' If the enemy had taken Leningrad and established a 'bourgeois, a white-guard government', Stalin continued, this would have given the imperialists 'a serious base for a civil war against Soviet power'.[29]

Negotiations broke down quickly after the Soviets had made demands unacceptable to Finland: a naval base with artillery, armour, infantry and two air-force regiments on Finnish territory and a re-drawing of the borderlines.[30] Thus, on 30 November 1939, Stalin unleashed the mighty Red Army towards his northern neighbour. His eastern front was calm after victory at Khalkhin Gol and his western front, likewise, was stable under the pact with Hitler and the Western powers' unwillingness to punish Stalin for it. He could expect his soldiers to march into the country as easily as they had done in Poland. 'The objective was to annihilate the Finnish Army and swiftly occupy the country', as recent research into the Soviet war plan has shown. In preparation of Soviet victory, Stalin organized a puppet government under the leadership of the refugee Finnish Communist Otto Kuusinen. From Terijoki, a sleepy town in Karelia, just 50 kilometres from Leningrad across the Soviet–Finnish border, he declared the People's Government of Finland (1 December). Another piece of paper was issued the following day: a 'Treaty of Mutual Assistance and Friendship' between this imaginary state and the Soviet Union. Then Kuusinen settled down to wait for Soviet victory.[31]

Kuusinen waited in vain. Unlike Poland, whose military was torn apart in a two-front war where the Germans had already done most of the dirty work, Finland resisted efficiently. Defences had been prepared; the troops were well trained, knew the terrain and were excellently motivated. Highly mobile on skis, nearly invisible in winter camouflage, in control of prepared fortifications, they inflicted terrible damage on the numerically superior enemy. In 105 days of fighting, the Red Army lost 333,000 men to wounds, burns or frostbite, 65,384 of them died.[32]

However, a nation of 3.7 million had little chance against the Soviet behemoth, which sent in nearly a million armed men supported by 63 per cent of the entire Soviet bomber fleet, and 38 per cent of its fighter planes.[33] By February 1940 the main Finnish defence line had been breached, opening up the path to Helsinki. Stalin, however, suddenly hesitated. Spring was just around the corner, and with it the period of 'roadlessness', which affected Finland as much as the Soviet Union. The cause of valiant Finland had become a global concern. Finland's government had quite patently not collapsed. There were no Slavic minorities in need of salvation. So why were the Soviets there? They were so plainly the aggressors that the Soviet Union was thrown out of the League of Nations, returning to a kind of diplomatic isolation just overcome when it had joined in 1934.

Moreover, French and British plans to intervene in the conflict were alarming. Whether or not an expeditionary force could actually have been deployed in practice is a moot point (Norway and Sweden would not consent to let troops pass through their territory). A confrontation with the British and French Empires could have opened new fronts in the south of the Soviet Union as well. Britain had an air base in Iraq and stood in India and could thus potentially threaten Tajikistan in Central Asia and Armenia and Azerbaijan in the Trans-Caucasus. Syria and Lebanon were a French mandate and could become a jumping off point for a campaign against the Caucasus. Had such plans eventuated, they would have made the old Bolshevik nightmare of 'capitalist encirclement' a reality. They threatened to nullify the entire attempt to avoid a two-front war, replacing it with an even more horrifying threat of fighting on multiple frontiers. The British and French had a record of intervening in Russia, as Stalin remembered from the years of warfare after 1917. Maybe they would try again? The dictator decided to cut his losses.[34]

The Moscow Peace Treaty of 12 March 1940, was, nevertheless, harsh. The Finns lost more territory than the Soviets had asked for before the war. Most of Finnish Karelia, including much of the industrial heart of the country as well as important timber producing areas, went to the Soviet Union. Altogether, a tenth of Finnish territory was lost alongside 13 per cent of national wealth. Stalin also got his naval base on the Hanko peninsula.[35]

The outcome of the Finnish war was ambiguous. It showed the Soviet Union's neighbours that Stalin was willing to risk offensive war if his territorial demands were not met. It improved the tactical situation around Leningrad, now further from the border with Finland. But it also pushed the Finns into an alliance with Hitler, which would come back to haunt Stalin in the summer and fall of 1941. The poor performance of the Red Army, moreover, helped to further convince Hitler that the Soviet Union was a giant with feet of clay. The Great Terror seemed to have destroyed whatever competence there had been and a repeat of the experience of the First World War seemed plausible: 'Russia' would collapse once confronted with decisive German military action.[36]

Gobbling up the Baltics, Bessarabia and Northern Bukovina

Finland was not the only misjudgement. In the first half of 1940, Stalin's strategy underwriting the pact with Germany began to fall apart. According to the plan, Germany was to be engaged in the west in a protracted war with France and Britain, which would weaken not only Hitler's state but also global capitalism. Instead, Stalin was confronted with a shocking performance of the Western Allies. It took Germany only forty-six days to occupy France. The British Expeditionary Force was thrown into the ocean and escaped only by the skin of its teeth in the 'miracle of Dunkirk'. On 22 June, the humiliated French signed an armistice agreement. This unforeseen German success left Stalin in a precarious position. Rather than weakened, Hitler's Reich emerged strengthened from this war. With the division of Poland, Nazi troops now stood at the border of the Soviet Union.

In this situation, military bases and friendly regimes in the Baltic states would no longer do. Instead, they needed to be annexed to buffer the Soviet Union against potential German aggression. Soviet forces stationed inside the Baltic republics as well as massed on the borders totalled well over half a million, ready to invade a region inhabited by fewer than six million people with peacetime armies of a combined 73,000 soldiers.[37] The governments of the three small states decided to avoid pointless heroics. On 15 June, the Red Army crossed the Lithuanian

ILLUSTRATION 5 Red Army enters Vilnius, 15 June 1940. © United States Holocaust Memorial Museum (public domain).

border unopposed. A day later, it was Latvia's and Estonia's turn. The annexations reiterated the pattern established earlier in Poland: rigged elections followed by official requests to join the Soviet Union. The difference was that the Polish regions had been attached to existing Union republics – Belarus and Ukraine – while the three Baltic republics became their own republics within the USSR.

The last victim of Stalinist aggression was Romania. After much bullying from Moscow, an armed conflict was averted and the Romanian government, now devoid of its ally France, conceded territory. On 28 June the Red Army crossed the border and by 4 July it had occupied Bessarabia and the Northern Bukovina, adding 50,762 square kilometres and 3.8 million people to the empire. There were some minor losses from accidents and very few fire fights with retreating Romanian forces, but by and large it was an eventless occupation. Again, the reasons for the acquisition were strategic: it pushed the borders to the west, gave access to a locally important railway line, opened up the possibility for airstrikes on Romanian oil fields – important suppliers of the German army. Again, historical, revolutionary and national reasons were mixed in the legitimation of this annexation. Romania had 'torn away' Bessarabia 'by force from the Soviet Union (Russia) at the start of 1918', wrote *Pravda* the day after the invasion, ignoring the fact that there was no Soviet Union at the start of 1918 and that 'Russia' had been falling apart in war and revolution. Now the old empire was mobilized to legitimize conquest by the new one. But the same logic could not apply to Northern Bukovina, which had never been part of the Russian Empire. No matter: like Bessarabia, it was settled 'predominantly by Ukrainians', the 'blood-brothers and sisters of the inhabitants of Soviet Ukraine'. They thus came home to their 'Homeland-Mother', the 'dream of the laboring masses of Bessarabia and the Northern Bukovina'.[38]

Again, many rank and file Soviets found this reasoning compelling.[39] And again, the subject populations were 'very apprehensive, excided and divided', as Markus Lecker, a native of Bukovina noted in his unpublished memoirs.

There were those who were sorry to see the Rumanians go. But others were glad to get rid of the Rumanians and welcomed the Russians with open arms. These were part of the working class and sympathizers of the Communists from way back. These people would have the shock of their lives because of the disappointing economic performance of the Soviets. But also because of the political terror the new administration instituted with arrests and detentions of all kinds for, what we considered, no reason at all.[40]

Revolution from abroad

Notwithstanding all national and imperial rhetoric, then, the Soviet Union remained a revolutionary state. The activities of the Red Army, said Stalin, were 'a matter of world revolution'.[41] Hence conquest and annexation was not enough. Once the new borders had stabilized, the acquired territories needed to be Sovietized: industries had to be nationalized, peasants collectivized and enemies eliminated – a replay of Stalin's revolution from above as a 'Revolution from Abroad'.[42]

Agrarian policies in this period differed between the newly acquired regions. In the formerly Polish territories, large landowners were expropriated and some of their holdings distributed to the rural poor. Collectivization began in the spring of 1940 but proceeded slowly. At the eve of the German attack, only 13 per cent of western Ukrainian and 7 per cent of Western Belarusian peasants had been collectivized. Those subject to the collectives were as unhappy with the results as their equivalents had been in the old Soviet Union at the start of the 1930s. 'How terribly we suffer from poverty now, like never before', wrote one of the victims in a letter opened by state security. 'We only live from day to day, waiting that someone liberates us from this Ukraine. After all, this is not a Ukrainian state but a Russian illness. If you don't want to work, they immediately ship you off to Siberia, where they torment people, forcing them to live in pits.' Hopefully, 'Mr Hitler' would read this letter and soon come and 'take us under his power'. On the other side of the frontlines of this Civil War against the rural population, the local young communists sent out to bully the peasantry into the collectives also experienced what their predecessors in the 'old' Soviet territories had a decade before. 'We were faced with terrible resistance from the farmers. In one of these villages, while staying the night after a meeting, I was almost killed when shots were fired through the window of my room.'[43]

Meanwhile, in the Baltic states, the Northern Bukovina and Bessarabia only the first step of the Soviet land reform was instituted: the expropriation of large landowners, and the transfer of their lands to small-scale farmers. In Russia, this step had been an integral part of the Bolshevik revolution of 1917 – a tactical concession to the rural poor to align them with the new, 'proletarian' power. In the long run, of course, it would give way to forced collectivization. But for the time being, Stalin judged these regions not ripe for his agricultural revolution from above. In the cities and towns of the three Baltic republics, as elsewhere in the newly acquired territories, however, house owners lost their tenements and medium and large enterprises were nationalized.[44]

The third and most important plank of the revolution from abroad was the elimination of enemies, both real and imagined. This purging of the new territories took many forms. One was arrests followed by labour camp sentences in Siberia and elsewhere in the Soviet hinterland. One target were activists of political parties other than the communists. These included organization of the left – such as the Jewish socialists of the Bund in Poland – and of the right. Top-level civil servants, policemen, officers and capitalists were arrested as class enemies and pillars of the old regime. Arrests affected tens of thousands of people. A total of 14,467 people had been arrested in the three Baltic republics by 17 June 1941.[45] In the regions taken from Romania, the corresponding number was 6,250 by 13 June 1941.[46] And in the formerly Polish territories of Ukraine and Belarus, 107,140 people were arrested between the arrival of Soviet troops in 1939 and the German attack in June 1941; of these, 40 per cent were Polish, 23 per cent Ukrainians, 22 per cent Jewish and 8 per cent Belarusian. These arrests made up 52 per cent of all arrests in the same period in the Soviet Union overall, indicating how repression was focused on the newly acquired regions.[47]

In Western Ukraine and Western Belarus, the arrests began immediately after occupation by Soviet troops in September 1939. In May 1941, the repressions expanded to the newly acquired Baltic republics. The Soviet government ordered the security services of Latvia, Lithuania and Estonia to arrest the 'criminal element', as well as all kinds of 'socially dangerous' people. The list of targets included 'active members of counterrevolutionary parties and participants in anti-Soviet, nationalist, white-guardist organizations', former policemen and prison guards, factory owners, large-scale land owners, high-level state functionaries of the old regime and officers of the old army. They received five to eight years labour camp sentences with confiscation of property. If they survived the camps, they were to be exiled for another twenty years 'in remote regions of the Soviet Union'.

Their families were subject to the second tool of Soviet cleansing: deportation. It also extended to the kin of 'counterrevolutionaries' in hiding, of those sentenced to death, of repatriates to Germany and of people who had registered to emigrate.[48] In contrast to those arrested, who were accused of lawbreaking, there was no such suggestion for deportees. Like the Koreans deported in 1937, they were removed preventatively, not because of anything they had done but because of who they were and what they therefore might do in the future. They were another example for the inability of Stalin's warfare state to develop efficient methods: deportations were an extremely costly policing tactic. They tied up manpower, trains, tracks and administrative resources. They led to extreme human suffering and did nothing to endear the victims to this regime. They led to social and cultural conflicts in the regions the deportees were sent to. But they were effective in suppressing or preventing resistance, as Stalin had learned ever since his war with the peasantry in the early 1930s.

In their modus operandi, too, the deportations from the western borderlands resembled those of the Koreans earlier in the war. Trucks or horse-drawn carts pulled up in front of the victims' residences, NKVD officers entered family homes and people were told to pack. They could only take essential goods. They would then be loaded on the waiting vehicles and driven to the train station, where, after more or less delay, they would be forced into the ubiquitous box cars which carted deportees, mobilized soldiers, evacuees, repatriates and returning POWs across Soviet space throughout the years of the Second World War.

'I took with me only my sheepskin and two suitcases of clothes', remembered Irena Protassewicz, a Polish victim who was deported just two days before the Germans attacked the Soviet Union in the summer of 1941. Not knowing what lay ahead, she 'left behind my long fur', a decision she would come to regret. Deportation was the latest in a long line of tribulations. Her family had lost their manor when the Soviets had invaded in September 1939, first to looting Belarusian peasants who let their pent-up resentment against the Polish lords' free rein, then to confiscation by the new Soviet masters. Now she had been awoken at night, told to get her things and was bundled onto a waiting peasant cart. She travelled through the 'beautiful June night', talking with the soldier who had come to collect her about whether or not God existed (she thought yes, he thought no). 'The conversation was conducted with great Soviet courtesy', she added. The idyll ended when they arrived at the train station. It was in 'a state of turmoil: lots of people, general weeping and wailing'. She would spend three weeks in a box car en route to Siberia.[49]

Overall, some 383,000 people were deported between 1940 and the summer of 1941 from the newly acquired western borderlands. Most of them came from the former Polish territories of Ukraine and Belarus: military colonists, foresters, families of arrested and POWs, refugees (mostly Jewish) from the German occupied territories who did not want to accept Soviet citizenship and other 'alien elements', like Protassewicz.[50] From the three Baltic republics, a total of 49,331 people, or nearly 1 per cent of the population, was deported.[51] The remainder came from the formerly Romanian territories.

The surviving descriptions of travel to the east of these deportees resemble those from the earlier Korean operation and would repeat themselves in later instances throughout the Soviet Second World War: of the Finns and Germans in 1941, the Kalmyks and Karachay in 1943, the Chechens and Ingush, Balkars and Tatars, Greeks, Kurds, Turks and others in 1944, repatriated soviets shipped to verification camps after the war ended in Europe or the renewed deportations from the western borderlands in connection with dekulakization and counter-insurgency in 1944–9. Deportees did not know where they were going. Conditions in the wagons were cramped and unsanitary. A bucket or a hole in the planks served as a toilet. People were rarely let out at the stations and the amount of food and drink was inadequate. Children and old people were particularly likely to die: from exposure, accidents, malnutrition or disease. Once they arrived, the survivors had to adjust to heavy labour in special settlements. These were essentially gulags without barbed wire or supervision by guards, where the victims were allowed to live with their family. Some were specially constructed, others tagged on to existing collective or state farms. Inmates had to work hard for small rations or meagre pay; they were not allowed to leave; death rates were high.[52]

The newly minted Soviet functionary Goldberg in Pinsk tried to make sense of these events. His confidence in the Soviet paradise had already been shaken by his visit to Minsk in late 1939, but by 1940 it would receive further hits. His work as 'the main political controller' of a tailoring cooperative was taxing. 'We had great difficulties in obtaining supplies because the entire economy was in shambles', he wrote. Goldberg had 'to push the workers to produce, knowing meanwhile what meagre pay they received'. He also had to 'advocate the political line, which in the winter of 1940 became difficult for my conscience'. The Finnish war and the increasing repression 'brought a crisis in my thinking. I saw things I could not explain to myself, not just to the workers'. Goldberg was impressed by the 'heroic resistance of the small Finnish nation' and more and more often also noticed the heavy hand of the Soviet police closer to home. 'First, during the night, portions of the Polish population of Pinsk started to disappear and were deported to Siberia. After that came the deportations of Jewish people who were suspected of being members of socialist and Zionist organizations under the Polish rule.' Finally, he was sent out to the countryside in the summer of 1940 to help with collectivization, which further disillusioned him. Eventually, a friend advised him to resign from his position and find a less exposed job. 'The higher I went', Goldberg summarized a law of Soviet careers, 'the harder I was bound to fall'. He thus resigned and became a worker in a chemical plant – 'the best months I had during the Soviet rule.'[53]

Mass murder

What Goldberg did not know at the time was that arrest or deportation were by no means the most radical ways the Soviets dealt with presumed or real enemies. They also used 'the highest measure of punishment': death by shooting. We do not have numbers of how many of the people who were arrested in 1939–41 in the western borderlands were sentenced to death. We do know that they were a minority: 221 among those arrested in Western Ukraine between 1939 and early April 1941.[54]

We also know one particularly gruesome statistic. On orders by the Politburo (that is, Stalin and his closest comrades), Soviet policemen shot 21,857 Polish officers, policemen, military settlers and other presumed enemies of the new regime. The executions took place in April and May 1940 in several sites. Most famous became the forest of Katyn in Smolensk region where 4,421 victims were buried.[55]

This mass murder was reminiscent of the shooting operations of the Great Terror. In the basement of the NKVD building in Smolensk the victims were led into a room, a trap door in the floor was opened, the executioners forced the condemned to the floor and shot him in the back or the side of the head, 'depending on the tastes of the shooter', as a witness reported. At least one officer resisted, wrestling the weapon out of the killer's hand, shooting him in turn. Such heroics just delayed the inevitable. In the prison in Kharkiv, the procedure involved a senior policeman, who did the shooting, a state prosecutor to verify the identity of the condemned and a guard to bring the prisoners into the execution chamber one by one and then remove the corpses. 'You had to wrap something around the head, so that their blood would not flow on the ground', he remembered. In a third shooting site, a prison in Kalinin, the executions were conducted by a veteran of the Great Terror. Vasily Mikhailovich Blokhin was a specialist in such matters. He had brought a suitcase of pistols as well as special protective clothing made of leather: apron, cap and long gloves reaching over the elbows. Thus attired he and his associates shot between 250 and 300 people a night, exchanging weapons several times during a shift, as they quickly overheated. At the end of a night's work, he handed out vodka to his associates, who drank themselves into oblivion. But first, they washed themselves with perfume, hoping to get rid of 'the smell of blood and decomposition'. This procedure was unsuccessful, as one of them later remembered: 'Even the dogs avoided us.'[56]

Soviet legalese gave this entire process a veneer of legitimacy. 'Based on the fact', Stalin's police chief Lavrenty Beria wrote to Stalin, 'that they are all hardened, irremediable enemies of Soviet power', a 'special procedure' was to be used to examine their cases and 'apply to them the supreme punishment'.[57] Given that the result of these 'examinations' was already clear from the outset, given that these men had not broken any Soviet laws, given that their only crime was loyalty to their state and arrogance towards their interrogators, and given that most of them were prisoners of war, protected by international law, customary rules of warfare, and even Soviet regulations, this gruesome episode was a war crime of immense proportions. Nothing the Soviets did later in their Second World War would compare to this gross violation of both formal and informal rules of warfare.[58]

But given that it remained secret, it did accomplish its aim: the destruction of a significant part of the Polish elite who could no longer mount resistance against Soviet rule.

Ambiguous expansion

Thus, by early 1941 a strictly Machiavellian observer might have concluded that Stalin had played his cards rather well. After stabilizing the eastern front against Japan in 1937–9, he waged his own campaigns in the west behind the shield of the Hitler–Stalin pact. These forgotten wars of the Second World War continued the collection of the Romanov lands the Bolsheviks had never entirely completed after the breakdown of 1917. This re-gathering of historically Russian lands as well as some that had never been part of the empire expanded the Soviet Union westwards, growing it from eleven Union republics inhabited by 167 million people to sixteen republics, covering 22 million square kilometres and housing more than 190 million people at the eve of the German invasion.[59]

However, while Stalin's accomplishments at the eastern front were unambiguous improvements of the security of his state, his record in the west was decidedly mixed. The westward expansion added new populations that could be mobilized for labour and defence, but they also were of dubious loyalties. The annexations stretched the security forces thinner than before and made fortifications at the old border useless. The new demarcation line remained poorly protected from the German hordes lurking on the other side. The Nazis could now attack directly without having to first fight their way through third parties' territory.

Even worse was the record in regard to Finland. The relatively minor territorial gains Stalin felt compelled to settle on in the end were hardly worth the blood of the dead and wounded this war cost him. Soviet aggression pushed the Finns into a closer alliance with Germany than they otherwise might have entertained. This alignment added to Hitler's strike-force in the summer of 1941.

Domestically, too, the expansion was a two-edged affair. Since the mid-1930s, the regime had wagered on Russian nationalism as the mobilizing ideology. But now, because of the incorporation of regions inhabited largely by other nationalities, the share of Russians in the empire decreased from 58 to 52 per cent of the population. Having stamped out any kind of potential opposition in the mass shooting operations of the Great Terror, Stalin in effect welcomed new enemies into his gates. The westward expansion brought organized Ukrainian, Polish and Baltic nationalists into the Soviet sphere. They would cause the Soviets significant troubles for the rest of the Second World War. In the first half of 1941 in Western Ukraine alone, the Soviet security forces 'liquidated' 38 'political' and 25 'criminal gangs'. A total of 485 people were either arrested or killed in these operations, which included at times sustained fire fights. Another 747 'illegals' were arrested during these months and 1,865 members of the Organization of Ukrainian Nationalists (OUN) were deported.[60]

The continuing relevance of the Asian theatre

Meanwhile, Soviet fears of a two-front war never entirely vanished. China remained an important part of the means to avoid it. In June 1939, the Soviet Union granted another large loan to buy military equipment, which soon followed. When in late 1940 Vasily Chuikov received his marching orders to serve as military advisor in China, Stalin told him: 'The most important thing is to unite all forces in China to repel the aggressor.' The goal of Soviet aid to China remained 'to tie down Japanese aggression', to 'tightly bind the hands of the Japanese aggressor'. The reasons were strategic, the dictator explained: 'Only if the hands of the Japanese aggressor are bound can we escape war on two fronts, if the German aggressors attack our country.'[61]

Only time would tell whether this strategy would work. For the moment, the Soviet leadership remained nervous. A 11 March 1941 General Staff document

ILLUSTRATION 6 Machine gunners of Far Eastern Army, 1941. The Soviet 'eastern front' against Japan continued to play an important role during the Second World War. © Library of Congress (public domain).

warned against a possible war in the west with Germany, Italy, Hungary, Romania and Finland, and at the same time in the east with Japan. The authors recommended to concentrate most forces in the west. Here, the largest number of enemy troops and materiel was expected. But significant forces should remain in the east, where a secondary threat was pinpointed.[62] Chuikov received instructions around the same time to evaluate the evidence he could find for Japanese intentions. Were they preparing for an attack on the Soviet Union?[63] The Japanese–Soviet nonaggression pact of 13 April 1941 did not alleviate this nervousness: would the Japanese honour the pact?

The eastern front also remained relevant because the Trans-Siberian Railway became an important lifeline for aggressors and victims alike. To fight its war in Europe, Germany needed supplies from Asia, in particular natural rubber for the tires of heavy military trucks. Japan could provide it, but given the Allied naval blockade was unable to ship it. After the Molotov–Ribbentrop pact and subsequent economic agreements, the Trans-Siberian Railway became the answer. On average 300 tons of natural rubber daily crossed along its tracks from Manchukuo to Berlin via Vladivostok and Moscow.[64] The final trainload with supplies crossed the Soviet–German border on the morning of the 22 June, just as German soldiers left their jump-off points to begin their ill-conceived war against the Soviet Union. And although the Soviets tried to put a brave face on the economic interaction later on, the fact of the matter was that on balance Germany benefited much more than the Soviets.[65]

Economic impact of the war

Indeed, Soviet civilians did worse as a result of the Soviet involvement in the war. The decline in living standards was most dramatic in the newly acquired borderlands in the west, who suffered in particular because of Soviet plunder, the confiscation of private property and the inevitable drop in consumption levels entailed by the imposition of the Soviet command economy. 'Right after the Soviet army invaded our town', remembered one Polish boy, 'everything got scarce: salt, flour, bread, sugar, cloth, shoes etc.' But shortages increased in the Soviet heartland as well, as the shift of resources into defence production from 1938 and the food deliveries to Germany began to bite. Lines in front of stores became longer. In September 1939, a partial mobilization of men in the run-up to the Polish campaign had led to panic buying. Salt, matches and other products disappeared from the shelves and were hoarded in private stocks. By December 1939, it was difficult to find bread or flower in the stores. Workers started to leave their enterprises in search for better living conditions elsewhere in the large Soviet country. Market prices for foodstuffs climbed steeply, peasants descended on the cities to buy bread. Police informers and party stooges reported long queues in front of shops and increasing displeasure among the hungry crowds. In the collective farms, grain shortages became widespread. By April 1940, Stalin received reports about malnutrition in the villages.[66]

The government reacted in the only way it knew. While resisting the urge to allow rationing, it reintroduced closed distribution systems for food for strategic sectors of the economy. Queues were outlawed. Next came regimentation of labour and of mobility. On 26 June 1940 it became illegal to be absent from work or be late or change one's employer without permission. This law put industrial workers on a wartime footing: like soldiers, they were subject to severe discipline. Soon, local authorities and in many cases local people introduced rationing, because they saw no alternative. Leningraders, for one, already had to deal with rationing during the war with Finland. By the end of 1940, the country was on a wartime footing as far as labour, mobility and consumption were concerned.[67]

Eurasian displacements

While deliveries along the Trans-Siberian helped fuel Hitler's war machine, East-European Jews fled the Nazi onslaught via the same track, only in the opposite direction. In the interlude between the division of Poland and the Soviet annexation of the Baltic republics, some 2,700 Jewish refugees from occupied Poland managed to obtain Japanese exit visas from the Japanese vice-consul in Kaunas, in still independent Lithuania. Thus equipped, they travelled thousands of kilometres across Soviet space to Vladivostok and from there to survival, very often in the ghetto of Shanghai. More paradoxical still was the unintended consequence of Soviet deportations from the West to Siberia, Central Asia or the Far North: they removed tens of thousands of Polish Jews from the reach of German murder squads. And while life in Soviet exile was hard and often lethal, the chances of survival here were much higher than they were for Jews in Nazi-occupied Poland. 'This was a paradox', mused one whose family was forced onto a deportation train in Pinsk on the day the Germans attacked the Soviet Union further west. The brutality of Stalin's security forces spared him the experience of the ghetto and of its liquidation in October 1942. 'It turned out that the exile to Siberia saved our lives', he concluded. The image of the deportation train to safety encapsulates the political and moral ambiguity of the Soviet war effort in this period.[68]

As echelons of deportees moved east, they often had to wait for trains bearing other human cargo passing in the opposite direction. While Stalin could not believe that Hitler would be crazy enough to start a two-front war, his military did not entirely ignore the warnings. On 13 May the General Staff ordered to transfer troops from the hinterland to the frontier. Twenty-eight rifle divisions and four army directorates were moved west at short notice.[69] 'Every day', remembers one veteran the massive troop movement 'new echelons with troops passed by us on their way to the border'.[70] This phenomenon is sometimes misunderstood to be part of the preparation for offensive war against Germany, a thesis which goes back to Nazi propaganda at the time and has received a new lease on life after new evidence for troop dislocations and troop movements emerged after the breakdown of the Soviet Union.[71]

The troop movement was so obvious that the Soviet news agency TASS felt obliged to deny such 'rumours' on 14 June 1941. These were normal summer manoeuvres training both the troops and the railway workers, a statement published in the newspapers claimed. It was read to the troops and announced to the crowds in the cities via radio blaring from public loudspeakers.[72] It greatly confused sailors in the Black Sea Fleet, who just days earlier had been instructed to be prepared for the outbreak of war. Who were they to believe?[73] Elsewhere, troops preparing for an imminent attack by the enemy were told that this message was only meant as a diplomatic signal, and that they should continue with what they were doing.[74] Officers of the General Staff, too, first reacted with 'some amazement' at the message but then interpreted it like the agitators in the ranks: given that now 'fundamentally new directives' were given, 'it became clear that it did not apply to the armed forces or the country as a whole.'[75] Others, however, read the message literally. 'To be honest, we did not expect war', noted the then General Staff officer Aleksandr Mikhailovich Vasilevsky in his memoirs. 'We were reassured by the TASS report. . . . After it, everyone decided that there would be no armed conflict in the near future.'[76]

While soldiers struggled with mixed messages, the railway lines were overcharged with troops travelling west along with supplies for the Germans. Deportees moved in the opposite direction, all on top of the normal circulation of goods and people. Many of those sent to take up positions at the German–Soviet border thus had to walk. One veteran remembered how in the spring of 1941 his unit was ordered to leave its training camp near Belgorod in south-west Russia. The rifle division marched for weeks on end through Ukraine, avoiding cities for reasons of secrecy, making its way first to the Black Sea, then to Poltava. 'When we marched out into the steppe', he wrote, 'we saw that in parallel with us other divisions marched west'.[77]

They were not, however, allowed to attack. Stalin was too keen a student of history to believe that anybody in his right mind would risk a two-front war if he had the choice. Given that Hitler was still at war with Britain and given that there was no sign of this war ending any time soon, it would be madness to attack the Soviets at the same time. All the evidence he got from intelligence sources at home and abroad was just smoke and mirrors trying to get him to attack the Germans and thus provoke war. They were the mystifications of either war mongers among the German military or the perfidious English, whom he had earlier suspected of having tried to lure him into a confrontation with Germany. He, Stalin, would not be fooled by such attempts to make him do the imperialists' dirty work. 'Comrade

Merkulov', he wrote to the head of his spy agency less than a week before the German attack, 'you can send your "source" from the general staff of the German Air Force to his fucking mother.' The German who had warned of war preparations was, he continued, 'not a "source" but a disinformant'.[78] Millions of Soviet civilians, both soldiers and civilians, would soon pay with their lives for the dictator's refusal to understand that Hitler was no Stalin.

4 ARMAGEDDON, 1941–2

Chaos

'Lenin left us a great legacy', Stalin fumed, 'and we – his heirs – we have shat all over it!' It was a little over a week after the Germans had attacked without warning or declaration of war. From the early hours of 22 June, Hitler's strike force had overwhelmed Soviet defences and advanced in three prongs deep into Soviet territory. Army group North was on the way to Leningrad, Army Group Centre motored towards Moscow and Army group South advanced towards Kyiv. On the day of Stalin's outburst, Hitler's *Panzer* reached the outskirts of Lviv in the South and controlled the region south of Minsk in the middle. Army group North stood deep in Lithuania.[1] But Stalin had no clear sense of what was going on at his western front. He had met with his closest circle to discuss the situation: Viacheslav Molotov, Georgy Malenkov, Anastas Mikoian and Lavrenty Beria. A phone call to the Commissariat of Defense did not lift the fog. Hence Stalin had decided to pay the soldiers a visit. The meeting with Semyon Timoshenko, Nikolai Vatutin and Georgy Zhukov was tense. Stalin lashed out at his general staff for not knowing what happened at the frontline. Zhukov left the room in tears. 'Clearly, it was only now that Stalin really understood how serious his miscalculations had been regarding the likelihood, the timing, and the consequences of an attack by Germany and its allies', reflected Mikoian later.[2]

At the frontlines, chaos reigned. Michael Goldberg had awoken on 22 June to the thunder of bombing raids on Pinsk. When the family heard Molotov's speech on the radio, announcing that Germany had attacked, his father had few illusions about the fate of Jews: 'That will be the end of us.' Michael joined up, only to find himself in a school building waiting for further instructions. 'Suddenly, we were awakened by an alarm. When we ran outside, we saw the western sky aflame, and heard explosions.' The draftees, still in civilian clothes, were ordered to march east into the night. In the morning, the unarmed men came under fire but managed to link up with a column of motorized sailors.

ILLUSTRATION 7 Germans attack the Soviet Union. 22 June 1941. © Wikimedia Commons (public domain).

'They gave us guns and together we destroyed the German force.' Eventually, they made it to Lunietz where they were stationed at the train station, a target for enemy air strikes. 'By the end of the day, we suffered our first attack from the German planes, with no place to hide. I witnessed a massacre. This was my first war experience.'[3]

The alleged attack on Pinsk which had prompted their march east had been a false alarm (a military base had been bombed by German planes). They were sent back in cattle cars, dislocated in an old church in town, finally given uniforms, but otherwise neglected. 'We had nothing to do and there was still no leadership or training.' Soon, the remaining officers ran away, leaving the recruits rudderless. Seeking instructions from the town's party leadership only yielded the information that soon the town would be under German occupation.

Left to their own devices, most of the soldiers returned to their families. Only twenty-six 'hard-core communists' remained. Goldberg, after some wandering about trying to connect with his family, was arrested as a deserter, liberated after the intervention of the local party leader and, after a conference with his father, returned to these remnants of his unit. His father had convinced him to leave with the army 'as he was sure that due to my political record I would be one of the first to be hanged by the German invaders'. This advice reflected the widespread 'naïve attitude of the townspeople who believed that although the political activists were in danger, the average citizen was not'. Goldberg and his comrades then marched across the bridge out of town, which was blown up behind them.[4]

What followed was a nightmare. After a night of marching, the soldiers found themselves on a road 'filled with hundreds of civilian draftees who had left town before us from different mobilization points'. As the sun rose, the heat increased. It would be a hot day without access to drinking water. German planes controlled the skies and swooped down on the marchers to machine gun them at will. The groups disintegrated into small gaggles. Goldberg was in a group of five.[5]

By nightfall, they reached a village and managed to buy bread and milk and negotiate shelter. Goldberg suffered from blisters on his feet. The pain kept him awake and he left the hut to catch some air.

I then overheard a conversation among several farmers conspiring to later kill the Jewish Communists because they probably carried gold with them! This deed would also earn them commendation from the advancing Germans. I immediately awoke my friends with this news and in the middle of the night we again continued our journey. This episode was another blow to my belief in humans; these farmers were the kind of people who had lived side by side with us for hundreds of years.[6]

Eventually, the stragglers were collected by one of the few remaining officers and sent to a railway station to be shipped east. 'We were loaded on cattle car trains, 50-60 persons to a car and started on a long journey without any provisions or sanitary facilities.' Soon, the echelon had to change direction, as German forces had cut behind its path. The train then stood for days at a station, constantly harassed by Luftwaffe attacks. 'Thus', Goldberg mused, 'many of the draftees never got a chance to participate in the war'. Eventually, the survivors were brought to Orel. Two more weeks of pointless waiting followed, before they were sent to a military training camp in the woods. 'There were no facilities. Our only shelter were the trees.' Rations consisted of smoked herring and black bread. Many were still in civilian clothes. Nobody had a change of underwear and they had not washed since leaving Pinsk. Air attacks resumed and the draftees had nothing to defend themselves against the menace from the skies.[7]

Labour army

Eventually, the soldiers from the former Polish regions were evacuated east in 'our old friends, the cattle car trains', where they joined other deportees. 'I discovered people of different nationalities; Polish, Ukrainian, and Germans born in the Soviet Union, where their families had lived hundreds of years. We figured out that we were all people considered untrustworthy by the Soviet regime.' What he saw during the travel through the old Soviet Union destroyed whatever illusions the young communist had left. 'I discovered the poverty and the terrible conditions of the people in the areas we passed through . . . . They looked like people living in times of centuries past, both in economic and cultural terms. I was shocked at the poverty that still existed so many years after the Revolution.' Goldberg and his comrades travelled for weeks, 'filthy and hungry, fed on rations insufficient for survival', and suffering from a variety of ailments. Finally, they disembarked in Izhevsk in northern Russia, where the soldiers were assigned to the labour army.

The labour army was a 'peculiar phenomenon' which combined 'the mobilization of men and women through the military enlistment offices with militarized formations organized according to a three-tiered structure (labour detachment, labour colony, labour battalion).' It combined 'elements of military service, productive labour, and a Gulag-like detention regime'.[8] Such militarized labour was used for contingents deemed suspicious: Soviet Germans, Romanians, Italians, Finns, Chinese, Koreans, Greeks, Kalmyks and Crimean Tatars were among them, as were many from the western borderlands, altogether some 400,000 people.[9]

Jews from the newly annexed regions belonged to this category between 1941 and 1943. Living in tents in the woods, Goldberg's unit had to build the new factories which would be supplied with the evacuated equipment and workforce from the western edge of the Soviet empire. During their long and arduous workdays they also built their own 'homes' – the ubiquitous *zemlianki*, 'small underground huts', which we have already encountered during the Korean deportations of 1937 and will see again and again in this war. Food was terrible and insufficient. Many swelled from hunger.[10] 'The work was very hard and we were hungry', reported a Bessarabian Jew who was sent to work in a munitions plant in Cheliabinsk. 'We were all sick with malaria, but you had to continue working.'[11] Mortality was high among the labour-soldiers: in 1942, nearly 11 per cent, or 11,874 human beings, died; even with improving conditions in 1944 this number still stood at 2,832 or 3 per cent.[12]

Evacuation and flight

The sufferings of Goldberg's labour battalion were part of the wider effort to save industrial and other assets from the advancing Germans. Whole factories were dismantled and shipped to the hinterland, accompanied by their workforce.

Collective farmers were ordered to pack up their things and herd their cattle east. Evacuation of essential personnel – leading cadres and their families, the workforce of enterprises – as well as the equipment of factories went hand in glove with the preparation to destroy what was left behind. Some evaded evacuation orders, others tried to get themselves onto the trains to safety. Many attempted to flee the advancing Wehrmacht under their own steam. Others stayed put, either because they could not manage to organize transport or because they had small children or elderly family members to look after. Expectations of those who stayed behind varied: some waited for liberation from Bolshevism, others remembered the last German occupation in the First World War, which, compared to the horrors to follow in the Civil War had been relatively benign, and many simply thought they could arrange themselves with any dictatorship.[13]

Already by 15 September, the authorities had registered nearly 2 million evacuees, mostly from Moscow, Ukraine, Belarus and Leningrad, and overwhelmingly women (1.3 million) and children (42 per cent). More than half of them were Russians followed by half a million Jews (a quarter of the total) and 190,000 Ukrainians (about 10 per cent). By 21 October 1941, the overall number had risen to 3.2 million evacuees, the majority of them living now in the Russian Federation.[14] By December, the total reached 5.8 million. Altogether in 1941 and 1942 just below 10 per cent of the pre-war population of the Soviet Union fled or were evacuated: 10.4 million in the first wave from June 1941 to February 1942 and 8 million in the summer of 1942. For many, these were temporary or repeated evacuations, implying that the overall numbers are likely to be lower.[15]

Staying behind was, indeed, the default option: at least 65 per cent of those who lived in the regions overrun by Germany and its allies did so, more likely 77 per cent, between 55 and 65 million people.[16] Even those mobilized by the state to leave with their enterprises, dismantled and to be rebuilt in the east, sometimes refused. Workers who owned houses and had access to garden plots, as many outside the large cities in Ukraine did, were loath to abandon this access to shelter and food for their families for the vagaries of state-support.[17] Likewise, in the cities, 'workers . . . who owned their own homes, refused' to leave, reported Ukraine's Deputy Commissar of the Interior.[18] Conversely, fleeing on one's own steam was extremely difficult. There were few private motor vehicles in the Soviet Union at the time. People who fled by bike or on foot were often overtaken by the fast-moving German spearheads or strafed by airplanes from the skies. Only those who, as part of the Soviet elite, had access to transport, or those who could in one way or another attach themselves to the formally organized evacuation, had a real chance to get away. Young, unattached men were the most likely to succeed. Families with small children were the least successful, if they tried in the first instance.[19] Some of the refugees were picked up by retreating Red Army trucks, even if commanders prohibited taking civilians along. 'The peasant-soldiers', remembered one whose life was saved that way, 'winked to us, and called us in: "The young guys don't understand much of life"', they dismissed their commander's order. 'Tomorrow you will be our soldiers too.' And so, thanks to their disobedience, we were taken into pre-1939 Russia.'[20]

The least agency had prisoners. Places of detention in the path of the German armies were emptied of some 141,000 inmates. Only 21,000 remained behind and another 7,000 were freed during evacuation. Another 1,000 fled during the one or the other confusion and 346 were liberated by 'bandits'. A total of 9,817, however, were shot in the prisons and another 1,443 during the march east. Another 1,000 died for other reasons on the way.[21] While these murders took place within a catastrophic military situation, they followed the same logic as the Katyn executions of 1940 or the mass operations of 1937–8: if in doubt, 'liquidate' possible opponents who might end up siding with the enemy.

Terror

The executions were not always performed as an alternative to impossible evacuation. Take the example of the initial commander of the Soviet forces in the Battle of Lake Khasan in 1938: Georgy Mikhailovich Shtern. Accused of various doctrinal sins, including Trotskyism, as well as participation in the imaginary military conspiracy against Stalin, Shtern had been arrested on 7 June, just two weeks before the Germans attacked. Together with other late victims of the military purge, he was successfully evacuated from Moscow to Kuibyshev, then shot on order of Beria on 28 October.[22] In November, Beria asked Stalin for the authority to shoot another 10,645 prisoners who had been sentenced to death, but whose sentences had not been endorsed by higher judicial authorities. Many of them were located far behind the frontline, in places like Khabarovsk or in Uzbekistan. They were not likely to be occupied by the enemy any time soon. Still, better safe than sorry, thought Beria.[23]

Prisoner executions were not the only moment of Great Terror redux. During the year and a half of military catastrophe, over 30,000 people were executed for counter-revolutionary crimes: 8,001 in 1941, and a staggering 23,278 in 1942. While this spike was nowhere near the nearly 700,000 executions in the Great Terror of 1937–8, it was higher than in any other year between 1922 and 1953. Only during the years of the Civil War had similar numbers been shot.[24]

This new murderousness was driven from the very top. Stalin reacted in characteristic manner to the catastrophe his own policies had caused: he blamed others. On 16 July Stalin signed a secret order accusing the entire leadership of the western front of 'disgracing the title of commander through cowardice, inaction, mismanagement, disruption of command and control, surrender of weapons to the enemy without a fight, and unauthorized abandonment of combat positions'. In a breathtaking example of projection of his own failings, Stalin thus announced that he had arrested the former commander of the Western Front, Dmitry Grigorevich Pavlov, and eight other senior military leaders who had had the bad luck of being in command of troops savaged by the Wehrmacht in the summer of 1941. Pavlov was stripped of his military rank, sentenced to death and shot, as Stalin announced in an order of 28 July.[25]

In addition to such targeted murders, security troops also shot presumed traitors, spies, saboteurs, panic mongers, cowards and deserters: 10,201 by 10 October, a number which needs to be added to the above executions, bringing the accounted for murders to a total in the tens of thousands – to say nothing of those soldiers simply shot by their commanders without trial or reporting. Another 15,000 military personnel were arrested and sentenced to lesser punishments, while well over half a million stragglers were detained but returned to the front.[26]

Executions were only the tip of the iceberg. Together with the mass mobilization to fight and the order to hand in private radio receivers to the authorities (to cut off independent modes of information about the situation), it was 'the wave of arrests' which convinced Soviet citizens in the summer of 1941 'that the war had truly started.'[27] The scale of the repression was truly remarkable. In the years 1941–5 on average 3.2 million people per year were sentenced to prison, labour camp, death or other sentences – up from 1.8 million per annum for the years 1937–40. This wave crested in 1941–2 with 3.4 and 3.6 million sentences.[28]

In the summer of 1941, as little as uttering the undoubtedly true words that 'Germany is a strong state', that the 'German army has already beaten several states', that all the fighting thus far had been on Soviet territory, and that the enemy had 'already taken several of our cities' could earn ten years in concentration camp. These were, in the eyes of the authorities, 'counter-revolutionary, defeatist, slanderous statements directed at lowering the defensive capacity of the Red Army'. The 23-year-old Russian worker-turned-soldier whose loose tongue about the desperate situation sent him to the Gulag was not alone.[29] A wide range of entirely reasonable statements could lead to prosecution for the crime of 'anti-Soviet agitation': the claim that the executions of army officers during the Great Terror had led to an officer shortage; the notion that collectivization had bankrupted the country and had depressed living conditions to such a degree that there were few incentives to fight for the Soviet regime; the assumption that the government arrested innocent people; the analysis that the Hitler–Stalin pact had been ill-advised; or the conviction that Soviet media reports could not be trusted – all these were construed as 'counter-revolutionary fabrications'. Even 'drunken chatter' could lead to repression, 'including the death penalty'.[30]

But repression extended far beyond politics. By November 1941, there were 18,000 former soldiers in the Gulag who had been sentenced for minor offences such as leaving their unit without permission or arriving late. They lived under horrible conditions, as food and warm clothes were insufficient, housing cramped and they could often not be fully employed, which meant they had to live on cut

rations. As a result, the death rate of inmates more than tripled between July and
September 1941.[31]

The origins of catastrophe

While Stalin thus blamed others, later Soviet historians appealed to the superiority
of the Germans. In fact, however, the catastrophe of the summer of 1941 was
caused by neither. To begin with what one historian has called the 'myth of German
superiority': together, the three German army groups included 3.5 million men,
more than 3,000 tanks, 600,000 other motorized vehicles, 7,000 artillery pieces and
above 2,700 aircraft. The Germans were aided in the south by Romanian, Slovakian
and Italian forces and in the north by Finland, which began its 'continuation war'
against the Soviet Union on 25 June. A day later, Hungary added some 25,000
men, who became part of Army Group South. Later in the year, Croatian troops
joined the German effort, as did volunteers from all over Western Europe, most
famously the Spanish 'Blue Division'. Throughout the campaign, nearly 4 million
foreign troops would serve at the side of the Wehrmacht in the Soviet Union, just
under a quarter of them from Western and Northern Europe, the rest equally
distributed between Soviet and East European collaborators.[32]

Hitler thus mustered an awesome strike-force, but so did the Soviets
(Illustration 8): nearly 5 million men, 77,000 artillery pieces, more than 22,000
tanks and around 20,000 combat planes. Of course, not all of these soldiers and
not all of the material were available in the west: the possible eastern front against
Japan continued to command the Soviet military's attention. Nevertheless, with
about half of the total fighting force deployed at the western front, the Soviets
still matched the Germans. What aided the Germans in the summer of 1941 was
their tactical superiority based on excellent training and the routine acquired in
fighting since 1939.[33]

The Soviets, by contrast, were poorly prepared for the attack, as Stalin had
refused to let the soldiers do the obvious until the eleventh hour. Much of their
equipment was outdated, deployed in the wrong places and poorly maintained.
Many of the crews were insufficiently trained. Some of the best commanders had
perished in the Great Terror and their replacements were still finding their feet.
The bulk of the soldiers were peasants, who saw little to defend in Stalin's Soviet
Union, which had forced them into collective farms from 1929, had done nothing
to save them from starvation in 1932–3, and continued to squeeze them to create
strategic grain reserves throughout the decade. 'The basic topics of conversation
between soldiers', wrote Konstantin Petrovich Bunin, a recently mobilized professor
marching among 40–50-year-old peasants, 'is that they are treated as cannon
fodder, that they walk like lambs to the slaughter'. They planned to surrender
at the first possibility and did not believe the reports in the Soviet press about
German mistreatment of POWs. They disrespected their commanders, who were

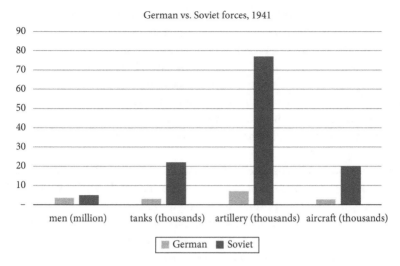

German vs. Soviet forces, 1941

ILLUSTRATION 8 German vs. Soviet forces, 1941.

'in reality still boys, straight from the school-bench'. Having to lead completely untrained soldiers into battle, they resorted to threatening the much older men with execution and yelled expletives at them. The overwhelming majority of the soldiers did not have 'modern combat training', Bunin pointed out. 'I also have never shot a rifle in my life.'[34]

Such troops confronted an enemy who controlled the skies, encircled Soviet troops in massive pincers, and then mopped up the resulting 'cauldrons' with lethal systematicity. No wonder that in the summer and fall of 1941, surrender was a mass phenomenon. During this first half year of the war with the Soviets, the Wehrmacht made 58 per cent of the total number of prisoners they would capture throughout the war. The Germans also encountered more defectors than anywhere else: men who did more than just passively surrender, but actively crossed the frontline to escape Stalin's war machine and at times to fight on the side of the Germans.[35]

Relentless counter-attack

Within the collapse, the disorientation, the defeatism, the despair and the desperate hope for a better life without Stalin, an entirely different war was fought, however. From the first days of the German attack elements of the Red Army fought bravely, tenaciously and aggressively. 'Enemy retreats only after tough resistance', reported the German fifty-sixth Infantry Division on 25 June from Army Group South. Red Army units did not just hold their positions. They counter-attacked. Relentlessly. 'Enemy fights doggedly and answers our infantry attacks with immediate counter-attacks', reported the seventy-ninth Infantry Division on 13 July 1941. Notwithstanding moments of panic, 1941 was no rout, but a fighting retreat. 'The enemy is in full retreat, which is secured by courageously led and bravely fighting rear-guards', reported the fifty-sixth Infantry Division on 28 June.[36] Even during cauldron battles, when incredible masses of prisoners were made in short periods of time, resistance did not cease. 'Despite the continuously tightening ring', reads one German report from the final days of the battle of Kyiv in September 1941, 'the surrounded enemy . . . fights doggedly and with grim determination. He continues to attempt to break through despite lacking artillery support.'[37]

It was the same everywhere: collapse, disorganization, lack of leadership, untrained troops and mass surrenders; at the same time: incredibly hard resistance. 'The enemy opposite us is a surprisingly active and tough guy', wrote Gotthard Heinrici, a German general with the apt nickname 'poison dwarf' to his wife from Army Group Centre on 30 July. 'He attacked the 134th Division early in the morning. . . . Seventy-five defectors approached us some time later. It is almost incomprehensible and always the same: on the whole the Russian fights with fanatical tenacity.'[38] And on 1 August, with rising anxiety, he put the following to paper:

We have all underestimated the Russian. It was always said that his leaders are pathetic. Well, they have proved their leadership skills. . . . A tremendous energy ruthlessly mobilizes all their forces and deploys them without mercy. . . . Our losses are substantial.[39]

The fighting was of a brutality the Germans had not encountered elsewhere. As one German soldier recounted the experience in early November 1941:

The heavy machine gun nearby burned belt after belt of gleaming ammunition through the feed tray, spent cartridges pouring from the hot receiver in an endless stream. Detonating mortar rounds erupted on the stony ground fifty meters before our defenses as our mortar teams behind us attempted to stem the advancing waves falling on us. Slowly the assault broke against our lines. The open ground before us was littered with the dark forms of the dead and dying. Only the cries of the wounded could be heard through the ringing in our ears . . .

Within minutes we again faced another onslaught, and the sun climbed above the horizon to reveal the full horror of the battlefield. . . . Over the din I heard the machine gunner cry, 'I can't just keep on killing' as he squeezed the trigger and held it tightly, sending a stream of bullets from the smoking MG barrel into the masses of attackers.[40]

A Soviet battalion commander remembered how such coerced attacks looked from other side of the trenches. His soldiers were partially unarmed and expected to acquire weapons from their dead comrades. They were urged forward by political officers armed with convincing arguments: pistols. Nevertheless, as the shelling started, most of the soldiers threw themselves to the ground and neither their commander's orders nor the political officers' obscenities, threats and kicks managed to get them up again. When German artillery began hitting the defenceless soldiers, panic ensued. People tried to escape every which way, only to be shot dead or ripped apart by explosives. Many raised their arms and tried to give up, but the Germans machine-gunned them; white flags did not help the aspiring POWs either. They were shot in cold blood.[41]

But not all counter-attacks were coerced. There were some highly motivated soldiers who fought extremely aggressively in 1941 without anybody forcing them to. Nachman Dushanski's combat group was one example. A Lithuanian Jew born in 1919 and a communist since he had joined the underground Lithuanian Communist Youth League at age fourteen, Dushanski had gone to prison for his politics only to be freed when the Soviets took over his country in June 1940. By the time of the German attack, he served in a counter-intelligence unit of the border guards, already a veteran of the security services: In 1940–1, he had caught border crossers ('We often had to shoot.'), enjoyed a holiday on Crimea, courtesy of the security organs, and was shipped back to Lithuania on 18 June, part of the last-minute scramble to get ready for the likely German attack. As the train rolled into the station during the night of 21–2 June, a nearby airfield was already under attack by the Luftwaffe. After what he learned later was an unsuccessful attempt to evacuate his parents, his group of security service troops fought a determined retreat from Lithuania to Russia in the summer of 1941. He survived with a shell fragment in his leg. 'The Germans were right to call us "communist fanatics"', he told a historian shortly before his death in Israel in 2008. 'None of us died in vain in June, and we avenged every one of our dead comrades.'[42]

Dushanski's group was typical: there were many in the Red Army in 1941 who fought with grim determination against the Nazi invaders. When German infantry, supported by tanks, penetrated Natan Gimelfarb's trench, his platoon leader, Lieutenant Ivan Skiba gave the order 'Beat the Fritzes, boys!', before throwing himself onto a 'healthy looking German who was shooting down our soldiers'.

With a blow of his sapper shovel to the giant's head he took care of him, immediately turning to another, whose machine pistol already pointed at Naum Dorfman. The red-haired German collapsed after the shovel's blade ripped into his neck. But the dying man's gun still discharged, killing Naum and his inseparable friend and protector Josef Boguslavsky.

Nearby, Lieutenant Skiba 'finished off the wounded' Germans 'with blows to the head'.[43]

Similar scenes played themselves out during the Battle of Moscow in December. Embittered Red Army men were sent on a bayonet attack during the engagement

ILLUSTRATION 9 Red Army soldiers at frontline near Leningrad, 1941. © Library of Congress (public domain).

at the village of Padikovo. Most of them were not equipped with cold weapons on their rifles, however, so they 'beat the Germans with their rifle butts, and once those broke, they beat them with their fists'.[44]

There were countless such counter-attacks, big and small. And there were major battles which the German generals portrayed as unambiguous victories after the war, to uphold their claim that they would have won the war if not for Hitler's interference, the mud or the cold. In reality, Germany lost the war as early as the battle of Smolensk, which raged from early July to nearly the middle of September. The Red Army's determined resistance, and the brutal counteroffensive of Yelnia, decisively delayed their advance into the Soviet heartland.[45]

When counter-attacks failed to stop the enemy, the Red Army scorched the soil it abandoned. In his radio address of 3 July 1941, Stalin demanded to leave nothing behind, 'not one locomotive, not one train car, . . . not a kilogram grain, not a litre of fuel'.[46] The Soviets evacuated whole villages, scorched the houses, transported factories east and blew up what had to be left behind. 'When we retreat', reported one participant, 'we destroy everything left behind, even warehouses full of valuables, even the crops, while the populace simply looks on. They beg, give it to us, don't burn it, we will die of starvation! But that would be going against orders. So we do what we must, and everything goes up in smoke!'[47] German soldiers regularly encountered the resulting wastelands and at times initial calm turned into hell. Such was the case in Kyiv in late September, when the apparently unharmed city began to blow up around them as time bombs exploded and booby traps activated.

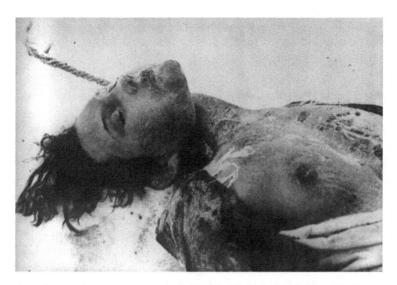

ILLUSTRATION 10 Zoia Kosmodemianskaia's body, as it was found by the Soviets in 1942. The Kommunist Youth League member had been sent behind the frontline in 1941 to burn down villages where German soldiers had taken refuge. The Germans tortured and then executed her. Her body was hanging in the middle of the village for over a month. Kosmodemianskaia would become one of the most popular heroines of Soviet wartime propaganda. © Wikimedia Commons (public domain).

The most famous implementer of Stalin's scorched earth order was the teenager Zoia Kosmodemianskaia. The 18-year-old had volunteered via the Moscow Communist Youth League, of which she was a member. In late November 1941 she was sent across the frontline with orders to burn villages where German troops had taken shelter from the cold. Armed with fuel bottles and a handgun, she managed to infiltrate one village and burn down three houses, which led to the death of twenty horses and one German soldier as well as the destruction of rifles and other equipment. She was caught when attempting to continue the job with a fourth hut. The Germans flogged her savagely, marched her around the snow for hours without shoes on until her feet were severely frostbitten, and eventually strung her up in the centre of the village. The Germans let her hang there for a month and a half, a sign reading 'Arsonist' around her neck as a warning to others. After liberation of the village her story quickly advanced to become one of the most celebrated examples of Soviet heroism. Villagers reported that when asked during interrogation where Stalin was, she answered 'Stalin is at his post!' and when she was dragged to the gallows, she had addressed the crowd with the words: 'Comrades! Victory will be ours!' She also exhorted the Germans to surrender: 'It's not too late.' There is no reason to doubt her devotion to the cause of Stalin: she was part of the hard core of supporters who made much of the difference in 1941. But the story was also more complex than later propaganda made it. Some villagers, whose houses had been burned to the ground by the partisan, abused her before her death, angry at their homelessness in the fierce Russian winter. The majority remained mute.[48]

Catastrophe

Rather than standing on feet of clay, then, the Soviet colossus stood firm, retreated reluctantly, fighting tooth and nail. The chances of the Wehrmacht defeating the Soviets thus became slimmer and slimmer. They had never been great in the first place. The Soviet empire was also a country extremely hard to fight in. The summers were scorching hot, and the winters icy cold. The distances were enormous: 580 kilometres from Brest to Kyiv; 700 kilometres from Vilna to Leningrad; 400 kilometres from Smolensk to Moscow. The roads were bad and became muddy in autumn and spring. The railroads ran on a different gauge than in Europe, were few and far between, and much of the track had been destroyed by the scorched-earth commandos. Wehrmacht enthusiasts often forget that the famed mechanized divisions were a minority in this army. The majority was still moving like their predecessors in the nineteenth century: as far as possible by rail, then by foot, carrying their personal equipment, their supplies and artillery hauled by horses. At the start of the campaign, the Germans mustered between 600,000 and 750,000 of them, as many or more than motor vehicles. As the campaign dragged on and trucks broke down, Hitler's soldiers became even more dependent on literal horsepower.[49]

For most of the invading force, this war was a nightmare of marching and fighting, of hunger, thirst and sweat, of aching legs, of blistered feet forever stuck in army boots. 'The infantry continued to march from sunrise to sunset', remembered one German veteran later. 'Dusty, sweaty, and clammy without relief from the brutal climate, we penetrated deeper into Soviet Russia.' The first encounters with the enemy – frightening at the time – seemed insignificant in retrospect, 'little indication of the nightmarish years of fighting marked by deprivation, sorrow, and countless victims that lay before us.' As summer turned into autumn, and the roads turned into mud, German soldiers began to realize 'that we were being consumed by this foreign land'.[50]

That the Germans nevertheless made progress, albeit slower than they had expected, was due to Stalin's botched war preparations. The army had been caught unaware in the middle of a major reform and during a large-scale redeployment. The newly acquired territories in the west had done little to stop the Germans. Army Group Centre overran Western Belarus in six days, taking Belostok on 27 June and Minsk on the following day. Army Group North reached the old eastern border of Latvia and Estonia between 4 and 11 July. Further north, the Finns moved slower through the marshes of Karelia, but reached the old border on 3 September. And in the south, the former Romanian and Polish territories were taken by the end of July.[51] And the advance continued to the gates of Leningrad and Moscow. Kyiv was lost along with the rest of Ukraine: some of the richest and most productive agricultural and industrial regions of Stalin's realm.

1941 was the worst military catastrophe of the Russian empire since Napoleon had taken Moscow in 1812. It was far worse that what tsarism had suffered in 1915–16, defeats which had triggered revolution, the fall of the Romanovs and the disintegration of their realm. Many on both sides of the frontline thought that something similar was in the offering now. By the end of the year, the pre-war army of 4.8 million had been wiped out: according to Soviet statistics, 1.3 million were wounded or sick, and 3.1 million were dead, missing in action, or captured by the enemy.[52] German numbers suggest even higher casualties.

'Long live Hitler!'

And yet, Stalin's regime did not buckle. This had been one German hope: that the story of 1917–18 would repeat itself, when Germany had won the war in the east, and occupied Ukraine, Belarus and the Baltics – all because the enemy's army had melted away in the chaos of revolutions and civil wars. Not so this time: the Soviet Union did not disintegrate, the government did not crumble, revolution did not break out. This result was partially due to people like Kosmodemianskaia, Dushanski and Skiba: highly motivated and ready to defend the Soviet Union cost what may. However, they were a minority in 1941. As we will see in more detail in Chapter 5, mobilization to work and fight was more important than volunteering. As time went on, the core of support surrounding Stalin's regime would grow in reaction to German brutality, its exploitation by a sophisticated Soviet propaganda campaign, and the realization that the Soviet Union was winning the war (see Chapter 7).

In 1941, by contrast, there was widespread opposition to Soviet mobilization, even moments of rebellion: in the Baltic republics, local guerrillas attacked retreating Red Army units, scorched earth commandos and garrisons.[53] In the Northern Bukovina, members of the Organization of Ukrainian Nationalists killed Soviet officials the moment the Red Army retreated, only to move on to killing Jews once the Germans arrived.[54] Overall, in 1941–4 over 7,000 armed gangs with some 54,000 participants operated all over the Soviet Union.[55]

In the south of Stalin's realm, resistance was particularly rife. In the Chechen-Ingush republic mass desertion of local functionaries paralyzed the administration. By the end of the year, most collective farms had been dissolved by the locals. Evasion of conscription was rampant. It grew in lockstep with the German threat. In August 1941, nearly 9 per cent of those called to the colours in Chechnya-Ingushetia failed to report to duty. By January 1942, this share had risen to 50 per cent. In the spring of 1942, out of 14,000 Chechens called up only some 4,000 reported and more than half of these would desert shortly thereafter. Overall, between 1941 and 1944, nearly 88 per cent of those conscripted in the region failed to comply with mobilization orders. Many of those who ran from the mobilization officers joined the armed resistance in the mountains, a phenomenon which preceded the German invasion. A 'small-scale, fragmented insurgency' had kept parts of the republic 'in permanent turmoil'. Over 1,500 insurgents and 'bandits' had been arrested or killed between 1937 and 1940. Now, German successes emboldened the guerrillas. By the end of 1941, every village in Chechnya had its small band of armed guerrillas. A major anti-conscription uprising erupted in October–November 1941 and had to be suppressed by Soviet troops supported by air power. Local uprisings continued to smoulder thereafter. By 1944, the Soviet security forces would capture or kill over 12,000 guerrillas. The counter-insurgency was exceptionally brutal and included the razing of villages, the execution of women and children and the burning down of houses. The government would eventually order the deportation of every single Chechen and Ingush in 1944. This operation, too, was more brutal than elsewhere. 'Untransportable' victims were shot on the spot. In at least one instance, hundreds of villagers were 'locked in a stable and burned alive'.[56] Further east, in Central Asia's Kyrgyzstan, a major but still little-known rebellion broke out in 1942. It too, had to be put down with force of arms.[57]

Elsewhere, resistance was less organized, but nevertheless ubiquitous. In Ukraine, peasants refused to herd their cattle east; workers resisted evacuation and prevented the destruction of their plants by scorched-earth teams.[58] Red Army men hailing from the newly acquired regions left their posts and went home, but soldiers from pre-1939 Soviet Ukraine deserted, too, reasoning that the Bolsheviks had 'sucked our blood for twenty-five years, enough already!' A group of 200 soldiers, including an outspoken Siberian, 'decided to force our way back, at all cost, toward the Germans'. When army commissars tried to stop them, '[w]e killed them and moved on'.[59] This group was not extraordinary, as defection to the enemy was a massive phenomenon in 1941. Those who actively sought to go over to the Germans came from all ethnicities and all walks of life. While non-Russian minorities were over-represented and the majority were from the labouring classes and from lower military rank, the largest group was indeed Russian. Members of all classes and military ranks could be found among defectors. There are no clear numbers for 1941, but the most conservative estimates for the entire war range from a conservative 119,000 to more likely tallies between 0.25 and 0.3 million.[60] Desertion and draft evasion was an even larger phenomenon, encompassing at least 1.5 million people throughout the war.[61]

Further East, collective farmers in the old (pre-1939) territories greeted the German 'liberators' in some localities, while displaying a 'wait-and-see' attitude in others.[62] Defeatism was widespread.[63] 'The war is lost', was a typical statement from the summer of 1941; 'the Red Army is in ruins and flees from the Germans on all fronts.'[64] Such attitudes shaded into more aggressive opposition at times. One man from Leningrad region threatened an official bearing a mobilization order with a revolver, yelling, 'I will not fight for Soviet Power, I will fight for Hitler!'[65] On the same day, in Moscow, workers celebrated: 'Good, the war's begun', they said, 'they'll kill the Jews'.[66] In Ivanovo, an old Russian centre of worker resistance, strikes broke out in late August and early September, and then again in October, when preparations for the dismantling and evacuation of the machinery were made. Officials were beaten, and workers discussed if life would be better under Hitler or Stalin. 'All you communists will be hung', threatened one striker. 'We won't allow you to take the machines', exclaimed another, 'let them remain for Hitler and we will work for him'. A third added: 'Down with Soviet power, long live little father Hitler.'[67]

Meanwhile, in Moscow, a panic had broken out on 16 October, when much of the state administration suddenly evacuated to Kuibyshev.[68] The most important inhabitant – embalmed Lenin – had already been brought to Tyumen in early July, but now the living representatives of the regime followed.[69] 'As military vehicles go towards the west', observed the Commissar for Aviation Industry, 'civilian cars drive east, packed to capacity with people, bundles, suitcases, spare cans of gasoline'.[70] While the dead leader left in secret, the fleeing functionaries and their families were all too visible. They were accosted by mobs shouting 'beat the Jews', pulled out of their cars and assaulted, their belongings scattered about and often 'confiscated' by the crowd. The old equation of 'Jew' and 'Bolshevik', which had emerged during the Civil War, was clearly alive and well before the Nazis could reinforce this stereotype with their own propaganda. 'Comrade Perventsev', one of the crowd explained to a famous Soviet writer, a Cossack, why they let him go and not others: 'we're looking for yids and we beat them.'[71] News of the 'massive beating up of Jews' in Moscow quickly spread at the frontline, where the state's enforcement agencies arrested soldiers voicing their discontent.[72]

The peasant majority in Russia, Ukraine and Belarus was particularly ill-disposed towards Stalin's regime. Throughout the 1930s, rumour had predicted war with the outside world, a welcome apocalypse to bring liberation from collective farms and communists.[73] Such sentiments did not disappear once Armageddon materialized. During the dark days of October 1941, quartermaster-technician of the First Rank Golosov remarked: 'The peasantry will not fight for Russia, because it has been ruined by the collective farms.'[74] Rank-and-file soldiers expressed similar sentiments during the first months of the war,[75] and in 1942, the soldier Doronin noted that it 'would be better if we were living now as we lived before 1929. As soon as they introduced the *kolkhoz* policy everything went wrong. I ask myself – what are we fighting for? What is there to defend?' Frontline soldiers complained 'about the collective farms, and how it was necessary to sweep them all away when the war was won'.[76] Knowing of such moods, generals approached even top party leaders, such as Nikita Khrushchev, advising 'that soldiers wouldn't die for land that they didn't actually own'.[77]

People not only talked. During the early phases of German occupation of Leningrad region, when Soviet control had collapsed but not yet replaced by its German equivalent, the spontaneous 'dissolution of *kolkhozi* from below' was widespread.[78] In another sector of the old Soviet heartland, Kalinin region to the north-west of Moscow, in November 1941, even Communist Party members distributed collective farm animals.[79] In Riazan, to the capital's south-east, the two weeks of German presence from late in that month, amounted to 'a period of . . . non-control' of the rural population. Peasants disbanded the majority of collective farms 'in a matter of days'. The unloved farms thus turned into 'the property of individual farmers'. The behaviour of rural people in spaces not controlled by either the Stalinists or the Nazis, concludes a leading historian, showed that 'peasants neither supported Soviet authority nor sought inclusion in the new German order'.[80] Most simply wanted to be left alone by ideological busybodies and get on with their lives. For many others, 'fear and uncertainty . . . overshadowed questions of political loyalties and patriotism'.[81]

There was even resistance in the Gulag in anticipation of German victory. Inmates from the western borderlands were particularly active. 'Hitler already stands 40 kilometers from Moscow', exclaimed a Latvian inmate 'soon we'll take rifles in our hands and come to his aid.'[82] But such 'new Soviets' were not isolated in the world of the Gulag: rumours of German victories and hopes for liberation were rife in the camp system in the fall of 1941. By 1944, the security organs claimed to have found 603 resistance groups totalling 4,640 people. A total of 10,087 camp inmates were sentenced to death as a result. Of course, we cannot take these numbers at face value, given the Stalinist tendency to invent conspiracies, but the existence of actual conspiracies in the Gulag is 'beyond doubt' as a leading scholar writes.[83] 'Decidedly fantastic plans were forged', remembered one Gulag survivor who dreamt about escaping both the Stalinist and the Germans and somehow make it from the Russian Far North to Scandinavia. 'The point of them always was the question of arming the prisoners and overpowering the guards.'[84]

Some went beyond planning. On 24 January 1942, an uprising broke out in the Gulag camp in Vorkuta, 'one of the most remarkable acts of mass resistance in the history of the Gulag'. The rebels were all from the 'old' Soviet Union and had planned their coup meticulously. According to the later police investigation, they intended to start a larger uprising to help the Germans, but according to their historian, they most likely tried to escape the mass shootings they expected were imminent because of the war – not an unreasonable expectation as we have seen. Led by a former inmate turned prison guard, they disarmed their guards, freed other prisoners, broke open the store-houses to supply themselves and left the camp. They attempted to take over the nearby town. They cut the phone lines and captured several strategic points, including the communications office. Soon, the first fire-fight with government forces killed nine of the rebels and wounded one. Sixty-one were captured or gave up. The remaining forty-one fled on sleds. On 28 January, the escapees won a battle with security forces before splitting up into smaller groups to try to get away. The last of the commandos was only mopped up in early March.[85]

The Gulag thus could become the basis for the organization of small groups rebelling against the official order of things in the context of the German successes. However, the significant number of individuals, both inside and outside the Gulag, who held grudges, nursed oppositional sentiments, and indulged themselves in fantasies about liberation from Bolshevism could not merge into a revolutionary challenge to Stalinism: there was nobody who could coordinate the opposition. The Great Terror had seen to that. 'If you went around to the factories now, people would rise up immediately and dismantle the Kremlin rock by rock', exclaimed one anti-Stalinist during the Moscow panic. But nobody went to organize people. 'You're right, nobody is', conceded the would-be revolutionary.[86] Where oppositional organizations existed – such as in the Caucasus, the Baltics, and Western Ukraine – they were too focused on their own region and too xenophobic to make common cause with anybody else.

Tenacity

And in Moscow, Stalin continued to hold the reins of power. 'Well, no big deal', he shrugged when told about the breakdown of order in Moscow on the 16th. 'I thought, it would be worse.'[87] True, he had both a train and a plane ready to whisk him away, but the news that he remained in the capital boosted the morale of pro-regime elements in the population. ('Stalin is at his post!' spat a defiant Kosmodemianskaia at her German torturers, repeating a prominent propaganda slogan.) The Man of Steel did have a short moment of nerves soon after his outburst about how they had 'shat all over' Lenin's legacy. He had holed himself up in his dacha outside Moscow pondering his next steps. His visitor book in the Kremlin remained empty on 30 June.[88] Some historians think he expected arrest, others believe that he gave his underlings a chance to show their loyalty. In any case, he knew that he was to blame for what had happened, and that it might cost him his job (and with it possibly his life). He said as much once the war was won, in a speech on 24 May 1945: 'Our government made quite a few mistakes', he admitted, remembering the 'desperate situation' at the start of the war. As the Red Army abandoned village after village, town after town in Ukraine, Belarus, Moldavia, the Leningrad region, the Baltics and the Karelo-Finnish republic, people 'might have said to the government: you have not fulfilled our expectations, go away, we'll put together a different government.'[89]

That such a revolution did not happen had little to do with the loyalty of 'the people', as the dictator claimed. In Stalin's totalitarian system, popular disaffection could not translate into power. The only people who had the ability to remove Stalin were his closest associates. But the members of the dictator's governing team could not yet conceive of themselves apart from their 'master'. And so they came to his dacha and begged him to come back, take the reins of power in his hands again and steer them out of this crisis. Stalin, the main culprit for the mess they were in, graciously accepted.

5 RECOVERY, 1941-2

Centralization

The scheme the dictator's underlings had dreamed up in his absence amounted to a further centralization of power. Until recently, Stalin had only been general secretary – the boss of the Communist Party. Viacheslav Molotov had served as chairman of the Council of People's Commissars (Sovnarkom – the Soviet government). In May 1941, Stalin had taken over this position as well, now officially serving as head of both the government and the party. In addition, of course, Stalin had long controlled, via the commissar for Internal Affairs, the secret police on which his rule of terror was based. After the German attack, Stalin's formal powers were further enhanced. On 30 June 1941 he became chairman of the newly founded State Committee of Defense (GKO). Over the course of the war with Germany, he would amass new titles: Commissar of Defense (July 1941), Supreme Commander of the Armed Forces (August 1941), Marshall of the Soviet Union (1943) and finally 'Generalissimus' as well as Hero of the Soviet Union (1945). But the mainspring of his power during the war remained the all-powerful GKO.

The GKO presided over all aspects of the political system. It brought together the state and party hierarchies and directed, via the highest military organ (Stavka), the armed forces. Besides Stalin, the members of the GKO included Molotov, Kliment Voroshilov, Georgy Malenkov and Lavrenty Beria – Stalin's kitchen cabinet. Other close members of Stalin's team were added later: Nikolai Voznesensky and Anastas Mikoyan on 3 February 1942, followed by Lazar Kaganovich on 20 February. On 22 November 1944, Voloshilov was replaced by Nikolai Bulganin.[1]

The GKO was a body of trouble shooters. GKO members or their delegates would be sent out to wherever a problem occurred – be it in food production, tank manufacture or a sector of the front. It was plenipotentiaries who organized the evacuation of factories to the east, away from the German menace; it was plenipotentiaries who held together the wartime state.[2] The war effort was a collective effort – team Stalin's 'finest hour'.[3] In February 1942, the division of labour within the GKO was fixed thus: Molotov was in charge of the production of weapons, Malenkov was to have an eye on the mortar forces and Beria was to make sure their mortars were produced in sufficient quantity and of acceptable quality. Together, Malenkov and Beria oversaw the production of aircraft and the Soviet air force more generally. Voznesensky was to solve any problems in the production of ammunition. Mikoian was responsible for Red Army supplies.[4]

Looking after their realms of concern, the GKO members were constantly on the move – fixing a problem here, plugging a bottleneck there, threatening a wavering commander somewhere else. A little army of lower ranking officials not part of the decision-making core of GKO did much the same. Stalin, with Molotov at his side, stayed put in Moscow, keeping an eye on everybody and making sure his underlings performed. Throughout the entire war he travelled very little: two trips close to the frontline, largely for propaganda reasons (October 1941 and August 1943); and the somewhat reluctant attendance of three major wartime conferences: Teheran (1943), Yalta and Potsdam (both 1945). Apart from these exceptions, he only shuttled back and forth between Moscow and his suburban dacha in Kuntsevo.[5]

Stalin remained fixed in an empire on the move, the eye of the storm of the wartime years, the only one not ever displaced by this war. His deputies, meanwhile, were in for an exhausting schedule. Lev Mekhlis, for one, Head of the Political Administration of the Red Army, never stood still in the first period of the war: in June and July he harangued people at the western front, in August he threated commanders at the central front, in September and October he made sure the army did its job at the north-western front before moving on to berate military staff of the reserve army and then again on the western front.[6]

Even the officers in the General Staff were constantly en route to and from the various frontlines. As one of them reported in his memoirs:

Contrary to established tradition, Stalin believed that a good staff officer would never let him down as a commander, and that to be a proper staff officer one must know life in the field. For this reason were all without exception sent out to the fronts very often and sometimes for long spells. This practice did, in some instances, noticeably deplete the General Staff and create additional difficulties in the day-to-day work.

At the top-level, representatives of Stalin, such as Georgy Zhukov or Aleksandr Vasilevsky, would fly into Moscow to report to the dictator, only to be asked 'as soon as he saw' them, 'how soon they intended going out to the front again.'[7]

Decentralization

Stalin's main job, meanwhile, was to motivate his people and keep them accountable. He was good at the task. In July 1942, he gave Nikolai Baibakov his marching orders. The GKO plenipotentiary for the delivery of fuel to the front was to go to the Caucasus and make sure that Soviet oil would not fall into the hands of the advancing enemy. 'If you leave even one ton of oil behind for the Germans to take', Stalin warned, 'we will shoot you. But if you destroy the oil fields, and the enemy does not manage to conquer this territory, and we will be left without oil ourselves', he added, 'we will shoot you as well'. Baibakov protested that Stalin did not give him any real choice, but the dictator disagreed: 'Young man', he told the 31-year-old functionary, 'there is a choice here. You fly down there, and . . . decide on the ground what to do and when to do it.' Baibakov did as he was told.[8]

The plenipotentiary system, then, relied on initiative and judgment of individuals, that is, on a significant de-centralization, empowering the dictator's team as well as officialdom more generally. It turned out that one could not deal with the catastrophe of the war with the tools of the totalitarian dictatorship as it had emerged after the Great Terror. Instead of deferring to the dictator, people like Baibakov had to reach decisions on the spot. In this system, empowered individuals circled like satellites around the stationary centre of the system: Stalin. It was this Janus-faced process of centralization and decentralization which allowed the war effort to continue under catastrophic conditions.

This decentralization extended far beyond the top of the system. In the GKO, Mikoian was making sure that the Red Army had the food, weapons and other supplies it needed, but nobody was put in charge of feeding the civilian population. This responsibility devolved down the hierarchy. The top body for the distribution of food to civilians was the Commissariat for Trade, which now effectively became the commissariat for rationing. Its head, Aleksandr Liubimov, was not part of the leadership group in GKO, and his administration remained outside its direct overview. His commissariat distributed food stocks through a centralized system including central, union republic, regional and city levels, from where they supplied enterprises and local distribution centres (stores). At first, it covered only Moscow, Leningrad and a few provinces, but by November 1941 most of the urban population was included. The peasantry, however, was left out of the system which, in 1942–3 covered at best 48 per cent of the population. Moreover, even those subject to rationing received only 79 per cent of their calories from central stocks in 1942, a share that fell to 68 per cent by 1944. The remainder came from 'local resources'. These included farms run by enterprises that also attempted to procure food directly from producers, gardens tended by workers and the collective farm markets. The latter – 'kolkhoz markets' – had been legal since the early 1930s, allowing collectivized peasants to sell surplus

ILLUSTRATION 11 Ration cards in Leningrad, 1941–2. Food rationing was an essential part of the resource mobilization which allowed the Soviet Union to win the Second World War in Europe. © Alexander Demianchuk / Getty Images.

produce from their private market gardens, which they tended in addition to the collective fields which produced for the state. Purchase on kolkhoz markets made up nearly half of these crucial local food sources during the war, which made 'the difference between starvation and survival'.[9] As a celebratory Soviet history of food supply put it: 'One of the specific features of the war economy in the USSR was the preservation of a market, where the producers of agricultural products could freely sell them.'[10]

The main food distributed by the state, meanwhile, was bread. Only 46 per cent of calories from other sources (meat, fish, fats, vegetables) in 1942 came from central stocks, 23 per cent from individual gardens and 19 per cent from purchase on the farm markets. By 1944, a quarter of these foods were grown by families and another quarter bought on the market. Moreover, in reality the role of local and non-state sources was significantly larger than these numbers imply, as the official tallies over-stated state-controlled stocks. They 'did not account for large gaps between what the Commissariat of Trade planned to supply and what local trade organizations actually received', as one historian has pointed out. 'Bakery stoppages, adulteration, decrease in quality, small-scale pilfering, large-scale embezzlement, wastage, spoilage, and other chronic problems' further depleted what was actually available through state supply.[11]

The crisis became acute by early 1942, when the government had to admit that central stocks were insufficient to feed even the urban population. Hence more of food production and distribution was delegated downwards, becoming the domain of regional and city administrations, enterprise directors and indeed families. Factories grew their own food in company gardens to feed their workforce; they struck deals with local farms to receive food; trade unions parcelled out land to families, so they could feed themselves. Everywhere one looked in the cities and towns of the wartime Soviet Union gardening and gardens proliferated as a means for survival as centralized food distribution to civilians became more and more strained. In 1940 4.1 million city dwellers had a total of 295.3 thousand hectares of private gardens at their disposal; by 1944 it was 10.4 million people and 755 thousand hectares.[12] In the extreme case of besieged Leningrad, public parks were transformed into cabbage and potato fields. In the villages, too, private plots began to grow beyond the legally permitted, but authorities turned a blind eye: as long as the workforce of women, old men and children delivered the required food for the Red Army, the villagers were allowed to feed themselves and also market produce in nearby towns.

The subsidiary market mechanisms that had enabled the command economy to function already during the 1930s, thus, expanded dramatically. The civilian population of the wartime Soviet Union was fed, clothed and otherwise supplied to a significant extent by the market. The urban population's income from the sale of 'goods and services' to the rural population grew from 1.3 billion in 1941 to 34.6 billion in 1942 to reach 111.4 billion in 1943. Meanwhile, city dwellers spent 17.7 billion on the collective farm markets in 1941, 51.6 billion in 1942 and 127.4 billion in 1943. Prices on the kolkhoz markets increased more than thirteen times between 1940 and 1943, and while they began to decline thereafter, by 1945 they still stood at five and a half times their 1940 level. And the date collected by the authorities of course did not reflect interactions with illegal middlemen, that is, buying and selling on the black market.[13]

Gardening and the growing reach of markets were only two symptoms of the increasing dispersion of power in the wartime Soviet Union. In the 'decentralizing dictatorship' or the war years, local officials gained far-reaching powers. The heads of local government – the party secretaries of regions or cities – 'became regional dictators', as a recent study of wartime administration has it. 'Local party and governmental administrations acted both as regional "state planning committees" and as independent governments. Not only did they regulate resource flows, they also changed the production plans of enterprises.' They thus effectively 'violated the planned centralized standards' in order to run the wartime economy which would defeat Hitler. Central authorities partly authorized and otherwise tolerated this power grab by the regions as long as they delivered what the centre needed: tanks, shells, uniforms, airplanes. Rather than a planned economy, then, the Soviet Union of the war years was a command economy: the centre demanded, the localities produced. This combination of central target setting and local problem solving was a war-winning approach.[14]

The intelligentsia, likewise, was given somewhat greater leeway to produce cultural products that would engage citizen and motivate them to work or fight. Enduring master pieces were produced as a result: in poster propaganda, poetry, song, even symphony music. Wartime culture utilized complex symbolism, combining the defence of home and hearth, women and children, family and nation, civilization, religion and the community into powerful representations of what there was to defend.[15]

Mobilization

Many patriotic Soviet citizens, therefore, experienced the war years as a time of personal agency, even freedom – despite the hardship and the repression. At the frontline individual responsibility for the war effort was felt most keenly. Soldiers and commanders gained more power to make decisions than they had been granted in the terror-laced years before. Military competence, professionalism and the production of results now counted more than ideological purity. Soldiers were admitted to the Communist Party because they were good at their job, had killed many Germans and could inspire their comrades. Whether they knew Stalin's writings by heart was now secondary. Between the start of the war and the middle of 1945, some 4 million soldiers were admitted to the party, the majority of them (2.7 million) Russians.[16]

The Soviet war effort, then, was driven by the commitment of a sizable 'core' in state, party and army.[17] In the summer of 1941, young women attempted to volunteer for the army, joining male volunteers of all ages. As Maria Starchukova remembered later:

Due to the warm summer weather, the military conscription office had set up tables on the street, illuminated with light-bulbs. There was a great crowd, everybody writing statements volunteering for the front. When our turn came, my girlfriend and I told them that we were born in 1924. . . . A military man at the table wrote everything down, then he asked the final question: 'Do you have an internal passport?' We answer: 'No, but we'll get it soon.' He cut us off: 'Once you have one, come back. Next!' We went to another table. Again, we stood in line. But everywhere we got the same answer. In general, in our class it happened this way: those who already managed to become seventeen before the 22 June, went to the front as Komsomols. They did not take me, because I became seventeen only in August 1941.[18]

Such adolescents could still join fire-fighter brigades or organize civil defence units. Others, some of them still children, attached themselves to retreating army units who 'adopted' them as mascots.[19]

But such volunteer effort, of course, accounted only for a fraction of those who would work or fight for victory. About 4 million Soviet citizens volunteered for the army during the war against Germany – about the same number as would join the Communist Party at the frontline.[20] They comprised below 12 per cent of those who served in the armed forces between 1941 and 1945, and included up to 0.8 million women. Another substantial, if smaller, minority actively resisted mobilization: between 1.6 and 1.8 million deserted, defected, or evaded military service despite the dangers these choices entailed. Meanwhile, the overwhelming majority of the 34.5 million soldiers Stalin could field against the Germans were mobilized whether or not they wanted to.[21]

Men of nearly all ages fought. When the Germans attacked, the Soviet armed forces stood at 4.8 million men: conscripts born from 1919 to 1922 as well as professional soldiers. Between July 1941 and February 1943, the rest of the 1922 cohort as well as men born in 1923 and 1924 were drafted. The birth years from 1925 to 1927 followed between 1943 and 1945. The rest of the armed forces – some 23.1 million or 67 per cent – were older men. The strength of mature men in the Red Army was also reflected in the casualty statistics. Nearly 42 per cent of Soviet military dead were men in their thirties and forties. Another 40 per cent were in their twenties and only 18 per cent were 20 years old or younger. Men over 50, meanwhile, served largely behind the frontline and therefore accounted for only a small fraction of the dead. [22]

Womanly face of war

Despite their visibility (and the existential terror they struck into many German men forced to contend with armed and lethal females), the 0.8 million army women were atypical of their gender. While uniformed women served as anything from sniper to telephonist, with a particularly high participation in the medical services, most of their sisters were mobilized not to fight but to work: in industry or on the collective and state farms, where they replaced the men departing into the Red Army's meat grinder. Between 1940 and 1943, overall female employment outside agriculture grew from 38 to 57 per cent. By late 1944, 53 per cent of the industrial workforce, 59 per cent government employees and 62 per cent of workers in trade were women. Only transport (which was partially militarized) and construction employed more men than women. The most dramatic feminization happened on the collective farms, which were bled dry of men: three-fifth of Red Army manpower came from the villages, which 'became the preserve of women, children, pensioners and evacuees'.[23]

The collective farms were increasingly populated by women, children and old or disabled men. The villages in the unoccupied Soviet hinterland lost at least 63 per cent of their adult able-bodied population between 1941 and 1945. If at the start of this period 52 per cent of the village workforce was female, by January 1945 this share had grown to 80 per cent. The few men who returned before the start of mass demobilization had been invalided out of the army. Often, they were unable to work altogether, or could only perform subsidiary tasks. The work was done by the women, who had to contend with catastrophic conditions: draft animals and the few tractors had disappeared into the army along with brothers, husbands and fathers. As the collective farmer Ulianova from Moscow region recounted later, the results were truly appalling, even by the low standards of Stalinist agriculture. 'During the war we had to pull the plough ourselves', she remembered. 'Nine or ten women harnessed themselves close together and pulled. . . . And one more woman, or a boy, walks behind the plow.'[24]

In the towns, meanwhile, women were commandeered to dig trenches or to build fortifications. 'We constructed antitank barricades – with crowbars, shovels, pickaxes, working twelve hours a day', wrote Valentina Bushueva, who had been mobilized in Leningrad immediately after the German attack. 'The regimen was very harsh and demanding – fifty minutes work, ten minutes break. Then the next shift followed, and so it went. Then the Germans began dropping bombs on us, and we left that place ahead of schedule.'[25]

And of course, many continued in their pre-war roles in administration, education or medical care. Now, they also took over collective farm chairs and other positions of relative power in the lower rungs of the state and party hierarchy. The wartime changes in the status of women, however, were not as dramatic as in other belligerents. In the Soviet Union, women in the workforce were no novelty – the First Five-Year Plan had already seen to that. Already by 1934, 37 per cent of industrial workers were women, and the overall workforce outside of collective farms followed suit with 38 per cent by 1940. The war then boosted this share to 55 per cent in 1945. But unlike elsewhere in Europe, this feminization was the continuation of a pre-war trend rather than a radical change.[26]

In addition to work in factory or enterprise, urban women also tended the proliferating gardens to feed themselves and their families. 'I worked night-shift in the factory', noted the worker Sivakova. 'It often happened thus: you finish work, rest for two or three hours, and off you run to the garden. In the fresh air', she added optimistically, 'your tiredness disappears'. The toll such double shifts and sleep deprivation took can hardly be over-estimated.[27]

It is thus women who shouldered the main burden of keeping their truncated families alive, be it at home, during flight or evacuation, or in exile in the hinterland. Often, this role fell to very young women, as families were robbed of men by the army and of parents by the terror. Inna Gaister was not yet 16 years old when the war broke out. She was visiting her mother in a concentration camp in Akmolinsk, where she was locked up as the wife of an 'enemy of the people'. Inna's father, a high Soviet official, had been arrested and shot in 1937, followed by many other kin. Other relatives felt unwilling or unable to help Inna, her two younger sisters Natalia and Valeria and her cousin Igor, roughly her age. After her return to Moscow and confronted with evacuation of the city, the panic, and the approaching Germans, she took the children on an odyssey. First they travelled to a state farm three days outside Irbit, in Russia's Sverdlovsk region, where neither work nor food could be found. Then they went on to Ufa, some 700 kilometres to the south-west, in Bashkiria, where Inna survived a severe bout of typhus; then on to Fergana in Uzbekistan, 2,500 kilometres to the south-east, where they nearly starved to death. By the time they were able to return to Moscow, both Valeria and Igor had died of the exertions of life in evacuation. Inna, however, managed to return her second sister home, catch up on her education while working full time, and enter Moscow State University just before the war ended.[28]

Displacement

Women were also central to the survival of the families which had been deported from the Far East in 1937 or from the new territories in the west in 1940–1. The Korean, Polish and Baltic deportees in Kazakhstan, the Far North and Siberia were now joined by other presumed 'enemy nations'. In 1941, some 89,000 Finns were sent to Kazakhstan, suspected of the potential to aiding the invading Finnish army on the northern front. The largest group for the entire war years was Germans, both those who had lived for centuries on the Volga and those who had fled the Nazis only recently. Vladimir Leonhard was one of the 749,613 who was deported to Kazakhstan and Siberia.[29]

Vladimir had been born in Vienna in 1921 to a communist mother married to the Soviet Ambassador to Austria. When the boy was 10 years old, mother and son moved to an artists' colony in Berlin. After Hitler assumed power in 1933, Susanne sent Vladimir – on a Soviet passport obtained through her now ex-husband – to boarding school in Sweden, while she joined the anti-fascist underground. During a visit to her son in 1935, her group was uncovered and Susanne was stuck abroad. Encouraged by old communist friends, including Alexandra Kollontai, the Bolshevik feminist now turned ambassador to Sweden, and the Moscow-based widow of the murdered German communist leader, Sonja Liebknecht, she decided to emigrate to the land of the Soviets. Vladimir, himself a young communist, insisted on coming as well. Thus, in June 1935 they moved to Moscow. Susanne was arrested in October 1936 – like many German communists falling victim to Stalin's Great Terror. After a gruelling 223 days in a Moscow prison she was sentenced as a 'counter revolutionary' to five years concentration camp. When war with Germany broke out, her sentence was prolonged for the duration.[30]

Her son experienced the witch hunt of the Great Terror, the shock of the Hitler–Stalin pact, the Soviet invasion of Poland, and 22 June 1941 in Moscow. On 28 September he was deported to Kazakhstan, at the tail end of the expulsion of the entire Moscow German population, which had started on 10 September. He was sent to 'Settlement No. 5' where he encountered deported kulaks openly discussing if Hitler would get as far as Kazakhstan and 'liberate us'. 'I went hot and cold all over', he remembered decades later, now an anti-Soviet defector in the West. 'I had never heard anything like this in the Soviet Union.'[31]

More surprises were to follow. Vladimir managed to talk the disinterested head of Settlement No. 5 to let him go find his educational institution, which had been evacuated to Alma-Ata. After making his way, without proper papers, to Karaganda, he was astounded by its poverty ('never yet had I encountered anything so completely wretched'). Eventually, he found an actual hotel and later the 'Karaganda Educational Institute', where he got himself admitted. He studied with the sons and daughters of deported kulaks, who 'had become Stalinists with the passage of time', decrying their parents' lack of understanding of why collectivization had been 'justified'. In the middle of June 1942, he then received a fateful telegram which mobilized him into a secret school which trained officials for the eventual establishment of satellite regimes in Eastern Europe.[32]

Leonhard's determined attempt to make the best of an impossible situation, evade wartime controls where possible and take opportunities where available might well have saved his life. Unbeknown to him, they helped him escape mobilization into the labour army. On 10 January 1942, the GKO had ordered the drafting of all male German deportees aged seventeen to fifty into labour colonies 'for the entire duration of the war'. The goal of this order was 'a rational use of the German resettlers'.[33] Subsequent decrees mobilized 'practically the entire able-bodies German population of the country' into the harsh world of the labour army.[34]

Leonhard and Gaister were not the only strong-willed individuals who navigated the mobilizational and coercive system of the wartime USSR to their least disadvantage. When Moshe Lewin, a refugee from Vilna who had been assigned to work in a steel mill and then mobilized to help with the harvest, deserted from the labour front and volunteered for active service in the army, he got away with it.[35] Adam Broner, another Jewish refugee from the western borderlands, fled the labour army by falsifying his papers during a stay in a hospital, attempted to join the new Polish army under General Berling, only to be judged to be not Polish enough and sent to a coal mine to work for victory. He again deserted, travelling on his own steam to an induction point and managed to join up in late 1943.[36] Finally, when Grigory Chukhrai, a gung-ho Russian paratrooper, was assigned, against his will, to a Red Army song and dance ensemble, he simply ran away and returned to his unit, which took him back, no questions asked. Like Leonhard he was a believing communist, whose wartime experience opened his eyes to the complexity of life in this country. He, too, encountered a former kulak not in love with Stalinism or the dictator, whom he imagined as a behoved demon. He also encountered a friend who thought collectivization had been a mistake – an opinion amounting to heresy.[37]

'You would know better'

A group with a particularly convoluted wartime trajectory between deportation, mobilization and spontaneous movement were those Polish citizens who had been arrested in 1939–41 in the newly acquired western borderlands or had been deported from there in 1940–1. Once Germany invaded the Soviet Union, Britain, relieved that it no longer had to fight Germany alone, quickly forgave Stalin's collaboration with the Nazis. From now on the British and the Soviet empires would fight shoulder to shoulder. But Britain also housed the Polish exile government. In his greatest hour of need, then, Stalin found himself an ally not only of the terrible British imperialists whom he had always suspected of trying to trick him into war with Germany, but also with the remnants of the Polish state he had himself helped to destroy – a truly odd alliance.

Polish–Soviet diplomatic relations were restored on 30 July 1941 in the Sikorski–Maisky agreement. In it, the Soviets repudiated the Hitler–Stalin Pact, allowed for the formation of a Polish army on Soviet soil (known later as the Anders Army after its commanding general) and agreed to an 'amnesty to all Polish citizens who are at present deprived of their freedom on the territory of the USSR either as prisoners of war or on other adequate grounds'. The amnesty was announced on 12 August and details of the military formation on Soviet soil were regulated in a follow-up agreement two days later.[38] Some embarrassing questions followed about the whereabouts of the officers Stalin had had murdered in 1940. Now he could not remember where they might be. 'They left the USSR', he claimed, when pressed by a Polish representative. 'Where to?', his interlocutor asked. 'Unknown', answered Stalin, 'You would know better.'[39]

Meanwhile, 389,382 Polish deportees and camp inmates were suddenly told they were free to leave their places of confinement, and most did.[40] Families and individuals had to figure out what to do and where to go. 'After the amnesty', remembered Irena Protassewicz, 'we were able to find work for ourselves. The Poles therefore made an effort to help the local collective farm workers dig potatoes on the workers' own smallholdings. . . . After several weeks I moved to the small town of Aban, northeast of Kansk.'[41] Many decided to go south, to warmer climes, where food was rumoured to be abundant and life better. Instead, an often lethal ordeal of wartime travel awaited them. 'Our route in Uzbekistan was marked with hundreds of graves', remembers one survivor of the typhus epidemic which hit the already weakened victims of deportation, forced labour and exile with full force.[42] Surviving men could join the Anders Army, which Stalin intended to use as cannon fodder. Its commander, General Władysław Anders, just released from the Gulag himself, objected. With the support of American diplomats, he managed to annoy Stalin long enough for the dictator allowing the unit to leave via Iran (which was jointly occupied by Soviets and Brits since August–September 1941) to fight with the Western Allies. Thus 119,865 emaciated survivors of the rigours of camp life and exile evacuated in 1942.[43] Among them was Menachem Begin, the later prime minister of Israel, one of the maybe 6,000–7,000 Jews leaving with Anders' outfit.[44]

The evacuation also included women and children who were dependents of the soldiers, or claimed such relationship. Other women evacuated as part of the Polish Women's Army Auxiliary Service. Among them was Protassewicz, who had made her way to Central Asia, had joined up, served in an anti-typhus quarantine station ('the sick started to die like flies'), fell ill with typhus herself only to tend to dysentery sufferers among the Polish soldiers once she had, barely, recovered. 'Those who had not been finished off by typhus', she described the terrible scenes in the Central Asian field hospital, 'now lay in pools of their own blood on the floors of the hospital barracks without any sheets. There they died like flies. . . . I choked from the stench of bloody diarrhoea.' Then came 'the miracle of getting out of this man-made hell'. The soldiers, nurses and accompanying civilians travelled by train to Krasnovodsk, a port on the Caspian. The final 7 kilometres from the train station to the port, the weakened arrivals had to walk. 'More than one exhausted Pole' was sent to the grave 'on that final stretch from the railhead to the port'. Irena made it and boarded the ship that would deliver her from 'this land clasped in Satan's embrace'.[45]

The timing of the evacuation was fortunate. Relations between the London Polish government and Moscow had deteriorated for a while. In January 1943, Moscow informed the Polish Embassy that it would again consider all former Polish citizens from the annexed territories as Soviet citizens, effectively removing them from the jurisdiction of the Polish exile government. The final straw was delivered by the Germans. From April 1943 they exploited their discovery of the mass graves at Katyn in a propaganda campaign designed to discredit the Soviet Union and sow discord among the allies. The Soviets, of course, strenuously denied that they had anything to do with the exhumed bodies, but few Poles believed the claims that these were really victims of German mass shootings. The Poles asked for an investigation, which would have meant direct cooperation with the Germans in this matter. In reaction, the Soviet government severed diplomatic relations on 25 April 1943. At this point, some 258,000 former Polish citizens amnestied in 1941 were left in the Soviet Union. Over 11,000 had died since their release.[46]

Hitting back

By now, Stalin had recovered his composure, which had been shaken by the catastrophe his bungled war preparations had caused. It was time he showed some leadership, took charge of the war effort and repair his mistakes. He first spoke, somewhat haltingly, to the population in a radio address of 3 July 1941, published in parallel in the newspapers. This was just a few days after he had first lost his temper about the military situation before accepting his appointment to the newly formed GKO. Many listeners were stunned to be addressed by the atheist Bolshevik former seminarian in the words frequent in Orthodox Church sermons: 'brothers and sisters'. This opening set the scene for what was to come in the years ahead: a mobilization around patriotism with frequent religious overtones and a stress on German occupation crimes. Stalin called for full mobilization of the country, for the destruction of deserters, panic and rumour mongers, and other enemies within, for determined defence of every metre of Soviet territory 'to the last drop of blood', and, where retreat could not be avoided, for the implementation of scorched earth tactics and the unleashing of partisan war behind the lines. 'The war against fascist Germany', he warned, was 'no ordinary war'. It was an 'all-people's patriotic war'. 'Forward! Towards our victory!', he ended.[47]

His decision to stay in Moscow in the dark days of October and November 1941 boosted morale: everybody else seemed to flee and a German reconnaissance unit had already reached the suburb of Khimki, but the supreme commander remained at his post! Defiantly, he held the traditional military parade on the anniversary of the October revolution with troops marching straight from Red Square to the frontline. On this occasion he gave a speech comparing the country's predicament with 1918. Back then, he reminded his listeners, things had been really bad. 'Three quarters of our country were then in the hands of foreign interventionists', he claimed in a statement mixing historical reality with myth making. By comparison, the current situation was 'much better than 23 years ago', he added optimistically. 'The enemy is not as strong as some frightened little intellectuals portray him.'[48] A day earlier, Stalin had given a much longer and more fiery speech, promising the Germans a taste of their own medicine. 'The Germans want a war of extermination with the peoples of the Soviet Union', he exclaimed. 'Well, then, if the Germans want a war of extermination, they can get one!' Once the loud applause and the cries of 'Correct!' and 'Hurray!' had died down, Stalin added: 'From now on our task . . . is to exterminate to the last man all Germans who have forced their way as occupiers onto the territory of our homeland!'[49]

In the background raged the Battle of Moscow. Soldiers listened to what their supreme commander said and took few prisoners.[50] The successful counteroffensive outside of Moscow, which started on 5 December, demonstrated that this war was winnable on a larger scale. The great Stalin had been right and the frightened little intellectuals had been wrong.

Several factors contributed to Soviet victory outside Moscow. One was the exhaustion of the German troops. After over five months of marching and fighting they were at the end of their tether. They were not equipped for winter warfare and had lived off the land for most of the campaign. The Soviets had resisted strenuously and counter-attacked with a ferocity which frightened the most hardened of Hitler's soldiers. And they seemed to have an endless supply of men, sacrificing them in often suicidal attempts to push back the invaders.

After such counter-attacks Wehrmacht soldiers 'hardly remained conscious'.[51] And then, barely recovered, the survivors had to march again, on and on, into the endless expanse of the Soviet Union, their horses pulling their guns and supplies first through the summer heat, then the autumn rains along muddy roads and on into a hostile winter. And now, outside of Moscow, the Soviets threw in new and rested troops. The counter-attackers were supported by tanks, a significant share of which – probably 30–40 per cent of the medium and heavy machines – came from Britain, delivered via the hazardous route around Norway to Archangelsk and Murmansk under the first Lend-Lease Protocol (signed 1 October 1941).[52] The strange alliance had already begun to work.

Will the east remain quiet?

Some of the men attacking the Germans outside of Moscow in December 1941 were battle hardened veterans of Khalkhin Gol, transferred from the Far East to help save Moscow from the fascists. At least two rifle divisions and one cavalry regiment were pulled out of the Transbaikal and Far Eastern Regions and made available to the defence of the capital from 5 December 1941.[53] 'It was not an accident', wrote Zhukov later, 'that the formations which had been in Mongolia in 1939–40 fought beyond any praise once they were thrown against the Germans outside of Moscow in 1941.'[54] More important in the medium term was the Far East's role as an immense troop training ground. In 1942–3, 300,000 draftees from Moscow region alone were sent here to be prepared for the front. This constant influx of raw manpower explains how the region could both maintain an immense number of soldiers facing Japan and send more than a million men to the army fighting the Germans and their allies.[55]

That this could be done was due to Stalin's successful attempt to avoid a two-front war. After the defeat in Mongolia and the shock of the German–Soviet pact in 1939, Tokyo had settled for a neutrality pact with Moscow, signed in April 1941. But would Japan honour the agreement? Fears only increased after the German attack of 22 June, as Vasily Chuikov remembered: 'A second front in the east could appear during the very critical time when we suffered serious losses in the west and retreated.'[56] Stalin's spy in Tokyo, Richard Sorge, reported on 12 and 15 August that Germany continued to pressure Japan to attack the Soviets. Six divisions were in Korea, ready to strike Vladivostok.[57] The Far Eastern troops were immediately put on high alert: 'the Japanese will begin military actions against the USSR in the second half of August without a declaration of war.' Get ready, the telegram read, and 'not a step back!'[58] The Soviet leadership could not know that the Japanese government had decided already in July for the 'southern strategy' and against an attack of Soviet lands.[59] Later in August, Sorge's reports became less alarmist and by 14 September he reported that Japan's government had decided not to attack in 1941, a conclusion strengthened by further reports in early October.[60]

Sorge's reporting is often seen as central to the decision to transfer fresh divisions from Siberia to Moscow, and hence to the first large-scale victory of the Red Army. This point should not be overstressed, however. Stalin was never convinced that he could leave his eastern front defenceless. Even during the Battle of Moscow, 1.3 million troops, over 3,000 tanks, above 4,000 aircraft, 94 warships and over 10,000 artillery pieces remained in the east. Later in the war, troops never dipped below the 1.1 million mark.[61]

Nevertheless, Stalin's manoeuvres to keep Japan from attacking paid off. After deciding against confronting the Soviet Union, Japan aggravated others. The attack on Pearl Harbor on 7 December 1941, two days after the start of the Soviet counteroffensive outside of Moscow, brought a reluctant United States into the war. Stalin was now in alliance with two of the major capitalist imperialists, to use his terms. This strange alliance forced both sides to compromise on their convictions. Britain and the United States had to overcome their long-standing anti-Bolshevism; Stalin gave up the Communist International, the organization which had allowed Moscow to coordinate the actions of Communist Parties worldwide. It was dissolved in May 1943 on Stalin's suggestion. Both sides had been ready for such steps: Churchill had already in 1939 seen the Soviet Union as the smaller evil and had given Stalin the benefit of the doubt even after the pact with Hitler. Stalin had contemplated the dissolution of the Comintern at least since April 1941. It was a small price to pay. The strange alliance with 'the imperialists' served Stalin well. Instead of a two-front war with Germany and its allies in the West and Japan in the east, he had to contend with the western front only, and had the largest economy of the world and the largest overseas empire on his side. From here onwards, Germany and Japan had no chance of winning this World War, if they ever had had one in the first place.[62]

1942

The Battle of Moscow, however, was only the end of a catastrophic beginning. The Germans regrouped and in the late spring of 1942 attacked again, this time towards the south, to try reach the Caucasus and the oil fields of Baku. Their advance excited the mountaineers of the Caucasus, who increasingly evaded mobilization orders and ran to the mountains to reinforce the insurgents. A group of heavily armed Chechen guerrillas linked up with a German special forces unit operating behind Soviet lines and caused considerable damage. They were not the only ones. The approach of the German frontlines spelled the start of the 'key period of the guerrilla war in Chechnya'.[63] Meanwhile, the German successes alarmed not only Stalin, who sent Baibakov and his team to destroy the oil wells, but also worried the allies. Fitzroy Maclean, who as a British diplomat had witnessed the Korean deportation in 1937, now served with the newly formed British special forces in the Middle East. From his vantage point, the fighting deep in the Soviet Union threatened the British position. The German drive towards Stalingrad and beyond, he wrote in his lively memoirs, was part of a 'vast German pincer movement' threatening Britain's hold on the Middle East. The one arm had reached 'less than one hundred miles from Cairo and Alexandria'. The other arm stretched through Soviet territory to Stalingrad. The ultimate goal was the Caucasus and maybe Iran and beyond. The situation looked so desperate that Maclean was sent to Iran to prepare guerrilla warfare in anticipation of a German invasion through the Caucasus.[64]

He did not need to implement these plans because Hitler's Sixth Army was decimated by Stalin's soldiers. The German troops, after a genocidal march through Soviet territory as part of Army Group South, arrived in the outskirts of Stalingrad on 23 August. Hitler could not resist the temptation to take the city bearing Stalin's name, the place where his opponent had learned the art of totalitarian rule during the Russian Civil War. And Stalin, of course, would defend it, cost it what may. Soon, the Germans were pinned down in the ruins of a city they had bombed to smithereens, only to take away their own ability to manoeuvre. Their tactical superiority gone, they were engaged in fierce, close quarter urban fighting.

The commander on the other side of the trenches was Chuikov, who had just left his post in China in May. He led his troops with panache. 'To tell the truth', he told a military history commission interviewing survivors after the battle, 'most divisional commanders were not very keen to die here. The pressure had barely increased and it already started: please allow crossing the Volga. You scream: "I am also still sitting here", and you send a telegram: "If you take as much as one step [back], I'll shoot you."' These were not empty threats either. 'On the 14th [of September 1942] I shot the commander and the commissar of one regiment, shortly thereafter I shot two commanders and commissars of brigades', recalled Chuikov. General Aleksander Rodimtsev, likewise, noted that a divisional commander and commissar were shot after retreating across the river. 'One' also 'had to shoot' the driver of a boat assigned to transfer troops across the river under fire, because 'the man became frightened'; and an entire group of Uzbeks – the exact number is unclear – was shot by their commander because they had not advanced under fire as ordered.[65]

Using such methods of encouragement, Stalin and his generals sacrificed the defenders of Stalingrad. Their role was to pin down the attackers while the Red Army prepared for their large-scale encirclement. The Soviets thus sent only as many men and weapons, soap and food, into this inferno, as was absolutely necessary to keep bleeding the German army white. This mission could be accomplished, essentially, by ordering the army 'to die in place', while 'spoon-feeding reinforcements' into the destroyed city, to make sure the soldiers 'died for a purpose'. This was a bloody, inhuman and dangerous game. Stalin and his team excelled at it.[66]

Living conditions on both side of the trenches were terrible. After a day of fighting, the Germans had to bring up 'field cooks and craftsmen' to man the night-time watch. The combat troops were either dead, wounded or so exhausted that they collapsed 'into a dead-like sleep'. Both sides struggled with lice, lack of food and seriously compromised personal hygiene. The Germans, who complained about 'a diet of "dry black bread, canned meat and dried vegetables"' and suffered from jaundice and infectious hepatitis were still well off. Their adversaries reported home that 'three days have passed since I have eaten'. 'I am within a hairbreadth of death', wrote another Red Army man. 'My guts are turning inside out and are severely bloated'. And not because of a battle wound, either: 'The reason for all of this is the accursed dumplings and even the wheat kasha. It would be better to go hungry and not eat this food. They have also given us what passes for flour to eat.' And the low quantity and poor quality of food was not the only reason, why the health of Stalin's heroes was compromised. 'We can never bathe, there is no soap. We have not bathed since the month of May.'[67]

The purpose of all this suffering was to gain time for a counter-attack on the German flanks which would encircle the sixth Army and cut it off from its supply lines. This was Operation Uranus, staring on 19 November. On 23 November, the two pincers met and the Germans, who had excelled in cauldron warfare from

ILLUSTRATION 12 Dead German soldiers outside Stalingrad, 1943. The battle of Stalingrad was a major turning point of the war. © Heritage Image Partnership Ltd / Alamy Stock Photo.

the start of the campaign, finally were subjected to it themselves. Despite explicit orders from Hitler to die like heroes, the remnants of the sixth Army surrendered, starving, cold and sick, between 31 January and 2 February. Of the 91,000 exhausted survivors only 5,000–6,000 would live through the ordeal of captivity and return to Germany.[68]

Hunger

Stalingrad was a much clearer turning point than the Battle of Moscow had been. From now on, the Red Army was advancing, taking more and more prisoners, chasing the Germans out of Soviet lands. But not everybody experienced this turning point. For Susanne Leonhard life in her gulag in the Far North continued to revolve around 'hunger and mosquitoes, mosquitoes and hunger.'[69] The craving for food pervaded the wartime Soviet population. One survivor describes his diet as a civilian in 1943 as consisting of 'soup made out of some kind of thick stems from something with no resemblance to an edible plant, bread, rarely herring. And for this "food" people work in the factories. They might get a little bit more at work, but not a lot either.' [70]

Anna Malginova, who had been evacuated from Moscow to Perm in the Urals, remembered the ubiquity of the empty stomach, both during evacuation and after her return to Moscow:

> We didn't live very well. It was a very unsuitable place for evacuation. Before we got there, children born before the war had never had a piece of sugar. It was a very hungry place and here we had evacuated people, nobody needed them. Half a year later the organization got permission to return its employees to Moscow and then we automatically went back to Moscow [on 5 April 1942]. . . .
> Food [in Moscow] was bad. . . . We were always a little bit hungry and when my daughter called me up at work, 'Mama, can I take another slice of bread?' I didn't enjoy that very much. We managed though.[71]

Thus, even relatively privileged, middle-class Soviets suffered from scarcity of food. Only at the very top of the hierarchy did people eat truly well. 'The variety of food and drink' at Stalin's dinners with comrades 'was enormous – with meats and hard liquor predominating', reported one witness, a visiting Yugoslav communist. 'Everyone ate what he pleased and as much as he wanted; only there was rather too much of urging and daring us to drink and there were too many toasts.'[72]

Lower down there was an elaborate hierarchy of consumption created by the interaction of ration card type, access to special canteens and closed distribution systems according to workplace and rank, and personal connections to those with access to the official food distribution system. An official in the Soviet government could obtain 'bacon, canned goods, butter, sugar, flour, salt pork – all brought in from the United States – as well a Soviet fish, fowl, smoked fish, vegetables, vodka, wine, cigarets [sic]', at a time when bread was the main source of calories for most urbanites. 'Special tailors, working exclusively for the highest officialdom, made suits to order for us out of American and British lend-lease cloth at a time when a second hand garment fetched thousands of rubles in the open market.'[73]

Outside of the absolute top groups, then, this was a hierarchy of want.[74] 'Only combat soldiers and manual workers in the most difficult and hazardous occupations', summarizes one historian the situation, 'were guaranteed sufficient nourishment to maintain health'. Everywhere else, 'malnutrition was general and pervasive'.[75] 'We are dying of hunger, we don't have any bread and no potatoes either', wrote a collective farmer to her Red Army husband on 14 December 1941. 'I'm already on my death bed and our daughter is also in bed, swollen from hunger.'[76] In cities and towns subject to rationing, the theft of a ration card (a frequent occurrence) was a 'catastrophe' a 'boundless horror' and a 'nightmare': the loss of the bread ration threatened starvation.[77] 'During 1943 and 1944', confirms a historian, 'starvation and tuberculosis . . . were between them the largest single cause of death among the non-child civilian population'.[78] Stalin received reports about starvation in Russian and Siberian regions in 1942–3, from Kazakhstan, Uzbekistan, Tatarstan, Mordovia, the Altai, Gorki and Sverdlovsk regions in 1944, and from Uzbekistan and Buriat-Mongolia in 1945.[79]

The worst situation occurred in the northern city of Leningrad, the cradle of the revolution. In 1941, the Finnish army had approached from the north-west, first stopping at the 1939 Finnish–Soviet border, then advancing on to Petrozavodsk. North-east of Lake Ladoga the Finns advanced further into Soviet territory, but north of Leningrad they stopped. By the autumn, most of the Finnish frontline had dug in and remained stationary until 1944, with only sporadic fighting. Meanwhile, the German Army Group North cut communication from the south and west, reaching Lake Ladoga on 8 September. From now on, the city was encircled. Hitler ordered to destroy it by hunger, artillery and air bombardment. To raze it to the ground. What followed was one of the worst crimes of the entire Second World War, an attempt at 'genocide through blockade-induced starvation and massive bombardment', as two historians have recently put it. Only the Holocaust exceeds the blockade's horrors. Food soon ran low and rations were reduced to starvation levels. People died of cold, exhaustion, hunger and hunger-induced disease. All domestic animals, even rodents like rats and mice, were eaten. Cases of cannibalism appeared. The siege lasted for 872 days, until January 1944. Overall between 1.6 and 2 million people died as a result of starvation, disease, bombardment and battle wounds. At least half of the victims were civilians.[80]

The most lasting monument to the siege is Dmitri Shostakovich's moving 7th Symphony, entitled 'Leningrad'. It was first performed on 5 March 1942 in

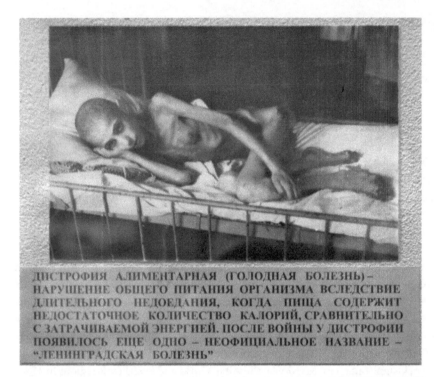

ДИСТРОФИЯ АЛИМЕНТАРНАЯ (ГОЛОДНАЯ БОЛЕЗНЬ) –
НАРУШЕНИЕ ОБЩЕГО ПИТАНИЯ ОРГАНИЗМА ВСЛЕДСТВИЕ
ДЛИТЕЛЬНОГО НЕДОЕДАНИЯ, КОГДА ПИЩА СОДЕРЖИТ
НЕДОСТАТОЧНОЕ КОЛИЧЕСТВО КАЛОРИЙ, СРАВНИТЕЛЬНО
С ЗАТРАЧИВАЕМОЙ ЭНЕРГИЕЙ. ПОСЛЕ ВОЙНЫ У ДИСТРОФИИ
ПОЯВИЛОСЬ ЕЩЕ ОДНО – НЕОФИЦИАЛЬНОЕ НАЗВАНИЕ –
"ЛЕНИНГРАДСКАЯ БОЛЕЗНЬ"

ILLUSTRATION 13 Victim of starvation in Leningrad. © Wikimedia Commons (public domain).

Kuibyshev, where the composer was in enforced evacuation. Starving musicians in Leningrad itself played it on 9 August 1942, broadcast by radio and listened to throughout the city through public loudspeakers. Another masterpiece was Anna Akhmatova's poem of 1941, describing in lyric quietude the devastating effects of German long-range artillery.[81] On 8 March 1942, already from evacuation in Tashkent, her words also reached the readers of *Pravda*. Remarkably for the organ of a regime which had silenced her as a bourgeois decadent and would denounce her after the war as a mix of 'whore and nun, whose lust is mixed with prayer',[82] the Communist Party's newspaper now allowed the proud aristocrat to rouse the patriotism of the Russians:

We know what today lies on the scales
We know what is happening today.
The hour of courage has struck,
And courage will not desert us.
We are not frightened of deadly enemy bullets,
We won't despair with no roof above,
But we will save you, Russian speech,

Mighty Russian word.
We speak you, free and clear,
We save you from captivity,
We pass you on to the grandchildren.
Forever![83]

6 TRIUMPH, 1943–5

The Soviet contribution to victory

Between 19 November 1942 and 9 May 1945, the Soviet Union won the war in Europe. The two dates mark momentous events: on the first of the two, the Red Army began its counter-attack outside Stalingrad (Operation Uranus), which would cut off the German sixth army and end with the most stunning Soviet victory of the entire war; the second was the day of Nazi Germany's unconditional surrender after the Red Army had taken the ruins of Berlin. Between these two moments, the war was punctuated by other battles, including the battle of Kursk (5 July–23 August 1943), the destruction of Army Group Centre during Operation Bagration (22 June–19 August 1944), the Vyborg-Petrozavodsk Offensive against German-supported Finnish forces (10 June–9 August 1944), which, while not succeeding in its objectives, did push Finland to make peace with the Soviets in September, or the Battle of Berlin (16 April–2 May 1945), which led to Hitler's suicide. These and many other battles were but episodes in a larger drama: the crushing of Nazi Germany by an overwhelming enemy. In these years of heavy fighting, the Red Army increasingly showed mastery of 'deep battle': the Soviet version of a modern war of movement based on sophisticated use of combined arms operations. The Soviets also continued to outgun and outman the enemy.[1]

The numbers are staggering. The Red Army was responsible for three quarters of all German soldiers killed and German military equipment captured or destroyed in the Second World War.[2] Illustration 14 shows these losses over time, demonstrating that the Red Army did most of the heavy lifting in Europe. And Stalin's allies knew it. 'Nothing would be worse', said US president Franklin D. Roosevelt in a private conversation in March 1942, 'than to have the Russians collapse'. In what would have scandalized his democratic allies, the US president added that he 'would rather lose New Zealand, Australia or anything else'. He was equally clear with British premier Winston Churchill in April: 'The Russians are today killing more Germans and destroying more equipment than you and I put

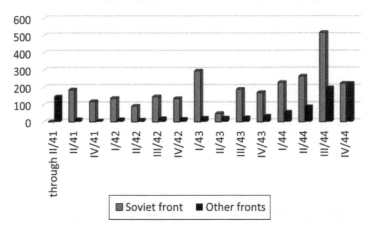

German personnel losses in WWII (thousands)

ILLUSTRATION 14 German personnel losses in the Second World War (thousands). Source: Mawdsley, *Thunder in the East*, 2016 edition, 390.

together.'[3] Churchill himself was even more categorical. On 2 August 1944 he rose in Parliament to proclaim

> that it is the Russian Armies who have done the main work in tearing the guts out of the German army. In the air and on the oceans we could maintain our place, but there was no force in the world which could have been called into being, except after several more years, that would have been able to maul and break the German army unless it had been subjected to the terrible slaughter and manhandling that has fallen to it through the strength of the Russian Soviet Armies.[4]

Thus even the old anti-communist war horse felt obliged to 'salute Marshal Stalin, the great champion'.

The Soviets and their allies

The great champion was not just saluted, but also supported by his allies. Despite the dictator's constant griping about the absent 'second front' in Europe, the Soviets never faced the Germans alone. Such loneliness had been the fate of Poland in 1939 and the British Empire in 1940–1, at a time when Stalin had delivered essential supplies to Hitler. Not so the Soviets, who always fought in a coalition. China kept their east safe by bogging down the Japanese from 1937. Of thirty-four Japanese divisions in the middle of 1938, twenty-four were fighting in China and an additional eight were securing Manchuria. The entry of the United States into

ILLUSTRATION 15 Roosevelt, Stalin and Churchill in Teheran, 1943: The strange alliance between the Marxist and anti-imperialist Soviet Union, the capitalist United States and the British Empire played a crucial role in the victory over the Axis. © Library of Congress (public domain).

the war in December 1941 added a maritime front to keep the Japanese fleet and air force busy, but the ground troops that could have invaded the Soviet Union continued to be stuck in the Asian land war. Sixteen Japanese divisions stood in China in 1942 and over one million men in the summer of 1945. These soldiers could have caused the Soviet eastern front significant trouble had they been free to do so. Together, then, the Asian land war and the Pacific maritime war kept Stalin's state from the potential catastrophe of a two-front war.[5]

Nor was Europe a quiet front. The British and US bomber war over Germany did disrupt production. 'From May 1943 onwards', writes one of the most accomplished economic historians of Germany at war, 'the RAF's night-time attacks on the Ruhr, the heartland of German industry, began to have a serious impact. The most serious setback to steel production since the beginning of the war halted the rapid ascent of German armament production in its tracks.'[6] The petroleum and chemical industries were hit as well, dramatically reducing the ability of Germany to supply its airplanes with fuel by 1944.[7] This contribution of the air war to the slowing of the German economy was particularly important as it came at a time when Soviet capacity began to hit a ceiling.

The air war also forced the Germans to pull fighters out of the Soviet front to defend their cities. Already by 1942, this transfer had a significant impact on the number of aircraft available against the Soviets and after June 1943 the planes deployed here dropped significantly. The bomber offensive over Germany thus indirectly helped the Red Army establish air superiority – an essential contribution to victory.[8] Other theatres of this global war also influenced the fighting in the depths of Eurasia. In 1941, when Britain threatened Italy in the Mediterranean, German air forces were transferred from Army Group Centre to help the Italians, easing the pressure on the Red Army at a crucial moment.[9] And with the Allied invasions in Italy in September 1943 and the massive D-Day landing in Normandy in June 1944, the pressure on the Soviet front was eased as Germany had to fight in the west as well as in the east.[10]

Nevertheless, the air war and the Allied invasions in Italy and France did not force Germany to surrender. They did not destroy morale, did not encourage a coup or a revolution against Hitler, and did not pulverize the German ability to resist. Unlike Japan, which surrendered after two atomic bombs were dropped but before its home territory was invaded, Germany did not give up until ground troops took Berlin in heavy fighting. These troops were Soviet. And while it did destroy aircraft, the Allied air offensive did not destroy a significant share of ground weaponry. This task was left to the Red Army.

ILLUSTRATION 16 Red Army tanks in the streets of Leipzig, March 1945 © United States Holocaust Memorial Museum (public domain).

As earlier in the war, the Western Allies understood this fact perfectly well. In January 1945 it became increasingly clear to them that unless the Soviets would break through soon, the war would drag on 'well into the summer and autumn'. Faced with such 'distasteful prospects' the allies redirected their air war in order to support the Red Army's advance. Attacks on Berlin, Leipzig and Dresden, wrote Churchill, would 'cause great confusion in civilian evacuation from the East and hamper movement of [German] reinforcements from other fronts'. The fire-bombing of Dresden, that 'most notorious' of Allied air raids in Europe made famous through Kurt Vonnegut's novel *Slaughterhouse-Five* (1969), was born out of Anglo-American frustration with their inability to end the war on the ground. But Dresden did not end the war either. The Red Army had to do the job.[11]

Lend-Lease

US and British ground troops were, thus, secondary to victory in Europe. When the allies landed in Italy in early September 1943 and in Northern France in June 1944, the Red Army had already established its dominance over the Wehrmacht. But the speed with which the Soviets could advance was due to the fact that the Germans now fought on multiple fronts in Europe and the Soviet elite infantry could now use a large number of trucks to follow their tanks. These trucks were, in their majority, American, delivered under the Lend-Lease scheme, another essential contribution of the Western Allies to the Soviet war effort.[12]

Lend-Lease was important but not essential to Soviet survival in 1941 or to its successes thereafter. 'The Red Army had already gained the upper hand . . . at the turn of 1942–43, before the full weight of Western assistance could be felt', writes a historian devoid of any sympathies for Stalin's state.[13] 'The vehicles supplied did not necessarily make the difference between defeat and victory', writes another. 'But without them victory would have taken much longer to arrive.'[14]

At first, such support came from Britain, which sent rubber from Malaya to Vladivostok, then military equipment via the perilous route along Norway to Archangelsk and Murmansk. These waters were not just hazardous to sail in, they were also haunted by German U-boats, surface vessels and planes despatched from the coast of Norway. Nearly all supplies in 1941 (99.6%) came through this path and still 84 per cent in 1942. These were important supplies during the most serious crisis of this war. By the end of December 1941, about a quarter of all medium and heavy tanks the Red Army had in service had been provided by Britain. During the Battle of Moscow up to 40 per cent of all medium and heavy fighting machines counter-attacking the Germans were of British origin.[15]

From 1943, shipment shifted from Britain to the United States and from the route around Norway to the Pacific. Overall, well over one-third (36 per cent) of all tonnage delivered to the Soviets came to Vladivostok, a sea-lane made possible by Soviet neutrality in the Pacific war (a result of both Chinese resistance since 1937 and Soviet victories in 1938–9). Nearly a quarter (21 per cent) came through Iran, jointly occupied in August–September 1941 by Britain (in the south) and the Soviet Union (in the north). A somewhat smaller share (18 per cent) came through the Norwegian route, and the remainder were distributed between the Baltic and Black Sea ports, the Arctic route from the east, and various land and air routes from Asia, Europe and Alaska.[16] Trucks were particularly important, making up 50–60 per cent of Soviet stocks. But food – spam, called 'second front' by Soviet soldiers – machines and tools were also essential, as was communications equipment which made the combined arms operations of the elite units of Stalin's army possible. These deliveries plugged important gaps in Soviet production, which allowed Soviet factories to focus on churning out tanks, guns and aircraft.[17]

Humble Australian and New Zealand sheep also did their bit for Soviet victory: the ANZACs delivered 'some 29,610 tons' of wool, according to one source. Sheepskins for Red Army coats (*polushubki*) were collected and sent by the Communist-affiliated Russian Medical Aid and Comfort Committee in Australia. These materials were among the 814.5 billion roubles worth of 'raw hides and leather goods' as well as 2,384.1 billion roubles of 'spinning materials and finished products' and 55.9 billion roubles of 'furs' the Soviets imported between the German invasion and the end of 1945. The Committee also sent medical supplies, probably of more tactical importance than the sheepskin rug, 'autographed with greetings', which the West Australian branch of the Committee sent to Marshal Timoshenko in 1944. But 'it is the gesture that counts', as the Hon. Organising Secretary of the Committee wrote in December 1944, 'the expression of the good-will from the citizens of the State of Western Australia'. This truly was a global war.[18]

Ending the war in the east

Help from Australian sheep or not: the Red Army's contribution to victory in Europe is undeniable. Its role in Asia, however, is much harder to assess. There were attempts to create buffer states to secure the eastern border. In Xinjang in north-western China, Stalin helped the anti-Chinese uprising of Uighurs and Kazakhs in 1944–5. Supported by Soviet ground troops and combat aircraft the rebels managed to control much of the north of that province by the summer of 1945.[19]

Meanwhile, the Soviets had remained neutral in the Pacific, honouring the April 1941 neutrality pact with Japan. This had the odd result that American airmen who crashed on Soviet territory after bombing missions against targets in Manchuria or Japan were detained by their allies, the Soviets, after rescue. In order to not provoke the Japanese, they were only let out in secret, after some diplomatic intervention.[20] Staying true to his commitment to avoid two-front war, Stalin resisted all attempts to draw him into the war against Japan before having dealt with Hitler. At the Allied conference at Tehran (November 1943) he committed himself to an attack on Japan, but only once the war against Germany was won. A little over a year later, at the Yalta Conference of February 1945, he then added that the Soviets would attack three months after the capitulation of Germany. And he kept his word to the Western Allies while breaking his 1941 treaty with Japan, which was still in force.

Soviet troops attacked Manchuria on 9 August 1945, followed by amphibious assaults on Sakhalin, the Kurile Islands and Korea. The fighting was at times heavy, especially on the Kurile Islands and on Sakhalin. Ten San Din, whose attempts to volunteer had been rebutted time and again because the army did not want Koreans, had finally been drafted in March 1945, sent to Vladivostok, where he celebrated the Soviet victory over Germany. Then, as part of a scouting unit of the marines he awaited things to come on their jump-off point on Russky Island, just south of Vladivostok. On 9 August 1945, he heard the news of war with Japan. 'I was overwhelmed with emotion, when I heard the news. My comrades-in-arms were confused by my reaction: listen, they said, we are already sick of war and long for peace, but you celebrate. . . . But I was happy because finally the hour of reckoning with the enemy of my [Korean] Motherland had arrived.' The marines were sent towards the Korean peninsula, already under heavy artillery bombardment. On 11 August they landed in six torpedo boats, each man equipped with an automatic rifle, a pistol, a knife, two hand grenades and 30 kilograms of ammunitions. 'How heavy that was!', he remembered the weight he had to carry. Ten San Din's group started to fight its way south, losing half of their comrades along the way. They fought for twenty-four days. Then the war was over. On 3 September 1945 he received the medal 'For Victory over Japan'.[21]

What Ten San Din did not mention in his interview was that in the wake of the frontline troops came the security forces, who arrested thousands of Russian émigrés who had worked with the Japanese. Peasants who had fled across the border to escape collectivization at the start of the 1930s were also rounded up, as were political leaders and intellectuals among the Russian diaspora. Denounced as traitors and collaborators, they were shipped to the Gulag.[22]

By now, of course, the Americans had successfully developed the A-bomb and had dropped one on Hiroshima on 6 August and a second one on Nagasaki on the day Soviet troops were set in motion. This coincidence led to controversy. Few historians deny that the Soviet entry had an impact on the Japanese decision to surrender. They disagree about the relative contribution of the Soviet attack and the atomic bombs. What we can say with certainty is that both the bomb and the Soviets were on the Japanese Emperor's mind in the final days of the war, although he chose to stress the one or the other depending on his audience. What is also clear is that the first bomb, on Hiroshima on 6 August, did not lead to surrender, but 'stunned and immobilized' the Japanese government. Then, on 8 August, 11.00 pm Tokyo time, the Soviets declared war, and in the early hours of 9 August the Red Army began its offensive. Later that day, the second bomb was dropped on Nagasaki. Only now 'did Japan's locked wheels of decision making become unstuck'. But they still ground slowly: 'Two atomic bombs, each of which destroyed a city, and the Soviet Union's declaration of war were not enough to produce a consensus to surrender.' The deadlock was broken by the Emperor's 'sacred decision' on 10 August which referenced neither the bomb, nor the Soviets. His renewed intervention on 14 August also remained silent on the issue, only stating that 'a continuation of the war promises nothing but additional destruction, . . . death to tens, perhaps even hundreds, of thousands of persons. The whole nation would be reduced to ashes.' In his Imperial Rescript, addressed to the Japanese public on the same day, he became more explicit: 'the enemy has begun to employ a new and most cruel bomb, the power of which to do damage is indeed incalculable, taking the toll of many innocent lives.' No mention of the Soviets. However, in a second rescript, of 17 August, directed towards the army, we find no mention of the bomb, but instead the statement that the 'Soviet Union has now entered the war, in view of the state of affairs both here and abroad, we feel that the prolongation of the struggle will merely serve to further the evil and may eventually result in the loss of the very foundation on which the Empire exists.'[23]

Untangling the Soviet entry into the war from the impact of the atomic bomb is thus impossible. What is clear is that roles were reversed in east and west. While in Europe the Soviets were the central player with the United States and Britain in supporting roles, in the Pacific and Asia the United States and China were the essential forces. To Stalin, however, victory over Japan was as necessary as victory over Germany. Finally, after all these nerve-wrecking years, the two-front threat to the birthplace of socialism had been neutralized.[24]

The war economy

How could Stalin's state win the war in Europe? The short answer is economic: the Soviet Union had more men, and way more machines, horses and guns from the start of the war (Illustration 8). Only a quick victory in 1941 could have saved Germany from defeat. Once Operation Barbarossa had failed to destroy the Red Army and the Soviet state, the Germans had lost the war.[25] Until 1944 the Soviet economy massively outproduced the Germans to replace losses and equip new divisions. The numbers in Table 1 show that in 1942 the Soviets produced twice as many combat aircraft, three times as many rifles, submachine guns, machine guns and artillery pieces, and four times as many tanks and self-propelled guns than the Germans. As time went on and German capacity increased, these ratios declined, but even by 1944 the German production of machine guns and artillery only slightly outpaced the Soviets, while the same number of rifles and combat aircraft rolled off German and Soviet conveyer belts. The major exception was tanks, where the Soviets retained an edge (see Illustration 17).

The centralized command economy Stalin's team had built in the 1930s was not very efficient, but nevertheless effective. It did not work as enthusiasts for economic planning had imagined (see Chapter 5), but it did churn out not only greater quantities but also much more standardized equipment than Nazi-occupied Europe. The Germans and their allies invaded with a cobbled together force including German, French and Czech tanks. The German machines came in a bewildering array of models. If one of them broke it could not be easily repaired by gutting another disabled *Panzer*. Providing replacement parts for this complex machine park in the depth of Eurasia was terribly problematic. The Red Army, by contrast, supplied a limited number of models in large quantities, which made replacement and maintenance much easier.

Soviet economic superiority was demonstrated particularly well during 1941. In the second half of the year, production plummeted dramatically, as much of Soviet war industry was either destroyed, in German hands, or dismantled on trains heading east. By November, the enemy had occupied territory which had housed two-fifth of the pre-war population, and produced one-third of industrial output, including at least half of the armaments. Nevertheless, the Soviets produced between one and a half and two times more equipment that year, mostly before the Germans attacked (Illustration 17). Once production capacity was recovered the following year, the Soviet Union's war industry took off (Table 1).[26]

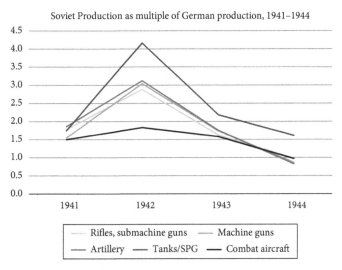

Soviet Production as multiple of German production, 1941–1944

ILLUSTRATION 17 Soviet production as a multiple of German production, 1941–4. Source: calculated from Mawdsley, *Thunder in the East* (2016 edition), 43.

TABLE 1 *German and Soviet war production, 1941–4 (thousands)*

	Germany 1941	USSR 1941	Germany 1942	USSR 1942	Germany 1943	USSR 1943	Germany 1944	USSR 1944
Rifles, submachine guns*	1,359	2,421	1,602	4,619	2,509	4,081	3,085	3,006
Machine guns	96	149	117	356	263	458	509	439
Artillery	22	41	41	128	74	130	148	122
Tanks/SPG	4	7	6	25	11	24	18	29
Combat aircraft	8	12	12	22	19	30	34	33

* 1941 is rifles only.
Source: Mawdsley, *Thunder in the East* (2016 edition), 43, 184.

Thus, the evacuation of people and machines, which had contributed so much to the chaos of 1941, turned out to be a war-winning venture, despite all the losses, the waste and the resistance the dismantling crews encountered. The 2,593 enterprises which were shipped east by December 1941 amounted to a 'permanent eastward shift in the Soviet defence industry's centre of gravity'. In the first year of the war, the share of the eastern regions in the production of war materiel rose from 19 to 76 per cent. By March 1942 they produced as much military equipment as the entire Soviet economy had before the Germany attack. But other industry moved east as well. By 1942, anything from steel, to tractors, to electricity was produced in the east of the empire. This geographic reordering was 'an indispensable achievement since, without it, the Red Army would have had nothing to fight with in 1942'.[27]

Once enough of the evacuated equipment had been re-assembled, new production capacity had come online due to conversion of civilian industries into armament factories, and because of the construction of entirely new enterprises, Soviet industry outperformed Germany multiple times in 1942 before reaching a plateau in 1943. With an increasingly exhausted population suffering from malnutrition, heavy losses and harsh working and living conditions, the Soviet economy hit a ceiling. In 1944, its output began to decline at a time when Germany and the Europe it controlled had finally switched to total war mobilization.

That the Soviets could produce so much was due to the size of the country, the large population and the wealth of resources. It was also the result of the industrial system built in the 1930s. And it was achieved by the dictatorial system that came with this command economy: the Soviet leadership could mobilize labour and suppress civilian consumption to an extent unthinkable elsewhere. It could coerce people to work despite tremendous suffering and widespread hunger. The food shortage further compelled people to participate in the war effort: if between 68 and 79 per cent of the calories you have to consume to stay alive come from centrally administered stocks, and if the ration cards necessary to get access to these essential supplies are linked to your employment, it does not really matter if you agree or disagree with the regime, its ideology, or its war aims: you either participate in the war effort as a soldier or a labourer, or you starve to death.[28]

The food crisis

Indeed, by the time the Soviet wartime economy started to decline in 1944, 'male defense workers, the country's best-fed civilians, *were* beginning to die of starvation.'[29] How could this happen? First, the collective farm system was terribly unproductive. In the wake of collectivization in the early 1930s, consumption levels had dropped massively and for the entire years of Stalin's dictatorship Soviet people would not eat as well as they had in 1928. Russians who grew up during the 1930s were shorter of stature than their peers born before the First World War. Children born under Stalin weighed less than those born under the last Tsar. On average, people consumed fewer calories and ate less animal fats and proteins than they had before or would later, from the late 1950s.[30] The Stalinist agricultural system was a failure even by its own reckoning. In 1928, Stalin had declared the country needed a grain reserve lasting for half a year in case of war; to establish this reserve was one of the goals of collectivization; by the summer of 1941, despite nearly wholesale collectivization of agriculture, he had only one month of supplies at his disposal.[31]

Political decisions, by comrade Stalin personally, made matters even worse. First, the food exported to Germany during the pact with Hitler in 1939–41 added to the scarcity created by the economic system. The dictator's poor preparation for war then allowed the Germans to occupy the most fertile regions of the country despite the Red Army's material superiority. The lost regions had produced half of the grain, 86 per cent of sugar beets, 70 per cent of potatoes and 60 per cent of all eggs; they had raised 68 per cent of Soviet pigs and half of its cows.[32] His decision to slow down the German advance by means of scorched earth prolonged the food crisis even after Soviet soil had been liberated. And then, there was of course the war itself, which destroyed food and production capacity as a matter of course but also because the Germans first plundered and then burned as much as they could when forced to retreat. The decision to draft horses and tractors into the Red Army also led to decreased productivity as did the disappearance of able-bodied men to the frontlines. Collective farms – unproductive and unpopular before the war – became places of immense suffering, coerced labour and malnourishment.

Gulag at war

The extreme case of the combination of the suppression of consumption and coercion to work was the Gulag. 'The prisoners' food portions depended on how much work they did every day. Those who did not fulfill the norm by 100 percent were given, for one twenty-four-hour period, in all 300 grams . . . of bread and a bowl of watery soup', thus summarized a former prison guard the connection between hunger and wartime production in the camps: 'So, in order not to die of hunger, everyone tried to fulfill the plan.'[33]

The authorities saw the sprawling camp system as a systemic part of the Stalinist war economy. When a group of young camp guards tried to volunteer for the army in the summer of 1941, the recruitment officer reminded them 'that the Gulag camp was integral to the war industry, and in sharp tones he lectured us about leaving our jobs at such a dangerous and crucial time. He told us to get back to work right away.' And indeed, Fyodor Vasilevich Mochulsky and the Gulag prisoners he controlled made a potentially essential contribution to the defence of the Soviet capital. They built a railway line from Vorkuta, a Gulag town north of the Arctic circle, to close to the port of Murmansk, in order to supply coal from the Gulag mines to re-fuel British ships bringing war supplies. These included British tanks which became such a crucial part of the Soviet strike force in the Battle of Moscow.[34] More generally, the Gulag produced massive amounts of coal, timber, oil and other raw materials, but also great numbers of army uniforms, artillery shells or gas masks. Gulag inmates built roads, railway lines, air-fields and factories, including the Chkalov Aviation Factory 153, which produced 12 per cent of all fighter planes the Soviets churned out during the war. In Novosibirsk, to cite an extreme example, up to 20 per cent of the workforce in the defence enterprises consisted of forced labour.[35] As far as Mochulsky and his prisoners were concerned, however, it is unlikely that their suffering contributed directly to the defence of Moscow. First shipments along the Northern Pechora Main Line they built began in late December 1941. By the time the line was completed in September 1943, Lend-Lease delivery had shifted to the Pacific.[36]

Elsewhere, too, the Gulag's role should not be overestimated. The system of camps and labour colonies held nearly 2.3 million people. Despite the mass repression at the start of the war, this number then plummeted to 1.2 million by January 1944. Not all of these people worked, while the economy as a whole employed 27.3 million in 1941, a number it recovered at war's end after a dip to 18.4 million in 1942. It was this workforce, made up in large parts of women and youth, which built the majority of tanks and guns, planes and shells which allowed Soviet victory. The share of forced labour in the total workforce remained constant at 2 per cent across the 1941 divide and in 1941–3 the Gulag produced below 2 per cent of the Soviet gross national product. Evacuees and their factories had a much larger impact on the war economy. Unlike Nazi Germany, 'the Soviet Union did not rely on its camp system more during wartime than in peacetime.'[37]

In the first three years of the war 2.9 million people left camps and colonies while 1.8 million new inmates arrived, changing the composition of the Gulag. Besides regular releases of non-political prisoners, a series of decisions was crucial, which transferred inmates to the armed forces to 'pay off their guilt with blood', as the saying went. Overall, nearly a million men left the camps for the frontline. Other groups, such as pregnant women, mothers of small children, disabled and those sentenced for 'unimportant crimes' were also released in the hundreds of thousands. New arrivals, meanwhile, included many women arrested for theft or desertion from the labour front. The Gulag population thus became more female. By 1 January 1945, 24 per cent of camp inmates and 38 per cent of those in colonies were women. The repression against non-Russian 'enemy nations' also contributed to the new population. By early 1945, nearly a third of the inmates of labour colonies were anything from Germans and Finns, to Koreans, Hungarians and Crimean Tatars.[38]

They entered a highly lethal environment. Between July and September 1941, the death rate in camps and colonies more than tripled as new arrivals could not be fully accommodated, clothed or fed.[39] In 1942, it reached nearly a quarter. 'If the Gulag can be considered akin to a system of death camps', writes one historian, 'the wartime Gulag . . . certainly comes closest'.[40] 'Prisoners had to work harder for less food', summarizes another scholar the situation. 'They were punished more severely for failures to meet production targets.' The result was 'mass starvation'.[41]

The camps became depositories of sick and dying humanity. As healthy men were released to fight and new inmates came exhausted from the evacuation of their prisons further west, the share of working inmates plummeted from 80 per cent in the summer of 1941 to 65 per cent by the start of 1943. Nearly a quarter were now classified as too sick to work (23 per cent).[42] Many never recovered. If in 1939, the Gulag administration had registered 47,000 deaths in custody, in 1941 this number exploded to 101,000 to peak at 249,000 in 1942. From then on, the body count started to decline but reached pre-1941 levels only in 1945.[43] Given the pervasiveness of sickness and death, Gulag labour was 'incredibly inefficient' and at best 'marginally useful'.[44]

Coerced labour

Indeed, the massive releases into the armed forces or the defence industry show that the Gulag was not essential for the proper functioning of the Stalinist wartime economy. But coercion to work certainly was. Gulag labour bled into other sectors of the mobilizational regime. We have already encountered the labour army, which overlapped to a significant degree with the camp system: 55 per cent of all workers drafted under this scheme 'served' in Gulag camps or associated construction sites; the rest were assigned to work under the oversight of other commissariats (as ministries were called until 1946).[45] Moreover, workers were under a strict regime everywhere. Already since 26 June 1940, lateness for work, unauthorized absence or changing jobs without permission could be punished with up to four months in prison. Between July 1940 and the end of 1945, 7.3 million people were convicted to docked pay and another 1.4 million went to prison. By Stalinist norms, these were relatively benign sentences, but cutting workers' pay by a quarter could leave their families 'on the verge of survival'. In December 1941, these regulations were toughened up for the war industry, where labourers were now liable for between five and eight years. The term 'war industry' was broadly defined and included not just weapons factories but also transport, coal, chemical, gasoline and even textile enterprises. Nearly 900,000 workers fell foul of this legislation by the end of 1945. More would follow, because this law remained in force until 1948.[46]

These draconian laws not only explain some of the changes to the Gulag population. They also had terrible consequences for individuals. As Iakob Glasse from Rostov-on-Don noted in his diary on 6 and 7 June 1941, just days before the German attack:

> The cleaning lady in my place of employment, a 60 year old woman, was ten minutes late to work due to flooded roads. At the entrance, Communist Youth League members control the arrival times of the employees. They had already caught her once, when she was five minutes late. Therefore, in accordance with the law, for repeated late arrival to work she was prosecuted.[47]

Given such laws and given the coercion involved it is indeed only slightly hyperbolic to call the Soviet Union 'one single forced labor camp'.[48] However, the metaphor of the countrywide Gulag ignores the significantly higher degree to which workers outside the camps could escape coercion. Unauthorized leave and change of job remained a mass phenomenon and many 'deserters from the labor front' evaded prosecution. Given the pervasive labour shortage, runaways could always find a company director who would look the other way and employ them despite their dodgy work papers.[49] In the end, patriotism, hatred of the enemy, the ration system and hunger were much better motivators for participation in the war economy than the law, as we shall see in more detail in Chapter 7.

Nevertheless, the image of the countrywide concentration camp is apt in one respect: it was a hungry, freezing, suffering and suppressed population which worked long hours in often horrible conditions, which produced the weapons necessary to crush the Wehrmacht. 'I was getting so much hot air and gases in my face that my brows burned down – as you can see', recalled a blast furnace operator who produced ferrochrome for tanks in the Urals.

> Worse – we would faint sometimes, mainly toward the end of the day (or night). I also saw how once, after the furnaces were loaded and closed to begin the melting process, the sturdy cover gave in to the pressure of the gas and heat from inside, and the glowing and melted metal and coal erupted like a volcano. There were quite a number of casualties. Another problem was that there was so much heat before you, blowing into your face . . . and your back was exposed to some 45–50 degrees Celsius of Siberian cold. No wonder lethal pneumonia – if that is what it was – plagued our barracks and cut down people suddenly and quickly during the night.[50]

Disease was rampant in the wartime Soviet Union. A weakened but hightly mobile population spread illness far and wide. A crude but effective public health response did manage to avoid the worst but it could not contain a typhus epidemic, which took off in 1942 with 368,000 sufferers, cresting two years later with 614,000 registered cases. Dysentery had peaked earlier, with 485,000 cases in 1941 and 390,000 in 1942, but trailed off thereafter.[51]

Suffering, deprivation and desperation extended to the armed forces. Despite being at the top of the supply chain for ordinary Soviets, Red Army soldiers often went hungry, lacked soap, uniforms or tobacco. Vodka was likely to be supplied, at the rate of 100 grams (later 200 grams) for frontline soldiers and smaller amounts for others. And the war provided ample opportunity to find more, once Stalin's soldiers marched beyond the Soviet borders. It was a drunken, ragged and despondent army that made its way into Europe in 1944–5 – but also a very well equipped one. Both sides of this equation – the poverty of the rank and file and the abundance of military hardware were a result of the totalitarian warfare state team Stalin had built in the 1930s.[52]

Learning to fight

As time went on, the Red Army also learned to marshal its resources more effectively. Progress was slow and painful, to be sure, but there was progress. First, Stalin began to stop micromanaging the military effort and began to trust the professionals. As a result of the Great Terror, the Red Army had started the war led by politically savvy military incompetents. Slowly but surely, they were replaced by professionals like Georgy Zhukov or Vasily Chuikov. These were hard men who used coercion liberally and were not above sacrificing their subordinates. But they also knew that a dead soldier can no longer fight. 'I demand', wrote Zhukov when serving as Commander of the Western Front in March 1942, 'that every unnormal loss of life is investigated thoroughly within 24 hours'. The commanders' 'reckless attitude towards the conservation of human resources' had to end, he decreed. Attacks were to be properly planned and infantry not sent against entrenched machine guns. Enemy strongholds had to be disabled first before foot soldiers would attempt to take them.[53] Even Stalin eventually came around to this idea. In May 1942 he admonished the political and military leadership of the South-Western Front that the country did not have 'new divisions ready for battle'. Throwing untrained troops into combat just handed victory to the enemy. 'Isn't it time that you learn to fight in a way that loses little blood, like the Germans?'[54] He also stopped ordering the execution of generals who had failed in battle, as he had done in 1941. Instead, he now replaced them with more competent soldiers.

Further down the hierarchy, a whole new generation of commanders was promoted through the ranks as they learned on the job. They gained more authority and a greater ability to make decisions as the Communist Party retreated from meddling with command and began to support professional leadership. During the catastrophe of 1941, Stalin had reintroduced dual command, modelled explicitly on Civil War precedents: each military leader would be shadowed by a political officer (called 'military commissar' in divisions and above and 'political leader', or politruk, in companies, batteries or squadrons). Rather than restrict their work to propaganda, they were to 'take responsibility for military work at the front' and serve as 'fathers' to their unit. They were meant to simultaneously support the commander and report on him to higher authorities. Any order had to be counter-signed by the commissar or politruk.[55] As the politicals were usually civilians mobilized by the party to serve in the army, this system not only lessened the authority of the commanders. It could also actively interfere in often critical decision-making. 'I shall tell you one case', said a former division commander, a career military man and veteran of the battle of Stalingrad, in a post-war interview:

> I received an order from the army command to start an attack against the Germans at six o-clock in the morning. I got this order the night before the attack was supposed to begin and worked all night on the plan of the attack. . . . Very little time was left but the commissar was not there [to counter-sign the order]. I decided to give the order myself and send it down to the unit. The commissar learned about it, he immediately took a car and drove to the command posts of the regiment. . . . 'Will you carry out this order?' The commander answered: 'How can I do otherwise, it comes from the division commander?' 'Do you see my signature on it?' The regimental commander calls me and tells me what happened, I say to him: 'Carry out the order', the commissar takes over the receiver of the telephone, I say to him: 'There are only two hours left, therefore I ask you not to hold back this order, afterwards I shall explain this order to you and you will sign it then, but meanwhile let the unit start the attack.' The commissar started to raise his voice and shout in the telephone: 'And what do you think I am here for, do you think I am just an idiot?'[56]

Eventually, Stalin understood the damage this system could inflict on the ability of his army to fight. The shortage of commanders also dictated using the more competent of the commissars as military rather than political leaders. On 9 October 1942 single command was restored and the political officers' position downgraded. Renamed 'deputy commanders for political affairs', they were now subordinated to the commander and more clearly directed towards political education and ideological indoctrination of the troops. The best prepared were made commanders themselves, taking over positions from their fallen comrades.[57]

The others now contributed to keeping morale, explaining the changing political line, and often also made sure that food, weapons, vodka or tobacco were supplied to the frontline troops. It soon became clear that it was the provisioning of these mundane objects of daily life rather than ideological pep talks which determined morale. 'When I came to the unit the first thing I wanted to know about was the daily life of the soldiers, whether they were being fed', recounted Lieutenant Colonel Afanasy Matveyevich Svirin, deputy commander for political affairs of the 308th Rifle Division in an interview right after the battle of Stalingrad. 'The first thing I'd do was ask the soldier whether he was getting enough to eat, was he getting his vodka, and then I'd get to talking with him about politics.' When food and tobacco were plentiful, it turned out, soldiers fought well; when they were scarce, incidents of desertion rose.[58]

The changing role of the Communist Party – from leader of the Soviet people to supporter of the military – was also reflected in admissions. Between 1941 and 1945 the vast majority of new members were admitted in the military. In the first two years of the 'Great Patriotic War' 2.4 million people had become candidate members, nearly all of them – 83 per cent – joined from the military. And although nearly a million communists had died or were missing in action, by the summer of 1943, such 'young communists' made up two-thirds of the party faithful.[59] New regulations eased this process by shortening the period between candidate status and full membership and by reducing the number of recommendations an aspiring communist needed to join the elect. On 19 August 1941, a Central Committee decree allowed the admission of soldiers with particularly good fighting record on the basis of three recommendations from members who knew the new candidate for less than a year and had themselves been in the party at least a year. This procedure contrasted to the earlier rule that only members with three years of party tenure could recommend a new candidate whom they had known for at least a year; and on 9 December, the time they needed to prove themselves as 'candidate members' was shortened to three months.[60] The result was a massive expansion of membership. By September 1943, the Party counted 4.6 million candidate and full members, over a million above the previous record of 1933 (3.5 million). 'Never before', noted an internal report, 'did the Party have in its ranks such a high number of communists'.[61]

Party admissions at the front were also entangled with what has been described as the 'hero strategy': the use of individual feats of bravery to inspire others.[62] Between the end of 1942 and January 1948, 10.3 million decorations rewarding military valour were awarded. A similar number of commemorative medals celebrating major victories also dangled from veterans' chests.[63] About half of the decorated soldiers were not party or Komsomol members and 49 per cent were infantry.[64] Party membership was more exclusive – it became a prize for outstanding soldiering. The Communist Party became an order of German slayers and ideological preparation fell by the wayside.

Professionalism thus rose in the army, but it was distributed unevenly. The bulk of the Red Army continued to be peasant conscripts armed with rifles and supported by horse-drawn transport. By 1 May 1942, Stalin's armed forces had a total of 9,000 tanks, 364,000 trucks and nearly 40,000 tractors at their disposal. The majority of the mobility of the 10.9 million men and women in uniform, however, was assured by 1.3 million horses.[65] Unlike the US or British Armies, but very much like the German Wehrmacht, the Red Army remained horse drawn to the very end of the war. The growth of the automobile park was matched by the growth of humans under arms, with the result that the ratio of people to machines remained constant. During Operation 'Bagration' in 1944 – one of the great examples of a successful 'deep battle' – the 43rd Army 'was forced to resort to transporting divisional artillery by horse', as a General Staff study noted later with irritation. It organized 'a cart battalion with 1,000 carts' in order to remain mobile. As the Red Army charged into Europe, infantry requisitioned peasant carts to rush after the motorized spearheads and even at the very end, when the Soviets prepared to join the war against Japan, they transported not only 2,000 fighting machines and 17,000 other motor vehicles along the Trans-Siberian Railway, but also 36,000 horses.[66]

The trucks, tanks and submachine guns the Red Army now had available were concentrated in elite mechanized units, recruited from the cities rather than the countryside. And it was from these elite units that the Communist Party overwhelmingly drew its new members.[67] It supported the 20 per cent mobile forces constituting the 'swift sword' of the Red Army rather than the 80 per cent of foot soldiers who made up its 'imposing bludgeon'.[68] Hence the wartime admissions concentrated on soldiers of white collar background, whose overall share in the party rose from 34 per cent in July 1941 to 45 per cent two years later. Meanwhile, workers dropped from 44 to 37 per cent and peasants from 22 to 18 per cent.[69]

The elite forces thus increasingly implemented the concept of combined arms mobile warfare, which pre-war planners had developed under the heading of 'Deep Operations' and which Zhukov had tried out at Khalkhin Gol in 1939. Meanwhile, tactics in much of Stalin's infantry remained relatively crude, although the command learned to use its fighting force more effectively, supporting infantry with massive artillery preparation (as Zhukov had demanded earlier). While the Red Army thus never really learned to fight 'like the Germans', as Stalin had hoped in 1942, it become much better at minimizing losses. Thus, the numbers of dead on both sides began to equalize. If it took ten dead or missing Red Army soldiers to kill one German in 1941, by 1942 this ratio was down to 6:1 to continue to decline to 3:1 in the following year. By 1944, the kill ratio was nearly even.[70]

7 WAR OF IDEOLOGIES

Regime support

As the Red Army thus learned to fight, it was also backed by larger and larger segments of the population. At the war's start, many had hedged their bets. Maybe the Soviet regime was at its end? Maybe the Germans came as liberators? In the summer of 1941, the civilian population had greeted the invaders with bread and salt (the traditional symbol of welcome). Flowers were thrown. Young women kissed their 'liberators'.

But from the very beginning, dissonances could be heard, as the German Secret Field Police of Panzer Group 3 reported from the operational area of Army Group Centre:

> The behaviour of the population towards the German soldiers in the regions occupied by Panzer Group 3 is friendly everywhere. Food is given willingly, if people have anything themselves. Everywhere one can hear that the population is pleased to have escaped the Bolshevik system. However, there are also complaints about the behaviour of individual German soldiers. People complain about indiscriminate requisitioning, the slaughter of cattle and the destruction of the interior of dwellings.

Nor were property crimes the only problem. 'We have also received complaints', the same report added dryly, 'that German Soldiers try to break into houses at night, in order to rape women'.[1]

Despite such early tastes of what life in occupation would be like, friendly sentiment towards the Germans was widespread in the western borderlands reeling from the red terror which characterized the first Soviet occupation. And it was far from absent elsewhere. In a town close to Leningrad, one diarist wondered on the day of the German invasion if 'liberation' was near. The Germans could not possibly be worse than the home-grown dictatorship.[2] In Siberia, young men mobilized into the army were 'singing loudly and rejoicing that they were going to surrender', as one witness remembered.[3] Even in far-away Tashkent, people waited for Hitler. 'Most of the Uzbeks were completely positive that they would be freed after Hitler came', remembered one evacuee. They would be 'freed from Communism . . . and it was a pity that these nice (Jewish) people who had come here would have to be killed'.[4] And in the camps of Komi republic in the Far North, the expectation that Hitler would free the prisoners remained alive well into 1944.[5]

The regime was saved by a second sizable minority rallying around the red flag, a group growing as the war went on. On 22 June 1941, a 17-year-old high-school student, chronicled the start of her war in her diary. Her personal writings until then had been filled with teenage angst, boy troubles, anxieties about trigonometry exams and longing for friendship and beauty in life. Now she wrote:

At 12 o'clock I listened to Molotov's address in the radio. Germany is bombing our country! . . . The country is in danger. How I felt when I heard this speech! My heart was ready to jump out of my chest from excitement. The country mobilizes its forces. Will I really remain quietly in my place? No! One has to be useful to the Motherland. Help her in her hour of need with everything we can. Victory must be ours.[6]

Ina Konstantinova joined a medical auxiliary to help look after wounded soldiers while continuing to study. Soon, she evacuated with her mother to Perm in the Urals but returned on 9 February 1942, only to learn that her boyfriend had died of battle wounds. The same day, the grieving young woman volunteered to the frontline. Her letter to the military registration office read:

Dear comrade!

I turn to you with a request, which I hope you can satisfy. I ask you to please take me into the ranks of the field army. Give me any work, any task, I will do everything possible to justify the trust you put in me. I will soon be eighteen years old. I completed the courses for medical auxiliaries. I have worked the entire autumn in the hospital. I shoot quite well.

Can I not be of use at the frontline? Maybe I could work in a field hospital? Or sent met to a partisan unit – just give me a chance to beat the Germans.

On 8 April, her impatient wait was over. 'What happiness', she noted in her diary. 'How I am happy, how happy, how happy, happy, happy!! Life was never so good! Today they have taken me on to work behind German lines. I am in heaven! Oh, how happy I am!' Less than two years later, on 4 March 1944, Ina Konstantinova died a hero's death while covering the retreat of her comrades from a trap set by the enemy. She was 19 years old.[7]

She was not alone in her determination to beat the enemy. Young women flocked to recruitment points en masse, trying to enlist to defend the socialist fatherland, as did men, old and young. Adolescents who were rejected by the enlistment officers joined fire-fighter brigades, organized civil defence units, and attempted to volunteer for the army. Children joined retreating army units who 'adopted' them as mascots.[8]

Moscow residents were optimistic. 'Hitler has miscalculated this time', noted the worker Mineev during the first days of the war, 'because the entire laboring people is ready for the defense of the Soviet Union. Every laborer will fight for victory over fascism'. Frontline soldiers and their commanders, meanwhile, resisted the *Wehrmacht's* onslaught doggedly, tenaciously, often in completely desperate circumstances. It seemed that pre-war divisions were forgotten and the country had come together in what one historian has called the 'crystallization' of Russian national consciousness.[9]

Russians indeed played a major role in the war effort. Among the new communists joining from the military, Russians were over-represented with 71 per cent as compared to 52 per cent in the population at large. Their prominence partially reflected an over-representation of Russians in the Red Army, caused by the amputation of western regions in 1941 and an initial reluctance to let men from the western borderlands to the frontline. In the Russian Republic, 19 per cent of the population was drafted into the army in 1941–5, compared to 17 per cent in Central Asia and the Transcaucasus, 13 per cent in Ukraine and 12 per cent in Belarus. But the over-representation in party admissions also reflected the stronger attachment of many Russians to the empire they defended. Since the 1930s, the Soviet Union had stressed its Russianness in a desperate attempt to shore up popular support. This propaganda now bore fruit, as a leading historian of the Red Army noted: 'Russians were more likely to stick with the fight and maintain their motivation.' They constituted part of the 'core' of dedication which held the army together. And the regime rewarded them not only with party membership but also with battle decorations, which overwhelmingly (71 per cent) went to Russians. Of the over 6,000 heroes of the Soviet Union – the highest military order – 67 per cent were Russians.[10]

There were of course members of other nationalities who dedicated themselves to the destruction of Nazism, the most obvious among them Jews. They, too, were over-represented among bearers of bravery awards, with about 2 per cent of decorated and fifty-nine heroes of the Soviet Union (just under 1 per cent). Just over 3 per cent of all party members in military party cells were Jews, who were admitted in disproportionate numbers: their share in the wartime army was about 1.5 per cent. A total of 142,500 Jewish Red Army soldiers died fighting the Nazis.[11]

Such tallies belie the myth of the 'Tashkent partisans', that is, the antisemitic story circulating in the wartime Soviet Union that Jews were hiding in evacuation while letting the Russians do the fighting. The bravery of many Jewish Red

Army men was rooted in a combination of Soviet patriotism with a reawakened consciousness of their Jewishness when confronted with both the Holocaust and the widespread antisemitism among Russian and Ukrainian servicemen. 'My dearest mother', wrote a thoroughly secularized young man from the frontline. He barely understood Jewish religious tradition and had married a non-Jew. 'When I married Nadia . . . you asked whether I would remain loyal to my Jewish origins.' Recounting a confrontation with traces of the Shoah he concluded: 'Today more than ever, I am yours and I know precisely to whom I belong!'[12]

The authorities eventually realized that they could not win this war on Russian patriotism alone, given that about half the population was not of that ethnicity. By war's end, some 8 million non-Slavic servicemen had been drafted.[13] In 1942, the propaganda organs began a campaign to mobilize the remainder more efficiently. The task was to answer a simple but profound question: 'Why should an Uzbek man risk his life to defend people in Leningrad, or an Armenian to liberate people in Minsk?' The answer was a celebration of the positive side of Soviet nationality policy: active state support for the development of non-Russian cultures; as well as highlighting the fighting traditions of non-Russian peoples. Whether or not it worked is hard to gauge, but the simple fact that commanders now got signals from above that non-Russians mattered made a difference: as with their Russian, Ukrainian or Jewish comrades, Uzbeks and Armenians fought better if properly supplied than if they were ignored, threatened or insulted by their superiors. Many learned Russian in the process, which also helped, both during the war and in post-war life.[14] Even Kyrgyz, who had rebelled in the summer of 1942 and 'in reality . . . could only be drafted via brute force' eventually began to identify with the common Soviet war effort. This Sovietization was partially the result of having men in the army, which elicited some kind of identification with the larger polity by their kin left behind; partially because Kyrgyz could feel superior to the many deported 'enemy nations' dumped in their homeland. These newcomers were both annoying and inconvenient to the locals and were clearly marked as inferior by the same state for which the drafted Kyrgyz fought. And finally, it turned out that the Soviets, which seemed weak in 1942, did in fact win the war and put down the local insurrection.[15]

Holocaust

Bit by bit, then, the group of Soviet citizens who fought or worked with some level of real motivation in defence of Stalin's state grew – be they Russian, Jewish, Korean or Kyrgyz. The regime's ideological accommodations played some role in this process, but more important became something else: anger, hatred and revenge animated larger and larger segments of the population. With every passing day, the utter brutality of the German occupation became clearer. As a secret police report from Latvia had it: the original expectation about liberation from Bolshevism 'soon wore itself out, as the population began to feel the reality of all the 'charms' of the German bosses', including 'open robbery' of goods from the cities and food from the countryside.[16]

Most well-known is the Holocaust. German policy makers had long marched towards more and more extreme measures to 'solve' what they perceived as 'the Jewish problem'. But it was in the Soviet Union where the 'final solution' first meant extermination. Despite the popular image of Auschwitz and the gas chambers as symbols of the Holocaust, scholars have long known that a large share of the victims were shot at close range.[17] In the scorching summer of 1941, police and SS forces, the so-called *Einsatzgruppen*, marched into the Soviet Union, following on the heels of the advancing *Wehrmacht*. They shot Jewish civilians from the first days of their war, radicalizing the practice over the summer and fall from shooting men of military age to executing every woman, man and child they could lay their hands on.[18]

However, this worst of the German atrocities could not be used fully to motivate the Soviet population and mobilize it behind the Soviet state. While it animated many Jewish soldiers, it had the opposite effect on others: the mass extermination of Jews turned out to be popular among a significant minority, making it useless for hate propaganda against the Germans. Indeed, in 1941, there was sometimes enthusiastic participation by locals in the newly acquired borderlands of Ukraine as well as in Latvia and Lithuania.[19] But the sentiment was far from absent in the Soviet hinterland. Historians have pointed to its particular virulence in destinations for evacuees.[20] In Kazakhstan in early 1942, for example, antisemitic incidents multiplied as social tensions over housing and other resources intensified with the mass arrival of those removed from the path of Hitler's army. 'No one go to the front until all the Jews have been killed!' yelled drunken soldiers in the city of Zhambyl, while beating evacuated Jews. 'Kill the yids, save Russia!'[21] But antisemitism was not just a response to the social stress caused the appearance of large numbers of new residents in already overcrowded cities of the periphery. It was a widespread and pre-existing sentiment all over the Soviet Union. In Russia, too, there were significant minorities of antisemites who saw this war as a chance. Muscovites rejoiced at the arrival of the long-awaited apocalypse, believing that 'the fascists kill Jews and Communists, but don't touch Russians.'[22]

Antisemitism in Leningrad is particularly well documented. In July and August both Party and police snitches reported a sharp increase in antisemitic speech. 'The Jews must be beaten', demanded one Leningrader, 'beat the Yids, crush the Yids, I will go to the front, I will beat the Jews'. Another resident of the city of Lenin added the well-worn cliché of Jews as draft dodgers: 'There are no Yids at the front, the day after tomorrow we will beat the Yids . . . the Yids drank our blood, and in three days we will get drunk on their blood.' In September, more and more leaflets were found asking for pogroms against the city's large Jewish community. In October, a handwritten leaflet was left in a Leningrad bomb-shelter. 'All against

ILLUSTRATION 18 'The Last Jew of Vinnitsa.' A Jewish man is about to be executed by a member of Einsatzgruppe D in Ukraine, 1941. The Holocaust by shooting was the worst aspect of a thoroughly criminal occupation regime. © Wikimedia Commons (public domain).

Stalin!' it proclaimed in the name of the 'Nationality of the Russian People'. The Soviet leader was a 'Georgian Jew, or Tatar, or Gypsy' and needed to be eliminated. 'Down with the convict! Bread and peace!' Nor was the Communist Party or the Red Army immune. 'The Jews are traitors and one can only despise them', claimed a Communist Party functionary in October 1941, his tongue loose with drink. 'My daughter of seven years was lying in bed, half-dead', wrote a Red Army soldier who visited his starving family from the frontline in November. 'The child started to cry when she saw me but soon fell asleep, weakened by hunger', he noted in distress. He then blamed not the Germans or even the Soviet authorities for the hunger, but the Jews: 'The hatred towards the Jewish traders is growing. They insult the people more every day, who are forced to run from store to store.' Antisemitism pervaded his diary: to this Russian, Soviet power was subjugation of the Slavs by the Jews; he gleefully waited for the moment of revenge, which he thought was close; and he did not believe in the talk of his 'Jewish politruk'.

By now, pre-existing antisemitism had fused with German propaganda dropped over Leningrad. The visibility of Jews among the city's elite further angered those left behind during evacuation. 'The Jews can go, they give them separate rail cars', one complained, 'but Russians have to sit wherever they can find a seat and go wherever. The Jews have been beaten, but only a little. They've got to be beaten more.' Wishful thinking about an end to hunger fused with violent phantasies. 'The Germans will come and give out sausages and potatoes', day-dreamed one Leningrader, 'and they will kill only Jews and communists'. Nor were better educated Russians immune to such resentments. 'Here the Jews have all rights – they are the ruling class, but we Russians are kept down and occupy a second place', uttered one professor. Another added: 'The people cannot understand that the Germans come to liberate Russia from the Jews and communists and from Soviet Russia to create the real Russia.'[23]

When news of the mass shootings reached antisemites in the unoccupied hinterland, they were pleased: 'You see what Hitler is doing to Jews!' exclaimed one newspaper reader in 1943 with eyes 'shining with delight'. Stalin knew about the Holocaust from the summer of 1941 and he knew about antisemitism in the population. Always pragmatic when it came to questions of propaganda, he decided in 1942 to cut his losses and downplay Jewish victimization. While it is not true that Soviet media never mentioned Jewish suffering, the overwhelming tendency was to obscure their nationality. Jewish corpses became 'peaceful Soviet citizens' – universal victims of the fascist occupiers.[24]

That this was a pragmatic move rather than an ideological imperative is illustrated by secret reports on the crimes of the Germans: the authorities knew exactly what was going on and they did not obscure anything in internal communications. A 1943 survey of the situation in occupied Latvia noted that 'Jews and gypsies' (together with 'communists and members of the communist youth league') were subject to mass shootings.[25] In the Latvian city of Daugavpils, read another report,

> groups of Jews between 500 and 2000 strong were marched out of the ghetto and shot *en masse*. As a rule the children were not shot, but the executioners grabbed them by their legs and hit their heads against a wall or against the pavement, then threw them into the pit. There was a slogan among the fascist executioners: don't waste bullets on children.

The Jewish population of Riga, the same report continued, was 'completely liquidated' by early 1944. Of 43,000 Riga Jews, only 170 survived. 'They were hidden by Latvians and Russians.'[26]

Prosecutors also minced no words behind the closed doors of their interrogation rooms where they went after collaborators and war criminals with Soviet citizenship. 'Did your commando of SS guards conduct shootings and arrests of citizens of Jewish nationality?', an investigator asked one such collaborator. When the answer was put in the passive voice – 'Yes, . . . Jews were shot' – he pressed on with 'Tell us in more detail about the shootings of Jews, which you conducted.'[27] After the war, a massive hunt was on for such executioners who had done some of the Germans' dirty work. Between 1943 and 1953, 257,000 Soviet citizens were prosecuted for treason and collaboration, 152,000 as accomplices, 63,000 as German police and other punitive agents, 28,000 for other help to the occupiers, 4,000 as war criminals and nearly 30,000 for participating in German sponsored organizations. Many more of the 1.6 million military and police collaborators the Germans had employed escaped prosecution, however.[28]

'The reality of German racial politics'

But the Holocaust was only the most extreme version of a criminal occupation. A recent statistical reconstruction of the human cost of the German occupations lists not only 2.1 million Soviet citizens who never returned from forced labour in Germany and 7.4 million as deliberately exterminated by the occupiers, but 4.1 million more as victims of 'the cruel conditions of the occupational regime (hunger, infectious disease, lack of medical services etc.).'[29] These large numbers were not accidental. German plans for the war had from the very start assumed the army would live off the land. German civilians were not to suffer from the war effort, the German army was never particularly interested in logistics, and distances were such that even if more thought had been spent on this crucial aspect of war making, resupply would have been close to impossible. Hence, an army whose members had been absolved from any responsibility for crimes against civilians was put in a position where units had to fend for their own provisions. Ideology made things worse. Jews were at the very bottom of the Nazi racial hierarchy, but Ukrainians or Russians, to say nothing of Central Asians, were not far behind. The invasion had never meant to liberate them from Bolshevism, although some German officers continued to convince themselves that this was what they were doing. Instead, Operation Barbarossa was to subjugate them in a most vicious, genocidal form of colonialism. 'Useless eaters' were to be starved, the rest exploited by the German master race. The Slavs were to be turned into slaves, their food, coal, oil and iron ore shipped to Germany to sustain the war effort. Eventually, German settlers were to take over the vast spaces of the east. To the most visionary genocidaires, indeed, the Holocaust was just a dress rehearsal for much more large-scale genocides.[30]

The reality was not far behind such plans. Prisoners of war faced highly lethal conditions in German camps, often not more than open air enclosures at first.

Soviet observers understood well that with this kind of treatment 'the Germans are helping us'.[31] Eventually, even the German army began to understand this simple fact. The needs for prisoner labour once the war of movement had transformed into a war of attrition further nudged the *Wehrmacht* to recalibrate its approach. From 1942, POWs were put to work, often facing high mortality and brutal bosses. Thus, initial hopes of joining forces with the Germans to liberate their homeland from Stalinist repression, 'soon melted away in gullible Russian hearts confronted with the reality of German racial politics', as one man remembered his own learning process. Even Russian peasants, while continuing to hate Stalin, came around eventually, turning into reluctant 'Soviet patriots', as the same memoirist observed: 'Although Stalin killed the people no less than Hitler, there [under the Bolsheviks] no one beat people with sticks in broad daylight and in plain sight.'[32]

Soviet press reports about German crimes against civilians and POWs initially met with scepticism. But soon they were confirmed by independent sources. 'It was hard to believe in all that was written about German atrocities. Sometimes I thought, these reports were exaggerated. However – it's all true!', exclaimed one such doubter. 'Recently, I received a letter from my sister from Kalinin province. She reported how the fascists humiliate the civilian population, how they hang and shoot completely innocent people.'[33] Once they started liberating German-held territory, Soviet combatants could see with their own eyes what the Nazis were doing. As the Red Army recovered region after region in 1942, 1943 and

ILLUSTRATION 19 Soviet propaganda posters at the frontline, Leningrad region, 1941. Propaganda played a crucial role in Soviet mobilization efforts. It worked not least because it was confirmed by lived experience. © Tass / Getty Images.

1944, the locals told the soldiers about their sufferings. 'They stole a cow and a calf from me, they took away the chickens, and they cleaned out the chest in my hut. Cursed robbers!', was the complaint of a 62-year-old woman. She admonished the soldiers who had liberated her: 'Beat them hard, boys!'[34]

Not always was this interaction as dramatic as in this case. 'The local inhabitants for some reason do not come out to greet us', wrote one anti-Stalinist veteran about his experience of freeing Soviet lands from German occupation. 'The few we encounter . . . are possessed by mixed, conflicting feelings: happiness and fear. They are afraid of us. Obviously, they know that we bring with us little that is good.' But even to soldiers such as this one, critical of the Soviet regime, still harbouring hopes that this war might open an escape from Stalinism, the German approach to the lives and the labour of the occupied population was shocking.

> In one of the villages I try to talk to a woman, who has a piece of cloth with a number on her chest. . . . 'What is that?' I say, pointing at the number. 'This is my working number,' timidly answers the woman. 'I work in the sawmill. . . . The German boss called us by number. We all sewed them on our clothes because the boss demanded it.'

> Somewhere deep in my soul resentment begins to boil. Involuntarily, I'm reminded of cattle breeding. I see oxen stamped with aluminium numbers. What a striking resemblance. Do they really look at our people only as working cattle? The Soviet regime makes animals out of us. But it does not stop addressing us like people.[35]

Scorched earth

Many combatants saw much worse. On 23 January 1944, Vitaly Novikov, a Soviet partisan operating in Leningrad region, noted in his diary: 'On the way to the base. Terrible: all villages are burned to the ground, the people are driven off into German slavery. The German fascists beat up little children. They shoot old men.'[36] What he witnessed was the German scorched earth retreat, which included not only destruction of what was left behind, but also the 'evacuation', as *Wehrmacht* sources called it euphemistically, of civilians. At the extreme, these operations removed all civilians who could be moved. One German officer boasted that when he had to retreat in March 1942 his troops had left only a few typhus sufferers and amputated POWs behind but forced everybody else along.[37] More often, only the able-bodied, working-age population was deported, leading to horrible scenes: 'Mothers were separated from their children; families were torn apart; men who refused to come were either treated as prisoners or shot on the spot.'[38]

What Novikov observed was one of the more brutal evacuations. 'All around burn villages', he noted on 2 February, 'the fascists drive the population to Germany and they set the villages alight. It's a horrible sight'.[39]

In Latvia in October, the Red Army found a population which had already been displaced once by the occupiers, who had deported them from Leningrad and Kalinin provinces during an earlier retreat. This time around, they left the women, older men and children behind. A good part of the younger male population, however, had been mobilized into the German army or deported as labourers to Germany (collaborators and fascists had left on their own accord, the report added).[40] When Vilnius in neighbouring Lithuania was evacuated in the same year:

> In connection with their retreat, the occupiers conduct mass removal of the population and extraction of property. The locals are herded to Lukia and Stafanovska Prisons, from where they are sent every day in echelons to Germany. Part of the detained population is kept to build fortifications in the city of Vilnius. Raids on the population are also conducted in the villages.[41]

These scorched-earth deportations were a radicalization of one of the policies that turned ordinary people against the occupiers: conscription to work in Germany. Originally, the recruitment of 'eastern workers' (*Ostarbeiter*) had been voluntary, but as news of atrocious treatment filtered back into the occupied territories, the supply of volunteers dried up. German authorities now forcibly mobilized youth, a process which often resembled manhunts. In August 1943, the Germans surrounded a park in Riga, and detained every single person they found in the park. A day later, the women were released, but all the men were shipped off.[42]

As such incidents multiplied in the occupied territories, those affected ran to the woods whence they joined partisan groups. Mobilization to fight on the side of the Germans, which was conducted in Latvia and Estonia, had a similar effect. As the Latvian Party leadership reported in 1943, it was 'the measures of total mobilization' which the Germans instituted in that year which 'heavily increased the number of partisan units on account of those who fled from the fascist mobilization'.[43]

Enchantment of success

German measures against this growing movement of Soviet irregulars, the so-called partisans, further increased tensions between occupiers and occupied. The partisan threat was first fairly small. In 1941, ineffectual partisan groups 'conspired, dug in, became filthy, grew beards, invented pseudonyms, so the population would not identify them as soviet activists', as one political officer complained.[44]

Nevertheless, German security forces conducted a most brutal anti-partisan war from the very beginning. Over-stretched, under-supplied and scared to death in a land they imagined as full of treacherous, bloodthirsty Bolsheviks, the German 'counter-insurgency' was indeed a war against civilians.[45] Already in April 1942, Hitler's propaganda minister, Dr Goebbels, pointed out to his diary that such behaviour did not win hearts and minds. The initially welcoming attitude 'has changed completely in the course of months'. Why? Because 'we have hit the Russians, and especially the Ukrainians, too hard on the head.'[46]

Finally, Soviet victories on the battlefield – what one historian has called the 'enchantment of success' – mattered for the growth of the partisan movement: people rallied to the winning side, no matter their ideological preferences. In 1941, this side seemed to be Germany; from 1943, it was increasingly clear that the Soviets would win.[47] In Leningrad region, where Novikov fought, significant numbers only attempted to join from the fall of 1943, when Soviet victory became all but certain.[48] In Belarus, too, the vast majority of partisans joined the movement in 1943 or 1944: they simply chose the winning side.[49] In Latvia, the number of partisans doubled in the first four months of 1944, from only 738 to 1,387 with another 1,481 'in reserve' because there were not enough weapons.[50] For the Soviet Union as a whole, numbers went from 30,000 in January 1942 to 120,000 a year later to reach nearly 139,000 in June 1943 and 181,000 in early 1944.[51]

Domestic consolidation

Slowly but surely, then, Stalinism turned out to be the lesser evil. Numbers on clothes and stolen chickens were the smallest complaints. Liberated peasants recounted how the occupiers had raped women, concluding that 'everything written about them in the newspapers, it's all true. They just go into a hut where a girl is and take her, saying she's ours for two hours. Then they leave.'[52] The destruction the Nazis left behind in the wake of their scorched earth retreats, the many dead, executed, carted to Germany to an unknown fate, all added up to an image of all-encompassing terror. The propaganda soldiers had been fed about the horrors of the German 'New Order' thus proved to be true. 'However much they write in the papers about atrocities', wrote an officer to his wife, 'the reality is much worse.'[53]

Together, the enchantment of success, the experience of German atrocities, their exploitation by a skilled atrocity propaganda, and the mobilizational regime of the Soviet state brought supporters and victims of Stalinism together. Elena Kozhina's wartime experience is one illustration of this process. The 8-year-old was close to death by starvation when she arrived in the Cossack village of Koshevka, 80 kilometres outside Rostov-on-Don. One of the survivors of a family that had endured, first, the blockade of Leningrad, the flight across frozen Lake Ladoga,

ILLUSTRATION 20 F. A. Modorov, 'In the Headquarters of the Soviet Partisan Movement'. The exploits of the Soviet partisans would be celebrated after the war as examples for the united resistance of the Soviet people against the occupiers as well as the leading role of the Communist Party in directing this resistance. The reality often looked quite different. © Album / Alamy Stock Photo.

and finally a lethal journey in cattle cars across the war-torn Soviet Union, the girl was at the end of her powers. A cart brought the evacuees from the train station to the house of the Cossack woman who was supposed to give them shelter. Kozhina was just able to drag herself to the entrance of the hut.

> When I reached the threshold of the house and tried to step over it, I could not. With surprise, almost with shame, I stared at this small wooden hurdle over which I could not raise my foot. I tried again, wobbled, and had to grab the doorjamb. Inside the house, on a bench along the wall, sat a row of old Cossack women: all straight and unflinching, with grim, unfriendly faces that were strangely dark under their white headscarves. They watched me dispassionately.[54]

The sons and husbands of these women were at the front, fighting in the Red Army against the Nazi invaders just as Kozhina's father did at the time. Yet they expressed no sympathy for the ragged Leningraders who had been placed among them. Starving children were not new. The Cossacks had seen them before, during the great famine of 1932–3. Only then it had been rural children, their children, who collapsed from malnutrition. And the last cattle cars they had witnessed had been full not of city people but of family members of 'kulaks', exiled to their northern plight and often to their deaths during the years of Stalin's war against the peasantry of 1929–32. Kushevka's train station had been a transit point for such trains full of unfortunates like the Cossack women themselves: villagers, peasants, people of the land; some of them were neighbours, family members, friends. Why should the Cossacks now feel compassion for these city people? The Leningraders were fools at best. 'Why do you stand up for your damn Bolsheviks?' the local women would say.

> Look, they starved your whole city to death, and those of you who survived were thrown in railcars like cattle and driven for months so that hunger could finish you on the way. Then they dumped you here without even a piece of bread. If you want to obey such people, go ahead, but we think differently. We remember our Cossack freedom.

To the locals, city folk were accomplices of 'the Bolsheviks', and indeed Kozhina's father was a Communist and an officer – that is, one of those cursed people who had imposed the devilish kolkhozes on the Cossacks.[55]

As time went on, however, Kozhina and her mother integrated into village life. They became, if never locals, then at least respected guests. As it turned out, the new masters – the Germans had occupied Kushevka on 31 July 1942, the eve of Elena's ninth birthday – brought neither Cossack freedom nor the abolition of the collective farms. Greeted with bread and salt by the villagers, the Germans were soon despised as exploiters, occupiers and murderers. Under the pressure of shared deprivation, the gap between the communist Leningraders and their unwilling hosts began to narrow. The locals 'had changed noticeably', wrote Kozhina in her memoirs, 'both in their demeanor toward us and in general. They asked about our lives more often and with more interest and talked about their own more willingly. Their remarks about the Germans became increasingly hostile.' After liberation by the Red Army in February 1943, the two worlds finally met in a common life: letters from the front arrived for both the Leningraders and the Cossacks, and reading them together formed a new bond between people who initially had felt 'separated by barriers without entrances and exits'.[56]

Civil war in the west

While in the Soviet heartlands the compact between different social groups and the state crystallized more and more, in the newly acquired borderlands in the west of the empire, the regime faced ideological competitors for the loyalty of the locals. In the formerly Polish territories of Ukraine and Belarus as well as in Latvia, Lithuania and Estonia national resistance to Soviet (understood as 'Russian') occupation entangled with dreams of ridding the nation of foreign elements, visions which had dovetailed well with the Nazi nightmare of the Holocaust, but which now turned decisively anti-Soviet. Pacification here had to wait until a further round of brutal deportations in 1949 upturned the soil in which the insurgency was rooted.

The most exclusionary national project was pursued in Ukraine. The Organization of Ukrainian Nationalists (OUN) and their fighting wing, the Ukrainian Insurgent Army (UPA), aspired to build an independent Ukraine free of Jews, Poles, Russians and Germans. Their 'Jewish problem' was 'solved' by the Nazi genocide in 1941–2, aided and abetted by local collaborators. In 1943, UPA forces manned by many of those same former Nazi supporters killed some 50,000 Poles in a bacchanalia of violence. Trying to find support and ways to revenge their slain family members, Poles ran into the woods to join the Soviet partisans or into the cities to join German auxiliary troops. A three-way struggle ensued between Ukrainian insurgents, German anti-partisan forces and Soviet guerrillas, which would evolve into a brutal counter-insurgency war from 1944, after the Red Army had chased the Germans back to the west.[57]

In Latvia, Lithuania and Estonia, too, the violence continued after the German retreat of 1944. 'For the Baltic states', write two historians, 'the Second World War did not end until the early 1950s'. What elsewhere were the post-war year here were 'years of hatred and deprivation' whose violent emotions would have a long afterlife.[58] Here, too, of course, the Jews were mostly gone, shot by the Nazi genocidaires and their local allies but at times also beaten to death by some of their Baltic neighbours, as had happened in a gruesome pogrom in Kaunas in June 1941.[59] Some nationalists initially boasted of their wartime exploits: 'When the Germans began to advance to the east, our partisans dispersed the red Jewish bandits and cleansed the country from them, which is why the German army marched so far to the east', read one leaflet from Lithuania. But later on, ethnic intolerance was much less pronounced here than in Ukraine. 'Ukrainian nationalists', writes the leading scholar of the Soviet counter-insurgency, 'regarded Russians, Jews, and Poles as enemies, whatever their attitude toward communism, but the Baltic resistance did not attack Russian, Belorussian, or Polish civilians' just because of their ethnicity.[60] As we shall see in Chapter 8, however, they did kill a lot of civilians in what amounted to a war after the war. As elsewhere in the Soviet Second World War, the majority of the population had to navigate the terrible terrain of minorities armed with lethal weapons and no less lethal ideologies.

8 THE WAR AFTER THE WAR, 1944–9

Revenge

As the Red Army was chasing the Germans to Berlin, Michael Goldberg, Adam Broner and others who had survived the war in the Soviet Union returned to their former homelands in what used to be the Baltic states or east of Poland. A few other Jews, such as Markus Lecker, had survived German occupation and the Holocaust hiding in the woods or with locals willing to take the risk. Both groups found their near and dear, and their entire communities, murdered. Many reacted by attempting to leave what had become the graveyard of their communities. Many succeeded in illegally crossing the border, while others were arrested. Still others stayed behind to make sure the murderers would not escape.[1]

Nachman Dushanski was among the latter. He had already had an eventful war by the time he returned, weapon in hand, to his homeland: Lithuania. After a hard-fought retreat in 1941, described in Chapter 4, he had helped protect the Kremlin in Moscow, followed by a stint in a logging camp, where the Baltic security troops were treated like members of the labour army. In the spring of 1942, they were transferred to a special school for further training (one of his teachers was Wilhelm Pieck, the German communist who would become the first president of the GDR, the east German satellite of the Soviets).

In the fall of 1943, Dushanski's well-prepared group of special security forces was sent to the front where they first hunted down German officers as 'tongues' who could be milked for intelligence. Later, their target was 'the local German government' in the occupied territories: 'the chief of police, the German district commandant, commanders of police punitive units and other such vermin'. Both types of operations required work behind the German frontlines, at times in coordination with Soviet partisans. They also mopped up 'traitors who had not managed to flee with the Germans' behind the advancing Red Army. The collaborators were put on trial and often executed immediately by a flying military tribunal, sometimes with active participation by the local population.

Dushanski helped liberate Vilnius in competition with partisan groups of the underground Polish Home Army (*Armia Krajowa*, or AK), who wanted Wilno to be Polish again. A Jewish guerrilla group from the woods around Vilnius supported the Soviet special forces against both Polish irregulars and retreating German troops. As they fought their way through the streets of Lithuania's capital, Dushanski happened upon survivors of the genocide of the Roma.

In Kaunas he encountered surviving Jews – an experience which changed his self-identification from 'Chekist who happens to be Jewish' to 'Jew who happens to work for the Cheka', a reaffirmation of Jewishness as a result of the Holocaust which was widespread, although not universal among Soviet Jews. Dushanski felt himself called to avenge his family and the community he hailed from (only one brother had survived the war):

> I went to the Ninth Fort, where the Germans had exterminated many tens of thousands of Jews and Soviet prisoners of war. As I was looking at the mass graves on that day, I swore to myself that I would not rest, that I would not stop destroying all these murderers and butchers, until I had avenged my lost family and all the murdered Lithuanian Jews. And if, until that day, I had felt that I was, in the first instance, a chekist, an officer, and a communist, and only after all that also a Jew; then now all of this changed. I said to myself: I'm a Jew first of all, and everything else is not so important any more. I promised myself, that I would not stop avenging my people, of whom only individuals had survived in Lithuania. I would not rest until every single one of these butchers would lie in a grave or rot in the snows of Kolyma.

Dushanski was a man of his word. And his position as a representative of Stalin's security services gave him the means to act on his righteous anger: he served for many years as the head of department for the fight against banditry in the Lithuanian Ministry of State Security (MGB), as one branch of Stalin's secret police was now called after yet another renaming. For a decade, he helped fight the Lithuanian partisans (the Forest Brothers) and prosecuted their leaders ('my war ended only ten years after Victory'). 'This was in fact a civil war', he told his interviewer, 'in which on our side fought people who believed deeply in the righteousness of our cause and in the purity of our ideals'. On the other side of the frontline he saw 'mostly former executioners and members of German-sponsored punitive troops'. Those hiding in the woods and operating in the Lithuanian underground, of course, saw things differently. Their views have become part of the official memory of today's Lithuania, as Dushanski complained: the media today present this war 'only from one, false perspective: "how the evil Soviets and the Russian-Jewish monsters from the NKVD strangled the Lithuanian people." That's not even close to what happened in reality.'[2]

Rescue

What was true, though, was that Dushanski began a war against the murderers of his people, a struggle that happened to coincide with the Soviet war against wartime collaborators and nationalist guerrillas. Dushanski indeed went well beyond such a tacit alliance with the Soviet state – typical for many Soviet citizens during the war, who had personal, family or national scores to settle. Dushanski, meanwhile, acted both as an agent of Stalin's state and as a Jewish resistance fighter to it.

The first time he broke Soviet laws in order to save Jews was in the summer of 1945, during the first deportation wave which came with re-Sovietization:

All Germans of Lithuania and Klaipėda region were subject to expulsion to Krasnoiarsk region, as was the criminal and anti-social element: professional thieves, prostitutes, and similar types. It was announced that these evictions were temporary. In all of Lithuania, six thousand people were subject to this expulsion, some 600 in Kaunas. I came home from work and saw that my wife, a medicine student, sitting with two of her student friends and they all cried. They usually studied together, all four of them, but now one of them was missing and the others are all in tears. I asked my wife: 'But where's Nadia? What happened?' 'Don't you know? They took her with her whole family . . . and will deport them to Siberia. They are Germans, it turns out!' 'What kind of Germans are they? She was in the ghetto! And she has a completely Jewish name!' 'Her mother is a German, and hence they all send them into exile!' I called two of my comrades. In uniform and carrying automatic rifles we drove to the train station. The entire station was surrounded by militiamen and NKVD soldiers, but we showed our identification papers which demanded that nobody could detain us. I found Nadia's family in the box car with those deported from Kaunas. I directed the family to follow us, but some major with an armed detachment ran after us: 'What right do you have!?' 'This one: Department for Fight with Banditry. They are our responsibility now!'

I wrote him a receipt for four persons, put the entire family in the car, drove them back home. Their apartment was already completely ransacked by their Lithuanian neighbours. . . . I told them: 'Go to Vilnius. Find the following man (I told them the name) in the synagogue and he will help you.' The man whose name I gave them was in touch with the organization 'Bricha'.[3]

About *Bricha* ('Escape' in Hebrew), the Jewish underground smuggling Jews out of Europe to Palestine, he had learned from old comrades he had grown up with. They had survived the war with the Soviet partisans or the Red Army and now tried to save as many of the remnants of the once vibrant Lithuanian Jewish community. They asked him to join them in Palestine to fight for a Jewish homeland. 'But I could not do that in 1945. I did not want to be a deserter. But the main thing was something else: I had to take revenge on the collaborators with the Germans. This was my main goal in life. And I also still believed in the Party and in the Soviet regime.' But he nevertheless helped the organization with false papers and also handed over materials about German war criminals, to be smuggled to the west to help with the prosecution of those who had escaped Soviet justice.

Had he been caught doing any of this he would have been lucky to get ten years in the Gulag. But this knowledge did not stop him. A few months later, he again abused his authority in order to save Jews from Soviet persecution. In November 1945 he found his headquarters full of Holocaust survivors from Kaunas who had tried to cross the border to Poland in an attempt to reach Palestine – and illegally crossing the border was prosecuted as treason. He made sure the women and children would be released and the remaining eleven men would only be charged with the lesser offense of illegally entering a border zone. The interview implies that these were not his only such actions.

Dushanski's interests as a re-born Jew thus intersected, but were not identical with those of the Soviet state – one of the many complexities antisemitic views cannot accommodate. Lamentably, tales of 'Jewish Chekists' and an alleged 'Jewish-Bolshevik conspiracy' have seen a revival in parts of Eastern Europe. But Dushanski's self-representation is also defective, if we take it as unaltered historical truth. After all, Dushanski was, by and large, a faithful implementer of the Stalinist occupation and Sovietization of Lithuania. To add yet another twist to this story, moreover, in the post-war years the very Soviet state Dushanski served at least part of his time turned antisemitic itself in the campaign against 'rootless cosmopolitanists'. Dushanski escaped, first because he was effectively hiding in the provinces once things heated up, but in the long term really only because Stalin died just in time in 1953.[4]

In the woods

Given Soviet resources, none of the nationalist resistance groups in Ukraine, Belarus, Latvia, Lithuania and Estonia ever had much of a chance in open confrontation with the Red Army or the security troops.[5] Dushanski's men included 'many former partisans and long-serving border guards, people with a lot of combat experience and great training. Thus the units of this regiment constituted a serious fighting force.' They were a multinational group of communists: Lithuanians, Lithuanian Russians, a few Jews and a Tatar. Communists of long standing were well represented, as were demobilized officers, in particular former scouts or military counter-intelligence men. They were specially trained for their new task in a secret police school in Kaunas, where they learned 'many aspects of the "anti-partisan war", from night-time orienteering in the forest to the organization of ambushes'.

Their opponents were much more poorly trained, organized and equipped. In 1944, maybe 33,000 Lithuanian guerrillas were hiding in the woods, not counting some 25,000 Polish AK troops operating in the Vilnius area.[6] The Lithuanian insurgents had less military experience. A few had served in German units during the war, but more had escaped serving in German forces for the same patriotic reasons they now refused to accept the new Soviet masters.[7] 'Some of those joining the partisans', writes a Lithuanian historian, 'had never held a gun in their hands.'[8] They suffered heavily from numerically not much stronger, but much better equipped, trained and led Soviet security troops – some 17,000 according to Dushanski and between 7,000 and 11,000 paramilitaries, the 'destruction battalions': not enough to wipe out the insurgents, but sufficient to reduce their numbers and keep the remainders locked down in their earth bunkers and other hiding spots.[9]

Between the liberation of Lithuania in July 1944 and 25 April 1946, the Soviets had killed 12,809 insurgents and detained another 15,309.[10] Others slipped out of the woods and legalized themselves in recognition of their hopeless situation – over 6,000 in 1945 alone.[11] Already by the summer of 1945, the Soviets counted only 6,200 Lithuanian guerrillas, and a year later the nationalists were down to some 4,500 fighters. They were militarily defeated now, once and for all. They thus reorganized into small cells hidden in bunkers in the woods and changed their tactics.[12] The other western borderlands (Estonia, Latvia, Belarus and Ukraine) followed a similar pattern: by the summer of 1946, the real military confrontation was over; from then the underground shifted to terrorist tactics, and most were liquidated by the end of 1949, although some continued to fight on into the early 1950s. We can thus take 1949 as the end-point to this war after the war, and with it as an end to the Soviet Second World War more generally.

Despite its early military defeat, the Lithuanian resistance proved remarkably resilient, continuously enlisting new recruits: overall, between 1944 and 1950, some 100,000 Lithuanians participated in the guerrilla force.[13] Dushanski blamed this tenacity on Winston Churchill's 'Iron Curtain' speech of 1946. And it was true that the nationalist underground fighters held out against all odds in the forlorn hope that the United States and Britain would come to their aid, that the Second World War against fascism would transform into the Third World War against Bolshevism and they could fight alongside Americans and Brits (and maybe also Germans?) for the liberation of their homelands and the destruction of communism. These were, of course, pipe dreams – although shared by large sectors of Ukrainian and Russian peasants, too: rumour was rife that a new war would sweep away the hated collective farms. But the nationalists were also successful in their recruitment of locals because re-Sovietization was again a very nasty affair. Many also ran to the woods to escape the draft into the Red Army, others to evade deportation and dekulakization.[14]

What awaited them in the woods was far from heroic. The activists spent most of their days doing little but hide, evading the increasing presence of Soviet security forces and occasionally terrorizing local supporters of Soviet power. One of them left a diary, found after one of his comrades was arrested in his hiding place by Dushanski's men. The diary is a chronicle of wasted time. Indeed, it seems that it was largely written in order to deal with the mind-numbing boredom of sitting alone or with a few comrades in a hole in the ground, waiting to be found by the enemy. At the start of the diary, 'Tigras', the tiger, as he modestly called himself, still fought with a reasonable size group – thirty-three people, as his diary noted on 18 February 1945. 'The majority of the men had not participated in the fighting at the frontline during the war, but had not even been in the army', he noted with some chagrin. There were a few veterans who had served with the Germans, and they took on leadership positions in battle. That day they lost eight men in an encounter with Soviet security forces, an unequal slaughter by machine gun fire. The survivors got help from villagers and made their way to a kinsman, in order to hide. Eventually, they linked up with three other survivors but soon split up into smaller groups again. The two wounded found locals to look after them. They somehow survived the winter.[15]

By the summer of 1945, the group had grown to sixteen. In order to survive they assailed collective farms for food. Besides such raids – robberies, really, legitimized by the fact that the farmers they stole from worked in Soviet kolkhozes – the only other operation they conducted was executing a Russian soldier who had plundered the locals. Otherwise, they were on the run. A constant problem was reconnaissance planes, which spotted the partisans. Large groups of Soviet security forces – some 100 of Dushanski's men – then suddenly emerged on the unsuspecting partisans, killing six in another unequal slaughter. In two other instances locals – or 'traitors' in the words of the diarist – gave away the hiding places of the group. More casualties followed. In another case, a spy found out where four partisans were hiding, and 300 security troops arrived to annihilate them: they burned to death after the farmhouse they had barricaded themselves in was set alight.[16]

Tigras was obsessed with traitors among the local population: a young Komsomol woman working as a nurse, whose brother (member of a destruction battalion) had been shot by the underground; a former neighbour who became a communist and who informed on the guerrillas etc. While he imagined himself supported by the population at large, he and his men were isolated and scared of their surroundings. In passing, he mentioned the beating of village communists – who then retaliated later. Attempts to get help from the locals increasingly failed. The diary chronicled a desperate struggle to stay alive: hiding, avoiding security forces and destruction battalions (or 'destroyers', as the members of these pro-Soviet militias were called), staying clear of spies. It was increasingly hard to move around, to get supplies. There was not much energy left for fighting. Thus, Tigras survived the winter of 1945–6 tucked away in a hiding bunker built next to the isolated farmstead of an old friend.[17]

By the summer of 1946, Tigras and his comrades operated in very small groups – two or three – and were under relentless pressure by Dushanski's troops. Their life was a constant game of hide and run, hide and run, all the while worrying about spies, who seemed to be everywhere among the civilian population. They planned to kill some 'destroyers', but failed because their targets were warned by one of the ever-present informers. Eventually, he did manage to kill one 'Bolshevik' who, he wrote dramatically, fell 'onto the Lithuanian soil'. Most other ventures failed. Tigras and his friends tried to rob a train station, for example, in order to be able to buy weapons and ammunition, but they got away with only 30 roubles and some cigarettes. Amid these disasters, Tigras left vignettes illustrating his world view: the train station was full of Russian beggars who had come to Lithuania to exploit the locals; on the wall were large portraits of Stalin and of 'other Bolshevik Jews'; the Bolshevik occupiers were 'mongols'.[18]

Deportations

Tigras survived into the spring of 1949 – bored senseless in his bunker much of the time, hungry, harassed and obsessed with spies in other moments. In March, he started to hear persistent rumours that deportations were imminent. The partisans listened but did nothing to try to disrupt them. They sat in their hiding place and complained that there were no women in the hut – nobody to prepare food. On 25 March, Tigras woke up to the news that people were already being deported: large number of trucks had arrived; in every truck, there were two to three families, guarded by Soviet security forces; six trucks drove off together in a convoy, to the train station where an echelon awaited. The partisans watched, angrily, but did nothing. At two in the afternoon, there was another convoy of seventeen trucks. Women and children cried. Men stared ahead sullenly. Later, there was another convoy of twelve trucks, then another ten. The partisans moved on because they could not watch any more. They believed the goal of the deportation to be the extermination of the Lithuanian people – a misreading which would have an afterlife as the claim that the Bolsheviks attempted 'genocide' in the Baltics.[19]

The real reason for these inhumane measures was counter-insurgency: ever since collectivization and dekulakization in the Soviet heartland at the start of the 1930s, the Soviet security forces had learned that the best way to stop an uprising was to remove potential trouble makers and their families. And they had perfected this technique during their long Second World War, beginning with the Koreans in 1937 and on to the many 'national operations' of the war years described in other chapters of this book. That they often deported the wrong people – because they selected by 'objective' criteria (social class or nationality) – did not mean that the tactic did not work: with everybody who refused to join collective farms threatened with removal, the popularity of collectivization suddenly increased in the western borderlands. And collectivized farmers could be controlled much better, both economically and politically, than individual families in charge of their own land and their means of production. As Tigras noted with resignation on 29 March 1949, writing in a bunker filled with civilians who had managed to escape the deportation: the agitation of the 'destroyers' for joining the kolkhozes now had much better results; people were afraid of deportation and joined.[20]

Dirty war

Eight months later, Tigras's luck ran out: on 20 November 1949, Albinas Milchukas, which was his true name, was arrested by the Soviets. He survived his capture and was sentenced to twenty-five years corrective labour camp (the death sentence had been abolished in 1947). He served his sentence in Karlag, in Kazakhstan, before returning to Lithuania.[21] Among his final acts before his arrest was terror against collective farmers. 'We spend nearly the entire day discussing what to do with the village of T., where nearly the entire population has already entered the kolkhoz', he wrote on 6 April. In particular the activists who joined first were a problem, providing an example to the rest. 'We thought all about what to do and then decided to pay these degenerates a visit.' As it got dark, intoxicated on account of some post-dinner drinking, they shouldered their weapons and marched through rain and wind to the hut of the village activists. 'These gentlemen had not expected such guests. . . . They thought, the partisans would leave them in peace and they could quietly build the kolkhoz. . . . We scared them a little . . . they promised to abandon the kolkhoz.'[22]

The targets of these 'conversations' were, of course, neither 'Russian occupiers' nor even 'Jewish Bolsheviks' but fellow Lithuanians, who had made the choice against deportation and for the collective farm. Like the 'spies' that turned in information to the authorities, they were part of the category of 'traitors' – collaborators with the occupiers. But as a Lithuanian historian admits, 'innocent civilians also perished as a result of such partisan activity'.[23] This is an understatement. As another historian has pointed out, the guerrillas' 'major victims' – in Lithuania as elsewhere in the Baltics or in Ukraine – were 'soft targets, the peasants who fit their definition of collaborator'.[24]

The statistics speak a clear language. In Lithuania, in 1944, the security forces killed 1,826 partisans but recorded only ninety-three own losses during these operations. Meanwhile, the partisans killed 582 supporters of the Soviets, 43.5 per cent of them activists of party or government, another 42.8 per cent other civilians. Only 13.7 per cent were security forces, police or army personnel. The kill ratio in Soviet counter-insurgency operations remained static in the years to come: during anti-partisan operation from 1944 all the way to 1948, only one security trooper was killed for every ten partisan. However, the guerrillas got better at shooting civilians:

in 1945, they executed 1,630 civilians and 575 activists; in 1946 the corresponding numbers were 2,029 and 432. Thus, after their military defeat, they killed more people than during the open confrontation with the occupying forces and the overall kill-ratios changed in favour of the insurgents: if in 1945, three supporters of the occupiers died for every ten dead partisans, already in 1946 fifteen did and in 1948 sixteen Soviets died for every ten killed Lithuanian resistance fighters. Nearly all of the 'Soviet' losses were local civilians, however. The Lithuanian guerrillas were not special in this regard: despite minor variations in particular in the size of the insurgencies (largest in Ukraine, smallest in Estonia), the overall numbers look very similar in Latvia, Estonia, Belarus or Ukraine. In their fight to free their countries from what they conceived of as 'Russian' or 'Jewish communist' occupation, the nationalists killed predominantly their own people.[25]

Soviet counter-insurgency combined covert operations, infiltration, intelligence gathering and search-and-destroy missions with the offer of amnesty and the threat of deportation of family members. Insurgents had the choice of turning themselves in and collaborating with the Soviets or being destroyed by an opponent with overwhelming firepower who would also deport their near and dear. These tactics were successful. They sowed internal discord, isolated the insurgents further from their social environment and forced them to choose between loyalty to their cause and to their families. The deportations in particular – victimizing some 203,737 people in Western Ukraine and 190,658 in the three Baltic republics – removed the soil in which the insurgency was rooted: people who could have supported the resistance were gone, had entered the collective farms, or were so scared now to be sent to Siberia that they avoided the insurgents like the plague. Eventually, thus, the borderlands were pacified.[26]

Counter-insurgency troops in the western borderlands committed many crimes: rape, random killings, murder, theft and destruction. On 22 October 1944, for example, a group of counter-insurgency troops operating in Ukraine took revenge for three soldiers they had lost by shooting ten uninvolved civilians and burning forty-five peasant huts.[27] On 13 March 1945, another group arrested a man in a village, whom they suspected of membership in the underground. The suspect was unable to walk, because he suffered from tuberculosis. The Soviets shot him. Two days later, another group got into a fire fight with nationalist guerrillas. They captured one of the survivors, but the soldier who was meant to bring him out of the woods to have him arrested instead executed the wounded man and returned to his group. On 8 April, another group marched through a village after a battle with 'bandits', and decided to burn down four peasant huts.[28] When the 10th Mechanized Division came under fire from 'unknown bandits' while passing through a Ukrainian village in the night of 10 January 1946, the soldiers responded by burning down twenty-three huts. Several inhabitants died in the flames. 'During the fire, the soldiers of this unit robbed the property of the population, raped women, and beat and killed citizens of the village', as the police report about the incident stated. This indiscriminate violence victimized war invalids as well as families of Red Army veterans.[29]

That such violence was committed by uniformed agents of the Soviet state does not mean that it was part of the totalitarian programme of social reconstruction. As the most accomplished historian of the Soviet counter-insurgency has it, 'senior party leaders and police commanders realized that pacification suffered immensely from arbitrary violence and the corruption of security forces.'[30] Hence, in Ukraine in 1944, 518 NKVD officials were prosecuted, including for illegal use of weapons, marauding and robbery. These included two officials who had burned down a hut and killed the son and mother of an underground fighter and were sentenced to ten years labour camp.[31] In 1945, another 391 officials were prosecuted,[32] including for torturing suspects.[33] The use of 'illegal investigative methods', that is, beatings and other forms of torture during interrogations, could also lead to exclusion from the Communist Party and ended long-standing Chekist careers.[34] The leadership in state and party thus 'never gave carte blanche to the security agencies during the counterinsurgency campaign in the borderlands', the same historian points out. 'It wanted repressions to be centralized and selective.'[35]

Liberation or occupation?

Nevertheless, such violence helped convince the locals that the return of the Soviets was no 'liberation' but rather a renewed 'occupation'. The case of Estonia is instructive in this respect. The small Baltic nation had suffered terribly under the first year of Soviet occupation in 1940–1. And it suffered less under the Germans than others. 'Compared to other parts of the Soviet Union', write two leading scholars, 'in Estonia the German occupation from 1941 to 1944 was relatively mild. Approximately 8,000 inhabitants were murdered', they point out, 'among them nearly all the remaining Jews and much of the Roma population'. But ethnic Estonians 'were better treated than other Eastern Europeans'. Moreover, the country lost significantly more due to Soviet actions: Estonians who died in detention, during deportation, in special settlement, in the Gulag, in labour battalions, were killed by the retreating Soviets in the bacchanalia of the summer of 1941, fell victim to counter-insurgency operations after their return or died due to the famine of 1946–7. Altogether, the war had killed at least 7.2 per cent of Estonia's population, mostly as a result of Soviet occupation and Sovietization. Many of these deaths, of course, were unintended: the Soviets did not plan to kill people in deportation trains, or to starve their population in 1946–7, but this fact does not mean that locals did not experience these as effects of the occupation. To many, the Nazis thus seemed the lesser evil. An astonishing 7 per cent of the population fought along the Wehrmacht against the Red Army in 1944, and 70,000 fled west with the retreating Wehrmacht in 1944.[36]

Those who remained had to brace for more of the same. During the years 1944–52, the level of repression in the western borderlands was breathtaking: the Soviets arrested, deported or killed in counter-insurgency operations nearly a million people from Western Ukraine and the Baltics. Measured against the overall population of these regions, these numbers mean that 6 per cent of the pre-Barbarossa population of Western Ukraine, Latvia, and Estonia fell victim to these three forms of repression. In Lithuania, this share reached an incredible 9 per cent. These are shocking percentages. The 'old' Soviet Union saw a similar war against the population only during collectivization and dekulakization at the beginning of the Stalin years.[37]

In parallel with the military operations against hidden guerrillas, Soviet security forces were engaged in detailed police work against collaborators with the Germans, including perpetrators in the Holocaust. They were helped by the fact that wartime crimes had happened very much in the open: there were ample witnesses of the rounding up and shooting of Jews and the neglect and execution of POWs. The Soviets had also often captured German archival documents which allowed to prove beyond doubt somebody's participation in German sponsored police or military formations as well as in the civil administration of the occupiers. Most historians who have worked with Soviet war crime trial records have concluded that these investigations, while not devoid of torture and other procedural irregularities (as even Dushanski acknowledged), by and large convicted actual war criminals rather than – as had been the case in 1937–8 – imaginary enemies of Soviet power. These war criminals often had become post-war freedom fighters, and Dushanski consistently conflated the two groups. This perception would be countered by a similarly one-dimensional celebration of the resistance by Lithuanian, Estonian, Latvian and Ukrainian nationalists, both then and today.[38]

The reality on the ground, meanwhile, was much more complex. Not every resistance fighter was a former Nazi collaborator and not every war criminal was a freedom fighter. The Germans had accounted for 180,000 armed collaborators in the Baltic states: policemen, Wehrmacht and SS troops, paramilitaries and auxiliaries, etc.[39] Many of them did not survive the war or fled with Hitler's retreating soldiers. After the war, the Soviets arrested as part of their counter-insurgency over 248,000 – a good 40 per cent more than had served the Germans in uniform. And this calculation does not account for the well over 23,000 killed in counter-insurgency operations, to say nothing of the 190,000 who were deported to the Soviet hinterland as family members of 'kulaks' and 'hidden' nationalists, or were accused of aiding and abetting the anti-Soviet resistance.[40]

Between hammer and anvil

At the same time, the resistance should not be conflated with the population at large. According to Lithuanian historians, about 4 per cent of the population 'was directly (as partisans) or indirectly (as supporters) engaged in the armed anti-Soviet resistance movement'. That this share was 'twice the percentage of people engaged in Vietnam's partisan war' might be true; but it was still just 4 per cent.[41]

The spectacular confrontation of Soviet security forces and local guerrillas can easily distract from the fact that outright supporters of Soviet power (like Dushanski) and outright opponents (like 'Tigras') were in the minority. As Dushanski rightly observed, a 'large part of the Lithuanian people wanted to live and work quietly and did not participate in the underground or "forest" war'. They adapted themselves to the new regime, however unhappily, secretly grumbling. Dreaming of liberation by the United States was one thing; taking up arms to endanger one's own and – more importantly – one's family's lives, was quite another.[42]

As historians have increasingly stressed, this statement was true more generally, and indeed throughout the war: there were strong minorities who supported the Stalinist regime or opposed it. The extremes of outright collaboration with the German occupiers and determined resistance to German occupation are both well documented. Pro-Soviet partisans and anti-Soviet nationalist guerrillas were both minority groups in the German occupied territories. The majority of the population, meanwhile, tried to evade to the best of their ability the violence of these groups as well as of the occupiers. On Soviet controlled territory, meanwhile, volunteers to the Red Army were a minority among Red Army recruits, as were those who evaded service or deserted. The majority was not asked for their consent and was instead drafted to fight or work.[43]

Likewise, after the return of Soviet power to the western borderlands, the population faced nearly impossible choices. 'The common peasants were in the worst situation', writes a historian of the Sovietization of the Baltic states. 'They found themselves "between hammer and anvil": if they sabotaged the state campaigns, they could expect repression from the authorities; but if they participated in these campaigns, they were punished by the "Forest Brothers."' Attempting to decide which one of these repressions was more legitimate, this scholar continues, is meaningless: 'For the peasants there was no choice between "better" and 'worse'.[44]

Crime wave

In the final analysis, then, the majority of the population wanted to live in peace, feed their families, survive and maybe even get ahead in life. It would side with whoever managed to monopolize the means of violence and thus establish a more or less predictable situation. That in itself was not an easy task, as violence and crime proliferated, and not just in the western borderlands. 'It has become impossible to go out into the streets', complained a Moscow resident in late 1945. 'I am more worried about my life now than during the war', he added. 'It became impossible to live because of the thieves and hooligans', grumbled another. 'Why is it not possible to take stronger action against them to protect the life of peaceful citizens?'[45] Not only in Moscow but also in the rest of Eurasia in 1945–9, the only force which could protect citizens from the violence of armed men was the Soviet state. This state worked hard to contain the war-induced orgy of lawlessness. Its geography is reflected in secret soviet statistics: in 1946, the security services liquidated 1,196 groups of nationalist resisters, nearly all in the western borderlands; but they also destroyed or detained the members of 2,895 criminal gangs: 84 per cent of these had operated in the 'old' Soviet heartland rather than the new territories.[46]

A central piece of legislation in this context was the 1947 theft law. Terrible penalties were imposed for the misappropriation of both state property and the things of private citizens (known as 'personal property' because, for ideological reasons, 'private property' could not exist in the Soviet Union). These laws were typically heavy-handed approaches to a real problem: the pervasive theft of grain from collective farms, bread from shops or individuals and items of daily use from both enterprises and private citizens. Theft from individuals was threatened now with five to six years in the labour camps. If it was committed by an organized gang or repeatedly, it attracted six to ten years. Robbery was punished with ten to twenty years in the Gulag, depending on the levels of violence and organization involved. Offenders of this crime also had their own property confiscated by the state. The equivalent decree protecting the property of state enterprises and collective farms imposed even heavier penalties: five to eight years for theft from collective farms and seven to ten years for theft from state enterprises and organizations, both with the option of confiscating the offender's property; eight to twenty years with confiscation of property if the illegal acquisition involved large quantities, happened repeatedly or was conducted by an organized group.[47] As a result, from 1946 to 1947, prosecution of theft of state property jumped from 378,500 in 1946 to well over half a million in 1947. In subsequent years, fewer people were prosecuted: 275,100 in 1948 and 234,000 in 1949, reflecting the decline in the number of offenses in these years.[48] Nevertheless, these laws swelled the numbers of prisoners in the Gulag system. If in January 1945 Soviet camps, prisons and labour colonies held 1.7 million people, by March 1953 this population had grown to 2.5 million. Nearly half of them served sentences for theft. Many of them were mothers who had stolen a piece of bred for their hungry children: women now made up 17 per cent of the Gulag population.[49]

Were these tough laws necessary? Table 2 summarizes now available top secret statistics on the war and post-war crime wave. These numbers show that crime peaked during the war in the west of 1939–40, when the western borderlands were annexed. It dropped in 1941 but then steadily increased to 1944, after which it dropped quite substantially with only a short upward movement during 1946, when mass demobilization and repatriation were at a height in the context of

TABLE 2 *Crime statistics for Soviet Union, 1939–49 (reported cases)*

	Murder	robberies	murder and robberies combined	Theft	Hooliganism	Other (including rape)	sum
1939	-	9,005	9,005	402,788	166,643	-	578,436
1940	8,086	18,758	26,844	518,270	14,473	282,681	842,268
1941	2,735	9,758	12,493	230,154	12,234	235,105	489,986
1942	4,485	7,932	12,417	312,861	5,991	186,734	518,003
1943	5,595	12,295	17,890	418,180	8,418	179,395	623,883
1944	9,935	18,259	28,194	481,191	15,731	150,773	675,889
1945	8,656	22,971	31,627	378,211	24,586	124,488	558,912
1946	10,304	29,427	39,731	355,996	87,603	122,856	606,186
1947	11,154	22,508	33,662	353,211	40,891	56,033	483,797
1948	5,514	9,761	15,275	162,320	45,559	19,460	242,614
1949	5,403	8,742	14,145	114,905	40,867	5,844	175,761

Notes: Crime statistics are notoriously problematic to analyse. They reflect not necessarily the reality on the ground and are subject to both under- and over-reporting depending on policing capacities. They also rely on changing categorization, which we see in this chart in the absence of 'murders' in 1939 (which were included under 'robberies' that year) and the puzzling absence of 'rape' in the same year. 'Hooliganism', a crime defined as defying social norms, suffered from two re-definitions during this period: in 1940 the category was toughened up and statistics from now on only counted cases including severe physical abuse. From 1947, the category was again relaxed, which makes the drop between 1946 and 1947 in this category all the more remarkable. The numbers in the table exclude cases registered by transport police. As trains were a space of high criminality, these numbers are thus lower limits.

Source: Top secret Ministry of the Interior report, 13 April 1955, reprinted in *Na 'kraiu' sovetskogo obshchestva. Sotsial'nye marginaly kak ob"ekt gosudarstvennoi politiki. 1945-1960-e gg*, ed. E. Iu. Zubkova and T. Iu. Zhukova (Moscow: Rosspen, 2010), 175–6, 184.

the post-war famine. Theft peaked in 1944, thus well before the tough theft laws came into existence. But as the war with Germany went on, crime became more violent. Murder and robberies combined as well as hooliganism were at their height in 1946. Murder continued to grow to 1947, when all other forms of crime were already in steep decline. Thus the perceptions of Soviet citizens that they were living in violent times were quite justified, but the state's 'iron fist' approach to theft was an over-reaction to a temporary crisis triggered by the famine and the massive population movements of 1945–6: repatriation, demobilization, the return of evacuated citizens and the transfer of troops from the European to the Asian theatre of operations.

Overall, then, outside the western borderland, the war-induced lawlessness was under control by 1946–7. What caused this crime wave? As far as theft was concerned, the most general underlying cause was the utter poverty and despair of most Soviet citizens after victory. The Soviet Union had never been a rich country, Stalin's revolution from above in the early 1930s had further depressed civilian consumption levels, and the Second World War in general, and the German–Soviet war in particular shifted the situation from bad to catastrophic, both because of wartime destruction and because of the single-minded way in which the Stalinist state concentrated all resources 'for the front, all for victory', to cite an ubiquitous propaganda phrase. Soviet citizens had always stolen – from the enterprise or collective farm where they worked and from each other – but the existential wartime emergency increased the phenomenon in a situation where almost everybody suffered from shortage of even the most basic means of life. At the same time, the population faced fewer police, first because the 1939–40 expansion of the empire stretched the existing security forces and after 22 June 1941, police were drafted to fight the invasion.[50] By 1946, writes an authority on Soviet policing, 'police ranks were stretched dangerously thin, more so than at any time since the early 1930s.'[51]

Many of those who ended up in the Gulag because of the new theft laws were convicted because they had picked up something that 'was lying around poorly', as the Russian phrase has it. But others were convicted because of seriously violent crimes. The many available weapons aided armed gangsterism among groups forged during times of war. The authorities made concerted attempts to collect these weapons. By 1 March 1945, security forces mopping up behind the advancing front lines had confiscated 1,506 machine guns, 1,895 automatic weapons, over 29,000 rifles, thousands of handguns, tens of thousands of hand grenades and over 23,000 pieces of ammunition from over 96,000 persons who had not been under the control of the authorities. Unauthorized weapons thus 'extracted' included forty-five mortars, sixteen artillery piece and 1,524 bombs, shells and mines.[52] Such large weaponry could not be easily hidden, but other arms made their way to the hinterland. Even the capital was not immune. In 1945, police in Moscow confiscated sixty-four machine guns, 365 automatic weapons, 975 rifles, 9,997 revolvers and 98,900 pieces of military ammunition.[53] In the following year, the authorities registered 11,860 cases of armed banditry all over the Soviet Union. This category included both nationalist attacks on activists, military or security forces in the western borderlands, but also large-scale armed robbery of trains, collective farms or enterprises. Over half of these 'non-political' cases took place in the 'old' Soviet heartland.[54]

Who were the perpetrators of crime? Youth and homeless children, displaced and disconnected by the upheaval of war, were one central group. Among those arrested and prosecuted in Vlamir province in 1946, between 65 and 70 per cent were young people, while in the Soviet Union as a whole close to half of all perpetrators were youth, often as members of gangs.[55] Soldiers were another prominent group of perpetrators. 'Taking advantage of the connivance of the command staff, some servicemen are engaging in robbery, theft, and hooliganism', reported a high-ranking Party official about the situation in the country in February 1947.[56] Such occurrences were continuations of the wartime situation. In 1939–45 and in the west again in 1945–9, Soviet troops were often poorly controlled and they frequently committed crimes. There was a multiplicity of victims: Soviet civilians, soldiers, enemy civilians and civilians of liberated countries, enemy combatants, in particular at point of capture.

A culture of violence

This brutality of soldiers towards others was an externalization of the ubiquitous culture of violence within the Red Army itself. 'The temper and morality of many military leaders', writes one historian, 'did not differ from Stalin's'. Georgy Zhukov's 'favourite method' of leadership was to threaten those he led with execution. Vasily Chuikov proudly reported his own use of such lethal intimidation to historians shortly after the battle of Stalingrad.[57] Further down the hierarchy, commanders punched their subordinates 'in the face' and the thus abused proceeded, likewise, establishing a 'chain of command of punching', as one war correspondent noted with dismay.[58] Others went further, wielding their handgun, threatening execution if troops would not advance under fire. 'Right away, our company commander warned us that, if we lay down, he would shoot all of us, and he really did shoot some', as one of his underlings reported. 'After that, we never tried to lie down again', he added dryly.[59] During the battle of Stalingrad, when an assault group of Uzbeks refused to go into a suicidal attack, the 'whole bunch of them were shot', as their commander reported matter-of-factly after the battle. 'The platoon commander just lifted them up by their collars and shot them.'[60]

As the war went on, this culture of brutality was institutionalized in small bands of armed men, bound together by rituals of violence. These groups existed in the army and the police forces employed to secure the hinterland, within irregular troops, pro- and anti-Soviet guerrillas, or as criminal gangs. They were as much about the survival of their members as about the violence they projected onto others. As long as these violent primary collectives could not be broken up – through demobilization, counter-insurgency and police work – they continued to violate others.

Besides surrendering enemy troops and anti-Soviet guerrillas, the main target of such violence was women: women in the armed forces, women among partisans, nurses tasked to look after war invalids on their way home, civilians – Ukrainians, Yugoslavs and liberated Ostarbeiter. Rapes and other brutalities are reported from Poland in 1939, from Yugoslavia in 1944, from Manchuria in 1945, and of course from Germany and Austria at war's end where they were particularly ubiquitous. Here, retribution for German sexual crimes in the occupied Soviet Union combined with a more general anger at their criminal conduct. Revenge became entangled with the oft-observed impulse of armed men to punish the enemy by violation 'his women'. This toxic cocktail of violent emotions was further stirred by a vicious campaign of hate propaganda designed to motivate exhausted troops to continue fighting beyond liberated Soviet territory. However, the bacchanalia in Germany was only an extreme form of a more generalized problem. Soviet penal battalions treated liberated Soviet villagers in the same barbaric fashion, cases where the perpetrators might well have been hardened criminals who had been enlisted from the Gulag. But in other instances, reported from the Soviet hinterland, regular Red Army soldiers, demobilizing veterans, or even students of military schools who had never seen combat behaved not much differently. Bands of deserters, draft dodgers and former collaborators with the Germans added to the volatile mix.[61]

During preparation for war against Japan and later during demobilization, these violent collectives travelled back to the Soviet Union.[62] In May 1945, Dushanski's men found an entire Lithuanian family murdered in their hut. Their investigation concluded that neither local troops nor nationalist guerrillas were responsible for this deed. 'Not far from the hut was a railway line', Dushanski remembered later. Along this line

> troop echelons rumbled past, one after the other, on the way to the east, to the coming war with Japan. We found out which trains had passed through Kaunas on this day and sent an encrypted telegram to the transport departments of state security. The killers were found only two weeks later, already beyond the Urals, a gang of seven military personnel.[63]

Further east, the security services reported in June of the same year 'cases of brutal behaviour from the side of servicemen, both rank and file and officers, who travel on the Siberian railway to the East'. They sold loot brought from Germany, the report continued, drank heavily, presumably from the proceeds of these sales and got into gunfights. They plundered and raped along the way.[64] Similar cases were reported during mass demobilization from the summer of 1945.[65]

The typical size of the violent collectives roaming the Soviet empire in the mid-1940s was around seven men – about the size, incidentally, of the spontaneously forming primary groups in the Red Army, which made life bearable and survival possible. Engaging in violence was a central part of the rituals which formed and re-created these groups. And they could proliferate because the state's grip on the population, its ability to police the vast spaces and the millions of armed men and women within them, was seriously impaired.[66]

The extent to which this post-war violence was rooted in a breakdown of the state's monopoly of force is illustrated by cases where one group of uniformed representatives of the Soviet state went after another such group: soldiers against police, in the most widespread constellation. One such instance happened on 7 July 1946 in the south-Estonian town of Viljandi, where some 6,000 locals celebrated a holiday in the town's main park. At about 6.00 pm, a fight erupted between two men, in the course of which one of them 'glassed' the other in the face. Blood was flowing and both fighters were arrested by the police. A drunk captain of a local anti-tank unit witnessed the arrest, went after the policeman and demanded to free one of the men, hitting the police in the process. When the police tried to arrest the hooligan in army uniform, the latter drew his Browning (a weapon he owned illegally) and threatened the policeman, before hitting him again and leaving the police station. He then proceeded to organize several soldiers into his own patrol of seven men. Armed with automatic weapons, they went after both regular militia and Ministry of Internal Affairs (MVD) forces present in the park. At around 9.00 pm they assaulted three MVD officers, and later a militia-man, the drunken captain yelling 'beat the Chekists!' Later, he wrangled a pistol from another MVD man, whom he also beat mercilessly. Then he emptied the entire magazine, shooting wildly into the air. When a local MVD boss tried to call the army commandant to get the perpetrator arrested, he only got his wife on the phone, who replied: 'The commandant is drunk. I will not wake him up.' The issue was still unresolved a week later, although the MVD knew the name of the ringleader.[67]

This incident was rather restrained. Worse had happened some months prior, on Victory Day (9 May) in a small town in Estonia. A red navy sailor and his girlfriend decided to cap the celebrations with a little love making. Having no place of their own, they broke into somebody's house and began to enjoy each other in the kitchen. The owner caught them in the act. It was bad luck for the lovers that he was a police (militia) man. He told them that his kitchen was no bordello and demanded the woman's papers. The lovers cursed him out in reply only to find the militia called to arrest them. But the police had underestimated the sailor, who managed to get some of his comrades to help him on the way: they beat the policeman, who ran only to get shot at. The sailors caught him in front of

ILLUSTRATION 21 Raising the Red Flag over the destroyed Reichstag in Berlin, 2 May 1945. This iconic photograph had to be retouched before publication, as the soldier to the right wears two wristwatches, an index of Red Army looting in Germany. After the offending evidence was removed, it became the most famous photo of Soviet victory. © SPUTNIK / Alamy Stock Photo.

the police building, beat him savagely, and threw him into a ditch. As they were already at it, they also assaulted another security official who tried to enter the building. He made a run for it, entered the police station with the words 'They want to kill me! Get your weapons!' A policeman then shot into the air, which turned the out-of-control soldiers around.

This might have been the end of this story, had the retreating twenty sailors not encountered one of their commanding officers, a major. The commander, who was not sober, told them to turn around and then oversaw a renewed assault on the police building. They broke down the door where the officials were hiding, hit one of them over the head with the butt of an automatic rifle, broke open the store room where evidence was kept, extracted six bottle of moonshine and an automatic rifle, and left only when a higher-ranking officer arrived and told them to get out of there.[68]

Many such stories could be added here – from archives in Latvia, in Lithuania, in Estonia, in Ukraine and in Russia. Occupied Germany yields a particularly rich trove of such stories, but they all come down to a similar line: there were a lot of armed men, often drunk, who were running amok in post-war Eurasia. Their main loyalty was to each other – to their immediate comrades. The stories resemble each other in mind numbing regularity: the anger, the alcohol, the utter brutality. Confrontations occurred between different arms of the Soviet state (army versus police, very often), between rival military units, and between gangs of armed men and the civilian population. Random destruction, assault for sport, theft, robbery and sexual violence were often intertwined. Aggression, sexual urges, alcohol and the satisfaction of material needs all congealed in violent rituals of male bonding in small groups.[69]

Ending the war after the war

The problem, then, was not the brutalization of individuals, but of groups and that the war had decreased the state's ability to properly police the vast spaces and the millions of people it nominally controlled. It would take until 1948–9 that Stalin's state re-established the control it had lost: over space, over people, over weapons, over violence. An essential part of this process was demobilization: an army of millions needed to be transported home, broken up and the men and women filling its ranks transferred to peacetime work and reintegrated into civilian society. Demobilization was not primarily motivated by the goal of pacifying the empire – the main reason was economic: an army of this size could not be sustained, the wartime economy was at its breaking point, and the country, its cities, villages, factories and collective farms needed to be re-built after the destruction of the war. All of this required labour and hence the soldiers needed to become civilians again. But demobilization, while sometimes accompanied by violence as well, did have the long-time effect of also breaking up many of the violent collectives which enabled troop violence.[70]

However, in the first instance, demobilization increased the already high level of population movement at war's end, which contributed to the further spread of violence. Everybody seemed to be on the move in the immediate post-war years. In the years from 1945 to 1948, in excess of 8.5 million soldiers returned to civilian life and millions more returned from evacuation in the hinterland to what was left of their homes (often occupied by others displaced by this war). At the same time, 5.4 million former prisoners or war or slave labourers to the

Germans were repatriated, screened by the security services and sent home (58 per cent), drafted into the army (19 per cent), the labour army (15 per cent) or were handed over as traitors or war criminals to the police for prosecution (7 per cent).[71] Meanwhile, well over a million people were encouraged to move across the newly drawn borderlines with Finland and Poland, or if they did not sign up themselves, were coerced to do so. These population exchanges were part of the 'unscrambling' of the ethnographic omelette, which had started in the wake of the Hitler–Stalin Pact of 1939 but which now fortified the new frontiers with ethnic boundaries: between 1944 and 1946, 483,000 Ukrainians moved from what was now again Poland to Soviet Ukraine, while 790,000 Poles (and Polish Jews) travelled in the opposite direction. Those 150,000 Ukrainians who had stayed behind were rounded up by Polish forces in the 'Vistula Action' of 1947 and deported to Ukraine.[72]

In the north, meanwhile, the end of the 'continuation war' had restored the 1940 border between Finland and the Soviet Union, with a few extra territories annexed by Stalin. Some 400,000 Finns were resettled elsewhere in their country, their houses taken over by voluntary re-settlers from the Soviet heartlands.[73] Moving in the opposite direction, some 56,000 Ingrian Finns, former Soviet subjects who had spent part or all of the war on the other side of the frontline, were returned to the Soviet Union. Never entirely trusted because they had spent the war on the Finnish side, those who had not been sent to remote parts of the Soviet Union in the first place would be expelled from Leningrad region in 1947 and not allowed to live in any major city of the Union.[74]

In the south, the year 1944 saw the wholesale deportation of some 750,000 people: Chechens and Ingush, Balkars, Crimean Tatars, Crimean Greeks, Bulgarians and Armenians and a variety of ethnic groups from Southern Georgia,[75] while Iranian Azerbaijanis moved to the Soviet side of the border in 1946, after Stalin had abandoned their uprising and the Red Army had retreated from Northern Iran.[76] During the next three years, they would be joined by 100,000 Armenians who had lived in the diaspora and decided to move their 'Soviet Homeland', as well as over 11,000 Greek communists who arrived in Georgia in 1949, after they had lost their Civil War. The latter were forwarded to Tashkent, where they were housed in camps just recently emptied of POWs and prisoners.[77]

In the east, in 1947–8 just over 6,000 émigré Russians from Shanghai and Tientsin repatriated from a neighbour embroiled in its own Civil War, and were sent to live in various regions of Siberia as well as the Bashkir and Tatar autonomous republics. Many of them would later be arrested, as would be several hundreds of 'naïve teenagers from Manchuria' who had crossed the border illegally to return to the victorious homeland.[78] In parallel to all of these movements, hundreds of thousands of presumed or real enemies of Soviet power were deported from the western borderlands to the Soviet hinterland, as we have already seen. Those who survived would not return until after Stalin's death.

ILLUSTRATION 22 Ukrainian resettlers from Poland to the Soviet Union, 1946. As part of the post-war consolidation of the Soviet empire the borders between Poland and the Soviet Union were made to conform more closely to ethnic lines. Poles were resettled from the Soviet Union, Ukrainians went the other way. In this picture, Ukrainian resettlers wait at a train station which had been destroyed by Ukrainian nationalist partisans who resisted both the Sovietization and the Polonization of regions they deemed Ukrainian. © Archive PL / Alamy Stock Photo.

ILLUSTRATION 23 A deported Ingush family mourns their dead daughter in Kazakhstan, 1944. Deportations of perceived 'class enemies' and 'enemy nations' were a central aspect of Stalinist war making. They brought untold suffering to millions of people. © Wikimedia Commons (public domain).

There would be some population movements later in the 1950s, but by and large, 1948–9 marks the end of this period of flux, violence, displacement and the start of some stability. Normalcy also returned in other respects: the final Soviet famine was over by 1947, rationing was ended at the end of that year in parallel with a currency reform which confiscated much of the extra cash peasants and black marketeers had managed to accumulate during the war, and the draconian labour laws of 1940–1 were abolished in 1948. The labour army was dismantled in steps between 1945 and 1949, its 'labour soldiers' allowed to return home (as in the case of Estonians), reassigned to become regular workers in their enterprises (as in the case of Russians) or transferred to the status of special settlers (as in the case of Germans). As the year 1949 came to an end, then, the Soviet Second World War was over.[79]

9   IMPACT AND AFTERMATH

Tortured, sick and tired

While fighting continued in the western borderlands and the violence of war continued to spill over into post-war society all over the Soviet Union, many exhausted Soviet citizens wearily celebrated the Red Army's triumph. 'A tortured, sick, and dead tired army had triumphed. Emaciated, coughing. With spinal injuries and arthritis, gastric ulcers. . . . That's how I remember victory', noted one of them later.[1] At the home-front, too, suffering defined the war's end. The war veteran Raban Idiev, who returned to his collective farm in Uzbekistan in July 1945, found that his wife, two of his children, and his two sisters all had not survived the war. His remaining 6-year-old son was covered in ulcers. He lived in a broken tent.[2]

These were not individual experiences – the archival record is littered with similar stories, results of the utter desolation of Stalin's empire in 1945. The Soviet Union had paid a heavy price for victory. About 12 per cent of the pre-war population had perished. Russia had sacrificed most men at the frontlines: 66 per cent of the military dead were Russians, who before the German attack had constituted some 52 per cent of the Soviet population. Ukrainians, whose republic was occupied in full and who were often kept away from the frontlines because the regime did not trust them, were underrepresented among military losses. In 1941, they had represented nearly 18 per cent of the population, while their share among military dead was 16 per cent. Belarusians, nearly 4 per cent of the population, fell in a similar ball park with 3 per cent of losses, and the under-representation of Jews, about 2.6 per cent of the population and 1.6 per cent of military losses, can also be explained by a combination of the physical location of many of them in the occupied regions and the Soviet reluctance to let 'new Soviets' from the annexed territories to the frontline.[3]

Among civilian losses, however, Russians were underrepresented with 38 per cent, while Ukrainians had suffered disproportionately under German occupation.

They made up 36 per cent of civilian losses, Belarusians 9 per cent. But the worst affected were Soviet Jews. Out of a 1940 Soviet Jewish population of some 5 million, 2.5 to 2.6 million had been murdered in the Holocaust and some 142,500 died at the frontlines. Thus, at least 52 per cent did not survive the war, not counting those who died in the Soviet hinterland, starved to death in encircled Leningrad, or were shot by Stalin's secret police.

Those who survived lived on scorched earth. Thousands of town and myriad villages had been bombed, burned and shelled to smithereens. The largest absolute war costs had been occurred by Ukraine, followed by Russia and Belarus. Overall, nearly a third of Soviet national wealth had been destroyed. Apartment blocks, factories and collective farms in the frontline zones needed rebuilding, those in the hinterland suffered from neglect and lack of upkeep and overcrowding. Millions were homeless, millions more were disabled and sick, traumatized by years of relentless misery and horror. Large numbers of orphans roamed the country. To make things worse, a terrible famine ripped through the war-weakened population in 1946–7. Much more widespread than the local instances of starvation of the preceding years, it killed between 1 and 1.5 million people.[4]

The Soviet leadership was aware of the level of destruction and attempted to re-construct the country and its economy as quickly as possible. This task was made more difficult by the US decision to stop Lend-Lease help once Japan was subdued in September 1945. Thus, the Soviet Union had to do it on its own, aided only by goods they confiscated (or, as locals would have it, 'robbed') from the countries they liberated – from Manchuria to Korea, from Poland to Czechoslovakia, and on to Hungary. Only in Germany, where it was particularly systematic, could such dismantling of infrastructure rightly be seen as collecting reparations.[5]

Consolidation

That there were troops in these places was not just an index of Soviet wartime success. It was also a problem. The Red Army's victories had over-extended Stalin's rule. By the end of 1945, the Soviet Union was as big as it ever would be. The Red Army had reconquered all that had been lost to the German advances in 1941 and 1942. The acquisitions of 1939–40 in the west were back in Stalin's hands: the Baltic states, eastern Poland and a strip of Finnish territory all remained part of the red empire. But there was more: Soviet troops occupied much of Eastern Europe and parts of Asia. They stood in Manchuria and Northern Korea, on the Kurile Islands at Japan's doorstep, in the far north of Norway and in the north of Iran. The Soviets had annexed the formerly independent republic of Tuva in the south in 1944 and even kept a presence on the Danish island of Bornholm. Stalin's power, then, extended from Berlin, Prague and Vienna in the west to Tabriz in the south, Pyonyang in the east and the Finnmark in the north.

This was a stunning reversal of fortunes, an expansion of the red empire which seemed to justify all Stalin had done since obtaining power by the late 1920s: collectivization, dekulakization and the five-year plans, the famine and the terror and all the suffering, heartbreak and death they had caused; his foreign policy gambles of the late 1930s, even the ill-fated pact with Hitler. Such an assessment, of course, required amnesia about all that had gone wrong along the way, not least the catastrophe of 1941. But dictators can forget their blunders more easily than politicians in open societies. Victory in the Second World War would become not only Stalin's greatest claim to fame but also the centrepiece of Soviet post-war identity. It haunts Russia and the other successor states of the Soviet Union to this day.

In 1945, however, this incredible expansion was dangerously close to having grown beyond the Soviet state's ability to govern. The situation in late 1945 was not sustainable. The expense of keeping current levels of military mobilization would cripple any ability to re-build the shattered economy. The share of military expenditures in the state budget had ballooned from an already high 33 per cent in 1940 to nearly 60 per cent in 1943. It still stood at 43 per cent in 1945 and needed to come down fast to free resources for civilian reconstruction. Stalin's empire was over-extended and exhausted from a long Second World War. Consolidation was clearly necessary and some lands which had been conquered had to be let go again. For those that remained in the Soviet orbit, the question was the extent to which they should be integrated into the empire – by annexation or by indirect control? This consolidation took place in parallel with demobilization and pacification.[6]

In deciding what should be in and what should be out of the borders of the post-war Soviet Union Stalin showed remarkable flexibility.[7] The exception was the gains made in 1939–40, which his Western Allies had grudgingly accepted as more or less legitimate throughout the years of the joint fight with Hitler. These were non-negotiable. Other potential sites of expansion could be let go, if allies pushed back or a deal could be struck. Japan's northern island of Hokkaido, for example, was on Stalin's list of places to occupy; but he pulled back when the United States opposed such a move – a remarkable back down, given that Japan had been the threat from the east in a similar way first Poland and then Germany had been from the west. But Stalin had no troops on the ground in Hokkaido and he did not want to risk western acquiescence to the occupation of the Kuriles and Sakhalin in the east, and much of Eastern Europe in the west.[8]

Stalin even retreated from places his army had managed to conquer. Northern Norway and Denmark's Bornholm went in 1945 and 1946, but these were relatively small fry. Larger prizes were given up as well: northern Iran, Xinjian and Manchuria. In Iran he had not only troops on the ground but also a local insurgency brewing in the north, which demanded this area to merge with Soviet Azerbaijan. Stalin wavered for a while, then drew back: this part of the world was not worth the fight, despite the possibility for oil exploration. Soviet troops left in 1946, the insurrection was quashed mercilessly by Iranian forces. Xinjiang, too, had looked as if it would become a Soviet satellite after Stalin's troops had supported rebel Uighurs and Kazakhs in 1944–5. With towering mountain ranges separating it from the rest of China and vast expanses of deserts it would have been 'just the sort of buffer Stalin needed to protect the vulnerable underbelly of Soviet Central Asia', as one expert has pointed out. But after the leader of the Chinese nationalists, Chiang Kai-Shek, had grudgingly accepted an 'independent' Mongolian republic (read: a Soviet satellite state), Stalin dropped the matter and abandoned his allies in Xinjiang just as he would the insurgents in Iran shortly thereafter. He even agreed not to support the Chinese Communist Party in its incipient conflict with Chiang's troops, and later forced its leader, Mao Zedong, to negotiate with Chiang.[9]

These negotiations failed, but that was clearly not Stalin's intention: he wanted to secure his eastern front, but did not know how. As in Europe in 1939, he made policy on the run, adjusting his tactics as matters evolved. The twists and turns of the Soviet position in Asia have created some headaches for historians who want to discern a clear ideological blueprint for Soviet behaviour, preferably an aggressive, expansionist one. The factual record makes such an interpretation hard to sustain, but that does not mean that we need to throw out the idea of ideological underpinnings of Stalin's decisions. The Soviet dictator was a revolutionary statesman: while his overall worldview was structured by Marxism–Leninism, his ideology was as flexible as his teacher Lenin's ideas had been. The Soviet Union was the bulwark of socialism; it was winning the war, but it had also suffered extreme losses and destruction; the security of this bastion of the coming world revolution was all that counted. This 'fusion of Soviet national interests with those of the world revolution', writes one historian, 'freed the Kremlin's hands for the most cynical Realpolitik, justified, ultimately, by allegedly *noble* utopian ends.'[10] Supporting ideological allies like Mao, whose peasant troops seemed to have no chance of winning a civil war against Chiang's troops, would have been unforgivable idealism. Bolsheviks were realists. Stalin stood for 'creative Marxism'. Increasingly, this meant whatever would safeguard the Soviet Union, which thus began to behave like an empire interested in stability rather than the revolutionary state obsessed with destabilizing the outside world.[11]

While good relations with Chiang were pragmatic, so was weakening his hand: who wanted a strong China at the doorstep after negotiations to include communists in the government had failed? Thus, from September 1945, Red Army command in Manchuria began to allow Mao's troops to take over strategic areas and informed them that in case of a Soviet withdrawal, the communists should take control of the abandoned regions. But clashes between communist and US troops worried Stalin, who did not want to be dragged into a conflict with his former allies. Hence in November he ordered the retreating Red Army to help Chiang's troops take over cities before they withdrew.[12] And when the Red Army retreated rather abruptly from Manchuria in May 1946, it had already handed over a large cache of Japanese weapons to Mao's troops, who clandestinely had moved in force into China's north.[13]

Thus, while officially neutral in the emerging Civil War, Stalin did help fuel it once the negotiations between communists and nationalists had failed. In a way, this was a continuation of the strategy followed since 1937: secure the eastern border by entangling potential opponents in war. In 1937, this meant to support China against Japan; after Japan's surrender, it could mean supporting the communist faction in the internal Chinese Civil War. As long as China was at war, it could not threaten the Soviet eastern front. Hence, a continuing confrontation rather than the victory of one side of the Chinese Civil War was one tactic to secure the eastern flank of the Soviet Union during the critical transition from war to peace.

But again, as in Europe in 1939, Stalin was wrong: Chiang would lose the war and Mao's communists would emerge victorious in 1949. Stalin now faced another communist leader with strong credentials to lead the movement in Asia if not globally. He first tried to put Mao in his place by treating him like an annoying poor relation when he came to Moscow in December 1949. But soon, he made sure that Mao would be busy elsewhere. The dictator encouraged his client Kim Il Sung – who had spent the war years in Soviet exile and emerged after the war as the leader of a communist North Korea – to invade the capitalist south of his country; and he made sure that China would support him. This was an incredible gamble, not unlike some of Stalin's antics of the 1930s. The Korean War (June 1950–July 1953) threatened to bring the Soviets into confrontation with the United States, which had transformed from an ally into a competitor in the Cold War between the two major victors of the Second World War: the United States and the Soviet Union, now both superpowers in a bi-polar world. The Korean war led to an undoing of much of the demobilization of the economy after the war: resources were redirected again to defence, reservists called up and the army expanded massively again. This war would continue throughout the final years of Stalin's rule and could only be ended by his successors after the dictator had died in 1953.[14]

In the west, Stalin also felt his way as he went along. Wary of increasing national tensions in his multi-ethnic empire, he did not gobble up the former tsarist domain of Poland. The country would be allowed the status of an independent nation-state friendly to the Soviets. Following the logic that had emerged when groping for a justification for the invasion of Poland in 1939, the borders were fixed along ethnographic lines – regions with large Ukrainian or Belarusian populations became Soviet. Poland shifted westward and became more Polish. Poles and Polish Jews were transferred from the Soviet Union, while Ukrainians and Belarusians were shifted east. Germans were expelled from newly acquired western regions, compensating the new Polish state for real estate lost to the Soviets in the east.

But Stalin did not leave it all to Poland. The formerly Prussian region of Königsberg – a strategically important region south-west of Lithuania – was annexed in 1946, purged of Germans and settled with demobilized Red Army soldiers and other Soviet citizens, overwhelmingly Russians. The fact that what was now called Kaliningrad region was an exterritorial part of the Russian Republic mattered relatively little – with Belarus, Lithuania, Latvia and Russia all part of the Soviet Union, Kaliningrad was integrated into a continuous territory. But today, after the former union republics of the USSR have become independent states, it has become a major anomaly and potential trouble spot in Eastern Europe – an exterritorial territory of Russia with access to the Baltic sea but not to the Russian heartland.[15]

There were some other adjustments to the Soviet borders, including annexations of Klaipėda region (which became part of the Lithuanian SSR) and parts of Finland (Karelia, Petsamo, Salla) in the north, of the Kuriles and Southern Sakhalin in the east and of parts of Czechoslovakia and Romania in the west. But the bigger story of post-war consolidation in the west of the Soviet Union was the creation of a ring of satellites of nominally independent states. At first, Stalin was content with letting each go its own way, with the respective Communist Parties taking more and more control. That, too, showed that the war was not really over: it was a continuation of the wartime policy of good relations and, where necessary, compromise with the Western Allies. After Churchill's 'Iron Curtain' speech of 1946 (which had encouraged Baltic and Ukrainian guerrillas to hold out despite their desperate position), however, Stalin started to lose patience. The turn came with the re-creation of the Comintern (abolished in 1943) as the 'Communist Information Bureau' (or 'Cominform') in September 1947. Between then and the end of the Berlin crisis in 1949, the dictator imposed uniform Stalinist dictatorships on all countries of what in 1955 would become the Warsaw Pact – the major competitor to the capitalist NATO. The pact included Eastern Germany, since 1949 a country in its own right. This year, then, saw the final consolidation of the gains of the war. The year 1949, then, marked the end of the Soviet Second World War not only in the now pacified western borderlands but also in the east of Europe more generally.[16]

Wartime de-Stalinization

If the years 1944–9 saw the pacification of the western borderlands and the period 1945–9 the creation of the ring of satellites in the west as well as the victory of the Chinese Communists in the east, the same period also witnessed a consolidation of Stalinism in the heartland. By 1945, the Soviet system had had evolved significantly from the totalitarianism which had entered the war. In the regions of the country which had remained in Soviet hands throughout the war, villagers had quietly privatized more of the collectively held lands than they were legally entitled to. Even worse, from the official standpoint was that in some areas which had been under German occupation after 1941, the collectives had been dissolved. And in much of the newly annexed territories (the Baltics and parts of Western Ukraine), collectivization had never been implemented in the first place. As a result, private ownership and private production of agriculture had increased compared to 1939. In the cities, meanwhile, many had gained access to garden plots to feed their families, removing one major incentive to stay in the village: the ability to grow your own food in an economy of extreme scarcity. The black market had encroached on the prerogatives of the state-run economy, reaching a high point of its development. The political system had evolved as well. At the top, Stalin's entourage had re-gained agency while running the war effort, and in the hinterland, local officials had also tasted the power which came with a more decentralized system. The intelligentsia had been on a somewhat shorter leash, experiencing the war as a period of freedom. Many thus hoped that the end of the war would bring a reconstruction of the destroyed country along with a reform of the political structure to fulfil wartime hopes.[17]

The ferment was intellectual as well as social. The top leadership considered transferring resources from the military and the heavy industry it depended upon to consumer goods. They also debated dialling back the dictatorship in order to allow the growth of 'socialist democracy'. If implemented, such plans would have amounted to a major deconstruction of the Stalinist warfare state in order to reward the population for victory. Further down the hierarchy even more radical ideas were circulating. State officials began to think it might be a good idea to legalize the black market, in order to tax it, the intelligentsia hoped for a liberalization of cultural production, and at the bottom of the hierarchy, rumours of the impending dissolution of the kolkhoz system swept both the demobilizing army and the countryside most of the soldiers initially returned to. Many of these soldiers had seen life outside the Soviet Union during the war and brought back stories of easy living and at times reports about political freedom existing elsewhere, 'abroad' (za granitsei literally: 'on the other side of the border').[18]

Stalinist reconstruction

Such hopes were bound for bitter disappointment. True, the state led an impressive reconstruction of the country. The number of people engaged in construction, which had collapsed from 1.7 million in 1940 to only 828,000 in 1943, was again up to 1.5 million in 1945. They built nearly 31 million square meters of housing space in 1944 and 1945, the majority (19.5 million) in the formerly occupied regions. Already at the start of 1945, there were more roads with hard covering to ease automobile transport than there had been in 1941. Turnover in transportation went from 259.7 billion kilometre-tons in 1942 to 374.8 billion in 1945. In 1945, train transport reached 67 per cent of 1941 indicators for goods transported and

63 per cent for passenger travel. Electricity production reached 1940 levels in 1946, coal in 1947, steel in 1948 and oil in 1949. In the same year, Soviet industry produced as much soap as it had in 1940, but foodstuffs such as sugar and meat, but also agricultural production in total took until 1950 to reach levels which had been common before the German attack. Some consumer goods, such as shoes or various fabrics for the production of clothes, had to wait until 1951.[19]

However, given the level of destruction, the state's reconstruction effort was far from sufficient. Houses had been damaged or destroyed not only in the former frontline regions. In the hinterland, too, housing stock had seen no upkeep, was in bad repair, lacked basic sanitation and was over-stuffed with suffering humanity. Twenty-five million people were homeless, at least two million lived in dugouts. Those who did not manage to crowd into cramped rooms in communal apartments lived in tents, dormitories, slept in kitchens or hallways. The vast majority of new homes were built by private citizens rather than by enterprises, state organizations or housing cooperatives: 60 per cent in 1941–6, rising to 64 per cent in 1946–50.[20]

The state's attention to the needs of the population was soon diverted to more pressing matters. The attempted stimulation of consumer goods industry was stifled by the emerging cold war. Life, both in the overcrowded cities and in the countryside remained extremely hard even after the famine of 1946–7 was over. The kolkhoz regime was reasserted in 1946 (and indeed re-imposed in those formerly occupied territories where the collectives had been disbanded); in the non-collectivized region of Western Ukraine collectivization was pressed upon the peasantry from 1947; a campaign to remove 'parasites' from villages all over the Soviet Union followed in 1948; and mass collectivization was imposed upon the Baltic republics from 1949. Thus, a central pillar of Stalin's revolution from above was re-constructed in the 'old', pre-1939 Soviet Union and exported as a 'revolution from abroad' to the new Soviet territories.[21]

Other aspects of this return to the Stalinist political and economic order proceeded in parallel: the black market was brought under control, and a currency reform confiscated wealth accumulated by 'speculation'. The intelligentsia was brought to heel in a campaign against all 'kowtowing before the west'. This 'anti-cosmopolitanism campaign' is often seen as antisemitic, which it was. But it was much more than that, targeting anybody with appreciation of, or links to the world outside the Soviet Union. The political system was re-centralized again, and just in case they had gotten cocky, Stalin's henchmen again threatened with terror by the dictator, who made sure they knew who was boss.[22]

A renewal of the Communist Party itself, backbone of the regime and major tool to manage the ambitious and the upwardly mobile, was part of this process. The war had brought people of dubious loyalty and poor ideological steadfastness into this very sanctuary of Stalinism. During the war, many of the old cadres died at the frontline and new recruits were selected largely on the strength of their fighting record. The lack of political preparation and ideological purity of many of the new recruits who had joined the Communist Party at the frontline now caused some consternation. A major (un-bloody) purge was conducted together with an education campaign for 'young communists'. In 1946–8, the majority of communists who were excluded from the Party in civilian party organizations had joined during the war with Germany (56 per cent, or 171,000 people). In the following period (1949–51) this share rose to 62 per cent, a staggering 188,000 people.[23]

In one word: the impact of the war had to be undone and pre-war Stalinism was re-built, a return to a strange kind of 'normalcy'.[24] This reconstruction was driven by the dictator. To Stalin the war proved that his revolution from above had been sound: collectivization had kept the peasants in check, industrialization had produced the arms necessary and the Great Terror had eliminated enemies who might have brought down the state during the war. This basic conviction that all the crimes and all the suffering of the 1930s had been historically necessary had been hidden during the war under patriotic slogans intended to mobilize a population at best lukewarm about defending this system which exploited the majority of them mercilessly. Nevertheless, sharp ears could hear the implications, when Stalin said, in his address at the Red Army Parade on Red Square on 7 November 1941, that 'today the situation of our country is much better than 23 years ago', at the start of the Civil War. 'Our country is several times richer in industry, foodstuff and raw materials than 23 years ago.' He did not say that this situation was caused by the Stalin revolution, but that implication was quite clear.[25] Two years later he became more explicit, when declaring that 'the workers of the Soviet Union' had built a 'highly developed, powerful socialist industry' which formed the basis of their wartime heroism. Again, it was clear that 'the years of peaceful construction' he talked about were the not-so-peaceful years of Stalinist industrialization of the 1930s.[26] A year later, again on the anniversary of the October revolution, the dictator further expanded on the topic, claiming that 'the socialist system' and the 'Soviet state' allowed the supply of the army even under conditions of occupation of some of the richest parts of the country. He stated that this system had been born in the October revolution, but everybody would have remembered that the type of Soviet system that actually was in place now had been created by the Stalin revolution at the start of the 1930s.[27] Similar hints were dropped throughout the war and the much quoted 1945 toast to the ordinary people, the '"little screws" of the great state mechanism', also implied that what had won the war was the totalitarian machine Stalin had built in the 1930s, which forced everybody to become a functionary of the warfare state.[28] The war was over. Stalinism had triumphed.

War-induced evolution of the system

While victory in war thus locked in the overall structure of the Soviet economic system, the years of consolidation after the conventional war was won also saw a subtle evolution of state administration. While an ageing Stalin retained dictatorial power, beneath his claim to totalitarian rule developed collective leadership and a more routinized bureaucracy. As we have seen in previous chapters, in the 1930s Stalin's immediate collaborators – 'team Stalin' – were terrorized into insignificance. After the Great Terror of 1937–8, Stalin truly was a 'totalitarian dictator' uninhibited even by his immediate entourage. The war proved too complex a problem to continue in this manner, and Stalin's henchmen gained considerable agency within a system of wartime crisis management. The result was a re-assertion of Stalin's team, which the dictator tried to undo after the war, without ever completely succeeding. Teamwork bubbled away under the surface and once Stalin died, his former lieutenants were ready to take power as a group.[29]

This war-induced evolution of the Soviet system away from totalitarian one-man rule and towards collective leadership found its equivalent further down the hierarchy. Here, a more and more professional, if often corrupt, bureaucracy worked according to rules and regulations in what began to look increasingly like a modern system. For the time being, this system was capped, like team Stalin, by the whimsical dictator. But once Stalin died in 1953, a more predictable dictatorship could emerge more or less instantly.[30]

Part of this development preceded the war. The Great Terror had removed (and often killed) an older generation of managers all over the Soviet system and replaced them with a new breed of functionaries, whose credentials were not revolutionary, but professional. But it was the wartime emergency that allowed these technocrats to come into their own. The partial decentralization of the political system during the war gave them the freedom necessary to make decisions and solve problems with less oversight than before. Thus civilian administrators, managers and directors emerged from the war no less tempered than the military.[31]

The professionalization of the state extended even to the branches most closely connected to Stalin's totalitarianism: the police. In the civilian sphere, terror was increasingly replaced by regular, if heavy handed, policing. Selective terror against the political elite continued between the war and Stalin's death, most spectacularly in the Leningrad affair when six prominent party leaders were sentenced to death. A large number of presumed supporters of the victims were expelled from the city, sent into exile, or incarcerated. Many of them died. More broadly, in the post-war years somewhere between 300,000 and 600,000 people were arrested as traitors. Another 20,000 old enemies (members of rival socialist parties or factions as well as 'white' counter-revolutionaries) shared their fate, and hundreds of thousands alleged or real enemies of Soviet power were deported from the newly acquired territories in the west. Nevertheless, political purging no longer formed the main task of security operations, in particular in the 'old' Soviet Union (in the borders of 1939). By the end of Stalin's rule, in 1953, nearly half of the inmates in the sprawling Gulag were victims of the incredibly tough theft laws of 1947, not of trumped-up political charges as during the Great Terror. Both the 'filtration' of repatriated citizens and the checking of the populations who had been under German occupation were remarkably differentiated and relatively rule bound.[32]

The war taught the Soviet leadership several important lessons. One was that all-out repression was undesirable when fighting for survival. It became clear soon enough that declaring each and every POW a traitor was absurd, counter-productive and wasteful. Only a minority turned out to have crossed the line voluntarily or had subsequently collaborated with the enemy. Their bodies were needed both in labour and in defence. Thus, the initial draconian rule was soon watered down and replaced with 'filtration' – an actual attempt at finding those who had actively sided with the enemy, a minority. The political leadership was painfully aware of the immense losses of the wartime years, a consciousness which encouraged a more careful approach to human resources. After Stalin's death, this consciousness was also extended to the Gulag, which was partially dismantled and fundamentally reformed, an evolution which one historian has linked directly to the experience of the devastation of the Second World War.[33]

In some instances, the link between the beginning normalization of repression and the war was made explicit. One was an amnesty, announced in a 7 July 1945 decree entitled 'On Amnesty in connection with Victory over Hitlerite Germany.' It freed several categories of non-political prisoners 'in commemoration of the victorious conclusion of the war',[34] the 'largest single release of prisoners' in Stalin's time.[35] Two years later, the death penalty was abolished, a decision motivated by 'the historical victory of the Soviet people over the enemy'. Victory demonstrated, the 26 May 1947 decree continued, not only the power of the Soviet state, but also 'the exceptional devotion of the entire population of the Soviet Union to the Soviet homeland and the Soviet State.'[36]

Celebrating the war and the Soviet system

The basic line Stalin trotted out after the war – that it was the Stalinist system created in the 1930s which won the war, and that everybody was devoted to this system and its leadership – would be reasserted by all of Stalin's successors. Despite all his criticism of the late dictator and his Cult of Personality, Nikita Khrushchev in his anti-Stalinist 'secret speech' of 1956, still claimed that the political line had always been correct. Without forceful collectivization and industrialization, he wrote, 'we would today not have a mighty heavy industry, we would not have any collective farms, we would be weak and unarmed in the capitalist encirclement.'[37] Khrushchev's reforms of the 1950s and early 1960s played themselves out within the confines of what the leadership had been discussing in the post-war years, but could not implement because Stalin would have none of these newfangled ideas. 'The Khrushchevite leadership', writes one historian, 'almost completely preserved the strategy of communist construction, which had been formulated in the [immediate] post-war period'.[38]

The victory of Stalin's system was celebrated in a war cult which became one of the major pillars of the late Soviet social and cultural order. It commemorated not just the war, but the victory of the Soviet system. When, under Khrushchev's successor as First (later General) Secretary of the Communist Party, Leonid Brezhnev, the war cult took off in a real sense, this message became even louder. The war became the major achievement of the Soviet Union, increasingly displacing the revolution as the foundational myth. Whatever had made success in war possible – the Soviet system – became sacrosanct. Victory thus proved that the Stalin revolution had been right, and it was part of the task of the Soviet war cult to drive home this point.[39]

To the Soviets, of course, 'the war' meant the Great Patriotic War (*Velikaia Otechestvennaia voina*), that is, the victorious and defensive war against Germany of 1941–5. Other, more problematic parts of the Soviet Union's Second World War were ignored, in particular the period on the side of Hitler's Germany of 1939–41. This narrative also required to suppress other memories – those of occupation rather than liberation, prevalent in the Baltics and the formerly Polish territories, those of Stalin's blunders of 1941, those of repression and starvation, exploitation and brutalization as well as those experiences where Soviet soldiers were perpetrators rather than victims, war criminals rather than heroic defenders of women and children. All of these stories would haunt and challenge the official narrative, but until the 1980s they could be contained to whispered conversations among family and close friends and to memoirs and histories printed outside the Soviet orbit (which could be dismissed, if anybody managed to get a hold of them, as anti-Soviet propaganda).

The official narrative had local variations, but they all followed a pattern.[40] It would move through several alterations in lockstep with the evolution of the political climate. Stalin's leading role was removed under Khrushchev (1953–64) but carefully reinserted under Brezhnev (1964–82). The latter's tenure as general secretary also saw the war cult move to new bombastic heights. Under Mikhail Gorbachev (1985–91), the narrative became destabilized by the liberalized atmosphere, which allowed critical voices to be heard. Indeed, during these years and after, a fully blown counter-myth emerged, which saw only the dark sides and the criminality of the Soviet war effort.[41]

These years, and in particular the three decades since the breakdown of the Soviet Union in 1991, also saw the re-emergence of suppressed regional memories: in the Baltics and Ukraine of the crimes of the Soviets during the occupation of 1939–41 and again during the re-establishment of Soviet power after 'liberation' from 1944; of the struggles of the Forest Brothers, the OUN and the UPA; of the participation of locals in the genocide against the Jews or the ethnic cleansing of Poles or Ukrainians. Just as many in Russia, with determined support of the state, tried to salvage the old tale of the Great Patriotic War as a heroic achievement, this time of the Russian people rather than the Soviet system. Others, in Ukraine, Latvia, Lithuania and Estonia, also supported by their respective governments as well as historians and activists from abroad, constructed national narratives focusing on victimization by Hitler and Stalin and national resistance to totalitarianism. Despite occasional outright falsifications, most of these histories were not, technically speaking, 'wrong'. But all of them were incomplete, drawing only on those aspects of the Soviet war which were useful for their present political purposes. In one way, this book is an attempt to restore at least some of the complexity of the real history of the Soviet Second World War. It thus refuses to take sides in the history wars which now threaten peaceful relations between nations in Eurasia.[42]

Veterans

Connected to the increasing prominence of the Great Patriotic War in Soviet society in the post-war years was the rise of veterans as a social group with high prestige and special privileges. This rise was not pre-determined but the outcome of political struggles. After an initial phase during demobilization (1945–8), veterans' welfare all but disappeared. War disabled retained some very basic welfare rights, but they were inadequate and geared towards mobilizing them to work if at all possible. To many veterans, the return home was a bitter disappointment.[43]

Why was the Soviet state so stingy towards those who had saved it from destruction? Part of the answer was ideological: to Soviet officials, trained to think in Marxist–Leninist terms, special privileges for veterans made no sense. Socialism was meant to make life better for the working masses, not for old soldiers. Veteran welfare always smacked somewhat of fascism, one of the reasons why the Soviet Union did not allow an organized veteran movement in the interwar years. As one custodian of ideological purity explained, veteran movements in the capitalist world were 'imperialist and anti-Soviet' as well as 'reactionary'. In the Soviet Union a veteran organization was unnecessary, as the government cared about the citizenry as a whole. 'The attempt to isolate a section of the Soviet people (those who have been in the army) from the rest (those who have not been in the army)', the ideologue from the Central Committee apparatus lectured, was 'absolutely unnecessary'.[44]

And then there was the issue of money. In 1945, there were between 20 and 25 million veterans alive in the Soviet Union. The state simply could not afford a major benefits system for such a large group, as officials found out to their slight shock when reviewing the allowances attached to wartime decorations (which as a result were cancelled). It took until the late 1970s, after enough old soldiers had died, that veteran welfare became financially feasible. Even then, however, when only 9 million combat survivors of the Second World War were still around, veteran activists lobbying for a benefits system were keenly aware that 'this is not a simple question, and not an easy question, and not a cheap question. We still need money', the functionary continued, in order 'to ensure the power of our state'.[45]

Eventually, however, in 1978, veterans did gain privileges enshrined in law. This new status was the outcome of a complex political process involving the persistent pressure from veterans, both within and outside of the new organization formed in 1956, the greater receptiveness to veteran issues by Brezhnev, who fancied himself a war hero, and decreased resistance from the Ministry of Finance, because the number of war survivors was more manageable now than it had been in 1945.[46] The decision to grant a special status, however, caused an ideological dilemma: how could one explain the existence of war veterans as a social group in ideologically consistent terms? It required a man of the genius of Gorbachev, general secretary from 1985, to find the answer. His solution was ingenious: he added veterans – who plainly existed as a socio-legal grouping now – to the list of Marxist–Leninist social groups Stalin had first declared the building blocks of Soviet society: workers, collectivized peasants and the intelligentsia. Clearly, veterans were different from them, but so were another problematic category of Marxist–Leninist thought: nations and nationalities. Gorbachev integrated veterans into this sociology by treating them as a 'generation', which made some sense by the early 1980s when the older combatants were dead and the privileges for war veterans had been extended, bit by bit, to former workers in the hinterland. Hence, the general secretary described Soviet society in 1987 as constituted by social class ('the working class, the kolkhoz peasantry, the intelligentsia'), gender ('women and men'), ethnicity ('nations and nationalities') and generation ('veterans and youth'). Old soldiers thus had found a legitimate place in the official order of the universe.[47]

Victory and welfare

In the Soviet Union, then, veterans did not serve as the avant-garde of the welfare state as they did in other contexts. It was only well after the more generalized Soviet welfare state had taken off in the 1950s that veterans gained a special status inscribed in law in 1978. Indeed, rather than rewarding veterans, the Soviet leadership endeavoured to reward the entire population for its effort in the war. This generalized welfare philosophy made perfect sense on a variety of levels. First, it fit ideologically much better than a special regime for veterans. Socialism was meant to make life better for the working masses, not for old soldiers, the preoccupation of fascists. By providing generalized welfare the regime finally made good on the promises of the Revolution for building a better life for working people. Moreover, it also reflected the fact that the suffering of war was not borne only by the soldiers at the frontline. Indeed, overall, more Soviet civilians died in this war than military personnel. Civilians were mobilized in one of the most total war efforts of history; civilian life was in many ways as regimented as life in the army; and working and living conditions were extremely hard.[48]

It thus was quite logical to see the entire population – with the exception of a few traitors, who had made common cause with the enemy – as deserving of state welfare. Indeed, this was the other aspect of Stalin's remark about the 'little screws' who made up the state: without them, he pointed out, he could not have won the war. He was even more explicit in an earlier speech, on 24 May 1945, where he acknowledged that 'the government' – that is, Stalin personally – had made 'more than a few mistakes' at the start of the war with Germany. These mistakes were so bad that they could have cost him his job.[49]

Stalin was not alone in this appreciation of the contribution of ordinary people to victory. Veterans were often seen as particularly deserving by mid-level functionaries, who had to make decisions about who should get access to housing and other scarce resources. But the appreciation of wartime achievement was much broader. The universalized suffering of the wartime years softened the pre-war trend among officials to see welfare recipients as shirkers rather than victims of circumstance. Disability, previously a minority concern, became linked to wartime sacrifice and hence raised its profile. Late Stalinism thus saw a revival of the welfare discourse of the Soviet 1920s, which had been abandoned in the 1930s. While overall policy only shifted after Stalin's death, these reforms were already conceptualized in the final years of the dictator's life, under the impact of war and victory.[50]

Indeed, one of Khrushchev's most iconic welfare programmes – the mass housing campaign of the 1950s and 1960s – was a direct response to the destruction of the war, which had led to homelessness on an unprecedented scale. Under Stalin, a significant part of the reconstruction of housing had been left to private initiative: in 1940, 154 million square meters of urban housing space was privately owned; in 1950, it was 173 million, more than one-third of the total. While the results were impressive for a country were any private activity had to overcome incredible obstacles, the outcomes fell far short of what was needed. Under Khrushchev, then, a massive building programme created what later would be called 'Khrushchev slums', but at the time was indeed 'the greatest housing program in the world'.[51]

Equally important was the pension reform of 1956 and its widening to the rural population in 1964. Together, they were part of an overarching – and highly utopian – programme to ensure 'an abundance of material and cultural values for the whole population', indeed the 'construction of communist society', as the 1961 Program of the Communist Party put it. It had first been outlined in the wake of victory, in 1947, but was then shelved as impossible. From the mid-1950s, it was implemented.[52]

Victory gardens

Not always did the results of the war, the demands from below, and the efforts from above interlock so neatly as in the case of the Khrushchevite welfare programmes. We have already seen how one result of the war – the new social group of war veterans – ran aground ideological sandbanks until these were removed much later, under Brezhnev and Gorbachev. The same was true for gardening – another mass phenomenon engendered by the war. Urban gardening for food by individuals, their families and enterprises was a reaction to the war-induced squeeze on civilian consumption during the war in Europe of 1939–41. Essentially, urban gardening was an extension to the cities of the private garden plot the collective farmers were allowed to keep. Already in 1939, more than a million urban dwellers were engaged in such self-provisioning, nursing close to one-third of all Soviet cows and pigs on their private or company plots. In 1940, the central government saw itself compelled officially to regulate what was already a reality: the distribution of land for garden plots in cities and towns. After the German attack, it began actively to encourage the phenomenon, when it became clear that the rationing system would be unable to keep workers from starvation. Mass gardening thus ensured the survival of civilians, while the central state could focus more of its attention on the provisioning of the armed forces.[53]

The emergence of this 'gardening state' – a state encouraging gardening and raising gardeners – was thus an ideological compromise engendered by war. The focus on the family which this policy implied, on self-sufficiency, and on keeping essentially private garden plots, clearly smacked of 'petty bourgeois' tendencies. No wonder that during the more purist years of Khrushchev's utopian tenure as first secretary, the state again cracked down on the practice. The Brezhnev years, however, which would bring finally legal recognition for veterans, also brought the final capitulation of the state to its citizen-gardeners. As food shortages returned in the 1970s, the regime turned 'from reluctant acceptance of private plots to their enthusiastic support'. So much so, indeed, that the 1977 'Brezhnev' constitution enshrined not only the right of citizens to farm in order to supply their own families, but even declared that 'the state and collective farms have to assist citizens in keeping their private plots'. This culture of gardening had wide-ranging implications well beyond the history of the Soviet Union. It was the food grown in the gardens of ordinary citizens which allowed the population in Russia, Ukraine and elsewhere to survive the catastrophic collapse of the economy in the early 1990s – a somewhat perverse return in peacetime of the crisis of war which had given rise to mass gardening.[54]

Victory Day, 1945–2045

There are other examples of similar processes. The day Soviet citizens could bask in the glory of victory and remember the war dead was Victory Day (9 May), a central holiday in the Soviet calendar. Originally celebrated as a non-working holiday during the years of demobilization, it was discontinued in 1947. Subsequently, there were still artillery salutes and parades in many cities, speeches and articles in the press, and formal and informal celebrations all over the country, but people had to go to work (whether much work was actually done on that day is a different matter).[55] This peculiar situation of the 'working holiday' existed until 1965, when the holiday in the proper sense – a day without work – was reinstated. The new status of the date was marked by a military parade on Red Square, just as in 1945. Victory Day remains the most important civic holiday of post-Soviet Russia.[56]

With the reintroduction of a work-free holiday celebrating Victory Day in 1965 the regime accommodated pressures 'from below': Victory Day was a truly popular holiday and people found it hard to understand why they should work on such an important date. The same is true for other delayed rewards for victory. Soviet people wanted to have dachas, pensions and housing. Veterans demanded respect and social support. The 'little screws' felt that it was they who had won the war and eventually the government bowed to their demands. Nevertheless, it was up to the government to decide which of the popular calls they would hear. Soviet people also dreamed of free elections, travel abroad and the abolition of the collective farms. Such demands were ignored, the dreamers persecuted.[57] It was one thing to build a socialist welfare state, which was completely consistent with overall ideology; it was quite another to fiddle with the fundamentals of the authoritarian economic and political order. The impact of war, thus, played itself out in the context of the system in place since the 1930s.[58]

It was only in 1991 that these shackles were removed. The breakdown of the Soviet Union began a new, a post-imperial, era in the lands once ruled by the Romanovs and later by the Communist Party of the Soviet Union. That command-state-socialism, which had caused so much suffering but had also won the war against Hitler, was gone, however, did not mean all of its history became irrelevant. The war, indeed, became the touchstone of much of the post-1991 struggles, both within each of the fifteen successor states to the Soviet Union but also between many of them. This war, thus, is still very much alive today in the lands once ruled by Stalin. But its echoes reverberate well beyond the region. This war's displacements did not stop at the changing Soviet borders. As we have seen again and again in this book, they transcended them: deported Poles left with the Anders Army to Iran in 1942; Russian, Ukrainian, Lithuanian, Latvian and Lithuanian displaced persons evaded repatriation and stayed in the west; Polish and Baltic Jews returned from the Soviet Union to their homeland only to leave once they found an antisemitic graveyard there. They all took their stories of this war to their new homes in Australia, Canada, the United States, Latin America or Israel. Anybody who teaches the history of this war in any of these places will regularly encounter students who are attracted to it because it is theirs: the history of their grandfather or grandmother, the history of their family, the history of their community. We cannot predict what will happen to our world between now and the centenary of victory over Germany and Japan in 2045. But what we can predict with confidence is that the Soviet Second World War will still be remembered then, although in different ways by different people.[59]

APPENDIX

MAPS

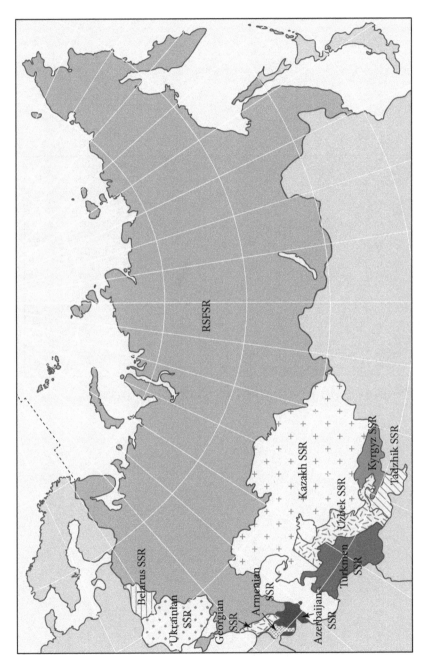

MAP 1 The Soviet Union in 1937.

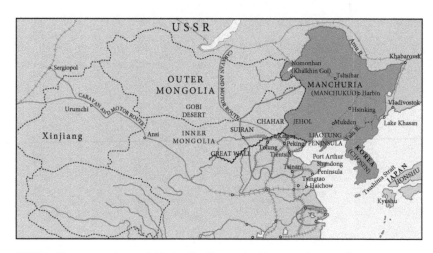

MAP 2 The eastern front, 1938–9 – Far East, Lake Khasan, Khalkhin Gol.

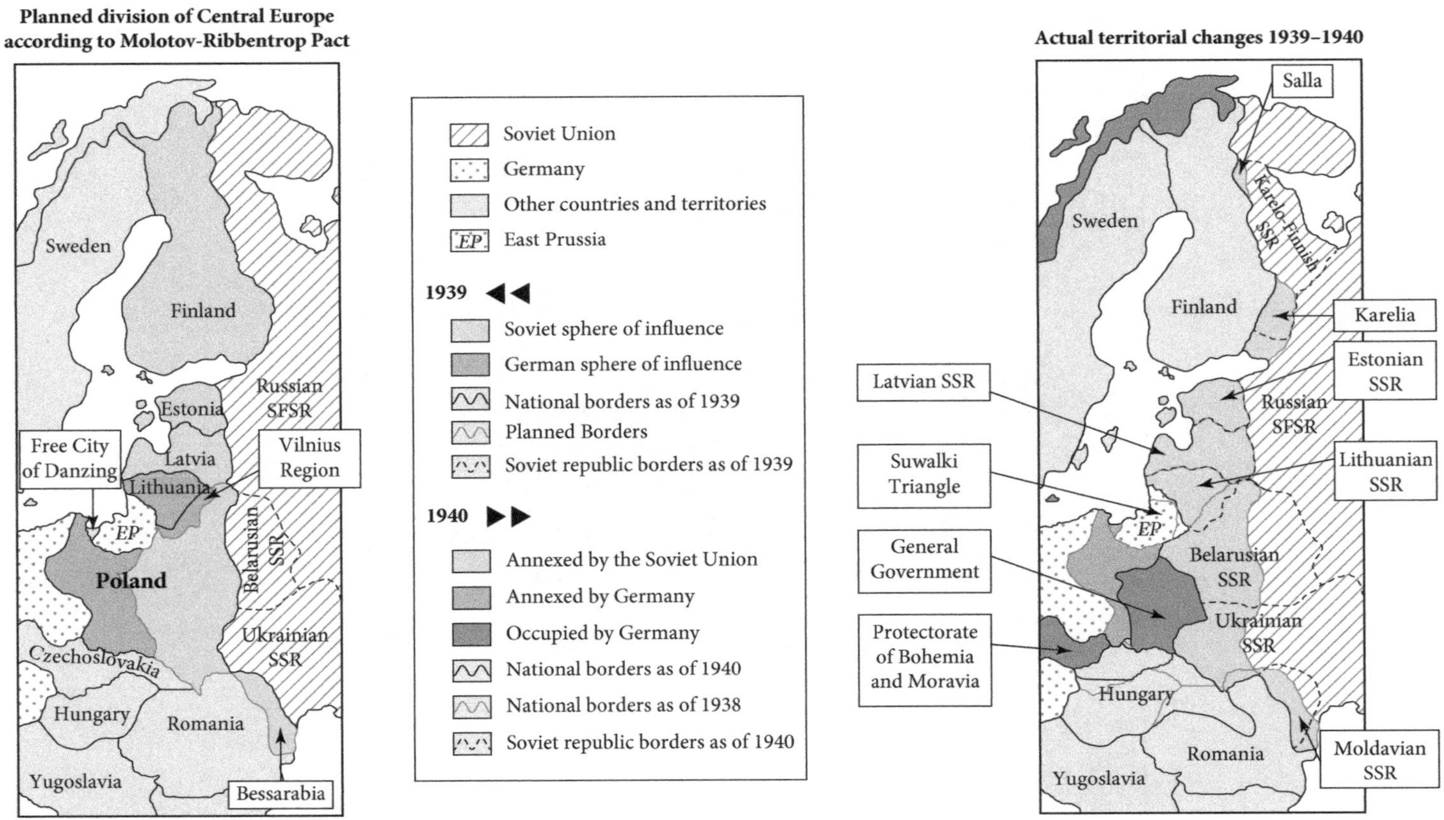

Planned division of Central Europe according to Molotov-Ribbentrop Pact

Sweden

Finland

Russian SFSR

Vilnius Region

Estonia

Latvia

Lithuania

Belarusian SSR

Free City of Danzig

EP

Poland

Ukrainian SSR

Czechoslovakia

Hungary

Romania

Bessarabia

Yugoslavia

Actual territorial changes 1939–1940

Salla

Karelo-Finnish SSR

Karelia

Estonian SSR

Russian SFSR

Lithuanian SSR

Belarusian SSR

Ukrainian SSR

EP

Latvian SSR

Suwalki Triangle

General Government

Protectorate of Bohemia and Moravia

Sweden

Finland

Hungary

Romania

Moldavian SSR

Yugoslavia

Soviet Union	
Germany	
Other countries and territories	
EP	East Prussia

1939

Soviet sphere of influence	
German sphere of influence	
National borders as of 1939	
Planned Borders	
Soviet republic borders as of 1939	

1940

Annexed by the Soviet Union	
Annexed by Germany	
Occupied by Germany	
National borders as of 1940	
National borders as of 1938	
Soviet republic borders as of 1940	

MAP 3 The western front, 1939–41.

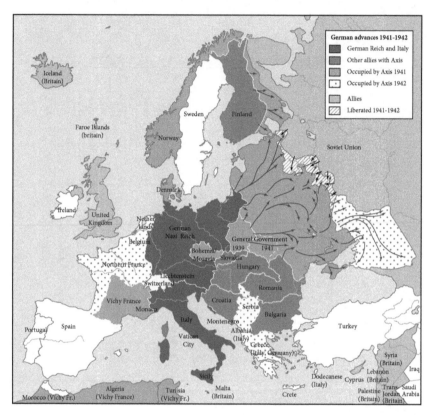

MAP 4 The frontline, 1941–2.

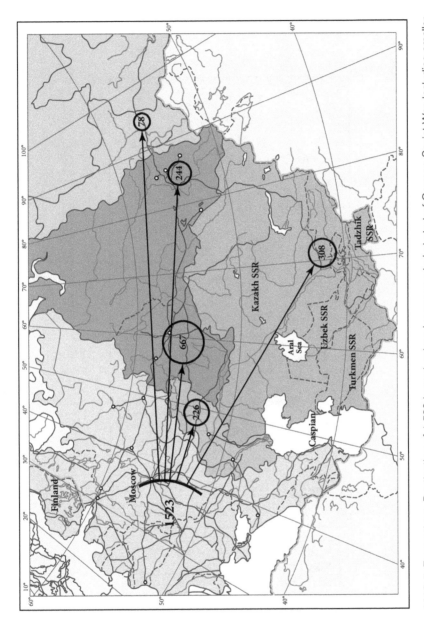

MAP 5 Evacuations. Destination of 1,523 largest enterprises evacuated at start of German-Soviet War. Including smaller plants, a total of 2,500 enterprises were relocated.

Territory liberated by the Red
Army from German occupation.

Liberated 23 June – 2 August 1944
Liberated by 22 June 1944
Liberated during Winter campaigns of 1942-43

MAP 6 Soviet successes in the west, 1943–4.

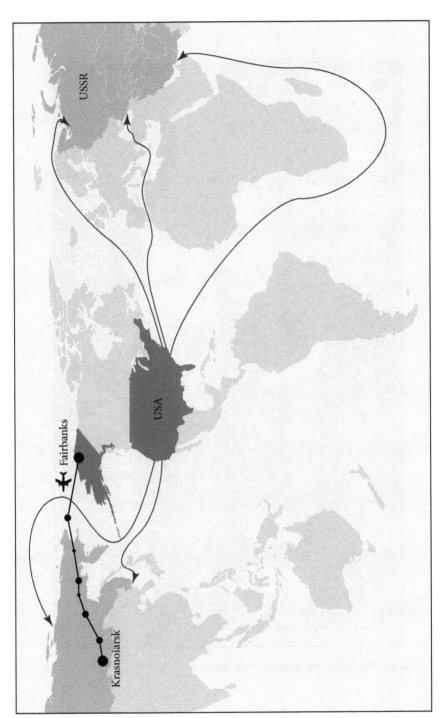

MAP 7 Lend Lease Routes.

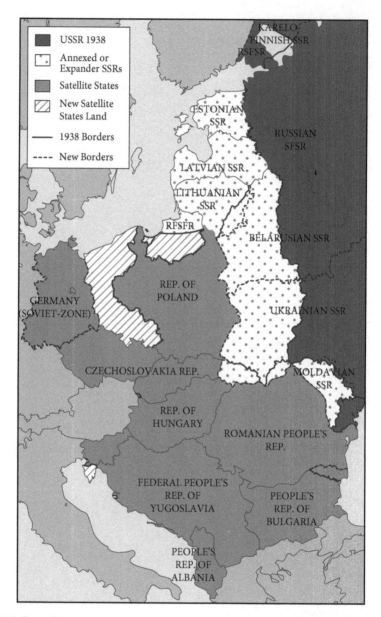

MAP 8 Soviet Empire in the West after the War.

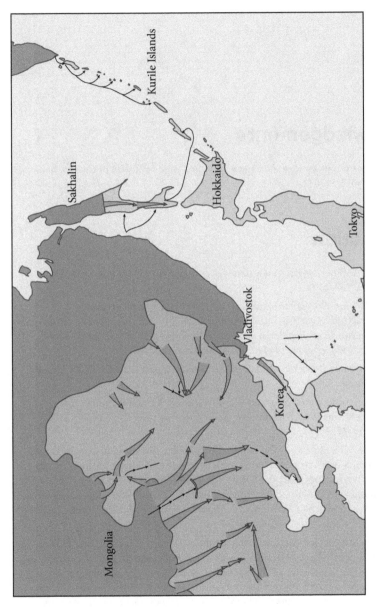

MAP 9 The eastern front: Manchuria, North Korea, Sakhalin.

NOTES

Acknowledgements

1 Revised versions of some of the papers presented were published in *Cahiers du monde Russe* 52, No. 2/3 (2011).

Introduction

1 I. Stalin, *O Velikoi Otechestvennoi voine Sovetskogo soiuza* (Moscow: Kraft, 2002), 157–9, here: 157, 159.

2 Manfred Zeidler, *Kriegsende im Osten. Die Rote Armee und die Besetzung Deutschlands östlich von Oder und Neisse 1944/45* (Munich: Oldenbourg, 1996); Antony Beevor, *The Fall of Berlin 1945* (New York: Penguin, 2003); Ian Kershaw, *The End: Hitler's Germany, 1944-45* (London: Allan Lane, 2011).

3 Richard B. Frank, *Downfall: The End of the Imperial Japanese Empire* (New York: Random House, 1999).

4 Mark Edele, 'Who Won the Second World War and Why Should You Care? Reassessing Stalin's War 75 Years after Victory,' *Journal of Strategic Studies* 43, No. 6-7 (2020): 1039–62.

5 Mark Edele, 'The Impact of War and the Costs of Superpower Status', in *The Oxford Handbook of Modern Russian History* (online version), ed. Simon Dixon (Oxford: Oxford University Press, 2015). DOI: 10.1093/oxfordhb/9780199236701.013.028. On the number of famine victims: Michael Ellman, 'The 1947 Soviet Famine and the Entitlement Approach to Famines', *Cambridge Journal of Economics* 24, no. 5 (2000): 603–30.

6 The quality of recent Russian scholarship on the war is mixed. Quality contributions include E. S. Seniavskaia, *1941-1945. Frontovoe pokolenie. Istoriko-psikhologicheskoe issledovanie* (Moscow: RAN institut Rossiiskoi istorii, 1995); V. A. Zolotarev and G. N. Sevost'ianov (eds), *Velikaia Otechestvennaia voina 1941-1945. Voenno-istoricheskie ocherki*, 4 vols (Moscow: Nauka, 1998); V. F. Zima, *Mentalitet narodov Rossii v voine 1941-1945 godov* (Moscow: RAN institut Rossiiskoi istorii, 2000); S. K. Shoigu (ed.), *Velikaia Otechestvennaia Voina 1941-1945 godov*, 12 vols (Moscow: Kuchkovo pole, 2015); and A. E. Larionov, *Frontovaia povsednevnost' Velikoi Otechestvennoi voiny*, 2 vols (Moscow: Zolotoe sechenie, 2015). Essential statistics for a wide variety of economic

and demographic indicators can be found in P. V. Malkov (ed.), *Velikaia Otechestvennaia voina. Iubileinyi statisticheskii sbornik* (Moscow: Rosstat, 2020). For two projects bringing together Russian and western scholars see Oleg Budnitskii and Liudmila Novikova (eds), *SSSR vo Vtoroi mirovoi voine. Okkupatsiia. Kholokost. Stalinizm* (Moscow: Rosspen, 2014); and Beate Fieseler and Roger Markwick (eds), *Sovetskii tyl 1941-1945. Povsednevnaia zhizn' v gody voiny* (Moscow: Rosspen, 2019).

7   Interview with Ten San Din (27 February 2015). https://iremember.ru/memoirs/r azvedchiki/ten-san-din/ (accessed 12 February 2019). Report of Commissar for the Interior N. I. Ezhov (29 October 1937), in *Istoriia Stalinskogo Gulaga: Konets 1920-kh – pervaia polovina 1950-kh godov. Sobranie dokumentov v semi tomakh* (Moscow: Rosspen, 2004), vol. 5: 237.

8   The connection between the two decisions was pointed out by Oleg Khlevniuk, 'The Reasons for the "Great Terror": The Foreign-Political Aspect', in *Russia in the Age of Wars*, ed. Silvio Pons and Andrea Romano (Milan: Fondazione Giangiacomo Feltrinelli, 2000), 159–69, here: 168.

9   Interview with Petr Fedorovich Katasonov (13 December 2013). https://iremember.ru /memoirs/pulemetchiki/katasonov-petr-fedorovich/ (accessed 14 December 2019).

10 For an argument to begin in 1931 and in Asia see S. C. M. Paine, *The Wars for Asia 1911-1949* (Cambridge: Cambridge University Press, 2012). For an argument to start in 1939 see Gerard L. Weinberg, *A World at Arms: A Global History of World War II*, 2nd edn (New York: Cambridge University Press, 2005). For an argument to begin in 1941 see Evan Mawdsley, *December 1941: Twelve Days that Began a World War* (New Haven and London: Yale University Press, 2012). For a critique of the '15 Year War' framework see Sandra Wilson, 'Rethinking the 1930s and the "15-Year War" in Japan', *Japanese Studies* 21, no. 2 (2001): 155–64.

11 For two sketches of this history see Mark Harrison, 'World War II', in *Encyclopedia of Russian History*, ed. James R. Millar (New York: Macmillan, 2004), vol 4: 1683–92; and Mark Edele, *The Soviet Union: A Short History* (Hoboken: Wiley Blackwell, 2019), 123–43.

12 Evan Mawdsley, *World War II: A New History* (Cambridge: Cambridge University Press, 2009). The case for why one should not start the history of the Second World War with the Japanese invasion of Manchuria in 1931, the Italian attack on Abyssinia in 1935 or the outbreak of the Spanish Civil War in 1936 is made on p. 7.

13 Good introductions to the military and economic histories include John Barber and Mark Harrison, *The Soviet Home Front, 1941-1945: A Social and Economic History of the USSR in World War II* (London: Longman, 1991); and David Glantz and Jonathan House, *When Titans Clashed: How the Red Army Stopped Hitler*, 2nd rev. and expanded edn (Lawrence: University Press of Kansas, 2015). Important works on the social and cultural history of the war years include William Moskoff, *The Bread of Affliction; the Food Supply in the USSR During World War II* (Cambridge: Cambridge University Press, 1990), now superseded by Wendy Z. Goldman and Donald A. Filtzer (eds), *Hunger and War: Food Provisioning in the Soviet Union during World War II* (Bloomington and Indianapolis: Indiana University Press, 2015); Robert W. Thurston and Bernd Bonwetsch (eds), *The People's War: Responses to World War II in the Soviet Union* (Urbana and Chicago: University of Illinois Press, 2000); Karel C. Berkhoff, *Harvest of Despair: Life and Death in Ukraine under Nazi Rule* (Cambridge and London: The Belknap Press of Harvard University Press,

2004); Donald A. Filtzer, *The Hazards of Urban Life in Late Stalinist Russia: Health, Hygiene, and Living Standards, 1943-1953* (Cambridge and New York: Cambridge University Press, 2010); Olga Kucherenko, *Little Soldiers: How Soviet Children Went to War 1941-1945* (New York: Oxford University Press, 2011); Julie deGraffenried, *Sacrificing Childhood: Children and the Soviet State in the Great Patriotic War* (Lawrence: University Press of Kansas, 2014); Vanessa Voisin, *L'urss contre ses traîtres. L'épuration soviétique (1941-1955)* (Paris: Publications de la Sorbonne, 2015); Olga Kucherenko, *Soviet Street Children and the Second World War: Welfare and Social Control under Stalin* (London: Bloomsbury Academic, 2016); Masha Cerovic, *Les enfants de Staline. La guerre des partisans soviétique (1941-1944)* (Paris: Editions du Seuil, 2018); and Brandon M. Schechter, *The Stuff of Soldiers: A History of the Red Army in World War II through Objects* (Ithaca: Cornell University Press, 2019).

14 Archives I have worked in physically include the State Archive of the Russian Federation (GARF), the Russian State Archive of Socio-Political History (RGASPI), the Russian State Archive of the Economy (RGAE), and the Russian State Archive of Contemporary History (RGANI), all in Moscow; the Ukrainian KBG Archive (GDA SBU) and the former Communist Party Archive of Ukraine (TsDAGO), both in Kyiv; the German Military Archive (BA-MA) in Freiburg; the National Archives of Estonia in Tallinn (ERA) and Tartu (ERAF); the Latvian State Archives (LVA) in Riga; the Lithuanian KBG archives (LYA) in Vilnius; the Bakhmeteff Archive at Columbia University; and the United States Holocaust Memorial Museum (USHMM) in Washington, DC. Some archival holdings I have accessed in multiple locations, including online. For example, the Stalin archive can be accessed in RGASPI but since I moved to the University of Melbourne in 2017, I could also use its subscription to the Stalin Digital Archive (https://www.stalindigitalarchive .com/). Some holdings from TsDAGO and GARF I first worked on in Kyiv, then in USHMM, which had acquired a copy. And some selected archival documents have been published on http://istmat.info and http://sovdoc.rusarchives.ru/#main (the latter only accessible from Russian IP addresses).

15 For the contemporary interviews see Jochen Hellbeck (ed.), *Stalingrad: The City That Defeated the Third Reich* (New York: Public Affairs, 2015); and S. V. Zhuravlev (ed.), *Vklad uchenykh-istorikov v sokhranenie istoricheskoi pamiati o voine. Na materialakh Komissii po istorii Velikoi Otechestvennoi voiny AN SSSR, 1941-1945 gg.* (Moscow: Tsentr gumanitarnykh initsiativ, 2017); transcripts of the Harvard project are available online at https://library.harvard.edu/collections/hpsss/index.html; the recent oral history database is https://iremember.ru. For memoirs and diaries see the endnotes throughout.

16 The best pre-archival biographies which include the war years are Isaac Deutscher, *Stalin: A Political Biography*, 2nd edn (New York: Oxford University Press, 1967); and Adam B. Ulam, *Stalin. The Man and His Era*, expanded edn (Boston: Beacon Press, 1989). The best works drawing on the new archival evidence now available are Dmitrii Volkogonov, *Stalin: Triumph and Tragedy* (London: Weidenfeld and Nicolson, 1991); and Oleg Khlevniuk, *Stalin: New Biography of a Dictator* (New Haven and London: Yale University Press, 2015). For a discussion of the wider literature on Stalin see also Mark Edele, *Debates on Stalinism* (Manchester: Manchester University Press, 2020), chapter 5.

17 Essential diplomatic histories include Jonathan Haslam, *The Soviet Union and the Struggle for Collective Security in Europe, 1933-1939* (London: Macmillan, 1985);

Silvio Pons, *Stalin and the Inevitable War 1936-1941* (London: Frank Cass, 2002); Geoffrey Roberts, *Stalin's Wars: From World War to Cold War, 1939-1953* (New Haven: Yale University Press, 2006); Robert Gellately, *Stalin's Curse: Battling for Communism in War and Cold War* (New York: Knopf, 2013); Alfred J. Rieber, *Stalin and the Struggle for Supremacy in Eurasia* (Cambridge: Cambridge University Press, 2015); and Norman Naimark, *Stalin and the Fate of Europe: The Postwar Struggle for Sovereignty* (Cambridge, MA: The Belknap Press, 2019). An essential military history of this war is Evan Mawdsley, *Thunder in the East: The Nazi-Soviet War 1941-1945*, 2nd rev. edn (London: Bloomsbury, 2016).

18 Mark Edele, 'The Second World War as a History of Displacement: The Soviet Case', *History Australia* 12, no. 2 (2015): 17–40, here: 29; G. F. Krivosheev, *Rossiia i SSSSR v voinakh xx veka. Poteri vooruzhennykh sil. Statisticheskoe issledovanie* (Moscow: Olma-Press, 2001), 595.

19 'Spravka 1 spetsotdela MVD SSSR o kolichestve arestovannykh i osuzhdennykh v period 1921-1954 gg'. (11 December 1953), reprinted in *GULAG (Glavnoe upravlenie lagerei) 1917-1960*, ed. A. I Kokurin and N. V. Petrov (Moscow: Demokratiia, 200), 431–4, here: 433.

20 Jan T. Gross, *Revolution from Abroad: The Soviet Conquest of Poland's Western Ukraine and Western Belorussia*. expanded edn (Princeton and Oxford: Princeton University Press, 2002). Krivosheev, *Rossiia i SSSR v voinakh xx veka*, 187, 214, 595. The number for those who saw the outside world is a lower limit. It comprises only those troops who took part in the Polish operation in 1939 (466,516) and the troops stationed in the Baltic countries by 1 January 1940 (58,055).

21 Sarah Davies, *Popular Opinion in Stalin's Russia: Terror, Propaganda and Dissent, 1934-1941* (Cambridge: Cambridge University Press, 1997), chapter 5; Timothy Johnston, *Being Soviet: Identity, Rumour, and Everyday Life under Stalin 1939-1953* (Oxford: Oxford University Press, 2011), chapter 1. Edele, 'The Second World War as a History of Displacement', 24 (numbers). Elena Osokina, *Za fasadom 'stalinskogo izobiliia'. Raspredelenie i rynok v snabzhenii naseleniia v gody industrializatsii 1927-1941* (Moscow: Rosspen, 1999), 206–13. On the shift into defence see R. W. Davies, Mark Harrison, Oleg Khlevniuk and S. G. Wheatcroft, *The Industrialisation of Soviet Russia 7: The Soviet Economy and the Approach of Ware, 1937-1939* (London: Palgrave Macmillan, 2018), esp. chapter 9; and Peter Gatrell and Mark Harrison, 'The Russian and Soviet Economies in Two World Wars: A Comparative View', *Economic History Review* 46, no. 3 (1993): 424–52, here: 438. On the labour law see Martin Kragh, 'Stalinist Labour Coercion During World War II: An Economic Approach', *Europe-Asia Studies* 63, no. 7 (2011): 1253–73.

22 Harrison, 'The Second World War', 244–5; 256–60; Donald Filtzer, 'Starvation Mortality in Soviet Home-Front Industrial Regions during World War II', in *Hunger and War: Food Provisioning in the Soviet Union during World War II*, ed. Wendy Goldman and Donald Filtzer (Bloomington and Indianapolis: Indiana University Press, 2015), 265–335. The best discussion of the available numbers is Michael Ellman and S. Maksudov, 'Soviet Deaths in the Great Patriotic War: A Note', *Europe-Asia Studies* 46, no. 4 (1994): 671–80.

23 See, for example, the interrogation report of one of them, accused of too close relationships with the nationalist underground: Latvian State Archive (LVA) f. PA-101, op. 9, d. 69, l. 147-49.

24 Alexander Statiev, *The Soviet Counterinsurgency in the Western Borderlands* (Cambridge and New York: Cambridge University Press, 2010), 7 (number of NKVD troops in counter-insurgency, 1945–47), data for losses is Krivosheev, *Rossiia i SSSR v voinakh xx veka*, 594.

25 Statiev, *The Soviet Counterinsurgency*, 128.

26 Calculated from top secret monthly MGB reports for 1948. Lithuanian KGB Archive (LYA) f. K-41, op. 1, d. 278, ll. 35, 66, 71, 73, 75, 77, 79, 81, 84, 86, 154, 162.

27 Sheila Fitzpatrick, 'Postwar Soviet Society: The "Return to Normalcy," 1945-1953', in *The Impact of World War II on the Soviet Union*, ed. Susan J. Linz (Totota: Rowman & Allanhead, 1985), 129–56; Elena Zubkova, *Russia after the War: Hopes, Illusions, and Disappointments, 1945-1957* (Armonk and London: M. E. Sharpe, 1998); Donald Filtzer, *Soviet Workers and Late Stalinism: Labour and the Restoration of the Stalinist System after World War II* (Cambridge, New York and Melbourne: Cambridge University Press, 2002); Yoram Gorlizki and Oleg Khlevniuk, *Cold Peace: Stalin and the Soviet Ruling Circle, 1945-1953* (Oxford and New York: Oxford University Press, 2004); Juliane Fürst (ed.), *Late Stalinist Russia: Society between Reconstruction and Reinvention* (London and New York: Routledge, 2006); Jeffrey W. Jones, *Everyday Life and the 'Reconstruction' of Soviet Russia During and after the Great Patriotic War, 1943-1948* (Bloomington: Slavica Publishers, 2008); Mark Edele, *Soviet Veterans of the Second World War: A Popular Movement in an Authoritarian Society, 1941-1991* (Oxford: Oxford University Press, 2008); Karl Qualls, *From Ruins to Reconstruction: Urban Identity in Soviet Sevastopol after World War II* (Ithaca and London: Cornell University Press, 2009); Juliane Fürst, *Stalin's Last Generation. Soviet Post-War Youth and the Emergence of Mature Socialism* (Oxford: Oxford University Press, 2010); Robert Dale, *Demobilized Veterans in Late Stalinist Leningrad. Soldiers to Civilians* (London: Bloomsbury Academic, 2015); Martin J. Blackwell, *Kyiv as a Regime City: The Return of Soviet Power after Nazi Occupation* (Rochester: University of Rochester Press, 2016); Mark Edele, 'The Soviet Culture of Victory', *Journal of Contemporary History* 54, no. 4 (2019): 780–98.

28 The state of our current knowledge is Seth Bernstein, 'Ambiguous Homecoming: Retribution, Exploitation and Social Tensions during Repatriation to the USSR, 1944-1946', *Past & Present* 242 (2019): 193–226.

29 Sheila Fitzpatrick, *Everyday Stalinism. Ordinary Life in Extraordinary Times: Soviet Russia in the 1930s* (New York and Oxford: Oxford University Press, 1999); Katrin Boeckh, *Stalinismus in der Ukraine. Die Rekonstruktion des sowjetischen Systems nach dem Zweiten Weltkrieg* (Wiesbaden: Harrassowitz Verlag, 2007); Olaf Mertelsmann, *Everyday Life in Stalinist Estonia* (Frankfurt: Peter Lang, 2012); George O. Liber, *Total Wars and the Making of Modern Ukraine, 1914-1954* (Toronto: University of Toronto Press, 2016).

30 N. P. Sutskov et al., *Krasnoznamennyi dal'nevostochnyi. Istoriia Krasnoznamennogo Dal'nevostochnogo Voennogo Okruga*, 3rd rev. edn (Moscow: Voennoe izdatel'stvo, 1985); Jonathan Haslam, *The Soviet Union and the Threat from the East, 1933-41: Moscow, Tokyo and the Prelude to the Pacific War* (Basingstoke: Macmillan, 1992); B. N. Slavinskii, *Pakt o neitralitete mezhdu SSSR i Iaponiei: diplomaticheskaia istoriia, 1941-1945 gg.* (Moscow: Novina, 1995); David M. Glantz, *The Soviet Strategic Offensive in Manchuria, 1945: August Storm* (Portland: Frank Cass, 2003); David Holloway, 'Jockeying for Position in the Postwar World. Soviet Entry into the War with Japan in August 1945', in *The End of the Pacific War: Reappraisals*, ed. Tsuyoshi Hasegawa (Stanford: Stanford University Press, 2007), 145–8; E. A. Gorbunov, *Vostochnyi rubezh. OKDVA protiv iaponskoi armii* (Moscow: Veche, 2010); Tsuyoshi Hasegawa, 'Soviet Policy toward Japan During World War II', *Cahiers du monde russe* 52, nos. 2–3 (2011): 245–71. For the numbers deployed: V. I. Achkasov (ed.), *Istoriia Vtoroi Mirovoi voiny 1939-1934. Vol. 11: Porazhenie militaristskoi Iaponii. Okonchanie Vtoroi Mirovoi voiny* (Moscow: Voenizdat, 1980), 184 (table 7).

31 For a manifesto see Mark Edele, 'The New Soviet Man as a "Gypsy": Nomadism, War, and Marginality in Stalin's Time', *REGION: Regional Studies of Russia, Eastern Europe, and Central Asia* 3, no. 2 (2014): 285–307. Essential literature includes: Peter Gatrell and Nick Baron, 'Violent Peacetime: Reconceptualizing Displacement and Resettlement in the Soviet-East European Borderlands after the Second World War', in *Warlands: Population Resettlement and State Reconstruction in the Soviet-East European Borderlands, 1945-50*, ed. Peter Gatrell and Nick Baron (New York: Palgrave Macmillan, 2009), 255–68; Peter Gatrell, *The Making of the Modern Refugee* (Oxford: Oxford University Press, 2013). Besides deportations, which are treated in the classical overview by J. Otto Pohl, *Ethnic Cleansing in the USSR, 1937-1949* (Westport: Greenwood Press, 1999), the phenomenon which has received most attention is evacuation. For the most recent literature see V. M. Kovalchuk, 'Evakuatsiia naseleniia Leningrada letom 1941 goda', *Otechestvennaia istoriia* 3 (2000): 15–24; L. I. Snegireva, *Vo imia pobedy: evakuatsiia grazhdanskogo naseleniia v Zapadnuiu Sibir' v dokumentakh i materialakh*, 3 vols (Tomsk: Izd-vo TGPU, 2005); or M. N. Potemkina, *Evakuatsiia v gody Velikoi Otechestvennoi voiny na Urale: Liudi i sud'by* (Magnitogorsk: MaGU, 2006). English language literature includes Rebecca Manley, *To the Tashkent Station: Evacuation and Survival in the Soviet Union at War* (Ithaca and London: Cornell University Press, 2009); Larry E. Holmes, *War, Evacuation, and the Exercise of Power: The Center, Periphery and Kirov's Pedagogical Institute, 1941-1952* (Lanham: Lexington Books, 2012); Natalie Belsky, 'Encounters in the East: Evacuees in the Soviet Hinterland during the Second World War' (PhD diss., The University of Chicago, 2014); Erina Therese Megowan, 'For Fatherland, for Culture: State, Intelligentsia and Evacuated Culture in Russia's Regions, 1941-1945' (PhD diss., Georgetown University, 2016); and Larry E. Holmes, *Stalin's World War II Evacuations: Triumph and Troubles in Kirov* (Lawrence: University Press of Kansas, 2017). For a path-breaking study of migration in the Soviet context more broadly see Lewis Siegelbaum and Leslie Page Moch, *Broad Is My Native Land: Repertoires and Regimes of Migration in Russia's Twentieth Century* (Ithaca and London: Cornell University Press, 2014).

32 Important contributions to a multinational history of this war include David M. Glantz, *Colossus Reborn: The Red Army at War, 1941-1943* (Lawrence: University Press of Kansas, 2005), chapter 13; and Roberto J. Carmack, *Kazakhstan in World War II: Mobilization and Ethnicity in the Soviet Empire* (Lawrence: University Press of Kansas, 2019).

33 Richard Overy, *Russia's War* (New York: Penguin, 1997); Amir Weiner, 'Saving Private Ivan: From What, Why, and How?' *Kritika: Explorations in Russian and Eurasian History* 1, no. 2 (2000): 305–36; Catherine Merridale, *Ivan's War: Life and Death in the Red Army, 1939-1945* (New York: Metropolitan Books, 2006).

34 For example: Il'ia Altman and Leonid Terushkin, *Sokhrani moi pis'ma . . . : Sbornik pisem i dnevnikov evreev perioda Velikoi Otechestevenoi voiny* (Moscow: MIK, 2007);

Oleg Budnitskii, 'The Intelligentsia Meets the Enemy: Educated Soviet Officers in Defeated Germany, 1945', *Kritika: Explorations in Russian and Eurasian History* 10, no. 3 (2009): 629–82; Julie Chervinsky, Aaron Kreiswirth, Leonid Reines and Zvi Gitelman (eds), *Lives of the Great Patriotic War: The Untold Stories of Soviet Jewish Soldiers in the Red Army during World War II* (New York: Blavatnik Archive, 2011); Harriet Murav and Gennady Estraikh (eds), *Soviet Jews in World War II: Fighting, Witnessing, Remembering* (Boston: Academic Studies Press, 2014); David Shneer, *Through Soviet Jewish Eyes: Photography, War, and the Holocaust* (New Brunswick: Rutgers University Press, 2011); Mark Edele, Sheila Fitzpatrick and Atina Grossmann (eds), *Shelter from the Holocaust: Rethinking Jewish Survival in the Soviet Union* (Detroit: Wayne State University Press, 2017); Eliyana Adler, *Survival on the Margins: Polish Jewish Refugees in the Wartime Soviet Union* (Harvard, MA: Harvard University Press, 2020).

35 Oleg V. Khlevniuk, 'The Objectives of the Great Terror, 1937-1938', in *Soviet History, 1917-53: Essays in Honour of R. W. Davies*, ed. Julian Cooper, Maureen Perrie and E. A. Rees (New York: St. Martin's Press, 1995); Olaf Mertelsmann and Aigi Rahi-Tamm, 'Soviet Mass Violence in Estonia Revisited', *Journal of Genocide Research* 11, nos. 2–3 (2009): 307–22, esp. 310, 312–13, 315; David R. Shearer, *Policing Stalin's Socialism: Repression and Social Order in the Soviet Union, 1924-1953* (New Haven and London: Yale University Press, 2009); Oleg Budnitskii, 'The Great Terror of 1941: Toward a History of Wartime Stalinist Criminal Justice', *Kritika: Explorations in Russian and Eurasian History* 20, no. 3 (2019): 447–80.

36 The centrality of the border war of 1938–9 was pointed out by Alvin D. Coox, *Nomonhan. Japan against Russia, 1939* (Stanford: Stanford University Press, 1985); and Stuart D. Goldman, *Nomonhan, 1939: The Red Army's Victory That Shaped World War II* (Annapolis: Naval Institute Press, 2012).

37 David Stahel, *Operation Barbarossa and Germany's Defeat in the East* (Cambridge: Cambridge University Press, 2009).

38 For a concise account of the Soviet leadership at war see Sheila Fitzpatrick, *On Stalin's Team. The Years of Living Dangerously in Soviet Politics* (Melbourne: Melbourne University Press, 2015), chapter 6. A more detailed account is provided by Viktor Cherepanov, *Vlast i voina. Stalinskii mekhanizm gosudarstvennogo upravleniia v Velikoi Otechestvennoi voine* (Moscow: Izvestiia, 2006).

39 The question of loyalty has occupied historians of Stalinism for decades, and has recently moved to centre stage of the debate for both the 1930s and the war years. For the discussion about the 1930s see Choi Chatterjee and Karen Petrone, 'Models of Selfhood and Subjectivity: The Soviet Case in Historical Perspective', *Slavic Review* 67, no. 4 (2008): 967–86. For the war years see Mark Edele, '"What are we fighting for?" Loyalty in the Soviet War Effort, 1941-1945', *International Labor and Working Class History* forthcoming 84 (2013): 248–68. Recent contributions include Mark Edele, *Stalin's Defectors. How Red Army Soldiers Became Hitler's Collaborators, 1941-1945* (Oxford: Oxford University Press, 2017); and Johannes Due Enstad, *Soviet Russians under Nazi Occupation: Fragile Loyalties in World War II* (Cambridge: Cambridge University Press, 2018).

40 Alfred J. Rieber, 'Civil Wars in the Soviet Union', *Kritika: Explorations in Russian and Eurasian History* 4, no. 1 (2003): 129–62.

41 Stephen Lovell, *The Shadow of War: Russia and the USSR 1941 to the Present* (Oxford: Wiley-Blackwell, 2010).

Chapter 1

1 Stalin, 'The Tasks of the Business Executives: Speech Delivered at the First All-Union Conference of Leading Personnel of Socialist Industry, February 4, 1931', in J. V. Stalin, *Works*, vol. 13: July 1930–January 1934 (Moscow: Foreign Languages Publishing House, 1955), 31–44, here: 40–1.

2 For growth numbers see the tables in R. W. Davies, Mark Harrison and S. G. Wheatcroft (eds), *The Economic Transformation of the Soviet Union, 1913-1945* (Cambridge: Cambridge University Press, 1994), 282, 292. On life in the cities see Sheila Fitzpatrick, *Everyday Stalinism. Ordinary Life in Extraordinary Times: Soviet Russia in the 1930s* (New York and Oxford: Oxford University Press, 1999); on popular opinion: Sarah Davies, *Popular Opinion in Stalin's Russia: Terror, Propaganda, and Dissent, 1934-1941* (Cambridge, New York and Melbourne: Cambridge University Press, 1997). For numbers on caloric decline see R. W. Davies, Mark Harrison, Oleg Khlevniuk and Stephen G. Wheatcroft, *The Soviet Economy and the Approach of War, 1937-1939* (London: Palgrave Macmillan, 2018), 120–1.

3 On the debate about the great famine of 1932–3 see Mark Edele, *Debates on Stalinism* (Manchester: Manchester University Press, 2020), chapter 9.

4 Walter Duranty, *Stalin & Co. The Politburo – The Men Who Run Russia* (New York: William Sloane, 1949), 57.

5 Robert Gerwarth, *The Vanquished: Why the First World War Failed to End, 1917-1923* (London: Allan Lane, 2016); Laura Engelstein, *Russia in Flames: War, Revolution, Civil War, 1914-1921* (Oxford: Oxford University Press, 2018).

6 Davies, Harrison and Wheatcroft, *The Economic Transformation of the Soviet Union*, 321; S. A. Smith, *Russia in Revolution: An Empire in Crisis, 1890 to 1928* (Oxford: Oxford University Press, 2017).

7 Sheila Fitzpatrick, Alexander Rabinowitch and Richard Stites (eds), *Russia in the Era of Nep: Explorations in Soviet Society and Culture* (Bloomington and Indianapolis: Indiana University Press, 1991); Oscar Sanchez-Sibony, *Red Globalization: The Political Economy of the Soviet Cold War from Stalin to Khrushchev* (New York: Cambridge University Press, 2014).

8 Robert C. Tucker, 'Stalinism as Revolution from Above', in *Stalinism: Essays in Historical Interpretation*, ed. Robert C. Tucker (New York: W. W. Norton & Company, 1977), 77–108; Sheila Fitzpatrick, 'Stalin and the Making of a New Elite, 1928-1939', *Slavic Review* 38, no. 3 (1979): 377–402; Sheila Fitzpatrick, *Education and Social Mobility in the Soviet Union 1921-1934* (Cambridge: Cambridge University Press, 1979); Sheila Fitzpatrick (ed.), *Cultural Revolution in Russia 1928-1931* (Bloomington: Indiana University Press, 1984); Jochen Hellbeck, *Revolution on My Mind: Writing a Diary under Stalin* (Cambridge, MA and London: Harvard University Press, 2006); Roger Reese, *Why Stalin's Soldiers Fought: The Red Army's Military Effectiveness in World War II* (Lawrence: University Press of Kansas, 2011), 312.

9 On Stalin's thought see Eric van Ree, *The Political Thought of Joseph Stalin: A Study in Twentieth-Century Revolutionary Patriotism* (London and New York: Routledge Curzon, 2002).

10 Matthew E. Lenoe, *The Kirov Murder and Soviet History* (New Haven: Yale University Press, 2010); Alexander Hill, *The Red Army and the Second World War* (Cambridge:

Cambridge University Press, 2017), 60–1; Roger Reese, *Red Commanders: A Social History of the Soviet Army Officer Corps, 1918-1991* (Lawrence: University Press of Kansas, 2005), 121. Numbers from statistical report on repressions 1921–53, prepared by Ministry of the Interior in 1953, reprinted: *GULAG (Glavnoe upravlenie lagerei) 1917-1960*, ed. A. I. Kokurin and N. V. Petrov (Moscow: Demokratiia, 2000), 433; and S. G. Wheatcroft and R. W. Davies, 'Population', in *The Economic Transformation of the Soviet Union, 57–80*, here: 76. That it was only the mass operations which made the terror 'great' was pointed out by Mark Junge and Rolf Binner, 'Wie der Terror 'gross' wurde: Massenmord und Lagerhaft nach Befehl 00447', *Cahiers du Monde russe* 42, nos. 2/4 (2001): 557–613. The most recent history of the terror is James R. Harris, *The Great Fear: Stalin's Terror of the 1930s* (Oxford: Oxford University Press, 2016).

11 'Materialy fevral'sko-martovskogo plenuma TsK VKP(b) 1937 goda', *Voprosy istorii*, no. 3 (1995): 3–15, here: 12.

12 Oleg V. Khlevniuk, 'The Objectives of the Great Terror, 1937-1938', in *Soviet History, 1917-53: Essays in Honour of R. W. Davies*, ed. Julian Cooper, Maureen Perrie and E. A. Rees (New York: St. Martin's Press, 1995); id., 'The Reasons for the "Great Terror": The Foreign-Political Aspect', in *Russia in the Age of Wars*, ed. Silvio Pons and Andrea Romano (Milan: Fondazione Giangiacomo Feltrinelli, 2000), 159–69; Mark Edele, *Stalinist Society 1928-1953* (Oxford: Oxford University Press, 2011), 112–18; for the national aspect: Terry Martin, 'The Origins of Soviet Ethnic Cleansing', *The Journal of Modern History* 70, no. 4 (1998): 813–61.

13 For the numbers: G. F. Krivosheev, *Rossiia i SSSR v voinakh xx veka. Poteri vooruzhennykh sil. Statisticheskoe issledovanie* (Moscow: Olma-Press, 2001), 213; 595; Jamil Hasanli, *At the Dawn of the Cold War: The Soviet-American Crisis of over Iranian Azerbaijan, 1941-1946* (Lanham: Rowman & Littlefield, 2006), 3; Mark Edele, 'Militaries Compared: Wehrmacht and Red Army, 1941-1945', in *A Companion to World War II*, ed. Thomas W. Zeiler and Daniel M. DuBois (Oxford: Wiley-Blackwell, 2013), vol. 1: 169–85, here: 174; G. F. Krivosheev, *Soviet Casualties and Combat Losses in the Twentieth Century* (London Greenhill Books, 1997), 227.

14 M. I. Mel'tiukhov, '9 dnei boevogo puti krasnoarmeitsa Bunina i ego razmyshleniia o poriadkakh v armii (1941 god)', *Voenno-istoricheskaia antropologiia* (2005/2006): 142–51, here: 143; Elena Siniavskaia, interview with Danil Fedorovich Zlatkin (13 July 2006). https://iremember.ru/memoirs/pekhotintsi/zlatkin-daniil-fedorovich/ (accessed 13 February 2019). On officer shortage: David Glantz, *Colossus Reborn: The Red Army at War, 1941-1943* (Lawrence: University Press of Kansas, 2005), 466–9. On lack of training: Roger Reese, *Stalin's Reluctant Soldiers: A Social History of the Red Army 1925-1941* (Lawrence: University Press of Kansas, 1996), chapter 4; on inability to read map or use compass: 140, 149, 157. On military preparation more generally: Seth Bernstein, *Raised under Stalin: Young Communists and the Defense of Socialism* (Ithaca and London: Cornell University Press, 2017), esp. chapter 7.

15 Report from 1st Far Eastern Front (9 August 1945), reprinted in: *Russkii arkhiv/ Velikaia Otechestvennaia* (Moscow: Terra, 1997) [henceforth: *RA/VO*] vol. 18–17, no. 1: 340.

16 John Erickson, 'Red Army Battlefield Performance, 1941-45: The System and the Soldier', in *Time to Kill: The Soldier's Experience of War in the West 1939-1945*, ed. Paul Addison and Angus Calder (London: Plimco, 1997), 233–48. Edele, 'Militaries Compared', 172–3. For life in the infantry: Gabriel Temkin, *My Just War: The Memoir* *of a Jewish Red Army Soldier in World War II* (Novato: Presidio, 1998). On the use of artillery see also David M. Glantz and Jonathan House, *When Titans Clashed: How the Red Army Stopped Hitler* (Lawrence: University Press of Kansas, 1995), 100–1; and Glantz, *Colossus Reborn*, 117–20.

17 Reese, *Stalin's Reluctant Soldiers*; id. *Red Commanders*, 134–57. On the impact of the Great Purges on the military see also Hill, *The Red Army and the Second World War*, 52–76.

18 Alexander Statiev, *At War's Summit: The Red Army and the Struggle for the Caucasus Mountains in World War II* (Cambridge: Cambridge University Press, 2018), quotation: 39.

19 Kenneth Slepyan, *Stalin's Guerrillas: Soviet Partisans in World War II* (Lawrence: University Press of Kansas, 2006), 17–21, quotation: 20.

20 James T. Sparrow, *Warfare State: World War II Americans and the Age of Big Government* (Oxford: Oxford University Press, 2011); David Edgerton, *Britain's War Machine: Weapons, Resources, and Experts in the Second World War* (Oxford: Oxford University Press, 2011). Britain, of course, had the luxury of an empire to exploit for the best of the metropole: Madhusree Mukerjee, *Churchill's Secret War: The British Empire and the Ravaging of India during World War II* (New York: Basic Books, 2010).

21 Davies, Harrison, Wheatcroft, *The Economic Transformation of the Soviet Union,* 300.

22 Mark Harrison and R. W. Davies, 'The Soviet Military-Economic Effort During the Second Five-Year Plan (1933-1937)', *Europe-Asia Studies* 49, no. 3 (1997): 369–406, here: 382, 372 (figure 1), 371.

23 Harrison and Davies, 'The Soviet Military-Economic Effort', 377.

24 Roberta Manning, 'The Soviet Economic Crisis of 1936-1940 and the Great Purges', in *Stalinist Terror: New Perspectives*, ed. J. Arch Getty and Roberta T. Manning (Cambridge: Cambridge University Press, 1993), 116–41, here: 132, 133 (citation); 134 (table comparing military strengths internationally).

25 Edele, *Stalinist Society*, chapter 8.

26 David R. Stone, *Hammer and Rifle: The Militarization of the Soviet Union, 1926-1933* (Lawrence: University Press of Kansas, 2000), 216.

27 Mark Harrison, 'Industry and the Economy', in *The Soviet Union at War, 1941-1945*, ed. David R. Stone (Barnsley: Pen & Sword, 2010), 26.

28 *Tragediia sovetskoi derevni: kollektivizatsiia i raskulachivanie. Dokumenty i materialy, 1927-1949,* ed. V. Danilov et al., 5 vols (Moscow: Rossiiskaia politicheskaia entsiklopediia, 1999), vol. 1: 327.

29 Nicholas Ganson, 'Food Supply, Rationing and Living Standards', in *The Soviet Union at War, 1941-1945*, ed. David R. Stone (Barnsley: Pen & Sword, 2010), 70, 88 (quotation).

30 Harrison, 'Industry and the Economy', 23–4.

31 Andrea Graziosi, *The Great Soviet Peasant War. Bolsheviks and Peasants, 1917-1933* (Cambridge, MA: Harvard University Press, 1996).

32 Sheila Fitzpatrick, *Stalin's Peasants: Resistance and Survival in the Russian Village After Collectivization* (Oxford: Oxford University Press, 1994), 288.

33 Jeffrey J. Rossman, *Worker Resistance under Stalin: Class and Revolution on the Shop Floor* (Cambridge, MA and London: Harvard University Press, 2005), 151.

34 Edele, *Stalinist Society*, 140.

35 David Brandenberger, *Propaganda State in Crisis: Soviet Ideology, Indoctrination, and Terror under Stalin, 1927-1941* (New Haven and London: Yale University Press, 2011). The Stalin quotation is from Stalin's speech at the first All-Union Conference of Stakhanovites, 17 November 1935, in J. Stalin, *Problems of Leninism* (Moscow: Foreign Languages Publishing House, 1943), 546–60, here: 552. The 'Three "Good" Years' is Naum Jasny's term. See his classic: *Soviet Industrialization, 1928-1952* (Chicago: The University of Chicago Press, 1961), chapters 6 and 7.

36 Karel C. Berkhoff, *Motherland in Danger: Soviet Propaganda during World War II* (Cambridge, MA: Harvard University Press, 2012), 277. For more on popular reactions and changes to popular support see chapters 4 and 7 later.

37 *Vsesoiuznaia perepis' naseleniia 1939 goda. Osnovnye itogi. Rossii* (Moscow: Blits, 1999), 31, table 2.

38 P. Charles Hachten, 'Property Relations and the Economic Organization of Soviet Russia, 1941-1948' (PhD diss., The University of Chicago, 2005), 50.

39 On policing: Paul Hagenloh, *Stalin's Police: Public Order and Mass Repression in the USSR, 1926-1941* (Baltimore: The Johns Hopkins University Press, 2009); David R. Shearer, *Policing Stalin's Socialism: Repression and Social Order in the Soviet Union, 1924-1953* (New Haven and London: Yale University Press, 2009). On propaganda state: Peter Kenez, *The Birth of the Propaganda State: Soviet Methods of Mass Mobilization, 1917-1929* (Cambridge and New York: Cambridge University Press, 1985). That the Red Army was effective but inefficient is a central insight of Reese, *Why Stalin's Soldiers Fought*.

40 On peasants: Lynne Viola (ed.), *The War against the Peasantry, 1927-1930* (New Haven: Yale University Press, 2005). On workers: Donald Filtzer, *Soviet Workers and Stalinist Industrialization: The Formation of Modern Soviet Production Relations, 1928-1941* (Armonk and New York: M. E. Sharpe, 1986). On the effects of the terror: Brandenberger, *Propaganda State in Crisis*. The impact on the army is discussed in Reese, *Red Commanders*, chapter 3; Hill, *The Red Army and the Second World War*, chapter 3; and Peter Whitewood, *The Red Army and the Great Terror: Stalin's Purge of the Soviet Military* (Lawrence: University Press of Kansas, 2015).

41 While the German GDP per head was over twice as large as the Soviet equivalent, the ratio of the Soviet to the German GDP in 1940 was 1.1 to 1. The US GDP, meanwhile, was 2.3 times the Soviet equivalent and the GDP per head was 3.5 times larger. See Davies, Harrison and Wheatcroft, *The Economic Transformation of the Soviet Union*, 270 (GDP per head); and Mark Harrison, 'The Economics of World War II: An Overview', in *The Economics of World War II: Six Great Powers in International Comparison*, ed. Mark Harrison (Cambridge: Cambridge University Press, 1998), 10 (GDP).

Chapter 2

1 For a state-of-the-art military history of the Sino-Japanese war see Mark Peattie, Edward Drea and Hans van de Vee (eds), *The Battle for China: Essays on the Military*

History of the Sino-Japanese War of 1937-1945 (Stanford: Stanford University Press, 2011).

2 Christopher D. O'Sullivan, 'Colonialism in Asia', in *A Companion to World War II*, ed. Thomas W. Zeiler and Daniel M. DuBois (Chichester: Wiley-Blackwell, 2013), vol. 1: 63–76, here: 63.

3 Jay Taylor, *The Generalissimo: Chiang Kai-Shek and the Struggle for Modern China* (Cambridge, MA: Harvard University Press, 2009), 47.

4 On the complexity of the 'Russian' Civil Wars see Jonathan D. Smele, *The 'Russian' Civil Wars, 1916-1926: Then Years That Shook The World* (Oxford: Oxford University Press, 2015); and Laura Engelstein, *Russia in Flames: War, Revolution, Civil War, 1914-1921* (Oxford: Oxford University Press, 2018).

5 For a lively history of the Trans-Siberian Railway see Harmon Tupper, *To the Great Ocean. Siberia and the Trans-Siberian Railway* (Boston: Little, Brown & Co, 1965).

6 This book thus follows scholars who see the debate about whether Stalin was a realist or driven by ideology as based on a false opposition: he was both. See Silvio Pons, *Stalin and the Inevitable War 1936-1941* (London: Frank Cass, 2002).

7 R. W. Davies, *Crisis and Progress in the Soviet Economy, 1931-1933* (Houndmills: Palgrave, 1996), 80–1, 113–18; David R. Stone, *Hammer and Rifle: The Militarization of the Soviet Union, 1926-1933* (Lawrence: University Press of Kansas, 2000), chapter 8; 1931 quotation: 185. 1936 quotation: Stalin in conversation with US journalist, transcript reprinted in *Dokumenty vneshnei politiki SSSR*, ed. Ministry of Foreign Affairs of USSR (Moscow: Politicheskaia literatura, 1974), vol. 19: 105–14; here: 107. Numbers: A. AM Buriakova and O. V. Shinin, *Deiatel'nost' organov bezopasnosti na Dal'nem Vostoke v 1922-1941 godakh* (Moscow: Kuchkovo pole, 2013), 234.

8 Komkor Lapin, report of 27 March 1937, *RA/VO* 18–17, no. 1: 74–8, here: 78; border incidents: V. V. Naumkin et al. (eds), *SSSR i strany vostoka nakanune i v gody Vtoroi Mirovoi voiny* (Moscow: IV Ran, 2010), 75–6.

9 'Treaty of Non-Aggression Between the Republic of China and the Union of Soviet Socialist Republics. Signed at Nanking, August 21st, 1937', *League of Nations Treaty Series: Treaties and International Engagements Registered with the Secretariat of the League of Nations* (1937-1938) (London: Harrison & Sons, 1938) , vol. 181: 103–5; Zhang Baijia, 'China's Quest for Foreign Military Aid', in *The Battle for China*, 289–90.

10 K. M. Pokrovskii, 'V efire Kitaia', in *Po dorogam Kitaia. 1937-1945. Vospominaniia* (Moscow: Nauka, 1989), 205–21, here: 205–6 (quotation), 209–10.

11 Memoirs by Andrei Rovnin, in *Ia dralsia s samuraiami. Ot Khalkhin-Gola do Port-Artura,* ed. A. Koshelev (Moscow: Iauza, Eksmo, 2005), 168–9.

12 Report of head of intelligence within General Staff of Red Army on results of the work of the Soviet advisors in the Chinese army (October 1939 to February 1941) (7 March 1941), *RA/VO* 18–17, no. 1: 224–9, here: 225; Zhang, 'China's Quest for Foreign Military Aid', 290; Hagiware Mitsuro, 'The Japanese Air Campaigns in China, 1937-1945', in *The Battle for China*, 244–5. Quotation of historian: Stephen R. MacKinnon, *Wuhan, 1938: War, Refugees, and the Making of Modern China* (Berkeley: University of California Press, 2008), 102.

13 Zhang, 'China's Quest for Foreign Military Aid', 290–1. G. F. Krivosheev (ed.), *Rossiia i SSSR v voinakh xx veka. Poteri vooruzhennykh sil. Statisticheskoe issledovanie*

(Moscow: Olma-Press, 2001), 168; Stalin speech at Kremlin reception of members of the Supreme Soviet of the USSR, 20 January 1938, in *Zastol'nye rechi Stalina. Dokumenty i materialy,* ed. V. A. Nevezhin (Moscow: AIRO-XX, 2003), 178; Alvin D. Coox, *Nomonhan: Japan against Russia, 1939* (Stanford: Stanford University Press, 1985), 174.

14 V. S. Mil'bakh, 'Repression in the Red Army in the Far East, 1936–1939', *The Journal of Slavic Military Studies* 16, no. 4 (01 December 2003): 58–130, here: 64; E. A. Gorbunov, *Vostochnyi rubezh. OKDVA protiv iaponskoi armii* (Moscow: Veche, 2010), 141, 194, 214.

15 B. D. Pak and N. F. Bugai, *140 let v Rossii. Ocherk istorii rossiiskikh Koreitsev* (Moscow: IV RAN, 2004); A. Suturin, *Delo kraevogo masshtaba. O zhertvakh stalinskogo bezzakonia na Dal'nem Vostoke* (Khabarovsk: Khabarovskoe knizhnoe izdatel'stvo, 1991), 181–3; Iu. A. Poliakov et al. (eds), *Vsesoiuznaia perepis' naseleniia 1937 goda: obshchie itogi. Sbornik dokumentov i materialov* (Moscow: Rosspen, 2007), 88, 106. There were also 24,589 Chinese in Far Eastern Region (Poliakov et al., *Vsesoiuznaia perepis' neseleniia 1937 goda,* 106). Politburo Resolution of 21 August 1937: 'About the Koreans', reprinted in *Lubianka. Stalin i Glavnoe Upravlenie Gosbezopasnosti NKVD 1937-1938,* ed. V. N Khaustov, V. P. Naumov and N. S. Plotnikova (Moscow: Demokratiia, 2004), 325–6. Parallel resolution (with identical wording) of Council of People's Commissars and Central Committee of Communist Party (No. 1428-32 ss), 21 August 1937, 'On the expulsion of the Korean population from the border regions of the Far Eastern Region', (signed Stalin and Molotov) reprinted in *Stalinskie deportatsii 1928-1953,* ed. N. L. Pobol and P. M Polian (Moscow: Demokratiia, 2005), 83–4.

16 Mikhail Pak, 'Podlezhat vyseleniiu', in *Tuda, gde konchaetsia solntse. Vospominaniia, svidetel'stva, dokumenty,* ed. Anatolii Kim (Moscow: Druzhba narodov, 2002), 42–55, here: 51; I. Bolodin, 'Enemy Spies in the Soviet Far East', *Pravda,* 23 April 1937, 5.

17 Ezhov to Stalin, 5 July 1937, RGASPI f. 558, op. 11, d. 203, l. 93–7; 'Subversive Work of Japanese Intelligence', *Pravda,* 9 July 1937, 4–5; continued in *Pravda,* 10 July 1937, 4–5; 'Japanese Provocation in Northern China', *Pravda,* 9 July 1937, 5; continued in *Pravda,* 10 July 1937, 5.

18 Politburo Resolution of 21 August 1937: 'About the Koreans', 325; Resolution No. 1b47-377 ss of Council of People's Commissars of USSR, 28 September 1937 (signed Molotov and N. Petrunichev), reprinted in: *Stalinskie deportatsii,* 89, here: 45.

19 Stalin to Vareikis, Bliukher, Liushkov, 11 September 1937, 17.40 h, RGASPI f. 558, op. 11, d. 57, l. 72.

20 Interview with Ten San Din (27 February 2015). https://iremember.ru/memoirs/r azvedchiki/ten-san-din/ (accessed 12 February 2019).

21 Terry Martin, 'Stalinist Forced Relocation Policies: Patterns, Causes, Consequences', in *Demography and National Security,* ed. Myron Weiner and Sharon Stanton Russell (New York: Berghahn Books, 2001), 305–37, here: 321–2.

22 'In the Council of People's Commissars and the CC VKP(b)', *Pravda,* 20 December 1937, 6. Report of Commissar for the Interior N. I. Ezhov (29 October 1937), in *Istoriia Stalinskogo Gulaga: Konets 1920-kh – pervaia polovina 1950-kh godov. Sobranie dokumentov v semi tomakh* (Moscow: Rosspen, 2004), vol. 5: 237.

23 Vladimir Kim, 'V eshelon', in *Tuda, gde konchaetsia solntse,* 61–70, here 62. Quotations: G. N. Li, 'Deportatsiia koreitsev v 1937 g. i ee posledstviia na primere kolkhoza "Kantonskaia kommuna" Spasskogo raiona Primorskogo kraia', in *Politicheskie repressii na Dal'nem vostoke (20-50-3 gg.). Pervaia Dal'nevostochnaia nauchno-prakticheskaia konferentsiia*, ed. A. P. Derevianko (Vladivostok: Iz-vo Dal'nevostochnogo universiteta, 1997), 308–16, here: 310–11.

24 Fitzroy Maclean, *Eastern Approaches* (London: Penguin, 2009), 60.

25 Li, 'Deportatsiia koreitsev', 310.

26 Konstantin Ten, 'V studenuiu poru', in *Tuda, gde konchaetsia solntse*, 56–60, here: 57.

27 Ten, 'V studenuiu poru', 58.

28 Kim, 'V eshelon', 62.

29 Ten, 'V studenuiu poru', 59 (quotation). On barges: Kim, 'V eshelon', 63.

30 Report by head of Agricultural Bank of USSR, M. V. Vynosov (15 December 1937); collective letter to Molotov (29 January 1938); both reprinted in *Istoriia Stalinskogo Gulaga*, vol. 5, 238–40; quotations: Kim, 'V eshelon', 63; Li, 'Deportatsiia koreitsev', 312; Head of Department of labour settlements of GULAG, Konradov, to Deputy Commissar of Internal Affairs of the Soviet Union, Comrade Chernyshov (5 October 1939). Reprinted in A. N. Dugin, *Neizvestnyi Gulag. Dokumenty i fakty* (Moscow: Nauka, 1999), 84.

31 Politburo decree of 5 September 1937. Reprinteed in *Sovetskaia etnopolitika, 1930-40-e gody. Sbornik dokumentov*, ed. L. S. Gatagova (Moscow: Institut rossiiskoi istorii, 2012), 140–1; Kim, 'V eshelon', 61; Li, 'Deportatsiia koreitsev', 310; Sergei Iugai, 'O nashei sem'e', in *Tuda, gde konchaetsia solntse*, 33.

32 Anatolii Kim, 'Zheltye kholmy Kazakhstana', in *Tuda, gde konchaetsia solntse*, 23–9, here: 25.

33 Pak, '"Podlezhat vyseleniiu"' 46–7; Iugai, 'O nashei sem'e', 31.

34 Iugai, 'O nashei sem'e', 33; Kim, 'V eshelon', 63. Numbers: Pak and Bugai, *140 let v Rossii*, 258.

35 Kim, 'V eshelon', 64–5.

36 Li, 'Deportatsiia koreitsev', 312.

37 With 1926 as a baseline, their number increased by 93 per cent 1937 (pre-deportation) and by 1939 had, despite the deportations, more than doubled. Meanwhile, the number of Russians increased only by 28 per cent, while the tally of Ukrainians declined by 10 per cent and the equivalent for Koreans by 22 per cent. http://www.demoscope.ru/weekly/ssp/ussr_nac_26.php; Poliakov et al., *Vsesoiuznaia perepis' neseleniia 1937 goda*, 86; *Vsesoiuznaia perepis' naseleniia 1939 goda. Osnovnye itogi* (Moscow: Nauka, 1992), 57.

38 Alvin D. Coox, 'The Lesser of Two Hells: NKVD General G.S. Lyushkov's Defection to Japan, 1938–1945, Part I', *The Journal of Slavic Military Studies* 11, no. 3 (1998): 145–86, here: 151, 152, 159. On Liushkov and the Korean deportations: 155.

39 Peter Whitewood, *The Red Army and the Great Terror. Stalin's Purge of the Soviet Military* (Lawrence: University Press of Kansas, 2015), 209, 220. V. S. Mil'bakh, 'Repression in the Red Army in the Far East, 1936–1939', 58–130, 89–91, 123, quotation: 80.

40 *Lubianka. Stalin i Glavnoe Upravleni Gosbezopasnosti NKVD 1937-1938*, 643-44 n. 32; Mil'bakh, 'Repression in the Red Army in the Far East, 1936–1939', 113 (quotation). Death by beating was confirmed by the final report of the Communist Party of the

Soviet Union's Central Committee Commission on the reasons for the repression of the 1930s (1963), in *Rebilitatsiia: Kak eto bylo. Fevral' 1956-nachalo 80-kh godov,* ed. A. Artizov, et al. (Moscow: Demokratiia, 2003), 541–670, here: 589.

41 Coox, 'The Lesser of Two Hells . . . Part I', quotation: 160.

42 B. M. Shaposhnikov to Commissar of Defense K. E. Voroshilov, top secret report, 24 March 1938, published in 2019 by Russian Ministry of Defense online: http://pakt1939.mil.ru (accessed 17 December 2019).

43 Unless otherwise noted, this section draws substantially on three books: the magisterial Coox, *Nomonhan*; the more accessible and slightly updated Stuart D. Goldman, *Nomonhan, 1939: The Red Army's Victory That Shaped World War II* (Annapolis: Naval Institute Press, 2012); and the chapter on Khalkhin Gol in Geoffrey Roberts, *Stalin's General: The Life of Georgy Zhukov* (New York: Random House, 2012), an authoritative account avoiding mistakes in the other two studies, which were relying too heavily on Zhukov's memoirs and were unfamiliar with now available archival sources from the Soviet side.

44 Protocol of report by commander of First Red Banner Army, comrade Shtern, about Lake Khasan operation, at meeting of Military Council of the Commissar of Defense (with Stalin, Molotov, Kaganovich, Kalinin, Andreev, Zhdanov, and Mikoian in attendance), 26 November 1938. Reprinted in *Voennyi sovet pri narodnom komissare oborony SSSR. 1938, 1940 gg.: Dokumenty i materialy* (Moscow: Rosspen, 2006), 206–16, here: 210–11.

45 Gorbunov, *Vostochnyi rubezh*, 265–6 (quotation). For the Soviet superiority in men and artillery: Goldman, *Nomonhan*, 72. Originally, the Soviets admitted 236 dead and 611 wounded: *RA/VO* 18–17, no. 1: 103. Archival reports put the total losses at 960 dead and 3,279 sick and wounded: Krivosheev, *Rossiia i SSSR v voinakh xx veka*, 81. Japanese losses were 526 killed and 914 wounded: Goldman, *Nomonhan*, 73. Hence the ratios Japanese: Soviet were: 1:1.8 killed; 1:3.6 wounded. On the lack of coordination between arms: V. I. Korotaev, 'Reaktsiia Zapada na voennyi konflikt u ozera Khasan (po dokumentam inostrannogo proiskhozhdeniia RGVA)', in *'Na granitse tuchi khodiat khmurno' (k 65-letiiu sobytii u ozera Khasan): analiticheskie materialy,* ed. N. I Reznik (Moscow: Kuchkovo pole, 2005), 107; Voroshilov quotation: Gorbunov, *Vostochnyi rubezh*, 265–6.

46 'Tri tankista/Three Tank Drivers', (1937), text in Russian and English in *Mass Culture in Soviet Russia: Tales, Poems, Songs, Movies, Plays and Folklore, 1917-1953,* ed. James von Geldern and Richard Stites (Bloomington: Indiana University Press, 1995), 318–19.

47 Roberts, *Stalin's General*, 47. On the packed bag: Roberts, *Stalin's General*, 46.

48 Order to the troops of the 57th Special Corps, No. 06 (11 July 1939), signed Zhukov, Nikishev, Testov, reprinted: Valerii Krasnov, *Zhukov. Marshal velikoi imperii. Lavry i ternii polkovodtsa* (Moscow: Olma Press, 2005), 112.

49 Report by Chief of Political Administration of the Red Army, Abramov, on moral-political state of affairs among personnel of 82nd Rifle Division (16 July 1939), *RA/VO* 18-7 (1): 124; Order to the troops of the 57th Special Corps, No. 012 (13 July 1939), signed Zhukov, Nikishev, Testov, reprinted: Krasnov, *Zhukov*, 113–14.

50 Quotation: Goldman, *Nomonhan*, 79, numbers 3. The Soviets lost 9,703 dead and 15,952 sick and wounded: Krivosheev, *Rossiia i SSSR v voinakh xx veka*, 179.

51 G. K. Zhukov, *Vospominaniia i razmyshleniia,* 2 vols (Moscow: Olma-Press, 2002), vol. 1: 167–8.

52 Alexander Hill, *The Red Army and the Second World War* (Cambridge: Cambridge University Press, 2017), 95–7, 106, quotation: 97.

53 Coox, *Nomonhan,* 189, 190, 191, 206, 207, 229, 231, 232, 248, 306, 576, 579, 667, 190–1; Artem Drabkin, interview with Aleksandr Filippovich Panuev (22 July 2006). https ://iremember.ru/memoirs/gmch-katiushi/panuev-aleksandr-filippovich/ (accessed 19 February 2019); Pozniakov and Voronin, top secret report on the battles at the river Khalkhin Gol from 15 May to 10 August 1939 (10 August 1939), reprinted: *Vooruzhennyi konflikt v raione reki Khalkhin-Gol. Mai – sentiabr' 1939 g. Dokumenty i materialy,* ed. A. N. Artizov et al. (Moscow: Novalis, 2014), 278–81, here: 280. On the opening skirmishes: Coox, *Nomonhan,* 190–1.

54 Stalin in front of top commanders of the Red Army, 14 April 1940, in *1941 god: v 2 kn. Kn. 2,* ed. V. P Naumov (Moscow: Demokratiia, 1998), 603.

55 For the border incidents: *RA/VO* 18–17, no. 1: 67–9, 72, 90, 111. Veterans' memories: Pavel Soklov'ev in *Ia dralsia s samuraiami,* 144; and N. I. Ganin, 'Neob"iavlennaia voina', in *Khalkhin-Gol: vzgliad na sobytiia iz XXI veka. Sbornik statei,* ed. E. V. Boikova (Moscow: Institut vostokovedeniia RAN, 2013), 23–4; numbers and comparison to Poland: Evan Mawdsley, *World War II: A New History* (Cambridge: Cambridge University Press, 2009), 72; Chinese preoccupations: Tobe Ryoichi, 'The Japanese Eleventh Army in Central China, 1938-1941', in *The Battle for China,* 217.

56 Lennart Samuelson, *Plans for Stalin's War Machine. Tukhachevskii and Military-Economic Planning, 1925-1941* (New York: St. Martin's Press, 2000), 202–3; on the shift towards defense production also: R. W. Davies, Mark Harrison, Oleg Khlevniuk and S. G. Wheatcroft, *The Industrialisation of Soviet Russia 7: The Soviet Economy and the Approach of War, 1937-1939* (London: Palgrave Macmillan, 2018), chapter 9. Voroshilov order to command of Soviet forces in Far East, 1 August 1939, *RA/VO* 18–17, no. 1: 125–6.

57 MacKinnon, *Wuhan,* 102; Goldman, *Nomonhan,* 74.

58 Veteran quotation: Nikolai Bogdanov in *Ia dralsia s samuraiami,* 151; Jonathan Haslam, *The Soviet Union and the Threat form the East, 1933-1941: Moscow, Tokyo and the Prelude to the Pacific War* (Basingstoke: Macmillan, 1992), 141 ('in these circumstances'); Coox, *Nomonhan,* xiii, 1078–9 (Khalkhin Gol as turning point); Goldman, *Nomonhan,* 5 ('most important . . . battle').

Chapter 3

1 The diary entries of 11 September and 17 September 1939 are cited from Jochen Hellbeck (ed.), *Tagebuch aus Moskau, 1931-1939* (Munich: dtv, 1996), 275–7. Iu. Trifonov, interview with Mariia Iakovlevna Starchukova (4 July 2013). https://ir emember.ru/memoirs/letno-tekh-sostav/starchukova-shebarshina-mariya-yakovle vna/ (accessed 19 February 2019). For newspaper reporting on Lake Khasan see 'The Japanese Warmongers Continue their Provocations', *Pravda,* 30 July 1938, 1; 'On the Events Near Lake Khasan', *Pravda,* 12 August 1938, 1. The first TASS report on Khalkhin Gol was published in *Pravda,* 26 June 1939, 2. For other examples, see: 'The

Japanese Provocateurs do not Clam Down', *Pravda*, 6 July 1939, 2; or the report on mopping up operations: 'The Liquidation of Leftovers of the Japanese-Manchurian Forces in the Border Region of the Mongolian People's Republic', *Pravda*, 1 September 1939, 3.

2 Most of the front page of *Pravda* was taken over by the news of this Pact on 24 August 1939. Also: *Pravda*, 29 August 1939, 1; 1 September 1939, p. 1, 3; 2 September 1939, 1; *Pravda*, 18 September 1939, 1.

3 Sara Davies, *Popular Opinion in Stalin's Russia: Terror, Propaganda and Dissent, 1934-1941* (Cambridge: Cambridge University Press, 1997), 97; Deputy Commissar of the Interior of Ukraine, A. Kobulov, top secret report to Party Secretary of Ukraine N. S. Khrushchev (27 August 1939), 968–70; and top secret report on reactions to Molotov's speech, 3 September 1939, in *Radians'ki orhany derzhavnoi bezpeky u 1939 - chervni 1941 r. dokumenty GDA SB Ukrainy*, ed. Vasyl Danilenko and Serhyi Kokin (Kyiv: Kijevo-mogilians'ka akademiia, 2009), 968–70, 974–80, quotations: 970, 977.

4 Both the Treaty and the Secret Protocol were first published in *Nazi-Soviet Relations 1939-1941: Documents from the Archives of The German Foreign Office as Released by the Department of State*, ed. Raymond James Sontag and James Stuart Beddie (New York: Didier, 1948), 76–8.

5 For a discussion of this historiography and its continued relevance today see Mark Edele, *Debates on Stalinism* (Manchester: Manchester University Press, 2020), 213–14.

6 Sergei Khrushchev (ed.), *Memoirs of Nikita Khrushchev. Vol. 1: Commissar (1918-1945)* (University Park: The Pennsylvania State University Press, 2004), 225–6.

7 For a discussion of the alternatives: M. I. Semiariaga, *Tainy stalinskoi diplomatii. 1939-1941* (Moscow: Vysshaia shkola, 1992), 57–9; on the British option: Robert Manne, 'The British Decision for Alliance with Russia, May 1939', *Journal of Contemporary History* 9, no. 3 (1974): 3–26; id., 'Some British Light on the Nazi-Soviet Pact', *European Studies Review* 11, no. 1 (1981): 83–102; for a more critical view: Louise Shaw, *The British Political Elite and the Soviet Union, 1937-1939* (London: Rank Cass, 2003), chapter 6. For an assessment of the newly available Soviet archival evidence see Silvio Pons, *Stalin and the Inevitable War 1936-1941* (London: Frank Cass, 2002), chapter 5, esp. 179–80.

8 *Memoirs of Nikita Khrushchev*, vol. 1: 225.

9 Ivo Banac (ed.), *The Diary of Georgi Dimitrov, 1933-1949* (New Haven and London: Yale University Press, 2003), 114 (entry from 7 September 1939). On the role of the fighting in the east on this decision see Jonathan Haslam, *The Soviet Union and the Threat form the East, 1933-1941: Moscow, Tokyo and the Prelude to the Pacific War* (Basingstoke: Macmillan, 1992), 134; and Stuart D. Goldman, *Nomonhan, 1939: The Red Army's Victory That Shaped World War II* (Annapolis: Naval Institute Press, 2012), 160.

10 Note on the conversation between Molotov and Polish Ambassador W. Grzyybowski, marked 'secret', 5 September 1939, in *Dokumenty vneshnei politiki* XXII (1939), (book 2: September-December 1939) (Moscow: Mezhdunaronye otnozheniia, 1992), [henceforth: *Dokumenty vneshnei politiki* XII, no. 2] 25–6.

11 *Dokumenty vneshnei politiki* XII, no. 2: 25.

12 Molotov speech in *Vneocherednaia piataia sessiia Verkhovnogo Soveta SSSR, 31 oktiabria - 2 noiabria 1939 g. Stenograficheskii otchet* (Moscow: Izdanie Verkhovnogo Soveta SSSR, 1939), 8.

13 Winston Churchill, 'The First Month of War' (Radio broadcast, 1 October 1939), in *Winston S. Churchill: His Complete Speeches 1897-1963*, ed. Robert Rhodes James (New York and London: Chelsea House Publishers, 1974), vol. 6: 6160-4, here: 6161.

14 Patrick R. Osborn, *Operation Pike: Britain versus the Soviet Union, 1939-1941* (Westport: Greenwood Press, 2000), 1-26.

15 G. I. Kulik to Stalin, Molotov, Voroshilov, 21 September 1939, top secret. Published in *Vestnik Arkhiva Prezidenta Rossiiskoi Federatsii: Sovetskaia armiia: gody reform i ispytanii*, ed. S. V. Kurdriashov (Moscow: IstLit, 2018), vol. 1: 166-7.

16 Report of Mechanized Cavalry Group to Stalin and Voroshilov, top secret, 1 October 1939, in *Vestnik Arkhiva Prezidenta Rossiiskoi Federatsii: Sovetskaia armiia: gody reform i ispytanii*, 170-4, here: 172; G. F. Krivosheev, *Rossiia i SSSR v voinakh XX veka. Poteri vooruzhennykh sil. Statisticheskoe issledovanie* (Moscow: Olma-Press, 2001), 187; Jan T. Gross, *Revolution from Abroad: The Soviet Conquest of Poland's Western Ukraine and Western Belorussia*, expanded edn (Princeton: Princeton University Press, 2002), 17.

17 H. Apolinary, 'My Experiences in Russia', in *War Through Children's Eyes: The Soviet Occupation of Poland and the Deportations, 1939-1941*, ed. Irena Grudziska-Gross and Jan Tomasz Gross (Stanford: Hoover Institution Press, 1981), 205; Nil Valentinovich Milovskii, unpublished memoirs, Bakhmeteff Archive, Columbia University, typescript, 46; Stanislaw H., in *War Through Children's Eyes*, 68.

18 M. I. Mel'tiukhov, *17 sentiabria 1939. Sovetsko-pol'skie konflikty. 1918-1939* (Moscow: Veche, 2009), 478-502; Gross, *Revolution from Abroad*, 45-8, quotation: 48.

19 Lev Mekhlis, encoded telegram to Voroshilov, Stalin, Timoshenko, Khrushchev and Borisov (21 September 1939), published by the Russian Ministry of Defense in 2019. http://pakt1939.mil.ru (accessed 16 December 2019); Michael Goldberg, 'Memories of a Generation', United States Holocaust Memorial Museum (USHMM) RG-10.120, 18.

20 Goldberg, 'Memories of a Generation', 20-1; Gross, *Revolution from Abroad*, 49.

21 Davies, *Popular Opinion*, 99 (quotation); and reports on mood of the population reprinted in *Radians'ki orhany derzhavnoi bezpeky*, 968-97, quotation: 977-8.

22 Molotov's radio address of 17 September. *Pravda* (18 September 1939), 1. Telegram No. 317 of Schulenburg to German Foreign Ministry, 10 September 1939, marked 'most urgent' and 'top secret'. Reprinted: *Documents on German Foreign Policy 1918-1945* (Washington: United states Government Printing Office, 1954), Series D, Vol. VIII: 44-5, quotation: 44. The Polish Ambassador to Moscow protested the Soviet claim when handed the note about Soviet intervention in the early hours of 17 September 1939, as Soviet Deputy Commissar for Foreign Affairs, V. Potemkin, reported shortly thereafter. *Dokumenty vneshnei politiki* XII, no. 2: 94.

23 Reports on the mood of the population with regards to Polish campaign. GDA SBU f. 16, op. 1, d. 381. Also: *Radyans'ki orhany derzhavnoi bezpeky*, 998-1045; V. I. Motorkin to Presidium of Supreme Soviet of the USSR, 1 November 1939. Published in: *Sovetskaia povsednevnost' i massovoe soznanie 1939-1945*, ed. A. Ia. Livshin and I. B. Orlov (Moscow: Rosspen, 2003), 15-16, quotation: 15.

24 *The Diary of Georgi Dimitrov*, 115-16.

25 See Serhii Plokhy's pathbreaking article, 'The Call of Blood: Government Propaganda and Public Response to the Soviet Entry into World War II', *Cahiers du monde russe* 52, nos. 2–3 (2011): 293–319.

26 Stalin to Grishuk, 3 July 1940, RGASPI f. 558, op. 11, d. 59, l. 2–4, here: l. 2.

27 *The Diary of Georgi Dimitrov*, 120 (entry from 25 October 1939). Dimitrov was the boss of the 'Komintern', Stalin's organization to control the international communist movement.

28 Richard Bidlack and Nikita Lomagin, *The Leningrad Blockade, 1941-1944: A New Documantary History from the Soviet Archives* (New Haven: Yale University Press, 2012), 17.

29 Stalin speech at the meeting of the military leadership, 17 April 1940, RGASPI f. 558, op. 11, d. 1124, l. 8–43, here: l. 9.

30 'Memorandum of the Government of the USSR Handed in Moscow on October 14, 1939', in *The Development of Finnish-Soviet Relations during the Autumn of 1939: Including the Official Documents*, ed. Ministry of Foreign Affairs of Finland (London: George G Harrap, 1940), 46–9, here: 47.

31 Historians disagree if the goal of the war was annexation of Finland or just moving the border. The existence of the Kuusinen 'government' can be interpreted either as an attempt to install a friendly government or a first step to outright annexation (as happened with the Baltic republics). That annexation was thinkable is demonstrated by the fact that Stalin's lieutenant Molotov asked Hitler in November 1940 if a 'settlement' of the Finnish question 'on the same scale as in Bessarabia' (which had just been annexed earlier that year) would be tolerated by the Germans. See the notes on the conversation between Hitler and Molotov, 13 November 1940 in *Nazi-Soviet Relations 1939-1941*, 240. On the war plan Pasi Tuunainen, 'The Finnish Army at War: Operations and Soldiers, 1939–45', in *Finland in World War II: History, Memory, Interpretations*, ed. Tiina Kinnunen and Ville Kivimäki (Leiden and Boston: Brill Academic Publishers, 2012), 139–88, here: 140 (quotation).

32 Krivosheev, *Rossiia i SSSR v voinakh XX veka*, 195. Some historians argue that losses were much higher. See Pavel Aptekar', *Sovetsko-finskie voiny* (Moscow: Eksmo Iauza, 2004), 329.

33 848,570 men, to be precise: Krivosheev, *Rossiia i SSSR v voinakh XX veka*, 197. Finnish historical population statistics are available here: http://www.stat.fi/tup/satavuotias-suomi/vuosisadan-vertailut_en.html (accessed 15 March 2019). On the planes: Top secret report on air-force performance in Finnish war, addressed to Voroshilov and Stalin, 19 March 1940, in *Vestnik Arkhiva Prezidenta Rossiiskoi Federatsii: Sovetskaia armiia: gody reform i ispytanii*, 227–435, here: 227.

34 On the plans see Llewellyn Woodward, *British Foreign Policy in the Second World War* (London: Her Majesty's Stationary Office, 1970), vol. 1: 31–106; and Osborn, *Operation Pike*. On the information Stalin received and how it influenced his decisions: Kommo Rentola, 'Intelligence and Stalin's Two Crucial Decisions in the Winter War, 1939-40', *The International History Review* 35, no. 5 (2013): 1089–112.

35 For the numbers: David Kirby, *A Concise History of Finland* (Cambridge: Cambridge University Press, 2006), 215–16.

36 On the wrong lessons learned by the Germans see Roger R. Reese, 'Lessons of the Winter War: A Study in the Military Effectiveness of the Red Army, 1939-1940', *The Journal of Military History* 72, no. 3 (2008): 825–52.

37 Mikhail Mel'tiukhov, *Upushchennyi shans Stalina. Skhvatka za Evropu. 1939-1941 gg (dokumenty, fakty, suzhdeniia)* (Moscow: Veche, 2008), 142, 147.

38 'Long Live Soviet Bessarabia and the Soviet Bukovina', *Pravda*, 29 June 1940, 1. For the data and the strategic reasons: V. A. Zolotarev (ed.), *Velikaia Otechestvannaia voina 1941-1945 godov*, 12 vols, vol. 2: *Proiskhozhdenie i nachalo voiny* (Moscow: Kuchkovo pole, 2015), 245.

39 Top secret NKVD report on the mood of the population in Kyiv (28 June 1940), *Radians'ki orhany derzhavnoi bezpeky*, 1161–3.

40 Markus Lecker, 'I Remember: Odyssey of a Jewish Teenager in Eastern Europe, 1939-1946', USHMM RG-02 (no pagination) [henceforth: Lecker memoirs].

41 *The Diary of Georgi Dimitrov*, 124 (entry of 21 January 1940).

42 Jan Gross's term.

43 Keith Sword, 'Soviet Economic Policy in the Annexed Areas', in *The Soviet Takeover of the Polish Eastern Provinces, 1939-41*, ed. Keith Sword (New York: St. Martin's Press, 1991), 86–101; Alexander Statiev, *The Soviet Counterinsurgency in the Western Borderlands* (Cambridge: Cambridge University Press, 2010), 41, 142; Top secret report on perlustration of letters, 6 June 1941, in *Radyans'ki orhany derzhavnoi bezpeky*, 1202–7; here: 1203; Goldberg, 'Memories of a Generation', 22.

44 Semiriaga, *Tainy stalinskoi diplomatii*, 246–7. On Bessarabia and Bukovina see the decrees of 14 August 1940, reprinted in *Sovetskaia etnopolitika, 1930-1940-e gody. Sbornik dokumentov*, ed. L. S. Gatagova (Moscow: RAN institute rossiiskoi istorii, 2012), 239, 243–4.

45 Top secret report by NGB SSSR chief V. N. Merkulov to Stalin, Molotov, Beria (17 June 1941), reprinted in *Istoriia stalinskogo Gulaga. Konets 1920-kh – pervaia polovina 1950-kh godov. Vol. 1: Massovye repressii v SSSR*, ed. N. Werth and S. V. Mironenko (Moscow: Rosspen, 2004), 404–5.

46 B. Z. Kovulov to Stalin, Molotov, Beria (13 June 1941), reprinted in *Istoriia stalinskogo Gulaga*, vol. 1: 401.

47 O. A. Gorlanov and A. B. Roginskii, 'Ob arestakh v zapadnykh oblastiakh Belorussii i Ukrainy v1939-1941 gg', in *Repressii protiv poliakov i pol'skikh grazhdan*, ed. A. E. Gur'ianov (Moscow: Memorial, 1997), 77–96, here: 82, 86, 89.

48 Reprinted in *Stalinskie deportatsii 1928-1953. Dokumenty*, ed. N. L. Pobol' and P. M. Polian (Moscow: Demokratiia, 2005), 215–17.

49 Irena Protassewicz, *A Polish Woman's Experience in World War II. Conflict, Deportation and Exile* (London: Bloomsbury, 2019), 95–132, quotation: 121.

50 Mark Edele, 'The Second World War as a History of Displacement: The Soviet Case', *History Australia* 12, no. 2 (2015): 17–40, here: 24; Mark Edele and Wanda Warlik, 'Saved by Stalin? Trajectories and Numbers of Polish Jews in the Soviet Second World War', in *Shelter from the Holocaust: Rethinking Jewish Survival in the Soviet Union*, ed. Mark Edele, Sheila Fitzpatrick and Atina Grossmann (Detroit: Wayne State University Press, 2017), 95–131, here: 106.

51 Semiriaga, *Tainy stalinskoi diplomatii*, 248. Size of population was a total of 5.9 million (2,880 thousand in Lithuania, 1,950 thousand in Latvia, and 1,120 thousand in Estonia) in 1940. Semiriaga, *Tainy stalinskoi diplomatii*, 254.

52 On the Polish experience of deportation see Katherine R. Jolluck, *Exile & Identity: Polish Women in the Soviet Union during World War II* (Pittsburgh: University of Pittsburgh Press, 2002); on the Polish-Jewish equivalent see Edele, Fitzpatrick and Grossmann, *Shelter from the Holocaust*.

53 Goldberg, 'Memories of a Generation', 22, 25.

54 NKGB lieutenant Tsvetukhin, top secret report on number of 'highest measure of punishment' in Western Ukraine, 22 April 1941, GDA SBU f. 42, op. 1, d. 46, l. 8.

55 A. Shelepin to N. S. Khrushchev, top secret report, 3 March 1959; reprinted in *Katyn: A Crime Without Punishment*, ed. Anna M. Cienciala, Natalia S. Lebedeva and Wojciech Materski (New Haven: Yale University Press, 2007), 332–3. Beria's proposal for the execution, before 5 March 1940, *Katyn. Plenniki neob"iavlennoi voiny*, 384–90. Politburo decision to implement this proposal (5 March 1939), *Katyn. Plenniki neob"iavlennoi* voiny, 390–2.

56 Thomas Urban, *Katyn 1940. Geschichte eines Verbrechens* (Munich: C. H. Beck, 2015), 43–7; R. G. Pikhoia (ed.), *Katyn. Plenniki neob"iavlennoi voiny* (Moscow: Demokratiia, 1999), 521–2.

57 Beria to Stalin, 5 March 1940, *Katyn: A Crime without Punishment*, 118–20.

58 The Soviets had not signed the Geneva Convention of 1929, but Russia had ratified the Hague convention of 1907 and during the war against Germany the Soviet Union announced that it felt bound by the latter – although in practice that was not always the case. Mark Edele, 'Take (No) Prisoners! The Red Army and German POWs, 1941-1943', *The Journal of Modern History* 88 (2016): 342–79. On the conventions: 348–9. On Soviet regulations regarding the treatment of POWs see 'Regulations about Prisoners of War', (19 September 1939), in *Katyn. Plenniki neob"iavlennoi voiny*, 78–83.

59 *Vsesoiuznaia perepis' naseleniia 1939 goda. Osnovnye itogi. Rossiia* (Moscow: Blits, 1999), 10–11; *Naselenie Rossii v XX veke. Istoricheskie ocherki,* 2 vols (Moscow: Rosspen, 2001), vol. 2: 6, 7, 12, 61.

60 NKVD report on fight against banditism in the western regions of the Ukrainian SSR, January to June 1941, reprinted in: *Ukrainskie natsionalisticheskie organizatsii v gody Vtoroi mirovoi voiny. Dokumenty* ed. A. N. Artizov (Moscow: Rosspen, 2012), vol. 1: 313–19, here: 314.

61 Agreement between USSR and China, 13 June 1939; contract for deliveries of 'special equipment' to China, 20 June 1939, both in *God krizisa 1938-1939*, vol. 2: *2 iiunia 1939 g. – 4 sentiabria 1939 g. Dokumenty i materialy,* ed. Ministry of Foreign Affairs of USSSR (Moscow: Politicheskaia literatura, 1990), 20–4, 43–4; V. I. Chuikov, *Missiia v Kitae. Zapiski voennogo sovetnika* (Moscow: Glavnaia redatktsiia vostochnoi literatury, 1981), 57–8.

62 V. P. Naumov (ed.), *1941 god,* 2 vols (Moscow: Demokratiia, 1998), vol. 1: 741–46.

63 Chuikov, *Missiia v Kitae,* 186–7.

64 Bernd Martin, *Deutschland und Japan im Zweiten Weltkrieg. Vom Angriff auf Pearl Harbor bis zur deutschen Kapitulation* (Göttingen: Musterschmidt Verlag, 1969), 155.

65 Report by S. Tochilin, 'Short results of trade of the USSR with Germany in 1941 (26 March 1942), Russian State Archive of the Economy (RGAE) f. 413, op. 12, d. 5515, l. 16-24. Quotation: l. 21. The Soviets received material worth 482.6 million German marks, the Germans 691.0 million. RGAE f. 413, op. 12, d. 5515,. l. 19.

66 Sergiusz M., in *War Through Children's Eyes*, 93; Elena Osokina, *Za fasadom 'stalinskogo izobiliia'. Raspredelenie i rynok v snabzhenii naseleniia v gody industrializatsii 1927-1941* (Moscow: Rosspen, 1999), 206–13.

67 Osokina, *Za fasadom*, 213–18. On rationing in Leningrad: Alexis Peri, *The War Within: Diaries from the Siege of Leningrad* (Cambridge, MA: Harvard University Press, 2017), 37.

68 Edele and Warlik, 'Saved by Stalin?' 103–4; Rozenberg interview by G. Koifman (25 April 2014). https://iremember.ru/memoirs/pekhotintsi/rozenberg-samuil-iosifovich/ (accessed 11 March 2019).

69 Georgii Zhukov, *Vospominaniia razmyshleniia* (Moscow: Olma-Press, 2002), vol. 1: 241.

70 Interview with Aleksandr Fedorovich Sobakin. https://iremember.ru/memoirs/artill eristi/sobakin-aleksandr-fedorovich/ (accessed 13 March 2019).

71 On this discussion see Evan Mawdsley, 'Crossing the Rubicon: Soviet Plans for Offensive War in 1940-1941', *The International History Review* 25, no. 4 (2003): 818–65.

72 'TASS Communique', *Pravda*, 14 June 1941, 2; I. Fleischhauer, *Diplomatischer Widerstand gegen 'Unternehmen Barbarossa': die Friedensbemühungen der Deutschen Botschaft Moskau 1939–1941* (Berlin and Frankfurt am Main: Ullstein, 1991), 336.

73 N. G. Kuznetsov, *Kursom k pobede* (Moscow: Olma-Press, 2003), 9–10.

74 I. A. Pliev, *Pod gvardeiskim znamenem* (Ordzhonikidze: Izdatel'stvo 'Ir', 1976), 12–13.

75 A. M. Vasilevskii, *Delo vsei zhizni* (Moscow: Politizdat, 1978), 109–10.

76 https://iremember.ru/memoirs/desantniki/lubentsov-aleksandr-grigorevich/.

77 Grigorii Chukhrai, *Moia voina* (Moscow: Algoritm, 2001), 29–32.

78 *Lubianka. Stalin in NKVD-NKGB-GUKR 'SmerSh' 1939-mart 1946*, ed. V. N. Khaustov et al. (Moscow: Demokratiia, 2006), 286–7.

Chapter 4

1 Hans-Adolf Jacobsen (ed.), *Kriegstagebuch des Oberkommandos der Wehrmacht (Wehrmachführungsstab)*, vol. 1: 1. August 1940–31 Dezember 1941 (Frankfurt am Main: Bernard & Graefe Verlag für Wehrwesen, 1965), 499–501.

2 G. Kumanev, *Govoriat stalinskie narkomy* (Smolensk: Rusich, 2005), 61–2, quotation: 62.

3 Michael Goldberg, 'Memories of a Generation', United States Holocaust Memorial Museum (USHMM) RG-10.120, 27, 35–6.

4 Goldberg, 'Memories of a Generation', 36, 38.

5 Goldberg, 'Memories of a Generation', 39.

6 Goldberg, 'Memories of a Generation', 39–40.

7 Goldberg, 'Memories of a Generation', 41, 42.

8 B. D. Pak and N. F. Bugai, *140 let v Rossii. Ocherk istorii rossiiskikh Koreitsev* (Moscow: IV RAN, 2004), 313.

9   C. Tischler, 'German Emigrants in Soviet Exile: A Drama in Five Acts', in *Russian-German Special Relations in the Twentieth Century: A Closed Chapter?*, ed. K. Schlögel (Oxford and New York: Berg, 2006), 92. On Estonians mobilized into the labour army in 1941 see Tiit Noormets, 'Estonians in Russian Armed Forces', in *Estonians in Russian Armed Forces in 1940-45*, ed. Leo Õispuu (Tallinn: The State Archive of Estonia, 2008), 12–14, and recollections: Noormets, 'Estonians in Russian Armed Forces', 34–40.

10 Goldberg, 'Memories of a Generation', 42, 44–5.

11 Leib Treitman, 'The School of My Life', recorded by Zina Ovis, translated by Irena Karshenbaum, in *Voices of resilience = Golosa stoikosti*, ed. Svetlana Shklarov (Calgary: Jewish Family Service Calgary, 2010), 216–17.

12 A. A. German, 'Sovietskie nemtsy v lageriakh NKVD v gody Velikoi Otechestvennoi voiny: vklad v pobedu', in *Voenno-istoricheskie issledovaniia v Povolzh'e. Vypusk 7* (Saratov: Nauchnaia kniga, 2006), 289.

13 Rebecca Manley, *To the Tashkent Station: Evacuation and Survival in the Soviet Union at War* (Ithaca and London: Cornell University Press, 2009).

14 Information on number of registered evacuees according to data of the resettlement departments, as of 21 October 1941, RGAE f. 4372, op. 42, d. 998, l. 19–22.

15 Numbers from P. V. Malkov (ed.), *Velikaia Otechestvennaia voina. Iubileinyi statisticheskii sbornik* (Moscow: Rossstat, 2020), 257 (evacuation numbers for 1941 and 1942), 259 (total registered evacuees by 15 December 1941), 24 (total population in 1940).

16 The available data do not allow to calculate exact shares, but we have access to some statistical signposts. The most recent estimate of the population under German occupation is between 55 and 65 million: Dieter Pohl, *Die Herrschaft der Wehrmacht: Deutsche Militärbesatz und einheimische Bevölkerung in der Sowjetunion 1941-1944* (Franfurt a. M.: S. Fischer, 2011), 124. Regions which were occupied had contained 84.5 million people in 1939: Malkov, *Velikaia Otechestvennaia voina. Iubileinyi statisticheskii sbornik*, 36. By the summer of 1941, these numbers would have changed because of labour migration, deportation, arrests, etc. but they can provide a first baseline. The total number who were removed before the Germans could get to them would then tally up to between 20 and 30 million. This number would include all those deported or arrested 1940–1, those who moved voluntarily 1939–41, those who evacuated or fled in 1941–2, and those deported after the German attack in 1941 (esp. Germans, Finns). (I ignore in-migration and natural population growth for this calculation). The deportations from the borderlands in 1940–1 amounted to some 0.4 million and arrests and executions to maybe another 0.2 million (see Chapter 3), the deportation of Germans and Finns in 1941 included some 0.9 million people: N. L. Pobol' and P. M. Polian (eds), *Stalinskie deportatsii. 1928-1953* (Moscow: Demokratiia, 2005), 792–3; evacuation in 1941–2 included 18.4 million (see above) – together around 20 million. Hence, the lower number of removals calculated here (20 million) seems more likely and hence the larger number of people remaining on occupied territory (65 million). Using this number, the share who stayed behind would be 77 per cent. Using the lower number (55 million) we would arrive at a more conservative estimate of 65 per cent.

17 Deputy Commissar of the Interior (Ukraine) Savchenko to Secretary of Ukrainian Communist Party Korotchenko (20 September 1941), GDA SBU f. 16, op. 1, d. 523, l. 474–77, here: 477.

18 Deputy People's Commissar of the Interior (Ukraine) Ratushnyi to Sergienko (25 August 1941), GDA SBU f. 16, op. 1, d. 523, l. 143–5; here: 144. Such refusal was not treated as resistance: 'Anti-Soviet manifestations ... were not recorded', noted the same report (l. 145). Similar: Savchenko to Meshik (20 September 1941), GDA SBU f. 16, op. 1, d. 520, l. 298–300a; here: 300a.

19 See the discussion in Mark Edele and Wanda Warlik, 'Saved by Stalin? Trajectories and Numbers of Polish Jews in the Soviet Second World War', in *Shelter from the Holocaust: Rethinking Jewish Survival in the Soviet Union*, ed. Mark Edele, Sheila Fitzpatrick and Atina Grossmann (Detroit: Wayne State University Press, 2017), 110–12.

20 Paul Buskovitch, 'Moshe Lewin', in *Visions of History: Interviews by Marho the Radical Historians Organization*, ed. Henry Abelov, Betsy Blackmar, Peter Dimock and Jonathan Schneer (Manchester: Manchester University Press, 1983), 281–308, here: 284.

21 NKVD report, 24 January 1942, reprinted: A. N. Dugin, *Neizvestnyi GULAG. Dokumenty i fakty* (Moscow: Nauka, 1999), 22.

22 A. Artizov, Iu. Sigachev, I. Shevchuk and V. Khlopov (eds), *Reabilitatsiia: kak eto bylo. Fevral' 1956-nachalo 80-kh godov* (Moscow: Demokratiia, 2003), vol. 2: 785–6, 906–7. Beria order (18 October 1941), and document confirming the executions (28 October), both reprinted: *Organy Gosudarstvennoi Bezopasnosti SSSR v Velikoi Otechestvennoi voine. Sbornik dokumentov*, ed. N. P. Patrushev (Moscow: Rus', 2000), vol. 2, book 1: 215–16, 248–9.

23 Beria to Stalin, 15 November 1941, reprinted in *Rodina*, no. 7 (1993): 61.

24 Internal and secret MGB statistics, 11 December 1953, reprinted: *Reabilitatsiia: Kak eto bylo*, vol. 1: 76–7.

25 GKO Decree No. 169ss (16 July 1941), top secret, signed Stalin, reprinted: *1941 god. Dokumenty*, vol. 2: 472–3; order of Commissar of Defense I. V. Stalin, No. 0250, 28 July 1941, reprinted: *RA/VO* 13–12, no. 2: 37–8.

26 S. R. Mil'shtein to Beria, top secret, October 1941, reprinted: *Lubianka. Stalin i NKVD-NKGB-GUKR 'SMERSh' 1939-mart 1946. Dokumenty*, ed. V. N. Khaustov, V. P. Naumov and Nd N. S. Plotnikova (Moscow: Demokratiia, 2006), 317–18.

27 Evgenii Antonovich Karpovich, memoirs (typescript), Bakhmeteff Archive, Columbia University, 1.

28 Statistics compiled for the Supreme Court of the USSR, 1937-1956 (21 January 1958), reprinted in *Istoriia stalinskogo gulaga. Konets 1920-kh – pervaia polovina 1950-kh godov. Sobranie dokumentov v semi tomakh*, ed. N. Werth and S. V. Mironenko (Moscow: Rosspen, 2004), vol. 1: 619–20.

29 His case file is in USHMM RG-75.001, box 1, folder 4.

30 Oleg Budnitskii, 'The Great Terror of 1941: Toward a History of Wartime Stalinist Criminal Justice', *Kritika: Explorations in Russian and Eurasian History* 20, no. 3 (2019): 455–6.

31 G. Safonov to A. A. Andreev, secret report, 4 November 1941, reprinted in *Istoriia stalinskogo gulaga. Konets 1920-kh – pervaia polovina 1950-kh godov. Sobranie dokumentov v semi tomakh*, ed. Iu. N. Afanas'ev (Moscow: Rosspen, 2004), 424–5.

32 Roger R. Reese, *Stalin's Reluctant Soldiers: A Social History of the Red Army 1925-1941* (Lawrence: University Press of Kansas, 1996), 195–7; Rolf-Dieter Müller, *An der Seite*

der Wehrmacht. Hitlers ausländische Helfer beim 'Kreuzzug gegen den Bolschewismus' *1941-1945* (Frankfurt a. M.: Fischer, 2010). Numbers: 242.

33 Mark Edele, 'Militaries Compared: Wehrmacht and Red Army, 1941-1945', in *A Companion to World War II*, ed. Thomas W. Zeiler and Daniel M. DuBois (Oxford: Wiley-Blackwell, 2013), vol. 1: 169–85, here: 170.

34 M. I. Mel'tiukhov, '9 dnei boevogo puti krasnoarmeitsa Bunina i ego razmyshleniia o poriadkakh v armii (1941 god)', *Voenno-istoricheskaia antropologiia* (2005/2006): 142–51.

35 Mark Edele, *Stalin's Defectors: How Red Army Soldiers Became Hitler's Collaborators, 1941-1945* (Oxford: Oxford University Press, 2017). For the numbers: chapter 2; for the motivations: chapter 6.

36 General Command of XVII Army Corps, Department Ic, 'The Campaign against the Soviet Union' (1941), BA-MA RH 24-17/155, folio 96, 107, 141.

37 General Command of XVII Army Corps, Department Ic, 'The Campaign against the Soviet Union' (1941), BA-MA RH 24-17/156, folio 63.

38 Johannes Hürter, *A German General on the Eastern Front: The Letters and Diaries of Gotthard Heinrici, 1941-1942*, trans. Christine Brocks (Barnsley: Pen & Sword, 2014), 73.

39 Hürter, *A German General on the Eastern Front*, 73–4.

40 Gottlob Herbert Bidermann, *In Deadly Combat: A German Soldier's Memoir of the Eastern Front* (Lawrence: University Press of Kansas, 2000), 57–8.

41 V. Valentinov, 'Wie ich ‚Kollaborateur‘ wurde', unpublished typescript, Bakhmeteff Archive, Columbia University, 10–14.

42 Interview G. Koifman with Nachman Dushanski, part one (23 January 2008). https://iremember.ru/memoirs/nkvd-i-smersh/dushanskiy-nakhman-noakhovich/ (accessed 10 February 2020).

43 Natan Gimel'farb, *Zapiski opal'nogo direktora* (Buffalo: Natan Gimel'farb, 1999), 64–5. Available at http://natan.gimelfarb.com/PART1.pdf (accessed 3 April 2019).

44 Abakumov to Beria, not before 11 December 1941, reprinted: *Lubianka v dni bitvy za Moskvu. Po rassekrechennym dokumentam FSB RF*, ed. V. K. Vinogradov et al. (Moscow: Zvonnitsa, 2002), 285–6, here: 285.

45 David Stahel, *Operation 'Barbarossa' and Germany's Defeat in the East* (Cambridge: Cambridge University Press, 2009).

46 *Pravda*, 3 July 1941, 1. This speech repeated verbatim a directive, signed by Stalin and Molotov, given to party and state organizations in the frontline regions on 29 June, reprinted: *1941 god. Dokumenty*, vol. 2: 446–8, here: 447.

47 Gennady Andreev-Khomiakov, *Bitter Waters: Life and Work in Stalin's Russia. A Memoir* (Boulder: Westview Press, 1997), 170.

48 See the archival documents on the case in *Mosvka prifrontovaia 1941-1942. Arkhivnye dokumenty i materialy* (Moscow: Mosgorarkhiv, 2001), 565–7; on the abuse: 579.

49 R. L. DiNardo, *Mechanized Juggernaut or Military Anachronism? Horses and the German Army of World War II* (New York: Greenwood Press, 1991), 40–1.

50 Bidermann, *In Deadly Combat*, 16, 18, 52.

51 Jacobsen, *Kriegstagebuch des Oberkommandos der Wehrmacht,* vol. 1: 421, 422, 424, 425, 427, 431, 432, 437, 442, 445, 486–7.

52 G. F. Krivosheev, *Soviet Casualties and Combat Losses in the Twentieth Century* (London: Greenhill Books, 1997), 91, 94.

53 Elena Zubkova, *Pribaltika i Kreml'* (Moscow: Rosspen, 2008), 196; Mar Laar, *War in the Woods: Estonia's Struggle for Survival 1944-1956* (Washington: The Compass Press, 1992), 11–15; NKGB report on work during Great Patriotic War, 28 September 1945, LYA, f. K-41, op. 1, d. 201, l. 88–124 here: 91.

54 Daria Rudakova, 'Civilian Collaboration in Occupied Ukraine and Crimea, 1941-1944: A Study in Motivation' (PhD diss., The University of Western Australia, 2018), chapter 4.

55 N. A. Kirsanov and S. I. Drobiazko, 'Velikaia Otechestvennaia voina 1941-1945 gg: Natsional'nye i dobrovol'cheskie formirovaniia po raznye storony fronta', *Otechestvennaia istoriia,* no. 6 (2001): 60–75, here: 64.

56 Alexander Statiev, 'The Nature of Anti-Soviet Armed Resistance, 1942-44: The North Caucasus, the Kalmyk Autonomous Republic, and Crimea', *Kritika: Explorations in Russian and Eurasian History* 6, no. 2 (2005): 285–318, here: 291 ('permanent turmoil'), 292–5, 299; Jeffrey Burds, 'The Soviet War against 'Fifth Columnists': The Case of Chechnya, 1942-4', *Journal of Contemporary History* 42, no. 2 (2007): 267–314, here: 291, 292, 295, 305 (shooting and burning of 'untransportables'), 307–8.

57 Moritz Florin, 'Becoming Soviet through War: The Kyrgyz and the Great Fatherland War', *Kritika: Explorations in Russian and Eurasian History* 17, no. 3 (2016): 495–516.

58 For example, Surkov (Dnepropetrovsk) to Sergienko (Kiev, NKVD USSR; August 1941), GDA SBU f. 16, op. 1, d. 523, l. 54-55; People's Commissar of the Interior of Ukraine Sergienko to Khrushchev (10 August 1941), GDA SBU f. 16, op. 1, d. 523, l. 69–71; Savchenko to Meshik (28 September 1941), GDA SBU f. 16, op. 1., d. 521, l. 357–9; Savchenko to Korotchenko (13 October 1941), GDA SBU f. 16, op. 1, d. 521, l. 373–5; I. O. Prokurora USSR R. Rudenko to SNK USSR Tov. Starchenko V. F; TsK KP(b)U tov. Korotchenko D. S. (Voroshilovgrad, 4 July 1942), TsDAGO f. 1, op. 23, d. 195, l. 6–8; 'Spravka o khode otseleniia naseleniia iz 30-ti kilometrovoi prifrontofoi polosy po krasno-limanskomu raionu, Stalinskoi oblasti' (no date, not before 5.7.1942), TsDAGO f. 1, op. 23, d. 195, l. 10–12.

59 Karel C. Berkhoff, *Harvest of Despair: Life and Death in Ukraine under Nazi Rule* (Cambridge, MA and London: The Belknap Press of Harvard University Press, 2004), 12–13.

60 See Mark Edele, 'Not an Ordinary Man: Ivan Nikitich Kononov and the Problem of Frontline Defection from the Red Army, 1941-1945', *Australian Journal of Politics and History* 62, no. 4 (2016): 546–60; id., *Stalin's Defectors,* numbers: 31, table 2.3. On Ukrainians: id., 'Why Did Ukrainian Red Army Men go over to the Germans? The Case of Defectors to the Wehrmacht's 296 Infantry Division, 1942-1943', *Ukrains'kyi istorychnyi zhurnal,* no. 5 (2019): 86–102.

61 G. F. Krivosheev, 'O dezertirstve v Krasnoi Armii', *Voenno-istoricheskii zhurnal,* no. 6 (2001): 94.

62 Theo J. Schulte, *The German Army and Nazi Policies in Occupied Russia* (Oxford and New York: Berg, 1989), 121; NKVD reports in *Lubianka v dni,* esp. 153, 168, 176.

63 Oleg Budnitskii, 'The Great Patriotic War and Soviet Society: Defeatism, 1941–42', *Kritika: Explorations in Russian and Eurasian History* 15, no. 4 (2014): 767–97.

64 Seth Bernstein, 'Rural Russia on the Edges of Authority: Bezvlastie in Wartime Riazan', November–December 1941', *Slavic Review* 75, no. 3 (2016): 560–82, here: 574.

65 Police report, June 1941, reprinted in *Iz raionov oblasti soobshchaiut . . . Svobodnye ot okkupatsii raiony Leningradskoi oblasti v gody Velikoi Otechestvennoi voiny 1941-1945. Sbornik dokumentov*, ed. A. R. Dzeniskevich (St. Petersburg: Dmitrii Bulganin, 2006), 15.

66 John Barber, 'Popular Reactions in Moscow to the German Invasion of June 22, 1941', *Soviet Union/Union Soviétique* 18, nos. 1–3 (1991): 5–18, here: 14.

67 Nicolas Werth et al. (eds), 'Smiatenie oseni sorok pervogo goda. Dokumenty o volneniiakh ivanosvkikh tekstil'shchikov', *Istoricheskii arkhiv* 2 (1994): 111–36 (quotation: 117); S. V. Tochenov, 'Volneniia i zabastovki na tekstil'nykh predpriiatiiakh Ivanovskoi oblasti osen'iu 1941 goda', *Otechestvennaia istoriia* 3 (2004): 42–7, quotation: 45, 46.

68 A pathbreaking study of the panic is John Barber, 'The Moscow Crisis of October 1941', in *Soviet History, 1917-53: Essays in Honour of R. W. Davies*, ed. Julian Cooper, Maureen Perrie and E. A. Rees (Houndmills: MacMillan, 1995), 201–18.

69 Act on the removal of the body of V. I. Lenin to Tiumen' (3 July 1941), signed N. Spiridonov and B. Zbarskii, reprinted: *Lubianka v dni*, 43–4.

70 Memoirs of A. I. Shakhurin (1970s), in *Mosvka prifrontovaia*, 266–7, here: 267.

71 Memoirs of G. V. Reshetin, in *Moskva voennaia 1941-1945. Memury i arkhivnye dokumenty* (Moscow: Mosgorarkhiv, 1995), 111–12 ('beat the Jews'); A. A. Perventsev, *Dnevniki. 1941-1945* (Moscow: Veche, 2011), 107. For other examples of cars hijacked, people beaten, and their things stolen by the crowd see top secret NKVD report, M. I. Zhuravlev to L. P. Beria (17 October 1941), reprinted: *Mosvka prifrontovaia*, 262–3.

72 *Lubianka v dni*, 231, 228–35.

73 Mark Edele, *Stalinist Society 1928-1953* (Oxford: Oxford University Press, 2008), 152–4.

74 NKVD report, 10 November 1941, in *Lubianka v dni*, 238–49, here: 248.

75 E.g., *Lubianka v dni*, 205.

76 Orlando Figes, *The Whisperers: Private Life in Stalin's Russia* (New York: Metropolitan Books, 2007), 438, 439.

77 William Taubman, *Khrushchev: The Man and His Era* (New York and London: W. W. Norton & Co., 2003), 150.

78 Alexander Hill, *The War behind the Eastern Front: The Soviet Partisan Movement in North-West Russia 1941-44* (London and New York: Frank Cass, 2005), 56–8, quotation: 57.

79 Daniel Stotland, 'Ideologues and Pragmatists: World War II, New Communists, and Persistent Dilemmas of the Soviet Party-State, 1941–1953' (Ph.D. diss., University of Maryland, 2010), 153. For pre-archival evidence see also: Thomas J. Greene, 'The End of the World Must be at Hand: The Collective Farm Peasantry and the Soviet State during the Great Patriotic War, 1941–1945' (Ph.D. diss., The University of Toronto, 1999), 103–14.

80 Bernstein, 'Rural Russia on the Edges of Authority', 560, 571.

81 Johannes Due Enstad, *Soviet Russians under Nazi Occupation: Fragile Loyalties in World War II* (Cambridge: Cambridge University Press, 2018), 42.

82 GULAG report, 22 December 1941, reprinted in *Istoriia stalinskogo gulaga. Konets 1920-kh-pervaia polovina 1950-kh godov*, vol. 6: 136-142, here: 140.

83 V. N. Zemskov, 'Gulag (Istoriko-sotsiologicheskii aspekt), chast' 1', *Sotsiologicheskie issledovaniia* 6 (1991): 10–27, here: 24.

84 Susanne Leonhard, *Gestohlenes Leben. Schicksal einer politischen Emigrantin in der Sowjetunion*, 5th rev. edn (Herford: Nicolaische Verlagsbuchhandlung Herford, 1968), 251, 259.

85 Alan Barenberg, *Gulag Town, Company Town: Forced Labor and Its Legacy in Vorkuta* (New Haven: Yale University Press, 2014), 45–52; quotation: 46.

86 Andreev-Khomiakov, *Bitter Waters*, 176.

87 Memoirs of A. I. Shakhurin (1970s), 267.

88 A. V. Korotkov, A. D. Chernev and A. A. Chernobaev (eds), *Na prieme u Stalina. Tetrady (zhurnaly) zapisei lits, priniatykh I. V. Stalinym (1924-1953 gg.)* (Moscow: Novyi khronograf, 2008), 340–1.

89 'Comrade Stalin's Speech', *Pravda*, 25 May 1945, 1.

Chapter 5

1 M. S. Astakhova, G. V. Gorskaia, N. A. Kirillova, A. K. Sorokin and O. V. Khlevniuk, *Gosudarstvennyi Komitet Oborony SSSR. Postanovleniia i deiatel'nost' 1941-1945 gg. Annotirovannyi katalog v dvukh tomakh* (Moscow: Rosspen, 2015), vol. 1: 5.

2 Pathbreaking: Sanford R. Lieberman, 'Crisis Management in the USSR: The Wartime System of Administration and Control', in *The Impact of World War II on the Soviet Union*, ed. Susan J. Linz (Totowa: Rowman & Allanheld, 1985), 59–76.

3 Sheila Fitzpatrick, *On Stalin's Team: The Years of Living Dangerously in Soviet Politics* (Melbourne: Melbourne University Press, 2015), 12.

4 GKO Decree of 4 February 1942. RGASPI f. 644, op. 2, d. 36, ll. 32–3.

5 Dmitrii Antonovich Volkogonov, *Stalin: Triumph and Tragedy* (London: Weidenfeld and Nicholson, 1991), 405–93, 487–8. On the travels to the front: 434–5; 480–2.

6 Iurii Rubtsov, *Alter ego Stalina. Kniga sozdana na osnove rassekrechennykh dokumentov iz arkhivnykh fondov* (Moscow: Zvonnitsa-MG, 1999), 177.

7 S. M. Shtemenko, *The Soviet General Staff at War. 1941-1945*, 2nd edn (Moscow: Progress Publishers, 1975), 119, 117.

8 G. Kumanev, *Govoriat stalinskie narkomy* (Smolensk: Rusich, 2005), 596. Baibakov went on to a distinguished career which earned him the award Hero of Socialist Labor in 1981.

9 Mark Harrison, 'The Second World War', in *The Economic Transformation of the Soviet Union, 1913-1945*, ed. R. W. Davies, Mark Harrison and S. G. Wheatcroft (Cambridge: Cambridge University Press, 1994), 262, 264 (quotations); Wendy Z.

Goldman, 'Not by Bread Alone: Food, Workers, and the State', in *Hunger and War: Food Provisioning in the Soviet Union during World War II*, ed. Wendy Z. Goldman and Donald Filtzer (Bloomington and Indianapolis: Indiana University Press, 2015), 50–3; 'Liubimov, Aleksadr Vasil'evich', in *Kto byl kto v Velikoi Otechestvennoi voine 1941-1945. Liudi. Sobytiia. Fakty. Spravochnik*, ed. O. A. Rzheshevskii (Moscow: Respublika, 2000), 156; *Gosudarstvennaia vlast' SSSR. Vysshie organy vlasti i upravleniia i ikh rukovoditeli. 1923-1991. Istoriko-biograficheskii spravochnik*, ed. V. I. Ivkin (Moscow: Rosspen, 1999), 131, 398–9.

10 U. G. Cherniavskii, *Voina i prodovol'stvie. Snabzhenie gorodkogo naseleniia v Velikuiu Otechestvennuiu voinu (1941-1945 gg.)* (Moscow: Nauka, 1964), 151.

11 Goldman, 'Not by Bread Alone', 55, 62–3 (quotation).

12 *Narodnoe khoziaistvo SSSR v Velikoi Otechestvennoi voine, 1941-1945 gg. Statisticheskii sbornik* (Moscow: Informationno-idatel'stkii tsentr, 1990), 109.

13 Price index: *Narodnoe khoziaistva SSSR v Velikoi Otechestvennoi voine*, 197; household spending: household budget report, Central Statistical Administration of Gosplan (30 December 1944), reprinted: *Sovetskaia povsednevnost' i massovoe soznanie 1939-1945*, ed. A. Ia. Livshin and I. B. Orlov (Moscow: Rosspen, 2003), 228–9. On the role of the black as well as of semi-legal and legal markets during the war see Julie Hessler, *A Social History of Soviet Trade: Trade Policy, Retail Practices, and Consumption, 1917-1953* (Princeton: Princeton University Press, 2004), 249–95.

14 Oleg Khlevniuk, 'Decentralizing Dictatorship: Soviet Local Governance during World War II', *The Russian Review* 77, no. 3 (2018): 470–84, quotations: 471, 473, 484.

15 Richard Stites (ed.), *Culture and Entertainment in Wartime Russia* (Bloomington and Indianapolis: Indiana University Press, 1995); Mark Edele, 'Paper Soldiers: The World of the Soldier Hero According to Soviet Wartime Posters', *Jahrbücher für Geschichte Osteuropas* 47, no. 1 (1999): 89–108; Lisa A. Kirschenbaum, '"Our City, Our Hearths, Our Families": Local Loyalties and Private Life in Soviet World War II Propaganda', *Slavic Review* 59, no. 4 (2000): 825–47. More sceptical on the freedom the war brought is Karel C. Berkhoff, *Motherland in Danger: Soviet Propaganda during World War II* (Cambridge, MA: Harvard University Press, 2012).

16 Computed from data for admission to candidate membership in the armed forces, third quarter 1941 through second quarter of 1945. Russian State Archive of Contemporary History (RGANI) f. 77, op. 1, d. 3 & 4.

17 Cf. Roger R. Reese, *Why Stalin's Soldiers Fought: The Red Army's Military Effectiveness in World War II* (Lawrence: University Press of Kansas, 2011), 312.

18 Iu. Trifonov, interview with Mariia Iakovlevna Starchukova (4 July 2013). https://iremember.ru/memoirs/letno-tekh-sostav/starchukova-shebarshina-mariya-yakovlevna/ (accessed 19 February 2019).

19 Olga Kucherenko, *Little Soldiers: How Soviet Children Went to War 1941-1945* (Oxford: Oxford University Press, 2011), 122–3, 151–3; Rodric Braithwaite, *Moscow 1941: A City and Its People at War* (New York: Knopf, 2006), Chapter 6. The best history of women in the Red Army remains Svetlana Alexievich's oral history, now reissued in an English translation: *The Unwomanly Face of War* (London: Penguin, 2017). For a guide to and critique of recent historiography see Steven M. Miner, '"Things Must Be Bad at the Front": Women in the Soviet Military during WWII', *MCU Journal* 9, Special Issue (2018): 41–65.

20 Reese, *Why Stalin's Soldiers Fought*, 104.

21 Numbers for overall armed forces and women: G. F. Krivosheev, *Soviet Casualties and Combat Losses in the Twentieth Century* (London: Greenhill Books, 1997), 91. Not all of the 0.8 million women were volunteers, but no clear data are available. For the number of evaders see Chapter 4.

22 See Mark Edele, '"What Are We Fighting For?" Loyalty in the Soviet War Effort, 1941-1945', *International Labor and Working-Class History* 84 (2013): 248–68, here: 257, figure 2 & chart 1.

23 Harrison, 'The Second World War', 259 (quotation); Susanne Conze, 'Women's Work and Emancipation in the Soviet Union, 1941-50', in *Women in the Stalin Era*, ed. Melanie Ilic (Houndmills: Palgrave, 2001), 219.

24 M. A. Vyltsan, *Krest'ianstvo Rossii v gody bol'shoi voiny 1941-1945 Pirrova pobeda* (Moscow: Rossiiskii nauchnyi fond, 1995), 23–4, 25. V. T. Aniskov, *Krest'ianstvo protiv fashizma 1941-45. Istoriia i psikhologiia podviga* (Moscow: Pamianiki istoricheskoi mysli, 2003), 87 (share of women in village workforce).

25 Interview with Valentina Il'inishna Bushueva, June 1995, in *Writing the Siege of Leningrad: Women's Diaries, Memoirs, and Documentary Prose*, ed. Cynthia Simmons and Nina Perlina (Pittsburgh: University of Pittsburgh Press, 2002), 133–40, here: 133–4.

26 Mark Edele, *Stalinist Society. 1928-1953* (Oxford: Oxford University Press, 2011), 179–82. Numbers: 179.

27 Euridice Charon Cardona, 'Dvizhenie ogorodnichestva v sovetskom tylu v 1941-1945 gg.', in *Sovetskii tyl 1941-1945. Povsednevnaia zhizn' v gody voiny*, ed. Beate Fieseler and Roger D. Markwick (Moscow: Rosspen, 2019), 48–68, here: 66.

28 Inna Shikheeva-Gaister, *Semeinaia khronika vremen kul'ta lichnosti 1925-1953* (Moscow: N'iudiamed-AO, 1998), 56–73.

29 J. Otto Pohl, *Ethnic Cleansing in the USSR, 1937-1949* (Westport: Greenwood Press, 1999), 5.

30 Susanne Leonhard, *Gestohlenes Leben. Schicksal einer politischen Emigrantin in der Sowjetunion*, 5th rev. edn (Herford: Nicolaische Verlagsbuchhandlung Herford, 1968), 1–50, 86–7, 241.

31 Wolfgang Leonhard, *Child of the Revolution* (Chicago: Henry Regnery Company, 1958), quotation: 162. Top secret Stalin order to deport Germans from Moscow, Moscow region, and Rostov to Kazakhstan (6 September 1941), reprinted: *Moskva voennaia. Memuary i arkhivnye dokumenty* (Moscow: Mosgorarkhiv, 1995), 77–8.

32 Leonhard, *Child of the Revolution*, quotations: 165, 169.

33 Top secret GKO decree of 10 January 1942, RGASPI f. 644, op. 1, d. 19, l. 49.

34 A. A. German and A. N. Kurochkin, *Nemtsy SSSR v trudovoi armii (1941-1945)* (Moscow: Gotika, 1998), 153.

35 Paul Buskovitch, interview with Moshe Lewin, in *Visions of History: Interviews by Marho the Radical Historians Organization*, ed. Henry Abelov, Betsy Blackmar, Peter Dimock and Jonathan Schneer (Manchester: Manchester University Press, 1983), 281–308, here: 284–5.

36 Adam Broner, *My War against the Nazis: A Jewish Soldier with the Red Army* (Tuscaloosa: University of Alabama Press, 2007), 43–107.

37 Grigorii Chukhrai, *Moia voina* (Moscow: Altoritm, 2001), 194–6, 228–30.

38 *Documents on Polish-Soviet Relations 1939-1945* (London: Heinemann, 1961), vol. 1: 141–2, 145, 147–8.

39 Meeting notes of conversation between Stalin and General Anders in Stalin's office in the Kremlin, 18 May 1942, marked 'secret', RGASPI f. 558, op. 11, d. 357, l. 2–15, here: l. 11.

40 Beria to Stalin, top secret report, 1 May 1944, in *Stalinskie deportatsii 1928-1953*, ed. N. L. Pobol' and P. M. Polian (Moscow: Demokratiia, 2005), 178. According to this report, by 1 September 1942 only 341 remained detained and were 'not amnestied'.

41 Irena Protassewicz, *A Polish Woman's Experience in World War II: Conflict, Deportation and Exile* (London: Bloomsbury, 2019), 126.

42 Hanka Swiderska in *War through Children's Eyes: The Soviet Occupation of Poland and the Deportations, 1939-1941*, ed. Irena Grudzinska-Gross and Jan Tomasz Gross (Stanford: Hoover Institution Press, 1981), 47.

43 Beria to Stalin, top secret report, 1 May 1944, in *Stalinskie deportatsii*, 178; American support: W. Averell Harriman to Stalin via Ambassador Laurence Steinhardt, 'Aide Memoire', 10 November 1941, RGASPI f. 558, op. 11, d. 377, l. 8–10 (at this stage, Harriman suggested to evacuate the Poles only temporarily, train and equip them, and then send them back to the Soviet front).

44 Menachem Begin, *White Nights: The Story of a Prisoner in Russia* (London: Macdonald, 1957). Numbers from Mark Edele and Wanda Warlik, 'Saved by Stalin? Trajectories and Numbers of Polish Jews in the Svoiet Second World War', in *Shelter from the Holocaust: Rethinking Jewish Survival in the Soviet Union*, ed. Mark Edele, Sheila Fitzpatrick and Atina Grossmann (Detroit: Wayne State University Press, 2017), 115.

45 Protassewicz, *A Polish Woman's Experience*, 133–45, quotations: 136, 140, 144, 145.

46 *Documents on Polish-Soviet Relations 1939-1945*, vol. 1: 473–4, 523–34. Data for end of 1943: Beria to Stalin, top secret report, 1 May 1944, in *Stalinskie deportatsii*, 178.

47 *Pravda*, 3 July 1941, 1.

48 Published the next day on the front page of *Pravda*, 8 November 1941, 1.

49 Report by comrade Stalin in commemoration of the XXIV anniversary of the Great October Socialist Revolution, 6 November 1941, Moscow, published in *Pravda*, 7 November 1941, 1, 2, quotation: 2.

50 Mark Edele, 'Take (No) Prisoners! The Red Army and German Pows, 1941-1943', *The Journal of Modern History* 88 (2016): 342–79.

51 Gottlob Herbert Biderman, *In Deadly Combat: A German Soldier's Memoir of the Eastern Front* (Lawrence: University Press of Kansas, 2000), 58.

52 Alexander Hill, 'British "Lend-Lease" Tanks and the Battle for Moscow, November-December 1941 – A Research Note', *Journal of Slavic Military Studies* 19, no. 2 (2006): 289–94.

53 V. I. Achkasov (ed.), *Istoriia Vtoroi Mirovoi voiny 1939-1945. Vol. 11: Porazhenie militaristskoi Iaponii. Okonchanie vtoroi mirovoi voiny* (Moscow: Voenizdat, 1980), 184.

54 G. K. Zhukov, *Vospominaniia i razmyshleniia*, 2 vols (Moscow: Olma Press, 2002), vol. 1: 181.

55 N. P. Sutskov et al., *Krasnoznamennyi dal'nevostochnyi. Istoriia Krasnoznamennogo Dal'nevostochnogo Voennogo Okruga*, 3rd rev. edn (Moscow: Voennoe izdatel'stvo, 1985), 149. The 1 million refers to 1941–5 as a whole.

56 V. I. Chuikov, *Missiia v Kitae. Zapiski voennogo sovetnika* (Moscow: Glavnaia redatktsiia vostochnoi literatury, 1981), 198.

57 Richard Sorge, reports transmitted to Moscow by radio, 12 & 15 August 1941: *RA/VO* 18–17, no. 1: 191.

58 Apanasenko and Iakovlev to the military command in the Far East, 15 August 1941, *RA/VO* 18–17, no. 1: 235.

59 Edward J. Drea and Hans van de Ven, 'An Overview of Major Military Campaigns during the Sino-Japanese War, 1937-1945', in *The Battle for China: Essays on the Military History of the Sino-Japanese War of 1937-1945* (Stanford: Stanford University Press, 2011), 41.

60 Richard Sorge, reports 23 August, 14 September, 23 September, 3 and 4 October 1941: *RA/VO* 18–17, no. 1: 192–4.

61 Achkasov, *Istoriia Vtoroi Mirovoi voiny 1939-1945*, vol. 11: 184 (table 7).

62 On Churchill's reaction to the Hitler-Stalin Pact see chapter 3. For Stalin and the Comintern see Alexander Dallin and F. I. Firsov (eds), *Dimitrov and Stalin 1934-1943: Letters from the Soviet Archives* (New Haven and London: Yale University Press, 2000), 226–53.

63 Jeffrey Burds, 'The Soviet War against "Fifth Columnists": The Case of Chechnya, 1942-4', *Journal of Contemporary History* 42, no. 2 (2007): 267–314, here: 292, 302.

64 Fitzroy Maclean, *Eastern Approaches* (London: Penguin, 2009), 263.

65 Jochen Hellbeck (ed.), *Die Stalingrad Protokolle. Sowjetische Augenzeugen berichten aus der Schlacht*, trans. Christiane Körner and Annelore Nitschke (Frankfurt am Main: S. Fischer Verlag, 2012), 337–8, 330, 361, 359, 370.

66 David M. Glantz with Jonathan M. House, *The Stalingrad Trilogy* (Lawrence: University Press of Kansas, 2009), vol. 2: 542.

67 Glantz with Jonathan M. House, *The Stalingrad Trilogy*, vol. 2: 399, 462, 464, 465, 463.

68 The standard account of the battle in English is Antony Beevor, *Stalingrad* (London: Penguin, 1998).

69 Leonhard, *Gestohlenes Leben*, 294, 258.

70 Evgenii Antonovich Karpovich, unpublished typescript memoirs, Bakhmeteff Archive, Columbia University, p. 107.

71 Transcript of interview with Anna Malginova, 4 September 1979, William E. Wiener Oral History Library of the American Jewish Committee: Oral Histories of Recent Soviet Emigres in America. New York Public Library, Dorot Jewish Division, 38–40.

72 Milovan Djilas, *Conversations with Stalin* (San Diego: Harvest Books, 1990), 75–6.

73 Victor Kravchenko, *I Chose Freedom: The Personal and Political Life of a Soviet Official* (London: Robert Hale, 1947), 412.

74 Goldman, 'Not by Bread Alone', 56–61.

75 Harrison, 'The Second World War', 263.

76 Vyltsan, *Krest'ianstvo Rossii*, 29–30.

77 Vladimir Kim, 'Eshelon', in *Tuda, gde konchaetsia solntse. Vosponimaniia, svidetel'stva, dokumenty*, ed. Anatolii Kim (Moscow: Druzhba narodov, 2002), 61–71, here: 69.

78 Donald Filtzer, 'Starvation Mortality in Soviet Home-Front Industrial Regions during World War II', in *Hunger and War*, 265–338, quotation: 266.

79 Vyltsan, *Krest'ianstvo Rossii*, 26.

80 Richard Bidlack and Nikita Lomagin, *The Leningrad Blockade 1941-1944: A New Documentary History from the Soviet Archives* (New Haven: Yale University Press, 2012), 1 (numbers), 36 (quotation), 52–3 (Shostakovich). Other recent excellent books on the blockade include Anna Reid, *Leningrad: Tragedy of a City under Siege, 1941-44* (London: Bloomsbury, 2011); and Sergey Yarov, *Leningrad 1941-42: Morality in a City under Siege* (Cambridge: Polity Press, 2017). On the Finnish advance: Pasi Tuunainen, 'The Finnish Army at War: Operations and Soldiers, 1939–45', in *Finland in World War II: History, Memory, Interpretations*, ed. Tiina Kinnunen, Ville Kivimäki (Leiden and Boston: Brill Academic Publishers, 2012), 139–88, here: 153–9.

81 Anna Akhmatova, 'Pervyi dal'noboinyi v Leningrade (First Long-Range Firing on Leningrad)' (September 1941), in *The Complete Poems of Anna Akhmatova*, trans. Judith Hemschemeyer, ed. Roberta Reeder (Somerville: Zephyr Press, 1990), vol. II: 182–3. Spelling adjusted.

82 Bidlack and Lomagin, *The Leningrad Blockade*, 68.

83 A. Akhmatova, 'Courage', *Pravda*, 8 March 1942, 3.

Chapter 6

1 For an excellent overview over the operational history of these years see Evan Mawdsley, *Thunder in the East: The Nazi-Soviet War 1941-1945*, 2nd rev. edn (London: Bloomsbury, 2016), chapters 9–13.

2 G. F. Krivosheev and M. F. Filimoshin, 'Poteri vooruzhennykh sil SSSR v Velikoi Otechestvennoi voine', in *Naselenie Rossii v xx veke. Istoricheskie ocherki. Tom 2: 1940-1959* (Moscow: Rosspen, 2001), 19–39, here: 21.

3 David Reynold and Vladimir Pechatnov (eds), *The Kremlin Letters: Stalin's Wartime Correspondence with Churchill and Roosevelt* (New Haven: Yale University Press, 2018), 94, 95–6.

4 Churchill to the House of Commons, 2 August 1944, *Parliamentary Debates (Hansard 1803-2005), Commons*, 2 August 1944, vol. 402, col. 1474.

5 Edward Drea, *Japan's Imperial Army: Its Rise and Fall, 1853-1945* (Lawrence: University Press of Kansas, 2009), 198, 228, 250. For the one million in 1945: Tohmatsu Haruo, 'The Strategic Correlation between the Sino-Japanese and Pacific Wars', in *The Battle for China: Essays on the Military History of the Sino-Japanese War of 1937-1945*, ed. Mark Peattie, Edward Drea and Hans van de Vee (Stanford: Stanford University Press, 2011), 423–45, here: 439.

6 Adam Tooze, 'The Economic History of the Nazi Regime', in *Nazi Germany*, ed. Jane Caplan (Oxford: Oxford University Press, 2008), 193. Also id., *The Wages of Destruction: The Making and Breaking of the Nazi Economy* (New York: Viking, 2006), chapter 18. See esp. fig. 22, p. 600.

7   Doris Bergen, 'Occupation, Imperialism, and Genocide, 1939-1945', in *Nazi Germany*, ed. Caplan, 241.

8   See chart in Phillips Payson O'Brien, *How the War Was Won: Air-Sea Power and Allied Victory in World War II* (Cambridge: Cambridge University Press, 2015), 290.

9   Mawdsley, *Thunder in the East*, 110.

10 Stephen G. Fritz, *Endkampf: Soldiers, Civilians, and the Death of the Third Reich* (Lexington: University Press of Kentucky, 2004).

11 Tami Davis Biddle, 'Anglo-American Strategic Bombing, 1940-1945', in *The Cambridge History of the Second World* War. Vol 1: Fighting the War, ed. John Ferris and Evan Mawdsley (Cambridge: Cambridge University Press, 2015), 485–526, here: 517–19.

12 Good introductions to Lend-Lease include Mawdsley, *Thunder in the East*, 182–99; and Alexander Hill, *The Great Patriotic War of the Soviet Union, 1941-45: A Documentary Reader* (London: Routledge, 2009), 163–92 (which also provides a list of further reading in English).

13 Norman Davies, *No Simple Victory: World War II in Europe, 1939-1945* (London: Penguin, 2006), 35.

14 Geoffrey Jukes, *Stalingrad to Kursk: Triumph of the Red Army* (Barnsley: Pen & Sword, 2011), 222.

15 Alexander Hill, 'British Lend-Lease Aid and the Soviet War Effort, June 1941-June 1942', *The Journal of Military History* 71 (2007): 773–808, here: 782, 785, 788, 791. On rubber deliveries from Malaya in August 1941 see Reynolds and Pechatnov, *The Kremlin Letters*, 34. On early deliveries also Avram Lytton, 'In the House of Rimmon: British Aid to the Soviet Union, June-September 1941', *The Journal of Slavic Military Studies* 26, no. 4 (2013): 673–704, esp. 691 and 694. Major casualties on the Norwegian route only began in 1942. See Evan Mawdsley, *The War for the Seas: A Maritime History of World War II* (New Haven: Yale University Press, 2019), 264–70. The Classic account of British aid is Joan Beaumont, *Comrades in Arms: British Aid to Russia 1941-1945* (London: Davis-Poynter, 1980).

16 P. V. Malkov (ed.), *Velikaia Otechestvennaia voina. Iubileinyi statisticheskii sbornik* (Moscow: Rosstat, 2020), 195.

17 Jukes, *Stalingrad to Kursk*, 220–3. Numbers of imported trucks: Malkov, *Velikaia Otechestvennaia voina*, 188.

18 ANZAC wool: J. A. Alexander, *In the Shadow: Three Years in Moscow* (Melbourne: The Herald and Weekly Times Ltd., 1949), 156. Sheepskin exports: Jessie Street's ASIO file: National Archives of Australia (NAA): A6119/360: 48–9, 62, 63, 88-91, 117, 118. Ruble import statistics: Malkov, *Velikaia Otechestvennaia voina*, 187. Rug for Timoshenko: Irene Greenwood to Australia's Minister of External Affairs Dr. H. V. Evatt (4 December 1944). NAA: A989/1944/845/5/2/26. On medical aid: Medical Aid from Australia for the Soviet Union, *Pravda*, 23 September 1944.

19 Sergey Radchenko, 'The Soviet Union and Asia, 1940s-1960s', in *Empire and After: Essays in Comparative Imperial and Decolonization Studies*, ed. Uyuma Tomohiko (Sapporo: Slavic Research Center, 2012), 99–116, here: 101.

20 George A. Larson, 'American Airmen Held as POWs in Far East Russia during World War II', *Air Power History* 59, no. 2 (2012): 24–31.

21 Interview with Ten San Din (27 February 2015). https://iremember.ru/memoirs/r
    azvedchiki/ten-san-din/ (accessed 12 February 2019).

22 Laurie Manchester, 'Repatriation to a Totalitarian Homeland: The Ambiguous
    Alterity of Russian Repatriates from China to the USSR', *Diaspora* 16, no. 3 (2007):
    353–88, here: 357–8.

23 Michael Kort, *The Columbia Guide to Hiroshima and the Bomb* (New York: Columbia
    University Press, 2007), 67, 69, 70, 323–4, 327–8, 330–1, 334.

24 A balanced assessment of the relative contributions of the bomb and the Soviet entry
    is Richard B. Frank, 'Ending the Pacific War: The Hew History', in *A Companion
    to World War II*, ed. Thomas W. Zeiler and Daniel M. DuBois (Chichester: Wiley-
    Blackwell, 2013), vol. 1: 387–401.

25 See David Stahel, *Operation Barbarossa and Germany's Defeat in the East* (Cambridge:
    Cambridge University Press, 2009); and Tooze, *The Wages of Destruction*.

26 On the catastrophic drop in production in the second half of 1941 see John Erickson, *The
    Road to Stalingrad. Stalin's War with Germany: Volume One* (New Haven: Yale University
    Press, 1975), 233. For the numbers regarding the occupied territories see next note.

27 Mark Harrison, 'The Second World War', in *The Economic Transformation of the
    Soviet Union, 1913-1945*, ed. R. W. Davies, Mark Harrison and S. G. Wheatcroft
    (Cambridge: Cambridge University Press, 1994), 253–4. Numbers: *Narodnoe
    khoziaistvo SSSR v Velikoi Otechestvennoi voine, 1941-1945 gg. Statisticheskii sbornik*
    (Moscow: Informatsionno-izdatel'skii tsentr, 1990), 14–15; G. A. Kumanev, 'Voennaia
    perestroika ekonomiki', in *Velikaia Otechestvennaia voina 1941-1945. Voenno-
    istoricheskie ocherki*, ed. V. A. Zolotarev and G. N. Sevost'ianov (Moscow: Nauka,
    1998), vol. 1: 385–95, here: 394.

28 For the percentages: Wendy Z. Goldman, 'Not by Bread Alone: Food, Workers, and
    the State', in *Hunger and War: Food Provisioning in the Soviet Union during World
    War II*, ed. Wendy Z. Goldman and Donald Filtzer (Bloomington and Indianapolis:
    Indiana University Press, 2015), 55.

29 Donald Filtzer and Wendy Z. Goldman, 'Introduction: The Politics of Food and War',
    in *Hunger and War*, 1–43, here: 43. Emphasis added.

30 S. G. Wheatcroft, 'The Great Leap Upwards: Anthropometric Data and Indicators of
    Crises and Secular Change in Soviet Welfare Levels, 1880-1960', *Slavic Review* 58, no.
    1 (1999): 27–60.

31 Chapter 1.

32 *Narodnoe khoziaistva SSSR v Velikoi Otechestvennoi voine*, 22.

33 Fyodor Vasilevich Mochulsky, *Gulag Boss: A Soviet Memoir* (Oxford: Oxford
    University Press, 2011), 80.

34 Mochulsky, *Gulag Boss*, 76–7.

35 Dmitrii Viktorovich Surzhik, 'Rol' GULAGa v gody Velikoi Otechestevennoi voiny:
    k istorii odnogo stereotipa', *'Belye piatna' rossiiskoi i mirovoi istorii*, no. 6 (2016):
    33–9; Beria to Stalin (top secret, not before 5 November 1944), reprinted in *Istoriia
    stalinskogo gulaga. Konets 1920-kh – pervaia polovina 1950-kh godov. Sobranie
    dokumentov v semi tomakh*, ed. Iu. A. Afanas'ev (Moscow: Rosspen, 2004), vol. 3:
    210–16; Wilson T. Bell, *Stalin's Gulag at War: Forced Labour, Mass Death, and Soviet
    Victory in the Second World War* (Toronto: University of Toronto Press, 2018), 64
    (Chkalov factory); 65 (Novosibirsk defence labour force).

36   Alan Barenberg, *Gulag Town, Company Town: Forced Labor and its Legacy in Vorkuta* (New Haven: Yale University Press, 2014), 36–7; B.B.R, 'The North Pechora Railway and the Development of the Pechora Coalfields', *Polar Record* 4, no. 29 (1945): 236–8; 'SZhD v gody voiny'. https://szd.rzd.ru/static/public/ru?STRUCTURE_ID=7269 (accessed 3 May 2020).

37   Bell, *Stalin's Gulag at War*, 51 (quotation); 76 (2 per cent of workforce and comparison to evacuation). *Narodnoe khoziaistvo SSSR v Velikoi Otechestvennoi voine*, 5 (number of people employed in the economy). Steven A. Barnes, 'All for the Front, All for Victory! The Mobilization of Forced Labor in the Soviet Union during World War Two', *International Labor and Working-Class History* 58 (2000): 239–60; here: 245 (1.9 per cent GNP 1941-43).

38   On releases and additions: Nasedkin to Beria, report on work of Main Administration of Labor Camps and Colonies during the Great Patriotic War (17 August 1944), reprinted in *Novaia i noveishaia istoriia* 5 (1996): 133–50, here: 134, 135; gender: V. N. Zemskov, 'GULAG (istoriko-sotsiologicheskii aspect)', pt. 1, *Sotsiologicheskie issledovaniia* 6 (1991): 10–27, here: 23; repressed nationalities: top secret Gulag administration report, 10 May 1945, in *Istoriia stalinskogo gulaga*, vol 4: 101–2. On categories and numbers of releases B. Bochkov to Stalin et al., 11 February 1942, *Istoriia stalinskogo gulaga*, vol. 1: 434–5.

39   G. Safonov to A. A. Andreev, secret report (4 November 1941), reprinted in *Istoriia stalinskogo gulaga*, 424–5.

40   Bell, *Stalin's Gulag at War*, 50.

41   Golfo Alexopoulos, *Illness and Inhumanity in Stalin's GULAG* (New Haven: Yale University Press, 2017), 24.

42   Top secret Gulag administration report, 10 March 1945, *Istoriia stalinskogo gulaga*, vol. 4: 98–101, here: 99–100.

43   Archival statistical table, not earlier than 1 January 1948, in *Istoriia stalinskogo gulaga*, vol. 4: 111.

44   Bell, *Stalin's Gulag at War*, 77, 78.

45   Nasedkin to Beria, 17 August 1944, 142.

46   Oleg V. Khlevniuk, 'Deserters from the Labor Front: The Limits of Coercion in the Soviet War Economy', *Kritika: Explorations in Russian and Eurasian History* 20, no. 3 (2019): 481–504, quotation: 484.

47   Iakob Glasse, unpublished diary, typed up ca. 1950. Bakhmeteff Archive, Columbia University, p. 157a.

48   Karel C. Berkhoff, *Motherland in Danger: Soviet Propaganda during World War II* (Cambridge, MA: Harvard University Press, 2012), chapter 3.

49   Khlevniuk, 'Deserters from the Labor Front', 492, 496; Martin Kragh, 'Stalinist Labour Coercion during World War II: An Economic Approach', *Europe-Asia Studies* 63, no. 7 (2011): 1253–73.

50   Paul Buskovitch, '[Interview with] Moshe Lewin', in *Visions of History: Interviews by Marho the Radical Historians Organization*, ed. Henry Abelov, Betsy Blackmar, Peter Dimock and Jonathan Schneer (Manchester: Manchester University Press, 1983), 281–308, here: 285.

51   Numbers: Malkov, *Velikaia Otechestvennaia voina*, 230. for the public health response: Donald A. Filtzer, *The Hazards of Urban Life in Late Stalinist Russia. Health,*

Hygiene, and Living Standards, 1943-1953 (Cambridge and New York: Cambridge University Press, 2010).

52   A good overview over life and supply in the Red Army is David M. Glantz, *Colossus Reborn: The Red Army at War, 1941–1943* (Lawrence: University Press of Kansas, 2005), 554–90. More details are in Catherine Merridale, *Ivan's War: Life and Death in the Red Army, 1939-1945* (New York: Metropolitan Books, 2006).

53   Directive of the Military Council of the Western Front, to all commanders and commissars of divisions and brigades. Signed Zhukov and Khokhlov (30 March 1942), reprinted in *Skrytaia pravda voiny: 1941 god. Neizvestnye dokumenty*, ed. P. N. Knyshevskii (Moscow: Russkaia kniga, 1992), 228–9.

54   Quoted in V. D. Danilov, 'Stalinskaia strategiia nachala voiny: plany i real'nost', in *Drugaia voina 1939-1945*, ed. Iu. N. Afanas'ev (Moscow: RGGU, 1996), 136–56, here: 154.

55   Decree of Presidium of Supreme Soviet USSR of 16 July 1941: 'On the reorganization of the organs of political propaganda and the introduction of the institution of the military commissars in the Worker-Peasant Red Army', *Vedomosti Verkhovnogo Soveta SSSR*, no. 33 (148) (26 July 1941): 1.

56   Harvard Project on the Soviet Social System. Schedule A, Vol. 13, Case 175 (interviewer A.P., type A4). Male, 50, Great Russian, Army Officer. Widener Library, Harvard University, 14–15. http://nrs.harvard.edu/urn-3:FHCL:950845 (accessed 13 January 2020). The interviewee mis-remembered the date of this episode as early 1943, when the politruks had been abolished.

57   Decree of Presidium of Supreme Soviet of USSR (9 October 1942): 'On the establishment of complete single command and the abolition of the institution of military commanders in the Red Army', *Vedomosti Verkhovnogo Soveta SSSR*, no. 38 (1942): 200–1.

58   Mark Edele, *Stalin's Defectors: How Red Army soldiers became Hitler's Collaborators, 1941-1945* (Oxford: Oxford University Press, 2017), 103. Svirin quotations: Jochen Hellbeck, *Stalingrad: The City that Defeated the Third Reich* (New York: Public Affairs, 2015), 183, 184.

59   Internal report on changes in composition of Communist Party in the first two years of the war, 1 July 1941-1 July 1943, RGASPI f. 17, op. 122, d. 56, l. 38–9.

60   Vinogradov to M. A. Suslov (16 July 1947), RGASPI f. 17, op. 122, d. 199, l. 109.

61   Shamberg to Andreev, Malenkov, Zhdanov, Shcherbakov (23 October 1943); RGASPI f. 17, op. 122, d. 56, l. 42–4, here: 42.

62   Hellbeck, *Stalingrad*, 47–50.

63   GARF f. r-7523, op. 40, d. 358, l. 12.

64   GARF f. r-7523, op. 40, d. 358, l. 17–18; 13.

65   David M. Glantz and Jonathan M. House, *To the Gates of Stalingrad: Soviet-German Combat Operations, April-August 1942* (Lawrence: University Press of Kansas, 2009), 47.

66   Hill, *The Great Patriotic War of the Soviet Union, 1941-45*, 232, 239, 235, 237; Gabriel Temkin, *My Just War: The Memoirs of a Jewish Red Army Soldier in World War II* (Novato: Presidio Press, 1998), 139, 189–90.

67   T. H. Rigby, *Communist Party Membership in the U.S.S.R. 1917-1967* (Princeton: Princeton University Press, 1968), 253. On the urban recruiting ground of elite

units see John Erickson, 'Red Army Battlefield Performance, 1941-45: The System and the Soldier', in *Time to Kill: The Soldier's Experience of War in the West 1939-1945*, ed. Paul Addison and Angus Calder (London: Plimco, 1997), 233–48, here: 234.

68 Glantz, *Colossus Reborn*, 618–19.

69 Secret statistical report on changes to Party membership, 1943, RGASPI f. 17, op. 122, d. 56, l. 45–77, here: l. 55.

70 Rüdiger Overmans, *Deutsche militärische Verluste im Zweiten Weltkrieg* (Munich: R. Oldenbourg Verlag, 1999), 277; G. F. Krivosheev, *Soviet Casualties and Combat Losses in the Twentieth Century* (London: Greenhill Books, 1997), 94. The massive losses of the Germans in the final period of the war plus losses by their allies fighting their Germans then further evened out the kill ratio, which for the entire war stood at 1:1.29 (Malkov, *Velikaia Otechestvennaia voina*, 273).

Chapter 7

1 Activity report Secret Field Police 703 for period 1 – 31 July 1941, BA-MA RH 21-3/437, folio 333–9.

2 O. V. Budnitskii (ed.), *'Svershilos. Prishli nemtsy!' Ideinyi kollaboratsionizm v SSSR v period Velikoi Otechestvennoi voiny* (Moscow: Rosspen, 2012), 65.

3 Irena Protassewicz, *A Polish Woman's Experience in World War II. Conflict, Deportation and Exile* (London: Bloomsbury, 2019), 128.

4 Alexander Meystel, Interview Transcript (24 December 1979), William E. Wiener Oral History Library of the American Jewish Committee: Oral Histories of Recent Soviet Emigres in America Dorot Jewish Division, New York Public Library, 7.

5 Susanne Leonhard, *Gestohlenes Leben. Schicksal einer politischen Emigrantin in der Sowjetunion*, 5th rev. edn (Herford: Nicolaische Verlagsbuchhandlung Herford, 1968), 259, 302.

6 Ina Konstantinova, *Devushka iz Kashina. Dnevnik i pis'ma Iny Konstantinovoi. Vospominaniia i ocherki o nei*, ed. G. Astaf'ev (Moscow: Moskovskii rabochii, 1974), 50.

7 Konstantinova, *Devushka iz Kashina*, 50, 68, 73, 9–10, 153.

8 Rodric Braithwaite, *Moscow 1941: A City and Its People at War* (New York: Knopf, 2006), Chapter 6; Olga Kucherenko, *Little Soldiers: How Soviet Children Went to War 1941-1945* (Oxford: Oxford University Press, 2011), 122–3, 151–3.

9 NKGB-NKVD information bulletin, 23 June 1941, *Moskva voennaia 1941-1945: Memuary i arkhivnye dokumenty*, ed. K. I. Bukov (Moscow: Mosgorarkhiv, 1995): 49; David M. Glantz, *Colossus Reborn: The Red Army at War, 1941-1943* (Lawrence: University Press of Kansas, 2005), 3–36, 93–170; Aron Shneer, *Plen. Sovetskie voennoplennye v Germanii, 1941-1945* (Moscow and Jerusalem: Mosty kultury, 2005), 93–172; Geoffrey Hosking, 'The Second World War and Russian National Consciousness', *Past and Present* 175 (2002): 162–86.

10 Admission data: RGANI f. 77, op. 1, d. 3; draft shares: G. F. Krivosheev and M. F. Filimoshin, 'Poteri vooruzhennykh sil SSSR v Velikoi Otechestvennoi voine', in

Naselenie Rossii v XX veke. Istoricheskie ocherki, Tom 2. 1940-1959, ed. Iu. A. Poliakov (Moscow: Rosspen, 2001), 19–39, here: 34. Quotations: Roger Reese, *Why Stalin's Soldiers Fought: The Red Army's Military Effectiveness in World War II* (Lawrence: University Press of Kansas, 2011), 253, 312; decorations: *Bloknot agitatora Krasnoi Armii*, no. 3 (January 1945): 28.

11 Mark Edele, *Soviet Veterans of the Second World War: A Popular Movement in an Authoritarian Society, 1941-1991* (Oxford: Oxford University Press, 2008), 137–8; Oleg Budnitskii, 'Jews at War: Diaries from the Front', in *Soviet Jews in World War II: Fighting, Witnessing, Remembering*, ed. Harriet Murav and Gennady Estraikh (Boston: Academic Studies Press, 2014), 57–84, here: 60.

12 Mordechai Altshuler, 'Jewish Combatants of the Red Army Confront the Holocaust', in *Soviet Jews in World War II*, 16–35, here: 25.

13 Glantz, *Colossus Reborn*, 549–50.

14 Brandon Schechter, '"The People's Instructions": Indigenizing the Great Patriotic War Among "Non-Russians"', *Ab Imperio* 3 (2012): 109–33, quotation: 119.

15 Moritz Florin, 'Becoming Soviet through War: The Kyrgyz and the Great Fatherland War', *Kritika: Explorations in Russian and Eurasian History* 17, no. 3 (2016): 495–516, quotation: 496.

16 Top secret NKVD report on the political and economic situation in German occupied Latvia (January 1943), LVA PA-101.5.6, l. 8-19ob, here: l. 8; on anti-Soviet feelings: l. 8ob.

17 Raul Hilberg's 1961 classic study described the process in detail and assumed that some 27 percent of the victims were shot. According to newer research, as many as 40 percent of Jewish Holocaust victims were killed in mass shootings. The term 'Holocaust by bullets' has been popularized by Father Desbois. See Raul Hilberg, *The Destruction of the European Jews* (New York: New Viewpoints, 1973), 177–256, 767. United States Holocaust Memorial Museum, 'Holocaust by Bullets'. https://www.ush mm.org/information/exhibitions/online-exhibitions/special-focus/desbois (accessed 17 January 2020).

18 Peter Longerich, *Holocaust: The Nazi Persecution and Murder of the Jews* (Oxford: Oxford University Press, 2010), chapters 10–13. Yitzhak Arad, *The Holocaust in the Soviet Union* (Jerusalem: Yad Vashem, 2009).

19 A good introduction to the large literature on this issue is Wendy Lower, 'Pogroms, Mob Violence and Genocide in Western Ukraine, Summer 1941: Varied Histories, Explanations and Comparisons', *Journal of Genocide Research* 13, no. 3 (2011): 217–46.

20 Sheila Fitzpatrick, 'Annexation, Evacuation, and Antisemitism in the Soviet Union, 1939-1946', in *Shelter from the Holocaust: Rethinking Jewish Survival in the Soviet Union*, ed. Mark Edele, Sheila Fitzpatrick and Atina Grossmann (Detroit: Wayne State University Press, 2017), 133–60.

21 Roberto J. Carmack, *Kazakhstan in World War II: Mobilization and Ethnicity in the Soviet Empire* (Lawrence: University Press of Kansas, 2019), 83.

22 John Barber, 'Popular Reactions in Moscow to the German Invasion of June 22, 1941', *Soviet Union/Union Soviétique* 18 (1991): 5–18, here: 13–14, citation: 14.

23 Richard Bidlack and Nikita Lomagin, *The Leningrad Blockade. 1941-1944: A New Documentary History from the Soviet Archives* (New Haven: Yale University

Press, 2012), 225, 223–4, 338, 340, 339, 342. The diary of the Red Army soldier was captured by the Germans: BA-MA RH 19 III/444, folio 239–46. Quotations: Entry of 27 November 1941 (folio 239); entry of 30 November 1941 (folio 241). On pre-existing antisemitism in Leningrad see Sarah Davies, *Popular Opinion in Stalin's Russia: Terror, Propaganda and Dissent, 1934-1941* (Cambridge: Cambridge University Press, 1997), 82–90.

24 Karel C. Berkhoff, 'Total Annihilation of the Jewish Population: The Holocaust in the Soviet Media, 1941-45', *Kritika: Explorations in Russian and Eurasian History* 10, no. 1 (2009): 61–105.

25 Top secret NKVD report on the political and economic situation in German occupied Latvia (January 1943), LVA PA-101.5.6, l. 8-19ob, here: 10ob.

26 'On the atrocities of the German-fascist occupiers on the territory of the Latvian SR' (marked 'secret'; November 1944), LVA PA-101.6.20, l. 5–10, here: 5, 7.

27 Excerpt from protocol of interrogation of I.S.B., Astrakhan, 20 November 1947, FSB Archives via USHMM RG-06.025*22, d. 1371, ll. 229–39, here: 233.

28 Mark Edele, *Stalin's Defectors: How Red Army Soldiers Became Hitler's Collaborators, 1941-1945* (Oxford: Oxford University Press, 2017), 141.

29 P. V. Malkov (ed.), *Velikaia Otechestvennaia voina. Iubileinyi statisticheskii sbornik* (Moscow: Rosstat, 2020), 274. The non-returnees from Germany include those who evaded repatriation, either because they found life better in the West or because they feared Soviet retribution.

30 For an excellent summary see Christian Hartmann, *Operation Barbarossa: Nazi Germany's War in the East, 1941-1945* (Oxford: Oxford University Press, 2013). On Holocaust as trial run for more ambitious genocides see Robert Gerwarth, *Hitler's Hangman: The Life of Heydrich* (New Haven and London: Yale University Press, 2011).

31 Alexander Werth, *Russia at War, 1941-1945*, 2nd edn (New York: Carroll & Graf, 2000), 422.

32 G. Bukhantsov, untitled, unpublished, typewritten memoirs (ca. 1953). Bakhmeteff Archive, Columbia University, 6–7 (quotation), 34–6 (quotation: 36).

33 Information bulletin on mood of population in Leningrad (16 April 1943), in *Leningrad v osade. Sbornik dokumentov o geroicheskoi oborone Leningrada v gody Velikoi Otechestvennoi voiny 1941-1944* (St. Petersburg: Liki Rossii, 1995), 476–9, here: 477, other expressions of disbelief in the reports: 478.

34 Ibragim Kinchegreevich Dzhenalaev, *Pod gravdeiskim znamenem* (Alma-Ata: Izd-vo 'Kazakhstan, 1970), 51.

35 'V boiakh za Rodinu i za Stalina', unpublished anonymous memoir, typescript, Bakhmeteff Archive, Columbia University, 355.

36 Diary of partisan commander Vitalii Vsil'evich Novikov (1944), Estonian State Archive, ERA f. 5039, op. 1, d. 4, l. 9.

37 AOK 4, Ia. Nr. 6201/42. geh., 'Die Kämpfe der 4. Armee im ersten Kriegsjahr gegen die Sowjets. 22 Juni 1941 – 22 Juni 1942' (8 October 1942), German Federal Military Archive Freiburg im Breisgau (BA-MA) RH 20-4/337, folio 39–40.

38 Dieter Pohl, *Die Herrschaft der Wehrmacht. Deutsche Militärbesatzung und einheimische Bevölkerung in Der Sowjetunion 1941-1944* (Frankfurt a. M.: S. Fischer, 2011), 327.

39 Novikov diary, 2 February 1944, l. 11.

40 A. Lobachev to Shcherbakov, marked 'secret' (October 1944), LVA f. PA-101, op. 6, d, 8, l. 21–31, here: 21.

41 Top secret NKGB report, July 1944, LYA f. K-41, op. 1, d. 9, l. 31.

42 Partisan reconnaissance report, 15 October 1943, LVA PA-101.5.5: 114–19; here: 119.

43 Jan Kalnberzin and V. Lapis to CC Secretary Malenkov (June 1943), LVA f. PA-101, d. 5, l. 5: 36–36ob.

44 Bogdan Musial, *Sowjetische Partisanen 1941-1944: Mythos und Wirklichkeit* (Paderborn: Schöningh, 2009), 70.

45 Ben Shepherd, *War in the Wild East: The German Army and Soviet Partisans* (Cambridge, MA and London: Harvard University Press, 2004).

46 Louis P. Lochner (ed.), *The Goebbels Diaries* (London: H. Hamilton, 1948), 135.

47 Oleg Budnitskii, 'The Great Patriotic War and Soviet Society: Defeatism, 1941–42', *Kritika: Explorations in Russian and Eurasian History* 15, no. 4 (2014): 767–97, here: 796.

48 Alexander Hill, *The War Behind the Eastern Front: The Soviet Partisan Movement in North-West Russia 1941-44* (London and New York: Frank Cass, 2005), 150.

49 Musial, *Sowjetische Partisanen*, 322.

50 Report on developments in Latvian partisan movement January through May 1944. LVA PA-101.6.11, l. 97–106, here: l. 98.

51 Kenneth Slepyan, *Stalin's Guerrillas: Soviet Partisans in World War II* (Lawrence: University Press of Kansas, 2006), 28, 35, 51.

52 Budnitskii, 'The Great Patriotic War and Soviet Society', 796.

53 Catherine Merridale, 'Culture, Ideology and Combat in the Red Army, 1939-45', *Journal of Contemporary History* 41, no. 2 (2006): 305–24, here: 319.

54 Elena Kozhina, *Through the Burning Steppe: A Memoir of Wartime Russia, 1942-1943* (New York: Riverhead Books, 2001), 3.

55 Kozhina, *Through the Burning Steppe*, 11–16.

56 Kozhina, *Through the Burning Steppe*, 1, 10, 11, 80, 83–7.

57 Timothy Snyder, 'The Causes of Ukrainian-Polish Ethnic Cleansing 1943', *Past & Present* 179 (2003): 197–234.

58 David Wolff and Gael Moullec, *Le KGB et les pays Baltes 1939-1991* (Paris: Belin, 2005), 42.

59 Ernst Klee, Willi Dreßen and Volker Rieß, '*Schöne Zeiten.' Judenmord aus der Sicht der Täter und Gaffer* (Frankfurt: S. Fischer Verlag, 1988), 35–44.

60 Lithuanian resistance leaflet (August 1944), in *NKVD-MVD SSSR v bor'be s banditizmom i vooruzhennym natsinalisticheskim podpol'em na Zapadnom Ukraine, v Zapadnoi Belorussii i Pribaltike (1939-1956)*, ed. N. I Vladimirtsev and A. I. Kokurin (Moscow: MVD Rossii, 2008), 177; Alexander Statiev, *The Soviet Counterinsurgency in the Western Borderlands* (Cambridge and New York: Cambridge University Press, 2010), 113.

Chapter 8

1 For an example of an arrest of eight Jews trying to cross the Lithuanian border in order to emigrate via Poland to Palestine see top secret NKVD report, 1946, Lietuvos ypatingasis archyvas (Lithuanian KGB archive – LYA) f. K-41, op. 1, d. 111, l. 11.

2 Interview G. Koifman with Nachman Dushanski, part one (23 January 2008). https://iremember.ru/memoirs/nkvd-i-smersh/dushanskiy-nakhman-noakhovich/ (accessed 10 February 2020).

3 This quotation and other quotations below are from part 2 of the interview, published two years after Dushanski's death. G. Koifman, interview with N. Dushanski (4 March 2020). https://iremember.ru/memoirs/nkvd-i-smersh/dushanskiy-nakhman -noakhovich-prodolzhenie/ (accessed 12 February 2020).

4 On the antisemitic campaign of Stalin's last years see Gennadii Kostyrchenko, *Out of the Red Shadows: Anti-Semitism in Stalin's Russia* (Amherst: Prometheus Books, 1995).

5 Unless noted otherwise, this section draws heavily on three standard works: Jeffrey Burds, 'Bor'ba s banditizmom v SSSR v 1944-1953 gg', *Sotsial'naia istoriia* (2000): 169–88; Elena Zubkova, *Pribaltika i Kreml'. 1940-1953* (Moscow: Rosspen, 2008); and Alexander Statiev, *The Soviet Counterinsurgency in the Western Borderlands* (Cambridge and New York: Cambridge University Press, 2010).

6 *NKVD-MVD SSSR v bor'be s banditizmom i vooruzhennym natsinalisticheskim podpol'em na Zapadnom Ukraine, v Zapadnoi Belorussii i Pribaltike (1939-1956)*, ed. N. I Vladimirtsev and A. I. Kokurin (Moscow: MVD Rossii, 2008), 146.

7 On the boycott of German mobilization efforts: top secret Soviet intelligence report from occupied Lithuania, 15 April 1943, LYA f. k-41, op. 1, d. 6, l. 9.

8 Vladas Terleckas, *The Tragic Pages of Lithuanian History 1940-1953* (Vilnius: Petro ofsetas, 2014), 92.

9 Numbers from Dushanski interview, part II. Lithuanian historians give a slightly larger number of security troops in 1945: 20,000. See Terleckas, *The Tragic Pages*, 96. Overall, for the years 1944–5, below 70,000 security troops fought in all of the western borderlands: Statiev, *The Soviet Counterinsurgency*, 7–8. For the entire period of 1940–56, Soviet losses in counterinsurgency operations amounted to 6,000: G. F. Krivosheev, *Rossiia i SSSR v voinakh xx veka. Poteri vooruzhennikh sil. Statisticheskoe issledovanie* (Moscow: Olma-Press, 2001), 594.

10 Minister of State Security of Lithuania, Efimov, top secret report about the results of work to liquidate bandit groups in the Lithuanian SSR (10 May 1946), LYA f. K-41, op. 1, d. 201, l. 244–7, here: l. 245.

11 Zubkova, *Pribaltika i Kreml*, 246.

12 *NKVD-MVD SSSR v bor'be s banditizmom*, 147; Terleckas, *The Tragic Pages*, 99.

13 Statiev, *The Soviet Counter-Insurgency*, 111.

14 Zubkova, *Pribaltika i Kreml*, chapter 4; Elena Zubkova, *Russia after the War: Hopes, Illusions, and Disappointments, 1945-1957* (Armonk: M. E. Sharpe, 1998), 61–2; Mark Edele, *Stalinist Society 1928-1953* (Oxford: Oxford University Press, 2008), 152–4.

15 Diary of the accused Albinas Milchuk, pseudonym 'Tigras', LYA f. K-1, op. 3, d. 336, l. l. 7–9, 10–15. [henceforth: Milchuk diary]

16 Milchuk diary, l. 17–23, 58.

17 Milchuk diary, l. 32, 52–3, 63–4.

18 Milchuk diary, l. 24, 66.

19 Milchuk diary, l. 92–5.

20 Milchuk diary, l. 96.

21 'Mil'chukas Albinas', entry in name index of *Virtual Museum of the Gulag*. http://www
    .gulagmuseum.org/ (accessed 13 February 2020).

22 Milchuk diary, entry of 6 April 1949, l. 101.

23 Terleckas, *The Tragic Pages*, 103.

24 Statiev, *The Soviet Counterinsurgency*, 128.

25 Data for Lithuania: *NKVD-MVD SSSR v bor'be s bantitizmom*, 151 (data for
    1944–46), and LYA f. K-41, op. 1, d. 278, l. 1, 35, 66, 71, 73, 75, 77, 79, 81, 84, 86,
    154, 162 (data for 1947 and 1948). Data for other regions for 1944–6: *NKVD-MVD
    SSSR v bor'be s bantitizmom*, 154 (Latvia), 156 (Estonia), 142–3 (Ukraine), and 145
    (Belarus).

26 Deportation numbers for 1944–52: GDA SBU f. 42, op. 1, dl. 97, l. 3; Zubkova,
    Pribaltika i Kreml, 257.

27 Report by Deputy Commissar for the Interior of Ukrainian SSR, Kal'nenko to (9
    January 1945), TsDAGO f. 1, op. 23, d. 2410, l. 1–3.

28 Top secret report by General-Lieutenant Strokach (27 May 1945), TsDAGO f. 1, op.
    23, d. 2410, l. l. 89–96; here: l. 91–2.

29 Commissar of State Security of Ukraine Savchenko to N. S. Khrushchev, GDA SBU f.
    16, op. 1, d. 562, l. 15–17, quotation: l. 15.

30 Statiev, *Soviet Counterinsurgency*, 273.

31 Top Secret NKVD report on prosecution of NKVD personnel in Ukraine in 1944,
    28 March 1945, TsDAGO f. 1, op. 23, d. 2410, l. 22–6.

32 Secret statistical report, 22 December 1945, TsDAGO f. 1, op. 23, d. 2410, l. 27–31;
    here: l. 27.

33 Top Secret Decree by Ternopil Obkom Bureau of KP(b)U (4 June 1945), TsDAGO f.
    1, op. 23, d. 2383, l. 2–5.

34 Top Secret Decree by Stanislav Gorkom Bureau of KP(b)U (25 May 1945), reprinted
    in *Ukrainskie natsionalsiticheskie organizatsii v gody Vtoroi mirovoi voiny. Dokumenty.
    Tom 2: 1944-1945*, ed. A. N. Artisov (Moscow: Rosspen, 2012), 661–3.

35 Statiev, *Soviet Counterinsurgency*, 308.

36 Olaf Mertelsmann, *Everyday Life in Stalinist Estonia* (Frankfurt: Peter Lang, 2012),
    70–1, 73; Mertelsmann, Olaf and Aigi Rahi-Tamm, 'Soviet Mass Violence in Estonia
    Revisited', *Journal of Genocide Research* 11, nos. 2–3 (2009): 307–22, here: 310, 311,
    314, 316, 322 n. 74.

37 Numbers of arrested, killed and deported in the three Baltic states: Zubkova,
    Pribaltika i Kreml, 256; pre-Barbarossa population: Rogachevskaia and Kabuzian,
    'Naselenie i territorii SSSR', in *Naselenie Rossii v xx vek*, vol. 2: 16; repression statistics
    for Western Ukraine: GDA SBU f. 42, op. 1, d. 97, l. 2, 3, 16; population statistics:
    TsDAGO f. 1, op. 23, d. 3970, l. 1. The comparison with the war against the peasantry

at the beginning of the 1930s is made by O. A. Gorlanov and A. B. Roginskii, 'Ob arestakh v zapadnykh oblastiakh Belorussii i Ukrainy v 1939-1941 gg', in *Repressii protiv poliakov i pol'skikh grazhdan*, ed. A. E. Gur'ianov (Moscow: Memorial, 1997), 77–113, here: 82, 96. Using the 1941 population as a baseline is a conservative choice: because of wartime losses, the 1945 population was lower and would thus lead to higher shares.

38 Among a growing number of investigations into the Soviet prosecution of war criminals two studies stand out: Diana Dumitru, 'An Analysis of Soviet Postwar Investigation and Trial Documents and Their Relevance for Holocaust Studies', in *The Holocaust in the East: Local Perpetrators and Soviet Responses*, ed. Michael David-Fox, Peter Holquist and Alexander M. Martin (Pittsburgh: University of Pittsburgh Press, 2014), 142–57; and Vanessa Voisin, *L'urss contre ses traîtres. L'épuration Soviétique (1941-1955)* (Paris: Publications de la Sorbonne, 2015).

39 Rolf-Dieter Müller, *An der Seite der Wehrmacht. Hitlers ausländische Helfer beim 'Kreuzzug gegen den Bolschewismus' 1941-1945* (Frankfurt a. M: Fischer, 2010), 242.

40 Numbers for 1944–52: Zubkova, *Pribaltika i Kreml*, 256.

41 Dalie Kuodyte and Rokas Tracevskis, *The Unknown War: Armed Anti-Soviet Resistance in Lithuania in 1944-1953* (Vilnius: Genocide and Resistance Research Centre of Lithuania, 2019), 34. Other historians make much lower estimates: about 0.5 to 1 per cent of the population in the Baltic republics actively participated in the insurgency: Zubkova, *Pribaltika i Kreml*, 198.

42 Dushanski interview, part 2.

43 The historiography this paragraph summarizes is discussed in Mark Edele, *Stalin's Defectors: How Red Army Soldiers became Hitler's Collaborators, 1941-1945* (Oxford: Oxford University Press, 2017), 173–8. More recently, see also Pavel Gavrilov, '"Naselenie stanovitsia ne za nas, a protiv nas": partizany Leningradskoi oblisti, sovetskaia identichnost' i natsistskaia okkupatsiia', *Neprikosnovennyi zapas* 131, no. 3 (2020): 70–95.

44 Zubkova, *Pribaltika i Kreml*, 242–3.

45 Report by Moscow City Committee officials, 2 November 1945, reprinted in *Moskva poslevoennaia. 1945-1947. Arkhivnye dokumenty i materialy* (Moscow: Mosgorarkhiv, 2000), 453–4, here: 454.

46 Zubkova, *Pribaltika i Kreml*, 210.

47 Decrees by Presidium of Supreme Soviet of USSR of 4 June 1947, 'On strengthening the protection of citizens' personal property'; and 'On the criminal liability for theft of state and public property', both published in *Pravda*, 5 June 1947, 1.

48 Report by Minister of Justice of USSR K. P. Gorshenin to Stalin, 5 June 1950. Reprinted in *Istoriia stalinskogo gulaga. Konets 1920-kh – pervaia polovina 1950-kh godov. Sobranie dokumentov v semi tomakh*, vol. 1: *Massovye repressii v SSSR*, ed. N. Werth and S. V. Mironenko (Moscow: Rosspen, 2004), 564–8, here: 564.

49 V. Zemskov, 'Zakliuchennie, spetsposelentsy, ssyl'noposelentsy, ssyl'nye i vyslannye', *Istoriia SSSR* 5 (1991): 151–65, here: 152, 153 (1945 numbers); L. P. Beria to G. M. Malenkov, 26 March 1953, top secret. Reprinted in *Lavrentii Beriia. 1953. Stenogramma iiul'skogo plenuma TsK KPSS i drugie dokumenty*, ed. V. Naumov and Iu. Sigachev (Moscow: Demokratiia, 1999), 19–21, here: 19, 20 (1953 number and percentage of women).

50 Louise I. Shelley, *Policing Soviet Society: The Evolution of State Control* (London and New York: Routledge, 1996), 35.

51 David R. Shearer, *Policing Stalin's Socialism: Repression and Social Order in the Soviet Union, 1924-1953* (New Haven and London: Yale University Press, 2009), 410.

52 Top secret NKVD report, Beria to Stalin, 3 March 1945, reprinted in: *Lubianka. Stalin in NKVD-NKGB-GUKR 'Smersh' 1939-mart 1946*, ed. V. N. Khaustov et al. (Moscow: Demokratiia, 2006), 490–3, here: 493.

53 Stenographic report of meeting of Moscow city Committee, 1 December 1945, reprinted in *Moskva poslevoennaia*, 455–62, here: 456.

54 Zubkova, *Pribaltika i Kreml*, 211.

55 Report by Party Control Commission plenipotentiary to Vladimir Province, A. M. Skol'nikov to G. M. Malenkov (12 March 1946), reprinted in *Sovetskaia zhizn' 1945-1953*, ed. E. Iu. Zubkova et al. (Moscow: Rosspen, 2003), 194–201, here: 195. For Soviet Union as a whole: see Molotov's special files: GARF f. r-9401, op. 2, d. 168, l. 349.

56 Report on the growth of hooliganism and crime, by head of the department for the checking of party organs in the Central Committee, I. I. Pozdniak to N. S. Patolichev, 10 February 1947, reprinted in *Sovetskaia zhizn. 1945-1953*, 202–6, here: 203.

57 Viktor Cherepanov, *Vlast' i voina. Stalinskii mekhanizm gosudarstvennogo upravleniia v Velikoi Otechestvennoi voine* (Moscow: Izvestiia, 2006), 486. On Chuikov see chapter 4.

58 Antony Beevor and Luba Vinogradova (eds), *A Writer at War: Vasily Grossman with the Red Army 1941-1945* (London: Plimco, 2006), 69–70.

59 From the political report of the 8th Guards Rifle Corps, 27 November 1942, quoted in David M. Glantz, *Colossus Reborn: The Red Army at War, 1941-1943* (Lawrence: University Press of Kansas, 2005), 585.

60 Transcript of interview with Major General Alexander Ilyich Rodimtsev, 7 January 1943, Stalingrad. Reprinted in: *Stalingrad: The City that Defeated the Third Reich*, ed. Jochen Hellbeck (New York: Public Affairs, 2015), 309.

61 Mark Edele and Filip Slaveski, 'Violence from Below: Explaining Crimes against Civilians across Soviet Space, 1943-1947', *Europe-Asia Studies* 68, no. 6 (2016): 1020–35, here: 1023–6; Mark Edele, 'Soviet Liberations and Occupations, 1939-1949', in *The Cambridge History of the Second World War. Vol. II: Politics and Ideology*, ed. Richard Bosworth and Joseph Maiolo (Cambridge: Cambridge University Press, 2015), 489–94. On Violence against surrendered enemy troops: Mark Edele, 'Take (No) Prisoners! The Red Army and German POWs, 1941-1943', *The Journal of Modern History* 88 (2016): 342–79. The classical account of the Red Army's sexual violence in Germany is Norman M. Naimark, *The Russians in Germany: A History of the Soviet Zone of Occupation, 1945-1949* (Cambridge, MA: Harvard University Press, 1995), chapter 2. For a comparative analysis of rape warfare in World War II see Mark Edele, 'Crimes against Humanity', in *The Routledge History of the Second World War*, ed. Paul R. Bartrop (London: Routledge, forthcoming 2021).

62 For Ukraine see NKVD report to Khrushchev, 24 August 1945, TsDAGO f. 1, op. 23, d. 3905, l. 1-10.

63 Dushanski interview, part 2.

64 Shamarin to Beria, 23 July 1945, top secret, GARF f. r-9401, op. 2, d. 98, l. 11–12, here: l. 11.

65 Mark Edele, *Soviet Veterans of the Second World War: A Popular Movement in an Authoritarian Society, 1941-1991* (Oxford: Oxford University Press, 2008), 26–8.

66 Edele and Slaveski, 'Violence from Below', 1022–7; Edele, 'Soviet Liberations and Occupations', 489–94; on primary groups in the Red Army see Roger R. Reese, *Why Stalin's Soldiers Fought. The Red Army's Military Effectiveness in World War II* (Lawrence: University Press of Kansas, 2011), 216–27.

67 Captain Laas to MVD of Estonia, secret report (13 July 1946) ERAF f. 17SM, op. 4, d. 36, l. 196–7.

68 ERAF, f. 1, op. 2, d. 10, l. 38ff.

69 On Germany: Filip Slaveski, *The Soviet Occupation of Germany: Hunger, Mass Violence, and the Struggle for Peace, 1945-1947* (Cambridge: Cambridge University Press, 2013).

70 Edele, *Soviet Veterans*, 21–78.

71 Total number of repatriated 1944–8: GARF f. r-5446, op. 50a, d. 6723 l. 20. Percentages for the outcome of repatriation are as of 1 March 1946, when nearly 96 per cent of all repatriated had arrived: V. Zemskov, 'K voprosu o repatriatsii sovetskikh grazhdan 1944-1951 gg', *Istoriia SSSR* 4 (1990): 26–41, here: 36. State of the art research on repatriation includes Vanessa Voisin, 'Retribute or Reintegrate? The Ambiguity of Soviet Policies Towards Repatriates: The Case of Kalinin Province, 1943-1950', *Jahrbücher für Geschichte Osteuropas* 55, no. 1 (2007): 34–55; and Seth Bernstein, 'Ambiguous Homecoming: Retribution, Exploitation and Social Tensions during Repatriation to the USSR, 1944–1946', *Past & Present* 242, no. 1 (2018): 193–226.

72 Kateryna Stadnik, 'Ukrainian-Polish Population Transfers, 1944-46: Moving in Opposite Directions', in *Warlands: Population Resettlement and State Reconstruction in the Soviet-East European Borderlands, 1945-50*, ed. Peter Gatrell and Nick Baron (New York: Palgrave Maxmillan, 2009), 165.

73 Ekaterina Melnikova, 'Making "Former" the Former Finnish Karelia', *Jahrbücher für Geschichte Osteuropas* 64, no. 3 (2016): 437–61, here: 447–8.

74 Secret report on the repatriation and reception of Ingrian Finns, Golikov to Malenkov, 20 January 1945, GARF f. A-327, op. 1, d. 8, l. 66–72: numbers l. 66; on the 1947 expulsion see top secret Order of Minister of Interior of Soviet Union, S. N. Kruglov, 21 May 1947, reprinted in *Stalinskie Deportatsii*, 634–5.

75 See table in Mark Edele, 'The Second World War as a History of Displacement: The Soviet Case', *History Australia* 12, no. 2 (2015): 17–40, here: 26.

76 David Wolff, 'Stalin's Postwar Border-Making Tactics', *Cahiers du monde russe* 52, nos. 2–3 (2011): 273.

77 Jo Laycock, 'Armenian Homelands and Homecomings, 1945–9: The Repatriation of Diaspora Armenians to the Soviet Union', *Cultural and Social History* 9, no. 1 (2012): 103; J. Otto Pohl, *Ethnic Cleansing in the USSR, 1937-1949* (Westport: Greenwood Press, 1999), 124.

78 Laurie Manchester, 'Repatriation to a Totalitarian Homeland: The Ambiguous Alterity of Russian Repatriates from China to the USSR', *Diaspora* 16, no. 3 (2007):

353–88, here: 354, 358. For one example of arrest – a man born in 1926 who arrived in Vladivostok from Shanghai in October 1946 only to be sentenced to ten years in the Gulag in early 1948 see the letter of his father inquiring about his fate and the answer by the authorities of 11 January 1949, both in GARF f. A-327, op. 1, d. 421, l. 31–2. For the destinations of the 'returnees': Dmitrev to Gritsenko, 18 November 1947, GARF f. A327, op. 1, d. 21, l. 67.

79 On the end of the labour army see Edele, *Soviet Veterans*, 118–20; and A. A. German, 'Nemtsy SSSR na spetsposelenii', *Izvestiia Saratovskogo universiteta. Novaia seriia. Seriia Istoriia. Mezhdunarodnye otnosheniia* 14, no. 2 (2014): 41.

Chapter 9

1 Svetlana Aleksievich, *Secondhand Time: The Last of the Soviets* (New York: Random House, 2016), 127.

2 Report by Party Control Commission Plenipotentiary to Uzbekistan on demobilization (24 August 1945), RGASPI f. 17, op. 122, d. 102, l. 96–104, here: 98.

3 The calculations in this and the following paragraphs are based on: O. M. Verbitskaia, 'Liudskie poteri v gody Velikoi Otechestvennoi voiny. Territoriia i naselenie posle voiny', in *Naselenie Rossii v xx veke, Istoricheskie ocherki. Tom 2: 1940-1959gg*, ed. Iu. A. Poliakov (Moscow: Rossiiskaia politicheskaia entsiklopediia, 2001), 128–65, here: 129; L. S. Rogachevskaia and M. V. Kabuzan, 'Naselenie i territoriia SSSR i RSFSR nakanune Velikoi Otechestvennoi voiny', in *Naselenie Rossii v xx veke*, vol. 2, 6–18, here: 15; G. F. Krivosheev, *Rossiia i SSSR v voinakh xx veka. Poteri vooruzhennikh sil. Statisticheskoe issledovanie* (Moscow: Olma-Press, 2001), 238 (table 121); L. L. Rybakovskii, *Liudskie poteri SSSR i Rossii v Velikoi Otechestvennoi voine*, 2nd. rev. edn (Moscow: Ekon-Inform, 2010), 95, 91; Viacheslav Konstantinov, *Evreiskoe naselenie byvshego SSSR v XX veke (sotsial'no-demograficheskii analiz)* (Jerusalem: LIRA, 2007), 33 (table 1.1); Yitzhak Arad, *The Holocaust in the Soviet Union* (Jerusalem: Yad Vashem, 2009), 252.

4 Number of famine victims: Michael Ellman, 'The 1947 Soviet Famine and the Entitlement Approach to Famines', *Cambridge Journal of Economics* 24, no. 5 (2000): 603–30.

5 Mark Edele, 'Soviet Liberations and Occupations, 1939-1949', in *The Cambridge History of the Second World War. Vol. II: Politics and Ideology*, ed. Richard Bosworth and Joseph Maiolo (Cambridge: Cambridge University Press, 2015), 487–506, here: 497–500.

6 Budget numbers: P. V. Malkov (ed.), *Velikaia Otechestvennaia voina. Iubileinyi statisticheskii sbornik* (Moscow: Rosstat, 2020), 165.

7 For an excellent overview see David Wolff, 'Stalin's Postwar Border-Making Tactics: East and West', *Cahiers du monde russe* 52, nos. 2–3 (2011): 273–91.

8 Sergey Radchenko, 'Did Hiroshima Save Japan from Soviet Occupation?' *FP*, 5 August 2015. https://foreignpolicy.com/2015/08/05/stalin_japan_hiroshima_occup ation_hokkaido/ (accessed 7 April 2020).

9 Sergey Radchenko, 'The Soviet Union and Asia, 1940s-1960s', in *Empire and After: Essays in Comparative Imperial and Decolonization Studies*, ed. Uyama Tomohiko

(Sapporo: Slavic Research Center, 2012), 99–116, here: 101–3, quotation: 101. On the negotiations: Sergey Radchenko, 'Lost Chance for Peace: The 1945 CCP-Kuomintang Peace Talks Revisited', *Journal of Cold War Studies* 19, no. 2 (2017): 84–114.

10 Vladimir Pechatnov, 'The Soviet Union and the World, 1944-1953', in *The Cambridge History of the Cold War*, ed. Melvyn P. Leffler and Odd Arne Westad (Cambridge: Cambridge University Press, 2010), vol. 1: 90–111, here: 91.

11 On 'creative' as opposed to 'dogmatic' Marxism see Stalin's reply to Preobrazhensky, VI Congress of VKP (b), 3 August 1917. Stalin, *Works* (Moscow: Foreign Languages Publishing House, 1954), vol. 3: 200.

12 Radchenko, 'Lost Chance for Peace', 109–10.

13 On the weapons: Michael M. Sheng, *Battling Western Imperialism: Mao, Stalin, and the United States* (Princeton: Princeton University Press, 1997), 110–11.

14 Yoram Gorlizki and Oleg Khlevniuk, *Cold Peace: Stalin and the Soviet Ruling Circle, 1945-1953* (Oxford and New York: Oxford University Press, 2004), 97–101.

15 On settlement of Kaliningrad region see report of the head of the Resettlement Administration D. Dmitriev on fulfilment of the resettlement plan for Kaliningrad region, 15 November 1946, GARF f. A-259, op. 6, d. 3805, l. 15–26; and annual report of Resettlement Administration, 1947, GARF f. A-327, op. 1, d. 19.

16 A good overview is Norman Naimark, 'The Sovietization of Eastern Europe, 1944-1953', in *The Cambridge History of the Cold* War, ed. Melvyn P. Leffler and Odd Arne Westad (Cambridge: Cambridge University Press, 2010), vol. 1: 175–97; for a series of case studies see id., *Stalin and the Fate of Europe: The Postwar Struggle for Sovereignty* (Cambridge, MA: Belknap Press, 2019).

17 Elena Zubkova, *Russia after the War: Hopes, Illusions, and Disappointments, 1945-1957*, translated by Hugh Ragsdale (Armonk and London: M. E. Sharpe, 1998).

18 Aleksandr Vladimirovich Pyzhikov, 'Sovetskoe poslevoennoe obshchestvo i predposylki khrushchevskikh reform', *Voprosy istorii*, no. 2 (2002): 33–43; Julie Hessler, 'A Postwar Perestroika? Toward a History of Private Trade Enterprise in the USSR', *Slavic Review* 57, no. 3 (1998): 516–42; Julie Hessler, 'Postwar Normalisation and Its Limits in the USSR: The Case of Trade', *Europe-Asia Studies* 53, no. 3 (2001): 445–71; Mark Edele, 'Veterans and the Village: The Impact of Red Army Demobilization on Soviet Urbanization, 1945-1955', *Russian History* 36, no. 2 (2009): 159–82; Timothy Johnston, *Being Soviet: Identity, Rumour, and Everyday Life under Stalin 1939-1953* (Oxford: Oxford University Press, 2011), 74–5, 136. Mark Edele, 'More Than Just Stalinists: The Political Sentiments of Victors 1945-1953', in *Late Stalinist Russia: Society between Reconstruction and Reinvention*, ed. Juliane Fürst (London and New York: Routledge, 2006), 167–91.

19 Goskomstat SSSR (ed.), *Narodnoe khozaisatvo SSSR v Velikoi Otechestvennoi voine 1941-1945* (Moscow: informattsionno-izdatel'skii tsentr, 1990), 153, 154, 155, 157, 172, 219, 220–2.

20 *Velikaia Otechestvennaia voina 1941-1945. Kniga 4: Narod i voina* (Moscow: Nauka, 1999), 294; Donald Filtzer, 'Standard of Living versus Quality of Life: Struggling with the Urban Environment in Russia during the Early Years of Post-war Reconstruction', in *Late Stalinist Russia*, 81–102; Mark B. Smith, 'Individual Forms of Ownership in the Urban Housing Fund of the USSR, 1944-64', *Slavonic and East European*

Review 86, no. 2 (2008): 283–305. *Narodnoe khoziaistvo SSSR 1922-1972. Iubileinyi statisticheskii ezhegodnik* (Moscow: Statistika, 1972), 365.

21 Donald Filtzer, *Soviet Workers and Late Stalinism: Labour and the Restoration of the Stalinist System after World War II* (Cambridge: Cambridge University Press, 2002); id., *The Hazards of Urban Life in Late Stalinist Russia. Health, Hygiene, and Living Standards, 1943-1953* (Cambridge: Cambridge University Press, 2010); Jean Levesque, 'Exile and Discipline: The June 1948 Campaign Against Collective Farm Shirkers', *The Carl Beck Papers in Russian & East European Studies* 1708 (2006); Elena Zubkova, *Pribaltika i Kreml* (Moscow: Rosspen, 2008), 165–90; Jan T. Gross, *Revolution from Abroad. The Soviet Conquest of Poland's Western Ukraine and Western Belorussia*, expanded edn (Princeton and Oxford: Princeton University Press, 2002).

22 For security services reports on liquidation of speculation in 1947, see Stalin's special files (*osobaia papka*), GARF f. r-9401, op. 1, d. 171, ll. 444–64, 471–86, 499–509; on currency reform: E. Iu. Zubkova, L. P. Kosheleva, G. A. Kuznetsova, A. I. Miniuk and L. A. Rogovaia (eds), *Sovetskaia zhizn' 1945-1953* (Moscow: Rosspen, 2003), 553–81; anti-cosmopolitanism: G. V. Kostyrchenko, *Tainaia politika Stalina. Vlast' i antisemitism* (Moscow: Mezhdunarodnye otnosheniia, 2003); S. Frederick Starr, *Red and Hot: The Fate of Jazz in the Soviet Union 1917-1991* (New York: Limelight Editions, 1994), chapter 10; Nikolai Krementsov, *Stalinist Science* (Princeton: Princeton University Press, 1997); Kiril Tomoff, *Creative Union: The Professional Organization of Soviet Composers, 1939-1953* (Ithaca: Cornell University Press, 2006), chapter 6; Juliane Fürst, *Stalin's Last Generation: Soviet Post-War Youth and the Emergence of Mature Socialism* (Oxford: Oxford University Press, 2010), 78–86; political system: Gorlizki and Khlevniuk, *Cold Peace*, chapter 1; Sheila Fitzpatrick, *On Stalin's Team: The Years of Living Dangerously in Soviet Politics* (Melbourne: Melbourne University Press, 2015), chapters 7 and 8.

23 'Sostav iskliuchennykh po partstazhu, po periodam (territorial'nykh partorganizatsii)', RGANI f. 6, op. 6, d. 25, l. 5.

24 Sheila Fitzpatrick, 'Postwar Soviet Society: The "Return to Normalcy," 1945-1953', in *The Impact of World War II on the Soviet Union*, ed. Susan J. Linz (Totova: Rowman & Allanhead, 1985), 129–56.

25 'Stalin Speech on Anniversary of October Revolution', *Pravda*, 8 November 1941, 1.

26 'Stalin Speech, 6 November 1943', *Pravda*, 7 November 1943, 1–2.

27 'Stalin Speech, 6 November 1944', *Pravda*, 7 November 1944, 1–2, here: 1.

28 'Kremlin Reception to Honour the Participants of the Victory Parade', *Pravda*, 27 June 1945, 2.

29 S. G. Wheatcroft, 'From Team-Stalin to Degenerate Tyranny', in *The Nature of Stalin's Dictatorship: The Politburo, 1924-1953*, ed. E. A. Rees (Houndmills: Palgrave, 2003), 79–107. Fitzpatrick, *On Stalin's Team*.

30 Yoram Gorlizki, 'Ordinary Stalinism: The Council of Ministers and the Soviet Neopatrimonial State, 1946-1953', *The Journal of Modern History* 74, no. 4 (2002): 699–736; on corruption: James W. Heinzen, *The Art of the Bribe: Corruption under Stalin, 1943-1953* (New Haven: Yale University Press, 2016).

31 Joseph S. Berliner, *Factory and Manager in the USSR* (Cambridge, MA: Harvard University Press, 1957).

32   David R. Shearer, *Policing Stalin's Socialism: Repression and Social Order in the Soviet Union, 1924-1953* (New Haven and London: Yale University Press, 2009), chapter 12; R. G. Pikhoia, *Sovetskii Soiuz: Istoriia vlasti. 1945-1991* (Novosobirsk: Sibirskii khronograf, 2000), 50–4; Tanja Penter, 'Local Collaborators on Trial: Soviet War Crimes Trials under Stalin (1943–1953)', *Cahiers du Monde russe* 49 (2008): 341–64; Mark Edele, *Stalin's Defectors:* How Red Army Soldiers Became Hitler's Collaborators, 1941-1945 (Oxford: Oxford University Press, 2017), 140–1; Elena Zubkova, 'The Soviet Regime and Soviet Society in the Postwar Years: Innovations and Conservatism, 1945–1953', *Journal of Modern European History* 2 (2004): 144–5; Pikhoia, *Sovetskii Soiuz: Istoriia vlasti*, 35–43, 50–4, 56–8; R. W. Davies, *Soviet Economic Development from Lenin to Khrushchev* (Cambridge: Cambridge University Press, 1998), 49; V. Naumov and Iu. Sigachev (eds), *Lavrentii Beriia. 1953: Stenogramma iiul'skogo plenuma TsK KPSS i drugie dokumenty* (Moscow: Demokratiia, 1999), 19; Katrin Boeckh, *Stalinismus in der Ukraine. Die Rekonstruktion des sowjetischen Systems nach dem Zweiten Weltkrieg* (Wiesbaden: Harrassowitz Verlag, 2007), 291–327; Igor' Vasil'evich Govorov, 'Fil'tratsiia sovetskikh repatriantov v 40-e gg. xx v. Tseli, metody i itogi', *Cahiers du Monde russe* 49, no. 2 (2008): 365–82; Vanessa Voisin, *L'urss contre ses traîtres. L'épuration soviétique (1941-1955)* (Paris: Publications de la Sorbonne, 2015).

33   For the realization that most Soviet POWs had not willingly collaborated with the Germans see, for example: Report from Political Administration of First Belarusian Front, 21 March 1945. RGASPI f. 17, op. 125, d. 323, ll. 37–42. On managing human resources: Mie Nakachi, 'Population, Politics and Reproduction: Late Stalinism and Its Legacy', in *Late Stalinist Russia: Society between Reconstruction and Reinvention*, ed. Juliane Fürst (London and New York: Routledge, 2006), 167–91; id., 'N. S. Khrushchev and the 1944 Soviet Family Law: Politics, Reproduction, and Language', *East European Politics and Societies* 20, no. 1 (2006): 40–68. Jeffrey S. Hardy, *The Gulag after Stalin: Redefining Punishment in Khrushchev's Soviet Union, 1953-1964* (Ithaca and London: Cornell University Press, 2016), 8.

34   Ukaz Prezidiuma Verkhovnogo Soveta SSSR, 'Ob amnistii v sviazi s pobedoi nad gitlerovskoi Germaniei', 7 July 1945, *Pravda*, 8 July 1945, 1.

35   Golfo Alexopoulos, 'Amnesty 1945: The Revolving Door of Stalin's Gulag', *Slavic Review* 64, no. 2 (2005): 274–306, here: 278.

36   Ukaz Prezidiuma Verkhovnogo Soveta SSSR 'Ob otmene smertnoi kazni', 26 May 1947, *Pravda*, 27 May 1947, 1. The death penalty was reintroduced in 1950.

37   N. S. Khrushchev, *Doklad na zakrytom zasedanii XX s"ezda KPSS. 'O kul'te lichnosti i ego posledstviiakh'* (Moscow: Gospolitizdat, 1959), 9.

38   Pyzhikov, 'Sovetskoe poslevoennoe obshchestvo', 41.

39   Nina Tumarkin, *The Living & the Dead: The Rise and Fall of the Cult of World War II in Russia* (New York: BasicBooks, 1994); Amir Weiner, 'The Making of a Dominant Myth: The Second World War and the Construction of Political Identities within the Soviet Polity', *The Russian Review* 55 (1996): 638–60; id. *Making Sense of War: The Second World War and the Fate of the Bolshevik Revolution* (Princeton and Oxford: Princeton University Press, 2000).

40   Lisa A. Kirschenbaum, *The Legacy of the Siege of Leningrad, 1941-1995: Myth, Memories, and Monuments* (Cambridge and New York: Cambridge University Press, 2006); Karl Qualls, *From Ruins to Reconstruction: Urban Identity in Soviet Sevastopol*

after World War II (Ithaca and London: Cornell University Press, 2009); Vicky Davis, *Myth Making in the Soviet Union and Modern Russia: Remembering World War II in Brezhnev's Hero City* (London: I. B. Tauris, 2018).

41 R. W. Davies, *Soviet History and the Gorbachev Revolution* (Houndmills: Macmillan, 1989), esp. 100–14, and id., *Soviet History in the Yeltsin Era* (Houndmills: Macmillan, 1997); Denise J. Youngblood, *Russian War Films: On the Cinema Front, 1914–2005* (Lawrence: University Press of Kansas, 2007); Thomas Sherlock, *Historical Narratives in the Soviet Union and Post-Soviet Russia: Destroying the Settled Past, Creating an Uncertain Future* (New York: Palgrave, 2007); Nikolai Koposov, *Pamiat' strogogo rezhima. Istoriia i politika v Rossii* (Moscow: Novoe literaturnoe obozrenie, 2011); Stephen Norris, *Blockbuster History in the New Russia: Movies, Memory, Patriotism* (Bloomington: Indiana University Press, 2012), chapter 6; Polly Jones, *Myth, Memory, Trauma: Rethinking the Stalinist Past in the Soviet Union, 1953–70* (New Haven: Yale University Press, 2013).

42 On Russia and Ukraine see Mark Edele, *Debates on Stalinism* (Manchester: Manchester University Press, 2020), Chapters 8 and 9. An incomplete guide to the literature on the memory wars in the successor states to the Soviet Union can be found in Mark Edele, 'Who Won the Second World War and Why Should You Care? Reassessing Stalin''s War 75 Years after Victory,' *Journal of Strategic Studies* 43, No. 6-7 (2020): 1039–62.

43 Mark Edele, *Soviet Veterans of the Second World War: A Popular Movement in an Authoritarian Society, 1941-1991* (Oxford: Oxford University Press, 2009), chapter 8. For a comparative view see Martin Crotty, Neil Diamant and Mark Edele, *The Politics of Veteran Benefits in the Twentieth Century: A Comparative History* (Ithaca: Cornell University Press, 2020).

44 G. Aleksandrov to A. A. Zhdanov (1946), Russian State Archive of Socio-Political History (RGASPI), f. 17, op. 125, d. 391, l. 74–6. On prohibition of veteran organizations during interwar years: Sheila Fitzpatrick, 'The Legacy of the Civil War', in *Party, State, and Society in the Russian Civil War: Explorations in Social History*, ed. William Rosenberg, Diane P. Koenker and Ronald G. Suny (Bloomington and Indianapolis: Indiana University Press, 1989), 385–98, here: 393.

45 Pavel Ivanovich Batov, chairman of Soviet Committee of War Veterans (SKVV), Stenographic report of SKVV Plenum, 23 October 1977, GARF f. r-9541, op. 1, d. 1484, l. 132; Edele, *Soviet Veterans*, 217, 191–4.

46 Edele, 'Collective Action in Soviet Society: The Case of War Veterans', in *Writing the Stalin Era: Sheila Fitzpatrick and Soviet Historiography*, ed. Kiril Tomoff, Julie Hessler and Golfo Alexopoulos (New York: Palgrave, 2011).

47 Gorbachev's report to Central Committee Plenum, 27 January 1987, *Pravda*, 28 January 1987, 1–5, here: 2–3.

48 Mark Edele, 'Veterans and the Welfare State: World War II in the Soviet Context', *Comparativ. Zeitschrift für Globalgeschichte und vergleichende Gesellschaftsforschung* 20, no. 5 (2011): 18–33.

49 Stalin Speech, *Pravda*, 25 May 1945, 1.

50 Claire L. Shaw, *Deaf in the USSR: Marginality, Community, and Soviet Identity, 1917-1991* (Ithaca and London: Cornell University Press, 2017), esp. chapter 3; Zubkova, 'The Soviet Regime and Soviet Society in the Postwar Years', 134–52; Maria

C. Galmarini-Kabala, *The Right to Be Helped: Deviance, Entitlement, and the Soviet Moral Order* (DeKalb: Northern Illinois University Press, 2016).

51 Mark B. Smith, *Property for Communists: The Urban Housing Program from Stalin to Khrushchev* (DeKalb: Northern Illinois University Press, 2010), 21. Numbers: Malkov, *Velikaia Otechestvennaia voina,* 240.

52 Mark B. Smith, 'The Withering Away of the Danger Society: The Pensions Reform of 1956 and 1964 in the Soviet Union', *Social Science History* 39, no. 1 (2015): 129–48; *Programme of the Communist Party of the Soviet Union: Adopted by the 22nd Congress of the CPSU, October 31, 1961* (Moscow: Foreign Languages Publishing House, 1961), 61–2; Pyzhikov, 'Sovetskoe poslevoennoe obshchestvo', 33–43, here: 41–2.

53 Stephen Lovell, *Summerfolk: A History of the Dacha, 1719-2000* (Ithaca and London: Cornell University Press, 2003), 163–78; Mark Edele, *Stalinist Society 1928-1953* (Oxford: Oxford University Press, 2011), 57–8. More recently also: Euridice Charon Cardona and Roger D. Markwick, 'The Kitchen Garden Movement in the Soviet Home Front, 1941-1945', *Journal of Historical Geography* 64 (2019): 47–59.

54 P. Charles Hachten, 'Separate yet Governed: The Representation of Soviet Property Relations in Civil Law and Public Discourse', in *Borders of Socialism: Private Spheres of Soviet Russia*, ed. Lewis Siegelbaum (New York and Houndsmills: Palgrave Macmillan, 2006), 65–82, here: 74–6; Pikhoia, *Sovetskii Soiuz: Istoriia vlasti*, 173–6; Lovell, *Summerfolk*, 178–85; Vladimir Shlapentokh, *Public and Private Life of the Soviet People: Changing Values in Post-Stalin Russia* (New York and Oxford: Oxford University Press, 1989), 161.

55 For example: *Pravda*, 9 May 1949, 1; 9 May 1950, 1; 9 May 1951, 1–2. A detailed study of Victory Day celebrations between 1947 and 1965 remains to be written.

56 Stephen M. Norris, 'Memory for Sale: Victory Day 2010 and Russian Remembrance', *Soviet & Post-Soviet Review* 38, no. 2 (2011): 201–29.

57 Edele, 'More Than Just Stalinists', 167–91; V. A. Kozlov and S. V. Mironenko (eds), *58-10. Nadzornye proizvodstva Prokuratury SSSR po delam ob antisovetskoi agitatsii i propaganda. Annotirovannyi katalog mart 1953-1991* (Moscow: Demokratiia, 1999).

58 An important study of the impact of the war is Stephen Lovell, *The Shadow of War: Russia and the USSR 1941 to the Present* (Oxford: Wiley-Blackwell, 2010).

59 For a study of the Polish path to Australia see Wanda Warlik, 'Displacement and the Second World War: Polish Refugees in Africa' (PhD diss., The University of Western Australia, 2019).

INDEX

air war 117–18
Akhmatova, Anna 112
Alma-Ata 31, 32, 102
Almaty, *see* Alma-Ata
Anders, Władysław 103–4, 191
Anders Army, *see* Anders, Władysław
appeasement policy 31, 41, 49
Archangelsk 106, 119, 198
Australia 115, 120, 191

Baibakov, Nikolai 95, 107
Baldwin, Stanley 48
Beijing 29
Beria, Lavrenty 65, 73, 78, 93–4
Bliukher, Vasily Konstantinovich 34, 39–40
Blokhin, Vasily Mikhailovich 65
Brezhnev, Leonid 186, 190
Britain, *see* Great Britain
Broner, Adam 102, 151
Buriat-Mongolian Autonomous Republic 3
Bushueva, Valentina 100

Chamberlain, Neville 49
Changkufeng Incident 39
Cheka, *see* Commissariat of the Interior (NKVD)
Chiang Kai-Shek 29, 178–9
China
    resisting Japan 29, 116–17
    role until 1942 7–8, 46, 67
    Soviet aid 30–3
    war in 2–3, 178–9
Chuikov, Vasily
    as commander 108, 166
    before Stalingrad 67–8, 106, 130

Chukhrai, Grigory 102
Churchill, Winston 52, 115–16, 155, 180
coerced labour 128–30
Commissariat of the Interior (NKVD)
    152, *see also* Ministry of Internal Affairs (MVD); Ministry of State Security (MGB)
    antiguerrilla operations 159–60
    terror 38–9, 63, 65
Communist Party 5, 15, 90, 132
    admitting soldiers 98–9
    changing role in the war 130–3, 140
    controlling population 55
    opposition within 25
    postwar renewal 182–3, 189
conferences
    Potsdam 1945 94
    Teheran 1943 94
    Yalta 1945 94
Cossacks 146–8

Daugavpils 141
deep operations 20–1, 133
deportations 2, 6, 34–8, 62–4, 69, 157–8, 171
Dunkirk 59
Dushanski, Nachman 83, 87, 151–5, 167

economy
    New Economic Policy (NEP) 15–16
    postwar reconstruction 181–3
    Soviet economic effort 45
    Soviet results by 1941 68–9
    Soviet war economy 122–5, 177
Einsatzgruppen 139
Estonia 2, 60
    arrests in 8–9, 62

human losses   160
  Soviet treaty with   56–7
  troop violence in   168–9
evacuation in 1941   76–8, 198

Fergana   101
Finland
  leaving the war   115
  restoring borders   171
  role in Siege of Leningrad   111
  Soviet negotiations with   57
  war with Soviet Union   27–8, 57–9,
    66, 80
Forest Brothers   152, 155–60, 186

Gaister, Inna   100
Gatrell, Peter   8
Germany
  1936   31
  invading Poland   44, 50–3
  negotiating with the Soviets   47
  occupation policy   142–4
  refusing to give up   118
  Soviet perception in 1939   48
  war experience in 1941   81–7
Glasse, Iakob   128–9
Goebbels, Joseph   146
Goldberg, Michael   54, 64, 73–6, 151
Gorbachev, Mikhail   186
Great Britain   22, 48–9, 50, 51–2, 58,
    59, 70, 103, 106, 107, 108, 118,
    119–20, 122, 155
Great Patriotic War   2–3, 7, 20, 26, 44,
    132, 186–7
Great Purge, see Great Terror
Great Terror   8, 17–18, 22, 25, 41, 59,
    101
Gulag   64, 110
  former soldiers   79
  labour   128–30
  numbers after 1945   163
  resistance in   90–1
  role in the war   126–8

Hangzhou   29
Heinrici, Gotthard   82
Hiroshima   1, 121–2
Hitler, Adolf   1, 10, 18, 49
Holocaust   3, 138–42
  revenge   152–4

Idiev, Raban   175

Japan
  at end of 1941   106–7
  march into Manchuria   31
  military strength   116–17
  neutrality with the Soviets   120–1
  pressured by Germany in 1941   106–7
  reaction to 1939   9
  Soviet perception of   39–40
  territorial claims   40
  troops in China and the Far East   29–30
  at war with Soviet Union   40–4

Katasonov, Petr Fedorovich   3, 8
Khalkhin Gol battle   19, 41–6, 50, 57
Khasan lake battle   19, 21, 39–40, 43
Khrushchev, Nikita   49, 90, 185, 189
Kim, Ivan   37
Klaipeda   180
Kollontai, Alexandra   101
Konstantinova, Ina   136
Koshevka   146
Kosmodemianskaia, Zoia   85–7, 91
Kozhina, Elena   146
Krasnovodsk   104
Kulik, Grigory Ivanovich   52
Kuomintang (KMT)   30–1
Kuusinen, Otto   58
Kyiv   73, 82, 84, 86, 87

labour army   76, 102, 128
Ladoga lake   111, 146
Latvia   6, 57, 60
  expecting liberation   90, 138–9
  living under occupation   141, 145
  partisans   146
League of Nations   58
Lecker, Markus   61
Lend-Lease   7, 106, 111, 119–20, 127,
    176, 199
Lenin   14–15, 73
Leningrad
  antisemitism in   139–41
  bordering Finland   57–8
  ration cards   96
  under siege   97, 111–13, 146–7
Leonhard, Vladimir (Wolfgang)   101–2
Lewin, Moshe   102
Liebknecht, Sonja   101

Lithuania
    Germans retreating from   145
    Holocaust in   152–3
    insurgency   6–7, 149, 155–9
    losses   161
    occupation of   57, 59–60
    role in Hitler-Stalin Pact   48
Liubimov, Aleksandr   95
Liushkov, Genrikh Samoilovich   34, 38–9
losses
    Khalkhin Gol   44
    overall Soviet   2
    ratio   19
    Soviet before 1941   6, 19
    Soviet in 1941–45   6, 19, 175–6

MacDonald, Ramsay   48
Maclean, Fitzroy   108
Malaya   119
Malenkov, Georgy   73, 94
Malginova, Anna   110
Mao Zedong   178, 179
Mekhlis, Lev   53, 94
Mikoian, Anastas   73, 94–5
Milchukas, Albinas   158
Ministry of Internal Affairs (MVD)   168
Ministry of State Security (MGB)   152
Mochulsky, Fyodor Vasilevich   126
Molotov, Viacheslav   8, 47–8, 50, 55, 68,
    73, 93–4, 136
Moscow
    1941 panic   89, 91
    Peace Treaty   59
Motorikhin, V. I.   55
Munich Agreement   48, 49
Murmansk   106, 119, 127

Nagasaki   121–2
Nanjing   29
Nomonhan incident, see Khalkhin Gol
    battle
Novikov, Vitaly   144

Operation Uranus, see Stalingrad
Organization of Ukrainian Nationalists
    (OUN)   67, 87, 149, 186

pact
    Anti-Comintern   31
    Hitler-Stalin   47–50, 55, 103

non-aggression with Japan   46, 68
Polish-Soviet   51
secret protocol   55–6
People's Government of Finland   58
Petsamo   180
Podlubny, Stepan   47–8
Poland
    deportees' experience   103–4
    fighting in 1939   53
    Soviet war against   50–4
Polish Home Army (AK)   152, 155
Protassewicz, Irena   63, 103, 104

railway
    Manchurian   31
    Northern Pechora   127
Red Army
    Baltic states   56–7, 59–60
    conditions of service   130
    culture of violence   166–70, 180–1
    defence in 1941   81–5, 105
    Finland   57–9
    invasion of Manchuria   121–2
    military effectiveness and
        structure   130–3
    Poland   53–4
    Stalingrad and after   110, 119, 132–3
    witnessing German crimes   144–5
repressions, see also Great Terror
    1941   78–9
    campaigns after the war   7–8
    collectivization and de-
        kulakization   24–5, 27
    death by shooting   64–6, 83, 105
    East   34–8
    occupied lands   62
Romania   60
Roosevelt, Franklin D.   115

Salla   180
San Din, Ten   2–3, 8, 121
scorched earth policy   144–5
Second World War
    disaster in 1941   80–1, 87
    nature   8
    paradox   28
    sources   4–5
    Soviet efficiency   20, 23
    Soviet participation   4, 115
    Soviet politics   8–10

Soviet recovery   10
Soviet victory   11
wars within   4
Shaposhnikov, Boris Mikhailovich   39
Shostakovich, Dmitri   111–12
Shtern, Georgy Mikhailovich   40, 78
Sikorski-Maisky agreement   103
Skiba, Ivan   83, 87
Smolensk   84
Sorge, Richard   106
Soviet
    agrarian policies   61–2
    aid to China   31–3, 67, 178–9
    antisemitism   139–41
    border war with Japan   39–42
    collaborators   142
    culture   26
    demobilization   171–3
    disease and illness   129
    enemies   27
    female roles and lives   99–101,
        136–7
    food crisis   125–6
    food production and
        consumption   24, 95–7, 110–11
    military spending   22–3
    patriotism   98–9, 135–8
    popular disaffection   87–91, 107,
        135–6
    post-war criminality   162–6
    preparation for war   25, 33–8
    propaganda   25–6, 34, 48, 70
    strength in the East   33
    suffering under occupation   144–8
    wartime administration   26
    welfare   188–9
Spanish Civil War   21
Stalin, Joseph
    accomplishments by 1941   66–7
    addressing the population   1, 13, 105,
        183
    as commissar for nationalities   16
    distrust of intelligence   70–1
    distrust of Western powers   49–50
    evolution of role in the political
        system   184–5
    getting rid of commissars   131
    outlook on future conflicts   14–15, 50
    outlook on Russia   13–14
    revolution from abroad   61, 64
    revolutions from above   16, 27
    shift towards nationalism   56
    strategy of   16–21, 24, 59
    style of leadership   94–5, 185–7
    support for China   30–3
    unease with non-Russians   35
Stalingrad   16, 115
    fighting   108–10, 131, 166
Starchukova, Maria Iakovlevna   47, 98
State Committee of Defence (GKO)
        93–5, 102, 105
Svirin, Afanasy Matveyevich   131

Terijoki   58
Timoshenko, Semyon   73
Tsaritsyn, see Stalingrad

United States of America (USA)   1, 3, 5,
        7, 9, 22, 28, 46, 107, 111, 116–17,
        119, 122, 155, 162, 177, 179, 191
Ukrainian Insurgent Army (UPA)   149,
        186, see also Organization of
        Ukrainian Nationalists (OUN)

Vasilevsky, Aleksandr   94
Vatutin, Nikolai   73
veterans in the USSR   187–8
Victory Day   190–2
Vladivostok   2, 7, 30, 68, 106, 119–21
Vorkuta   127
Voroshilov, Kliment   40, 45, 93
Voznesensky, Nikolai   93, 94

warfare
    irregular and guerrilla   21, 66, 87,
        107, 120, 145–6, 154–60
    mountain   21

Zhambyl   139
Zhukov, Georgy
    conduct in Mongolia   41–2
    reaction in 1941   73
    reporting to Stalin   94
    strategy   43, 133, 166